Advanced Social Research Series
The Center for the Study of Social Research for the Enhancement of Human Well-being
Kwansei Gakuin University, Nishinomiya, Japan
Volume 2

Frontiers of Social Research

Advanced Social Research Series
The Center for the Study of Social Research for the Enhancement of Human Well-being
Kwansei Gakuin University, Nishinomiya, Japan

Series editor: Eishō Ōmura

A Sociology of Happiness: Japanese Perspectives
Kenji Kosaka

Frontiers of Social Research: Japan and Beyond
Akira Furukawa

Advanced Social Research Series
The Center for the Study of Social Research for the Enhancement of Human Well-being
Kwansei Gakuin University, Nishinomiya, Japan
Volume 2

Frontiers of Social Research

Japan and Beyond

Edited by
Akira Furukawa

This English edition first published in 2007 by
Trans Pacific Press, PO Box 120, Rosanna, Melbourne, Victoria 3084, Australia
Telephone: +61 3 9459 3021 Fax: +61 3 9457 5923
Email: info@transpacificpress.com
Web: http://www.transpacificpress.com

Copyright © Trans Pacific Press 2007

Designed and set by digital environs, Melbourne. www.digitalenvirons.com

Printed by BPA Print Group, Burwood, Victoria, Australia

Distributors

Australia and New Zealand
UNIREPS
University of New South Wales, Sydney,
NSW 2052, Australia
Tel: +61(0)2-9664-0999
Fax: +61(0)2-9664-5420
Email: info.press@unsw.edu.au
Web: http://www.unireps.com.au

USA and Canada
International Specialized Book Services
920 NE 58th Avenue, Suite 300
Portland, Oregon 97213-3786
USA
Tel: (800) 944-6190
Fax: (503) 280-8832
Email: orders@isbs.com
Web: http://www.isbs.com

Asia and the Pacific
Kinokuniya Company Ltd.
Head office:
Shin-Mizonokuchi Bldg. 2F
5-7, Hisamoto 3-chome
Takatsu-ku, Kawasaki 213-8506
Japan
Tel: +81 (0) 44-874-9642
Fax: +81 (0) 44-829-1025
Email: bkimp@kinokuniya.co.jp
Web: www.kinokuniya.co.jp
Asia-Pacific office:
Kinokuniya Book Stores of Singapore
Pte., Ltd.
391B Orchard Road #13-06/07/08
Ngee Ann City Tower B
Singapore 238874
Tel: +65 6276 5558
Fax: +65 6276 5570
Email: SSO@kinokuniya.co.jp

All rights reserved. No production of any part of this book may take place without the written permission of Trans Pacific Press.

ISBN 978-1-876843-34-2 (Hardback)
ISBN 978-1-876843-35-9 (Paperback)

Cover illustration: A scene from *Dragon Ball Z*. Courtesy of the Japan Information and Cultural Centre, Melbourne.

Contents

Figures	vi
Photographs	vii
Tables	vii
Preface *Akira Furukawa*	viii
Contributors	xv

1. Overcoming the Predicament of Social Research
   Motoji Matsuda — 1
2. Explanation and Narrative: What Should Social Research Aim for? *Kazuo Seiyama* — 19
3. Rethinking Case Studies: Research as a Power to Construct Lives *Taisuke Miyauchi* — 39
4. Reflections on the Methodology of Seeing in *Kōgengaku* and the Study of Folklore *Makito Kawada* — 53
5. Drawing Sketches in the Field: Sketch Literacy for Social Research *Nobutaka Kamei* — 72
6. Opium and the Emperor: Anthropology, Colonialism and War during Imperial Japan *Kyung-soo Chun* — 100
7. Discovering the 'Sense of Co-Presence' in Urban Sociological Research *Michihiro Okuda* — 126
8. Through the Eyes of a Good Deed Investigator *Yukihiko Shigenobu* — 158
9. How Does the Village Express Local Knowledge *Akira Furukawa* — 183
10. Discovering Happiness through Environmental Research Conducted by Local Residents *Yukiko Kada* — 203
11. A Film's 'Power of Enlightenment' or Effect: An Exploration of the Film *Freaks* *Hiroaki Yoshii* — 233
12. Lessons on Human Rights Derived from an Epistolary Style: the Sociography of Structural Discrimination *Kōkichirō Miura* — 253
13. In Search of Evidence of a Child's Best Interests: Bridging Research and Practice in Social Work *Matsujiro Shibano* — 272

Notes	306
Bibliography	316
Index	337

Figures

2.1	Narrative and explanation	32
5.1	Cross-section sample of a sushi roll	75
5.2	Subject and number of sketches	80
5.3	Fieldwork sketches in the tropical forest region of the Republic of Cameroon	81
5.4	Sketches help to accurately understand the subject	82
5.5	Sketching allows accurate recording of a subject	83
5.6	Sketching forms rapport	85
5.7	Sketching makes the collection of samples smooth and easy	86
5.8	Sketches form a database	88
5.9	Sketches make verbal and written expression clearer	89
5.10	A simplified sketch. A sketch of a church in the Republic of Cameroon, March 2005.	91
5.11	Literacy education using sketching	93
5.12	Animation-based sociology 'Boryoku no fukei (Landscape of Violence)'	95
7.1	Typology of comparative analytic community study approaches	135
10.1	Environmental awareness of residents and scientists	210
10.2	Relationship between the firefly and me (Dynamic model)	215
10.3	Relationship between the firefly and me (Static model)	216
13.1	Process of permanency planning based on 1980 Act	276
13.2	The modified design & development (M-D&D) process	282
13.3	The Japanese-style management process in dealing with child abuse cases	288
13.4	The practical navigational database system's decision-making phase and risk assessment phase based on the phase-mode practice model	289
13.5	Fresno County due process 1: Referrals and investigation	290
13.6	Fresno County due process 2: Family maintenance	291
13.7	Fresno County due process 3: Family maintenance, protection hearing and family reunification	290
13.8	Fresno County due process 4: Permanency planning	291

13.9	Essential flow of the navigational database system based on the flow-mode practice model	293
13.10	Flow-mode navigation database system screening model	296
13.11	The CERAP module	298
13.12	Risk assessment module	300
13.13	On-the-spot-investigation module	301

Photographs

10.1.1	Morning on the Lake Biwa foreshore on 5 August 1956.	219
10.1.2	Okishima (same place and angle as photograph 10.1.1). Mrs Yoshiko Chatani and her daughter Aiko.	223
10.2.1	A mother doing the laundry and a baby in a pram, around 1955.	224
10.2.2	Mrs Kimi Nakano, who was doing the laundry in photograph 10.2.1.	225
10.3.1	Piers on Imazu beach.	226
10.3.2	The same place as in photograph 10.3.1, no pier remains.	226
10.4.1	A family photograph on the pier with some guests from Tokyo.	227
10.4.2	The same place as in photograph 10.4.1.	227

Tables

4.1	Visual methods in Kōgengaku	60
4.2	Comparative table of the three-part categorization of folklore materials of Kunio Yanagita	69

Preface

Akira Furukawa

The theme of the 'sociology of social research' remains forever an old yet new concern in sociology. Hot topics in recent debates on 'social research' in Japan are problems relating to the cognitive framework of social realism and social constructivism, and the relationship between researcher and social research subject, namely, the issue of 'politics and ethics.' Contrasting positivist social research methodologies, based on the assumption of a unique social reality that exists externally to the researcher, is the debate about whether social reality itself is constructed and arises out of the interaction between researcher and research subject. Another topic closely related, is that of the self in social research. This is a reflection on the research method that arises out of attention to the emergence of the individual, and from the focus on self-consciousness, the biases of researchers who are roused by that. It stands in contrast to the research method which has explicated social structure as elaborate relationships that demonstrate the universal and rule based nature of societies that have been the subject of research. This is to say, the self of researchers and the self of the research subjects, an issue thus far overlooked, has been taken up.

These two points of debate will lead to innovations in the various research methodologies used thus far, from research undertaken by questionnaire to participant based research. The praise heaped upon the technique of experimental ethnography in anthropology in the 1980s and 1990s and the life story method of sociology, were reflections of the variation in this epistemology. However, the development of these methods of research and description has not sufficiently addressed future issues.

Motoji Matsuda's thesis in Chapter One of this volume directly engages with these themes and considers a new perspective while being informed by the methodologies of Japanese anthropology and folklore. Matsuda conducts a review commencing with anthropological fieldwork of the 1920s and sketches the 'predicament of social research.' He proposes that this predicament came about most forcefully in the 1980s with the publication of the book, *Writing Culture: The Poetics and Politics of Ethnography* (Clifford and Marcus eds 1986). This work was seen to unmask the deception of the debates themselves, centered on cultural relativism and diversity as it applied to fieldwork, and its publication and the ensuing response, plunged the best part of anthropology into nihilism. It is the perception itself of the unbridgeable gap between researchers and the subjects of research that is at the root of this 'predicament.' Matsuda's own influences include Kunio Yanagita of Japanese folklore fame, the early Africanists and the sociological debates of the 1970s. He sets out the way for social research to overcome this impasse through the possibility of empathizing with and experiencing understanding of the other, in spite of an initial premise that the self and the other are heterogeneous and stand on either side of an unbridgeable gap.

In comparison to anthropology, Japanese sociology's response to *Writing Culture* was relatively minor and was seen through with little to no ill-effect. As seen in the word 'rapport,' it is possible to see this as due to the fact that from the outset most social research does not place the assumption of trust in the unbridgeable gap of researchers and fieldwork research subjects. This contrasts with anthropological research which has been based upon this foundation. Alternatively, it could also be said that the impact on Japanese sociology was not so great because most researchers do not perceive the unbridgeable gap itself as the most challenging issue facing sociological research.

This should not imply that there has not been debate in Japanese sociological circles on the introspective ethnographies of Paul Rabinow and colleagues (1977), or on cultural studies. Nor has debate been absent on the reevaluation of the unbridgeable gap between the self and the other or regarding new fieldwork initiatives, both of which have been brought about by experimental ethnography and similar endeavors since *Writing Culture*. In the same era as Rabinow and colleagues, Nitagai and Nakano—examined in detail by Matsuda in his article—were already confronting this issue, progressing to a point where the relationship between the researcher and research subjects is conceptualized as a 'joint project.' Following this, Nakano was central in making primary the sociology of life history and life story research, which carries on the awareness of these concerns. Further, symbolic interaction theory, phenomenological sociology and ethnomethodology have also made a profound commitment to the topic of the self and the other.

However, condensing the predicament of social research down to the issue of self and other may, in fact, work against our efforts to get to a resolution. In other words, in relation to the problem of the unbridgeable gap between the researcher self and the research subject other, if we leave the heterogeneity of the self and the other that stand on either side of an unbridgeable gap as is, Matsuda's aforementioned contention merely suggests inasmuch that the heterogeneity is suddenly overcome by the experience of empathy or understanding of the other. What is required to overcome the predicament of social research, the conundrum of fieldwork, is an actual logic and method for linking together the perception of heterogeneity with the experience of empathy and understanding. To this end, we need to consider the root of the problem of self and the other in fieldwork in a little more depth.

If we take pause to look back on the history of fieldwork epistemology, from the birth of anthropology until the existentialism of the 1960s up to Rabinow (and his introspective fieldwork), ethnographies were written in the form of an image of a collective other and the enigmatic self (researcher) that portrayed it. In contrast, the movement of the mid 1980s, stirred by the book *Writing Culture*, critiqued both the authority of the researcher who portrays the other by giving it substance and the authority that portrays the other not as an individual, but always as a collective entity. Anthropology in the aftermath of *Writing Culture* was plunged into confusion, so much so that the period has been referred to as the 'lost decade.' In the twenty years hence, Japan has also seen many endeavors including the development of experimental ethnography and material culture and undertakings that read all manner of relationships as political. It is possible to understand the debate on constructionism and the issue of 'politics and ethics' in research in the context of these trends. However, the shockwave created by *Writing Culture* has been constructed as critical logic with 'no exit' and hence any other efforts, particularly those on theories of fieldwork, were unable to make significant changes to the situation.

'No exit' refers to the following. Critiques of the authority that portrays the other collectively, find in the field, unique individuals.

The next inescapable development; however, is a criticism of the discoverer of this uniqueness and the authority that portrays the individual in this way. In other words, we need to overcome the nihilism that arises from getting stuck in the 'no exit' circuit that is interminable reiteration of a critique of the authority in which something is portrayed by someone.

Matsuda's thesis has found an exit from this circuit in the past experience of fieldwork where, through an analysis of images of the self in ethnographic descriptive accounts, he has acquired a context and a method where researchers and research subjects can empathize and experience mutual understanding. Here the issue of the self versus the other is not resolved by the discovery of a unique individual or a transparent researcher coming out as an individual. Rather, it is resolved by the issue of finding a context and a methodology for empathy and the experience of mutual understanding.

How about we try distancing ourselves, just the once, from the idea of separate images of the self? That is, the image of the selves that is intent on separating the researching self, which is afforded privilege, and the other, which is subject to research (the 'scribal self': Boon 1980) versus the image of selves intent on interconnecting the researching self which the other that is subject to research (see the 'tribal self' in Boon 1980, and Matsuda's article). Applying prescriptions to the self means, in the research arena, that it is possible for these two images of the self to simultaneously appear for both the researcher and research subject. A unilateral authority does not define the self. In the research arena, I think these definitions of self are mutually converted as they are paradigmatically selected by the logic associated with lifestyles in that context. They grasp that people who live in that context are the protagonists living life. From the depths of these lifestyles, people practice living by accumulating practice at living better. The journey starts from the idea that the selves of the researcher and research subject are defined by lifestyle practices.[1]

In consciously debating this problem of self and the other in research and painting either a positive or a negative picture, many of the arguments covered in this volume suggest new proposals towards reform of research methodology. These are not merely restricted to the method outlined above. The respective discourses pose questions in various contexts and suggest methodologies that can overcome them.

In his article (Chapter Two), Kazuo Seiyama attempts to overcome the classical issue of qualitative versus quantitative research by demonstrating that it is only by these both having a 'story' that they become shared knowledge. The debate is progressed by considering the issue of which scene gives the story a foundation where the researcher and the location of fieldwork interact.

In his article (Chapter Three), Taisuke Miyauchi considers what constitutes a case in research and ethnographic descriptive accounts. In his article (Chapter Eight), Yukihiko Shigenobu illuminates the violence inherent in bringing to light facts that emerge from research. He does this via an image of the selves of research committee members involved in the good deed research carried out after an earthquake catastrophe. Akira Furukawa's article (Chapter Nine) demonstrates that people and villages—elements of the field itself—are also protagonists in research. Yukiko Kada's article (Chapter Ten) proposes 'data displaying research' as a method of conducting empathic research. Kōkichirō Miura proposes a letter-styled sociography which would include readers of ethnographies in the picture, not just the self and the other involved in the research (Chapter Twelve). These articles confront the issue of the self and the other in research, head on, and feature new methodologies that take it into consideration.

Kyung-soo Chun's article (Chapter Six) advances into research ethics via the novel perspective of private encounters between colonized Japanese anthropologists and the research subjects. Michihiro Okuda proposes a dynamic comparative methodology that, within globalization, mutually references people's way of life transnationally rather than counting as attributes their nationality or ethnicity (Chapter Seven). These articles both suggest situational variability in images of the self and the other in research.

Another of the characteristics of this series of discourses in the present volume are their proposals for reframing research done thus far and innovating research methodology. The articles from Makito Kawada (Chapter Four), Nobutaka Kamei (Chapter Five) and Hiroaki Yoshii (Chapter Eleven) are attempts to overcome a research and ethnographic description methodology that has become staid by the superiority of research related language and text by an examination of the visual methodologies for research and description. It is possible to read Kada's 'data displaying research' and Miura's letter-based sociographies as similar attempts. Further, Matsujiroo Shibano's article (Chapter Thirteen) puts forward a specific proposal to reform the methodology of social welfare research that realizes a cycle which feeds back the results of research undertaken on practices to those very practices.

I have attempted to bring together the epistemology of the issue of the self and the other in research in line with my intent as editor to discover new possibilities for novel social research by taking pause to look back at the state of Japanese social research. However, the various articles have been written in the wider context of research and go beyond the issue of self and other in social research. It is my sincere wish as editor to encourage the reader to sample the multifarious flavors contained in the respective articles as they study this volume.

The present volume is one of the achievements of the '21st Century Centers of Excellence Program' (Program Leader: Kenji Kosaka) at Kwansei Gakuin University that was adopted by Japan's Ministry of Education, Culture, Sports, Science and Technology. This program is directed to 'studies of social research that contribute to human welfare.'

We are grateful to Ms Cathy Henenberg for her careful and thoughtful editorial assistance at every stage of the production of this book.

Contributors

Motoji Matsuda	Professor, Department of Sociology, Graduate School of Letters, Kyoto University
Kazuo Seiyama	Professor, Department of Sociology, Graduate School of Humanities and Sociology
Taisuke Miyauchi	Associate Professor, Graduate School of Letters, Hokkaido University
Makito Kawada	Professor, Graduate School of Sociology, Chukyo University
Nobutaka Kamei	COE Associate Professor, Graduate School of Sociology and Social Work, Kwansei Gakuin University
Kyung-soon Chun	Professor, Department of Anthropology, College of Social Sciences, Seoul National University
Michihiro Okuda	Professor Emeritus, Rikkyo University
Yukihiko Shigenobu	Associate Professor, Center for Fundamental Education, University of Kyushu
Akira Furukawa	Professor, Graduate School of Sociology and Social Work, Kwansei Gakuin University
Yukiko Kada	Governor, Shiga Prefecture (Formerly, Professor, Department of Environmental and Social Studies, Faculty of Humanities, Kyoto Seika University
Hiroaki Yoshii	Professor, Graduate School of Humanities and Social Sciences, University of Tsukuba
Kōichirō Miura	Professor, Graduate School of Sociology and Social Work, Kwansei Gakuin University
Matsujiro Shibano	Professor, Graduate School of Sociology and Social Work, Kwansei Gakuin University

1
Overcoming the Predicament of Social Research[1]

Motoji Matsuda

In recent years, there has been an increasing interest in ethnographies and life histories with attempts to innovate within social science methodology, including social research. Several background factors have led to a renaissance in the traditional concepts of qualitative research which includes 'thick description' and 'deep interviews.' One of these factors is, needless to say, the intensification of the deep-seated skepticism toward objectivism and positivism, established, conventional methodological standards for modern science. When the extent to which social research could objectify profoundly individual, inconsistent human behaviour and unconscious thought was raised, the view opened up by ethnographies and life stories once again came to the fore.

We can observe that another factor in the background to the re-examination of this methodology is the fact that it is interdisciplinary, trans-disciplinary even, and supersedes academic boundaries demarcated by increasing levels of specialization. When attempting to get an overview of a certain social phenomenon or issue, a valid approach recommended by present day thinking is the utilization of concepts from a range of disciplines without being restricted to narrow, fixed methodologies. This includes utilizing approaches from the natural sciences in addition to the humanities and social sciences such as the history of ideas, literature, economics and political science.

However, in stark contrast to the high regard held for this brand of qualitative social research, it is fair to say that, ironically, the negative viewpoint held toward this kind of methodology is increasingly coming to dominate the area of fieldwork theory. This appears in its most conspicuous form in the world of anthropology where fieldwork has become the mainstay of academic methodology while ethnographies have formed the essence of fieldwork descriptive accounts.

Following the shock that ensued the publication of *Writing Culture: The Poetics and Politics of Ethnography* in the mid 1980s, the earth suddenly shifted in the world of cultural anthropology and collided with the preexisting methodology. This ideological movement dismantled the political dynamics of portrayal which had been the mainstay of fieldwork and ethnographies by exposing them, and ousted empirical methods for conducting research in the blink of an eye. The rhetoric that claimed understanding from involvement in the field was completely rejected and the workings associated with the authority of portrayal which embellished 'field sense' were criticized as 'ethnographer's magic.'[2] Although it has spawned several backlashes and countercurrents, this trend has continued until the present day.

In some instances, a fieldwork based ethnographic approach is an effective way of conducting research on a society that has experienced serious destruction in, say, disaster, or of conducting research on groups in the social fringes (social deviants). However, this kind of research is fraught with harsh criticism. This is due to the assumption of securing a location where researchers can write up their accounts after they have removed themselves from the 'catastrophe' or 'marginality' which people find themselves in. This presumption is, without fail, identical to the epistemology of modern science which considers the researcher an epistemologically superior being. Some fieldworkers have shared life-threatening experiences with the people who live in the very societies dominated by fear and violence in reality. These fieldworkers have started to feel, for themselves, the limits to, and the smoke and mirrors associated with, the kind of human understanding and research ethics preached by fieldwork theory thus far.[3] This has lead to a rethink of the agency of research itself that moves beyond the dimension of the crisis of portrayal.

The interdisciplinary approaches that fieldwork has profited from have been rejected as mere 'myths.' For instance, Borofsky investigated all the 3,264 articles that have featured in the *American Anthropologist* which boasts more than 100 years of history. Of these, a mere ten percent employed an interdisciplinary approach. He highlighted that the discourse of fieldwork as a multi-faceted method for taking snap-shots of reality and analyzing society was sheer myth, conjured up by the likes of Malinowski and Lévi-Strauss (Borofsky 2002: 463–80).

In this sense, the criticism drawn by the qualitative research methods of ethnographies and fieldwork is diametrically opposed to the current renaissance these two methods are enjoying in sociology. What and how are we to think so we can break through this impasse and discover the potential for fieldwork research in the twenty-first century? This articles aims to find some answers to these questions.

Social research and the individual/figurative world

The promise field research makes of getting a direct handle on the thinking and behavior of human individuals is an attractive one indeed. However, in social research theory, research on these individual cases has often been relegated to the periphery. This fundamental tendency remains the same from the development of the classical methods of Tadashi Fukutake until the present day. Fukutake proposed the landmark idea, namely, that case study research be discarded as 'pseudo-science.' He set out the limits of the case study research method by commenting on the lack of a standardized record keeping format and the inaccurate descriptions littered with subjective terminology. He comments that case research, 'while being privy to the advantage of being able to study the totality of living reality, will not be able to make a sufficient contribution as long as it is not driven and backed up by statistical research' (Fukutake [1958] 1984: 68–70). Consequently, case research was sublimated to social research that was whole and complete by the reinforcement of formal statistical research.

This viewpoint has become more sophisticated in recent years with other arguments gaining currency. One argument suggests that statistical and case research should not be consigned to the statuses of lord and vassal, but that a combination of the two, where each is interdependent, would lead to the best outcome. Rather than arguing which is superior, research designs have been proposed that incorporate both methodologies. This could mean, for instance, inserting some survey research in an essentially field research design. Or it could mean starting with some field research, administering a questionnaire, and then supplementing it with some case research to follow up. Alternatively it could imply starting with survey research to get a sense of the overall picture, follow it up with some field research, and then conduct more quantitative research to verify the results. In this sense, aiming for a methodology that incorporates a combination of quantitative and qualitative research into the one method is one trend seen in present day theories on research (see, for example, Flick 1995).

Of course, it is possible to mount a critique of this argument by countering that the approach of dividing social research methods into qualitative and quantitative research is merely a run-of-the-mill dichotomy. Most people will be familiar with the observation that this traditional, dichotomous approach itself is a product of modern epistemology which separates subjective from objective and warps any understanding of society. However, it is necessary to confirm that the debate which criticizes this dichotomy has had no impact on how research is actually carried out. In the real world, quantitative and qualitative, subjective and objective violently spring up as opposing dichotomies. As long as we do not genuinely wrestle with the heterogeneity of the realities of the fieldworker who deals with the individual and the surveyor who collects and analyzes questionnaires, this type of dichotomous critique will not see any new developments.

Takashi Nakano has argued the case for qualitative research from a completely different perspective to the standpoint of identifying the lord and vassal in the relationship between quantitative and qualitative research, or developing new techniques by combining the two. In answer to Fukutake-esque critiques that cases are unique and exceptional, he claims that there is no need to pay heed to formalism or to universal laws which themselves are peppered with exceptions. He argues that all specific cases are unique and that if universal rules do exist, then they would show up in all specific, and therefore, unique cases (Nakano 1990: 33). In this way, Nakano sets out on a journey to research the unique, specific experiential world of particular individuals.

Here, what Nakano has clearly argued is the perception and objectification of the individual (cases) inherent in the research method known as quantitative research veils a heterogeneous potential that is not legitimized by conventional methodologies. He concludes that debating which approach is superior to which, or advocating combinations of the two without grasping this heterogeneity, is tantamount to a mere methodological doctrine of harmony that is static and lacks tension. However, since Nakano has launched himself into the fertile world of research on real individuals (cases), he has not sufficiently developed a close examination of the methodology associated with this heterogeneity.

When considering the individualism that forms the core of this methodological heterogeneity, one of the most fitting subject matters is the issue of the individual in social research. If you research a certain society, you will be able to acquire data in the form of stories and behaviors that are displayed by the individual human being in front of you and which are stupendous and, at times, inconsistent. So, to what extent can we manage this data? This question demands a fundamental reexamination of the position of the individual in social research methodology.

Say we take the example of field research which is a stereotypical type of qualitative research. The history of how the existence of the individual (unit) has been objectified is, surprisingly, quite new. In the period from the late 1930s until the early 1960s, fieldworkers belonging to the English anthropological school of structural functionalism conducted intellectual research where the individual was, in fact, consistently pushed into the background. This was because they turned their backs on the uniqueness and individuality in the social relations of specific human individuals they encountered in the field, and saw as their academic goal the description of social structures as a continuous, elaborate set of relationships that demonstrated generality and the nature of rules.

In response to this Radcliffe-Brownian point of view, it is inevitable that critiques will emerge declaring that it does not account for changes and fluctuations, or that the individual's autonomy is being ignored, with a variety of revised models now having taken the stage.[4] However, the period from the late 1960s to the early 1970s saw the emergence of initiatives that attempted to get closer to an understanding of the individual in the field more directly and without any revisions to this structural functionalism. The simple point of view of Barth and others that attempted to objectify the individual encountered in the field as actual, flesh and blood people identical to themselves, brought about far-reaching changes to fieldwork methodology. It set fire to a movement that shifted the focus of research to the existence of the self that had been intentionally discarded in the structural and normative system thus far. This included the individual's autonomous choices and self-interest, their sometimes inconsistent behavior and the logic that justified it (Matsuda 1995: 187–190).

This era of attention to the self brought about another change, namely, the objectification of the researcher's self-consciousness which was relevant to the relationship between the researcher and the subject of the research. The history of initiatives that consider the researcher's self-consciousness dates back to the 1950s and to the publication of the monographs by Redfield and Lewis. They focused on the workings of the researcher's 'individual biases' and recommended public accounts of these biases be made. However, with the 1970s came the advent of harsh critiques not only of the absence of self in the researchers themselves, but how this style functioned as a mechanism of suppression that actively preserved the political dynamics in the field which were inherently unequal. White fieldworkers who abstracted the concept of colonization and argued for the creativity of individual Africans were criticized. Calls were made for increasing awareness of the selves of researchers who continued scientific research without redressing the asymmetry between themselves and the subjects of their research. Nash and Wintrob, for instance, proposed a self-oriented ethnography in their claim that the critical relatedness of the selves of the observer and the observed was essential to ethnographies (Nash and Wintrob 1972: 527–542).

Against this background of thinking in the 1970s was a political critique targeting researchers who stood at the locus of political and economic power yet appreciated the marginalized and suppressed by unilaterally objectifying them. Scientific research, especially field research which had profited from human contact and interaction was exposed for concealing a system of inequality and for its contribution to an increasingly entrenched marginalization of the weak. Demands were made for self-reflection on the relatedness of the two. In a sense, this was how the issue of the self in field research finally came to be debated directly in the form of political self-reflection.

Fieldwork as a joint project: The Nitagai–Nakano debate[5]

The 1970s saw the emergence of a radical formulation of the problem of the self of the researcher and the self of the subjects of research and their relatedness, within the theory of fieldwork. Japan was home to a debate grounded in a conception of the issues that was identical in every regard, namely, the critiques exchanged between Kamon Nitagai and Takashi Nakano on the researcher's self-consciousness.

Nitagai's point of departure was in the perception that conventional theories of community and community studies had already lost touch with reality. The researcher and the subjects of research had been cleanly separated with the researcher's style of exploiting specialist knowledge to take, at whim, cuttings from objects which no longer held currency. The subjects of research harassed researchers about their relational style. In confronting the reality of the mistrust towards researchers being openly expressed, Nitagai became aware that the 'sham relationship of the researcher towards the object of research' had been exposed for what it was. He keenly felt what it was like for a researcher to wholly lack a self and be completely isolated from the reality of the field in contrast to the people being researched who had had individual characters and integrated thoughts. This was not an issue for individual researchers alone since it was partly due to a defective methodology of social science which had, in fact, been removed itself from reality by a system of scientific knowledge which was created through the arbitrary excising of only quantifiable items.

Feeling this way, Nitagai made a case positing social research as a joint project between the researcher and the subject of the research. To this end, he believed that researchers themselves should have everyday negotiations with participants in movements organized by the subjects of research, share knowledge and promote mutual understanding. He claimed that doing so would allow for participation by the individual, specific unadulterated activities carried out by people who lived in the field without being stymied by a universality model divorced from reality (Nitagai 1974: 1–7).

The critical awareness of the structural discrepancy between researchers and those they researched and the attitude of acknowledging the self of the subjects of research while admonishing the selves of the researchers was the most legitimate of the anti-fieldwork theories that swept the world in the 1970s. The ideal of a joint project between researchers and the subjects of research was proposed in light of the self-reflection by researchers. Of course it is easy to criticize the incredibly naive admiration researchers held towards the subjects of their research as the intellectual fieldworker's doctrine of field worship, especially when the subjects of research were involved in various social movements. However, there is no doubt that the efforts to problematize directly, the self of researchers which aspired to a new form of relatedness, were the best in this era and on equal footing with views from the likes of Nash, Wintrob and Barth.

It was Nakano who launched a scathing attack on this proposal from Nitagai, who was ahead of his time. Nakano was vehemently opposed to the concept of the joint project proposed by Nitagai, as the way research should be conducted. He claimed that the term joint project not only overlooked the tension filled heterogeneity that existed between the researcher and the subjects of research, but it embellished it with flowery language. Nitagai attempted to cut open the 'sham social relationships' the researcher had been demonstrating towards research subjects, but Nakano countered that no one would fall for such a sham. He also noted that there was no reason for research subjects to tell the truth since they were being deceived by the researcher. He criticized Nitagai himself for unconsciously putting the researcher in the dominant position epistemologically (Nakano 1975a, 1975b, 1975c, 1975d and 1975e).

Nakano takes the example where he and his students conducted research on perceptions of residents living in the Mizushima industrial belt and guessed what the response would be if they had conducted the research using language like 'our joint project' with residents in the research area. Let us quote him:

> If we had addressed them with 'We' as if they are walking along together, the residents in the pollution prone area would have curtly dismissed us with a "Don't suck up to me." Alternatively, they may have answered us politely with, "I'd rather you didn't come in" (Nakano 1975b: 5).

Nakano was not oblivious to the vestiges of the Enlightenment which researchers had let creep into the concept of joint project. Nitagai lamented researchers' lack of autonomy while research subjects who participated in movements had 'individual characters and integrated thoughts.' Unconditional admiration towards a self with a continually consistent thinking and logic on principle was the very essence of a strong, modern, individual awareness and completely differed to the self of the field which ducked and wove at whim according to circumstance. Nakano was critical of the fact that the theory of joint project was suffused with Enlightenment thinking which held up superman-like protagonists as missionaries while any other kind of selves were deemed behind the times.

This Enlightenment thinking often appeared in the language Nitagai used to flesh out the idea of a joint project. When he spoke of 'making at least one commitment to the actions of people responsible for the formation of culture in the populace,' he fixed in place the categorical assumptions of populace (subjects of research) and intellectuals (researchers), and of research subjects and researchers in the general population. We can see a structure where the former is the non-ego to be enlightened while the latter is the protagonist who educates. Subsuming this distinction with the phrase 'joint project' is either impossible or would bring about rather heated clashes and conflicts. However, Nitagai's theory of joint project made no attempt to objectify this tense relationship. It was on this point that Nakano stood in opposition.

However, Nakano did not hold to the position that the selves of the researcher and the subjects of research would not be on good terms. He subscribed to the premise that clear-cut differences existed between the two but saw the potential for various forms of social exchange after overcoming these differences. Human relationships are home to trust and mistrust. Building relationships involves each party shifting between both of these phases. There is no such thing as universal, invariant relatedness between selves that have integrated thinking and character. With regard to the relatedness of both, Nakano comments as follows: 'Real, intrinsic qualities are picked up on by passing through a period where the researcher's research lifestyle and the research subject's lifestyle interact on the basis of a discovered or created context of mutual trust between the two.'

Nakano himself rejects the idea commenting that this could not be referred to as a 'joint project.' However, I feel that referring to activities which seek to create something from an exchange (interchange) between the researcher and the research subject as a joint project is justified. From his opposition to Nitagai's theory of a joint project, which is embellished with notions of an ennobling Enlightenment, he rejects the phrase outright. However, the actual perception of heterogeneity between researchers and the subjects of research enabling cooperation between two differing entities is a type of joint project and moves closer to a mutual shifting and transformation over and above mutual differences. In this sense, an interchange between the two with differences left as is can be referred to as the crux of a theory of 'joint project' true to Nakano's ideas. Further, it is this that points to the potential of breaking through the dead end of the present day theory of fieldwork. This will be touched upon later.

Skepticism toward fieldwork

The activity of research is constituted upon the inequality between the researcher and research subjects. Researchers should reflect on this relatedness while aspiring to a joint project with the subjects of research, a view gained by research innovation movements that developed all across the world in the 1970s.

However, in the mid 1980s, these movements for innovation came to attract criticism as a new form of myth creation. This was due to the skepticism towards fieldwork that had gained prominence and fundamentally rejected actual attitudes like joint project. There is no doubt that the impetus for this came with the book, *Writing Culture: The Poetics and Politics of Ethnography*, edited by Clifford and Marcus (1986). Here, the relationship between researchers and research subjects was taken as an issue but from a different angle to the liberal political doctrines of the 1970s. The 1970s formulation of the issue was impervious to the inequality that existed between people at the heart of the political and economic system and those on the fringes (such as the Third World versus capitalist, developed countries, or rural versus urban communities). Moreover, fieldwork came under fire for the role it played in setting this in concrete.

However, the 1980s gave rise to a skepticism that spread the wings of critique a little further in producing a debate about the unfeasibility of fieldwork. The snap-shots of reality gained by 'working the field,' the mainstay of fieldwork thus far, was exposed as purportedly fraudulent while the arbitrariness of descriptive accounts and the style of nihilism itself were deconstructed. Malinowski confidently declared that the techniques of fieldwork and descriptive accounts were the 'ethnographer's magic.' His research lifestyle in Trobriand society being unreservedly brought into the light by his own diaries was a symbolic event. The simplistic ideas held up until then were completely thrown overboard; the idea that learning the language of the society targeted for research by a long period of stay and being recognized as a 'temporary member' of that society would lead to a 'discovery' of the various rules and structures that had been concealed from anyone from the outside. The loneliness and arrogance seen in the diary proved that Malinowski himself had become aware that he had not even been accepted as a 'temporary member' (Malinowski 1967). However, in some ethnographic descriptions, the researcher's self was cleanly erased with the putting together of standardized scientific descriptions. This type of vagueness and arbitrariness in ethnographic descriptive accounts resonated with the politics of portrayal that followed Edward Said's criticism of Orientalism and gave rise to debates about the unfeasibility of ethnographic descriptions (Said 1978).

In this way, the foundation for the existence of fieldwork, the 'working the field,' the 'being accepted by the locals,' was dismantled. Realism and empiricism were also cut down without mercy. Since it involved the editing of text and lacked scientific methodology, fieldwork very much came to be seen as a creative activity no different to the work of writing poetry or a novel. Important to this creative activity was subjectivity, metaphor, and rhetoric, the essential elements to creating fiction. The 'predicament' of fieldwork emerged.[6]

In this sense, once ethnography had morphed into a creative work as the text of a field description, interest was shown in its internal structure. Then, the rhetoric that would give the piece its authenticity became the core 'reality' of the text. In order to ensure the work's reliability, its credibility, its authority, its power to persuade the reader, techniques such as setting the types of characters, free indirect speech, narratives and dialogue were employed arbitrarily to reproduce, almost automatically, the product known as an ethnography. Naturally, this process activated the machinations of power where, as pointed out by Said, the marginalized non-ego is unilaterally portrayed and marginalized even further, thus reproducing the authority of knowledge and discourse that underscored the fieldworker. The knowledge system in its totality—the concepts and wording in descriptive accounts of reality in the field, the epistemology and ontology that propped them up—had already been input into the society to which the fieldworker belonged. It fixed and portrayed the 'reality' of the field by a massive, repetitive cross-referencing. Consequently, a series of activities, be they ideas, observations, analyses, understandings or descriptive accounts by individual fieldworkers, simply reproduced this 'reality' while pretending to be, at first glance, free, creative activity. The truth of ethnographies thus came to be regarded as always biased and political.

This skepticism swept through the world of fieldwork theory in the blink of an eye while the idea of a joint project between researcher and research subject was held up for ridicule. One group of skeptics, who criticized realism in the absolute, denounced all types of empirical reality as fabrications that should be dismantled and were not worthy of skepticism. We would be justified in referring to them as the 'sans-culottes' after the radicals positioned between the proletariat and the bourgeoisie who, during the French Revolution, ran wild proclaiming republicanism and paid the price.[7] The 'sans-culottes' who have dismantled fieldwork in one stroke solely based on ideology, were certainly a variant of the postmodernist thought that has deconstructed the categories of gender, race and ethnicity, one after the other.

However, they fall into an extreme version of nihilism in proclaiming they will 'banish realism from ethnographies.'[8] For instance, talking about real experiences is deemed to be poisoned by reactive, behind-the-times, cultural understanding while an unstoppable nihilism that rejects the generation and action of experience, existence and power has assumed the lead role in cultural research. The naive, everyday sense of reality—'that's how it is'—was shrugged off.

Thus the possibility of a joint project between researchers and the subjects of research in field research was completely rejected. All that remained were fieldworkers creating individual fictions in the context of the workings of power that overwhelmed.

Cooperativity to get beyond separation

It was imperative that a movement appear that would put the brakes on the wild self-dismantling in response to the position, pushed by the 'sans-culottes,' that fieldwork was untenable. Giddens, for instance, implored fieldworkers to confront the actual world of everyday lives (Giddens 1995: 272–7). From his point of view, shunning the empirical context of reality as a nod to a notional Romanticism and orienting meaning to the capriciousness of symbols was to be reduced to a position where meaning was sacrificed to fancy. The grunt work of confronting the context of reality, which comprised the complex and multilayered interplays of power, was demanded of ethnographies to save them from the world of mere 'creative pieces.'

How are we to escape the temptations of a sans-culotte self-dismantlement (the impossibility of cooperativity)? An analysis of cooperativity (between researchers and the subject of their research) requires that we return once more to the debate on the self. We understand well the differences in structural status (position) between researcher and research subjects. However, as with the 'sans-culottes,' here we need to stand riveted in front of this discrepancy and consider the structures of both selves rather than discard the structure of cooperativity. Let us consider the experience of the British school of social anthropology, which was the first to tackle this issue.

The British School of social anthropology conducted fieldwork in the sub-societies of Asia and Africa. Firstly they 'discovered' selves that were (thought to be) completely heterogeneous to the modern, Western image of self and related them to the 'primitive mentality.' These selves were unilaterally viewed by modern selves. However, in the next stage, the selves from these 'primitive' societies came to be valued for their hidden potential that stood in stark contrast to modern selves. For instance, Boon imagined an exclusive other. He referred to modern selves established by the mutual exclusion of other parties as 'scribal selves' and defined a manner of selves that were mutually complementary and interdependent as 'tribal selves.' Fieldwork then becomes a process where these two types of selves are at loggerheads. In line with this view, reports of established forms of various non-Western, modern selves came from all around the world. This also linked into the self-reflection of the modern ego and inquiries into an alternative self-consciousness (Boon 1982: 230–6).

In contrast to the assumptions made of, and praise afforded these non-Western selves; however, it was no surprise to see the emergence of critiques common to those of Orientalism, which claimed that these discoveries were only of romanticized, heterogeneous selves. The group of fieldworkers that maintained this position gave reports from non-Western regions of images of autonomous selves that clearly had self-consciousness and were freely choosing. Grounded in this ethnographic data, Rapport proposed that self-consciousness existed universally in human societies. At the core of this self-consciousness, he distinguished individuality from individualism, the latter of which was an historical and cultural ideology which only privileged individuality and vested it with transcendent value. He felt the former was the source of various attitudes, labels and creativity (Rapport 1997: 173–176).

Based on this individuality, cooperativity between selves came to be conceived of again. This cooperativity was, by no means, static nor fixed. It was not a partnership based on a meeting of the minds or rational consideration between free and autonomous individuals, nor was it a partnership in a restrictive, structured community. We can find a specific example from Reynolds who conducted research examining the attitudes of women living in black residential districts in England (Reynolds 2002: 591–606). She attempted an immanent critique on the points of view espoused by black feminists about the cooperativity of black women declaring them restrictive and structured. This was due to the fact that she felt it took as its unconditional premise, a homogenous, Enlightenment inspired, black women protagonist who separated herself from the diverse, specific lifestyles of the black community. In the unadulterated activities of real communities, solidarity based on being black or female was merely provisional and convenient in the extreme. This is to say, in contrast to the cooperativity between selves that came with being born into a lifestyle experience of community, women freely removed themselves from the structured cooperativity of being black or female and skillfully created a naturally emerging solidarity with white people and men, people who belonged to different categories.

Their self-consciousness was neither exclusivist nor absolutist. The communities they developed increased their sensitivity to selves other than their own through the accumulation of experiences such as sharing their emotional lives—the sadness, the anger and the joy—to experiences of understanding social difficulties such as poverty and sickness. The fact that cooperativity was not predefined according to race or gender and that the women had been able to shift between selves from external categories, was a characteristic of selves in the actual world. It was here that the potential for the construction of a naturally emerging cooperativity lay.[9]

This has given us a glimpse of the way towards the construction of cooperativity. Now, how can we enable the mutual understanding of parties at structurally different standpoints? Let us consider this at the end.

The first thing to consider is how to change the position of the self from one structural standpoint to another. In actual fact, Nitagai has conceptualized the potential for research as a joint project through a perpetual toing and froing where the research participates in movements involving research subjects while, on the other hand, activists move to the research analyst's camp and analyze the current situation (Nitagai 1986: 442–444). The shifting and melding of researchers and research subjects helps sublimate the opposition between the two. However, this development is too naive if it assumes it will eradicate structural differences. The result will be a restructuring and reinforcement of the relationship of control between some specialist groups (comprising the researcher and activist camps respectively), who will manipulate the logical and systematic discourse, and the vast majority of the locals.

Is there a movement that would not promote the melding or sublimation of the relatedness of the researcher and the research subject? Is there a movement that would not stand as a dead-end, the unbridgeable gap of the 'sans-culotte' anthropologists? It is conceivable that, on top of acknowledging the structural discrepancy that evidently exists and separates the researcher and the research subject, it would link into the potential for understanding or, as Nakano would put it, the 'picking up of reality through an interaction of lifestyles.' The field practice of the early Japanese Africanists, Morimichi Tomikawa, Yōichi Wazaki and others who studied African societies in the early 1960s comes closest to the perspective suggested by Nakano (Matsuda 1997: 210–6). Under the direction of the expedition chief, Kinji Imanishi, they divided into Junichirō

Itani's anthropoid team and Tadao Umesao's human team and launched into fieldwork in the societies of central Tanganyika prior to its independence. They were overwhelmed by the extraordinary cultural divide between the people in the sub-societies of Tanganyika and themselves. However, they were cognizant of the divide. While remaining self-conscious of their outsider status, they had the intense experience of sharing a foundation of mutual understanding. For instance, Wazaki affirmed that it is possible for two different parties to leave their differences as is, but experience mutual interaction and expand social interaction from there (Wazaki 1977: 65–75).

Their simple belief was that, by maintaining the heterogeneity with the subject of research and the categories of self and other, they could immerse and engross themselves in their research subjects, which allowed them to transcend the boundaries of self and other. Their belief was considered a form of primitive Romanticism in the ensuing debate on critiques of fieldwork and was paid no attention. This was due to the lack of acknowledgement as a 'theory' of fieldwork, the idea that a gap could be made bridgeable through the illogical yet intuitive process of stating a difference as a difference, then hurdling it to arrive at mutual understanding. Regardless, Wazaki and Tomikawa continued their fieldwork in defense of their style. On the one hand, they would gather snapshots in the field while continuing to carry out empirical research. On the other hand, they abandoned the idea of melding together the two worlds of the researcher and the research subject and reached mutual understanding by intuitive experience overcoming any differences.

The view of fieldwork as 'transcending differences through intuitive understanding' may, at first glance, be regarded as an indefensible, romantic, subjective impression. However, the roots of this view of the field based on sensibilities and intuitive understanding are remarkably deep. It was Masao Maruyama, a Japanese thinker and political scientist, who criticized this cognitive style as being the typically Japanese doctrine of supporting the status quo (Maruyama 1957: 206). Maruyama believed that Japanese society had, from time immemorial, a long history of relying on sensations and intuitive understanding as a physiological backlash following encounters with rationalist knowledge systems formed by universal reason and logic. In the tense situation where logic and logic were rivals competing with each other, the generation of perceptions was avoided, proclamations made that 'innate sensibilities would be respected,' but all the while justifying the 'passive adherence to a preexisting order of control.'

For Maruyama, Norinaga Motoori, a great thinker of the eighteenth century, was a typical proponent of this escapist research subject perception. Motoori's epistemology rejects all forms of rational logos in his fondness for his sense of intuition. It was a perfect match for the view of fieldwork espoused by Wazaki and other early Africanists. From Maruyama's standpoint; however, this kind of perception merely amounted to the unconditional worship of the 'practice of flapping your arms and legs about' and was the epitome of ideological opportunism. He felt that differences in structural standpoints should be disentangled as much as possible by logical analysis and could not be overcome in an instant by intuitive understanding.

It would appear that Maruyama had masterfully mowed down any attempt to conceptualize an understanding of fieldwork (and resolve the structural discrepancy between researcher and research subject) based on intuitive understanding and sensibilities.[10] However, we have seen the appearance of attempts to place the epistemology criticized by Maruyama and unique in Japanese ideology for its 'laxness,' at the core of the methodology in the self-hewn academic discipline involving histories of modern Japanese research. This was the folklore of Kunio Yanagita. Yanagita's explication that 'understanding only comes from appealing to the most nuanced mental sensation' (Yanagita [1934] 1990: 371) became the fundamental issue in folklore. He attempted to establish a vantage point, which positioned the human sensibilities espoused by Motoori as the self in an historical Gemeinschaft as opposed to the self of Maruyama's rational subject. Yanagita's methodology, which attempted to find a path to human understanding via sensation and the mind, has rarely been addressed in critiques of fieldwork theory in recent years,[11] but has been clearly reconstructed by Hiroyuki Torigoe, a proponent for the development of a new version of Japanese studies with a contemporary flavor.

Torigoe proposes reexamining Yanagita's style, which overflows with explanation and descriptive accounts that are neither positivist nor empirical at the level of an epistemology of human beings and society (Torigoe 1988). In contrast to the logocentrist view of humankind espoused by Maruyama, he avoids the schism between sensibilities and knowledge (reason) and conceives of a human perception that incorporates both. This has commonalities with observations by Hideo Kobayashi, a famous literary essayist, who holds regard for the Motoori-like perception where knowledge and sentiment are one in the same; that is, the setting up as an epistemology a 'complete perception where knowing and feeling are identical' (Kobayashi

1977: 144). It is fair to say that the idea of a 'complete perception' is a fundamental stance that gets to the crux of thinking traced back to Motoori through to Yanagita in its grasp of the relatedness with the research subject. If we take Motoori's notion of giving ourselves to the current of life's emotions, leaving any differences as they are and interacting cordially with research subjects as an epistemology rather than a theory of emotion, the mental world put forward by Yanagita comes into view. It prepares a circuit for an approach via the mind and the sensations of life which occupies a different dimension to contemporary scientific protagonists who approach the research subject by recording what they observe and what they hear.[12]

This allows us to witness the expansion of another world of perception. It is different to the hereto world of perception in which analytical reason sat at the throne and where anything which it could not objectify was labeled as sensations or as intuitive understanding and then marginalized (disparaged). This other world of perception should enable empathy with the other and the experience of understanding by leaving differences as is. This was the epistemology, arrived at by Nakano and Wazaki that became the mainstay for potential understanding between researchers and the subjects of research.

In place of a conclusion

Social research, particularly all qualitative research methodologies such as field research, has enjoyed a renaissance, following an introspective period in modern science. On the other hand, many observations have been made about the structural difficulties and unfeasibility of this methodology. Considerations of the relationship between researchers and research subjects could not be resolved by merely harking back to the political superiority or inferiority of the two, or to major and minor issues relating to specialist knowledge. There is no doubt that it is the individual in research who is listened to face-to-face. However, this brings us back to how the unit of the 'individual' is generated in specific societies and which will perhaps require us to reconfigure a theory of research. This is because there are no assurances that the 'individual' taken as the research subject in qualitative research is the same manner of self. In a similar vein, while structural discrepancies between researchers and research subjects exist, we need to reexamine how friendly relations between the two can be enabled by going back to the epistemological roots.

Viewing it this way, we can see that casting aside the infeasibility of field research and investigating the possibilities resonates with activities to innovate the epistemology and ontology of modern social sciences. If we are to assume that we can expect abundant achievements from social research in the twenty-first century, they are guaranteed to be found where the conundrum of fieldwork theory is overcome.

2
Explanation and Narrative: What Should Social Research Aim for?

Kazuo Seiyama

Neither law nor empirical generalization

The fallacy of nomothesis

There seems to be a lingering misconception that quantitative social research has nomothetic aims, though this view is arguably less common than before. As nomothesis is so recorded in social research textbooks regarded as classics, it is not easy to banish this misconception. (I did, however, make a feeble attempt to correct it in my own textbook (Seiyama 2004).

Of course, those who are actually conducting quantitative social inquiry, whether they are researchers or business people, know all too well that the reality of social research is far removed from nomothesis. Instead, survey data is usually considered to be mostly chaotic.

The works of early statisticians, such as Quételet's law of the average man and Galton's principle of regression, were originally responsible for the view that nomothesis should be the aim in the statistical analysis of quantitative survey data. The 'law of the average man' means that the 'statistical average' of people's physical, mental and moral traits signifies the 'representative individual.' Here, 'representative' is close in meaning to 'true.' It goes without saying that this law was underlain by the 'law of large numbers' in probability theory. (It is puzzling, though, how a mathematical theorem should be called a 'law'). If people's characteristics were in fact probabilistically scattered around 'common true value,' then Quételet should not necessarily be regarded as mistaken. However, of course, there is no such a thing as 'true value' in people's characteristics.

Galton's principle of regression proposes that the trait values of the sons of those fathers whose trait values diverge from the mean will tend to regress towards the mean. This proposition is correct. In fact, if this were not the case, and the sons' trait values were scattered around the same average value as their fathers, then over generations, the distribution of traits such as human height and weight would grow steadily broader. Conversely, when the mean and the variance of genetic traits within a group are stable across generations, the law of regression comes into play. (There are, of course, cases in which the law of regression does not come into existence, for example, in stochastic processes such as random walks). However, the law of regression is restricted to biological and genetic phenomena, as in Mendel's laws, and it is extremely rare, even among natural phenomena, to find such nomological phenomena.

Furthermore, it is absolutely impossible to derive laws from empirical generalization. Empirical generalization means that when some kind of statistical relationship is found to exist in regard to certain data, we may predict that basically such a relationship would also arise in regard to any alternative data. Anyone would see that such a prediction would be ridiculous, as predictions go, because it is no more than foretelling, based on an observation that an earthquake had immediately followed the leap of a catfish and that an earthquake would occur whenever a catfish leapt out of the water.

Excessive empiricism

Concepts such as nomothesis and empirical generalization are rooted in the 'excessive empiricism' that has haunted social research and sociology. Excessive empiricism considers that everything we should know is contained within observed empirical data itself, where various products of raw data processed in some way are also 'the data itself.' Examples of processed products are statistical indicators such as mean and variance, or correlation coefficient, regression coefficient and coefficient of determination. Also included are the results of calculations which employ such complex quantitative models as factor analysis and covariance structure analysis. The numerical values generated by such statistical treatment constitute 'the data itself' in the sense that these represent structural characteristics which were hidden in the original data, and extracted by means of some kind of algorithm.

A surprisingly large number of social researchers think that the objective of social research is to extract the structural characteristics of such data itself. There are also quite a few analyses of survey data which have been conducted just as if the researchers really did have that opinion, even if they themselves did not have such a clear idea. Even in qualitative surveys which do not use statistical analysis, the same tendency can be seen. For example, it is frequently insisted that in qualitative surveys the actual utterances made by subjects should be shown in their raw form, as far as possible, because the reality that we need to know is deemed to reside in them.

Such a tendency has arisen from the extreme, and bad, influence of empiricism. The proper, core meaning of empiricism might be expressed as: 'Our knowledge must be based upon things which are observed from an empirical standpoint.' However, as this 'based upon' wording is vague, it allows diverse interpretations. I think that it is sufficient to define the fundamental principle of empiricism, at most, as: 'Checks should be carried out, wherever possible, by means of things observed from an empirical viewpoint.' Hence, it does not matter at all if knowledge encompasses even those components which cannot themselves be observed empirically (such as 'gravity,' or 'energy'). Laws and theories are things, as Hume correctly pointed out, which are never able to be verified (to be proved of their 'validity') in empirical terms.

However, extreme empiricism considers that scientifically valid knowledge must be composed only of things which are able to be empirically observed. It also considers that only knowledge which is made up of things that can be observed empirically is worth us knowing. Old-time behaviorist psychology is one example of this.

Herein lays a view that things which have not been empirically observed are fictitious ideas that researchers have subjectively fabricated, and that such things are absolutely not worth knowing, and that any knowledge arising from them is false. Of course, among the elements which make up this view, the following point is entirely correct, namely that things which are empirically observed are not simply observed subjectively, but are the product of what is, for us, basically 'joint observation,' and which form a shared knowledge base. By comparison, knowledge about things which have not been empirically observed has a high degree of subjectivity which may not necessarily be shared.

However, this view is flawed on the following point, namely, that the idea is entirely mistaken that knowledge which is built up through subjective conjecture without empirical observation will always be fallacious, and will have no correspondence with the real world. In fact, this is not the case, because such knowledge as universal gravitation, energy, and genes before the discovery of DNA has been created by the subjective speculation of scientists, and yet there are also things in existence which can have proper correspondence with the real world. Moreover, generally speaking, the development of our knowledge consists of an accumulation of knowledge which, while being created by conjecture, is jointly acknowledged as being correct after having endured various examinations. It is not simply made up of an accumulation of observed facts.

Data, laws, and narratives

Let us return to the subject of social research. Nowadays, people who analyze survey data are well aware that 'formulating laws' and so on from such data is well-nigh impossible, even if that could be the goal. This is because the sort of schema which would enable a consistent understanding of complex and diverse observed facts in an intellectual way, as would a 'law,' is not just lying around among observational data in a form immediately visible.

Mostly, it is only in the far latter stages of the survey research process that some kind of 'understandable facts' become visible in quantitative social research data. When routine survey sheets are used, after the respondents' answers are entered into the sheets, the responses are recorded by some kind of electronic medium once they have gone through coding and have been assigned numeric values. During this process, the researcher is definitely unaware of the whole picture, though there are times when he or she is involved with interviews or coding in some of the cases. (This is the same even when the researcher was involved in all of the cases). The way we can find out things is by reading a data file, using statistical software. Until then, we have no way of knowing what is 'written' there.

This stands in complete contrast to qualitative surveys, which often make interviews, or observations, or written documents into their object of analysis. In this instance, the data is given in a form which we can directly read and understand. As a matter of fact, in many cases—especially with interviews, observations and so on—nothing more than what is understood by the interviewer and observer is recorded. That the data itself is in a form that can be directly read and understood in this way, means, in one sense, that the data itself is indicating its manner of 'reading.' Let me call this 'self-interpretation-presenting (*jiko-kaishaku-teiji-sei*).' Qualitative research is greatly aided by this self-interpretation-presenting of data. When the analyst goes to compose, as the outcome of survey data analysis, a 'narrative (*monogatari*),' the self-interpretation-presenting type of data on its own offers one part of that narrative, or presents the whole narrative itself. Undoubtedly, this involves some risk, and I shall discuss that later.

'Narrative' is mentioned frequently in recent years, especially in relation to qualitative research. However, the reporting of the outcomes of social research analysis as a narrative is by no means new, having been implemented long ago, though it was not widely regarded or recognized as an appropriate technique. For instance, a 'law' may also be regarded as a kind of 'narrative.' As we understand from the examples of Quételet and Galton, a 'law' gives a consistent outlook to a variety of facts. It can be said that amid the various types of 'narratives,' they proposed a type of narrative called a 'law.'

For qualitative studies, too, in an age when science was slave to excessive empiricism, it was considered that a correct research method was to record, as is, what had been observed. Anthropologists intended their records to faithfully mirror the raw facts of the societies they were studying, or else, at least, they made it look as if they did. However, as one can understand from reading Malinowski, Mead and their ilk, ethnography makes for an excellent 'narrative.'

The structure of 'anomie narrative' in Durkheim

For understanding the significance of 'narrativity' in sociological quantitative analysis, there is probably no more apt example than that of Durkheim's *On Suicide*. I want to confirm this by focusing upon his Chapter 5, 'Anomie Suicide.' This chapter has the following structure:

1. In the first section, Durkheim shows, in order, five tables which illustrate the link between economic factors and suicide rates, to accompany the explanation: 'If therefore industrial or financial crises increase suicides, this is not because they cause poverty, since crises of prosperity have the same result; it is because they are crises, that is, disturbances of the collective order' (Durkheim [1897] 1952: 246), by which a relationship between 'diminution of social regulation' and suicide is suggested.

2. In the following two sections, without showing any data, Durkheim's thoughts on the relationship between individual desire and social restrictions upon its fulfillment are developed. Firstly, the fundamental proposition is stated—that man cannot be free from all constraints, but is bound by that which he (sic) feels is superior to himself, in other words, by society. And when economic breakdown occurs, or, conversely, when he is blessed with a sudden upturn in fortunes, the constraints and regulation by society are lost and the concept of 'anomie' is exhibited, in the following style: 'The state of de-regulation or anom[ie] is thus further heightened by passions being less disciplined, precisely when they need more disciplining' (Durkheim [1897] 1952: 253).
3. Next, while showing data on suicide rates according to occupation, it is argued that 'anomie' is not something which only arises in situations of sudden peril, but also is always latent in daily social life.
4. In the fourth section, it is debated that anomie is related not only to economic life, but to all areas of social life, with a special focus upon family life. Here, again, all kinds of statistical data are employed, and in all, eight charts are shown, but there are many complex data displays which match marital status such as unmarried, divorced, separated, and widowed with age, sex, or region, etc. Here, using the concept of 'immunity' or 'inhibition ratio' towards suicide, it is emphasized that the change in inhibition ratio which accompanies divorce moves in reverse direction between wives and husbands.
5. Later in the same section, the issues of what married life is and what different meanings it has for men and women are discussed, leading to the following extremely interesting conclusion. That is to say, monogamy is beneficial to humans in that it tempers the passions and brings equilibrium to the spirit, but in the case of men, they are blessed with other opportunities to pursue their passions, in order to deal with the suffering generated by those restraints. By contrast, for women, it is claimed that 'there is no compensation or relief...The regulation therefore is a restraint to [them] without any great advantages' (Durkheim [1897] 1952: 272).

The above represents the bones of Durkheim's theories and proofs regarding anomic suicides. The issue here is neither the validity of Durkheim's interpretations regarding married life in the final section, nor that of his theories on the links between anomie and suicide. What is important is the 'narrativity' in Durkheim's method of argument. Here, there exist no less than three types of 'narrativity,' as outlined below.

Firstly, the entire structure has a splendidly dramatic composition. The parts which I divided into (1) to (5) above can be arranged as follows:

1. Introduction. While showing the data, a new intellectual problem regarding the link between economic conditions and suicide is posed.
2. Development 1. A theoretical schema (anomie theory) which can answer the problem posed in the Introduction is presented and developed.
3. Turn 1. The wide applicability of that theoretical schema is proven, along with new data.
4. Turn 2. Along with data, it is further proven that this theoretical schema is applicable even to married life, which is an altogether separate phenomenon.
5. Development 2. The theory of anomie which was posed in Development 1 is further expanded by tying it to the theories on marriage.

There is no part constituting a 'conclusion' here, but this is because after this chapter, the latter half of the entire volume, *On Suicide*, functions as a 'conclusion.' In any case, this layout of Chapter 5 strongly emphasizes to the reader the significance of the concept of 'anomic suicide.' Without questioning whether to use statistical data, one might say that it offers one model for the structure that a research thesis should adopt.

Secondly, different kinds of narrativity, as described below, are buried within it. These are the narrative of 'anomie' in Development 1, and the narrative of 'the difference in the meaning of married life for men and women' in Development 2. Anomie is the theme running through the whole of *On Suicide*, and the Development 1 part is, in a manner of speaking, the scene in which the protagonist makes a grand entrance. In the case of sociological research, it is concepts, theses and theories that constitute the protagonist and the other main characters, and these in themselves constitute narratives. The 'anomie' narrative is made up of the message that 'people cannot live under conditions of perfect liberty and without regulation.' This is demonstrated to us as an inescapable destiny for us human beings.

The other narrative, on the 'meaning of married life,' is also shown as a predestined pattern surrounding the relationship between men and women. The inescapable restraint or structure which is shown to be predestined or fated gives 'meaning' to existence. There is nothing more effective for giving a clear and solid basis to life than the verdict that 'it has to be the way it is.' The concepts of 'anomie' and 'married life' that Durkheim openly discloses in his sociological theories both also give similar verdicts.

Come to think of it, such properties of sociological theory are not confined to Durkheim. One might recall what a fatalistic tone Weber's writing employed, in such works as *The Protestant Ethic and the Spirit of Capitalism* (Weber [1920] 1996), *Politics as a Vocation* and *Science as a Vocation* (Weber [1919] 2004).

At any rate, in Chapter 5 of *On Suicide*, I must point out, there is a third kind of narrativity which is common to regular quantitative research theses. In this chapter, a total of fourteen sets of statistical data relating to suicide are presented—five in (1), one in (2), and eight in (3)—but none of those sets, by any means, directly show 'anomie' or 'the difference in the significance of marriage for men and women.' Nowhere in the suicide statistics do words like 'anomie' or 'the meaning of marriage' appear. For example, one table sorts French 'departments' by suicide rates, and is merely something which shows the 'average number of persons of independent means per one thousand inhabitants,' and simply suggests that 'the greater an area's economic prosperity, the higher its suicide rate' (Durkheim [1897] 1952: 245). From the beginning, any of the individual suicides which are supposed to form the basis of suicide statistics, has no accompanying special mark or evidence to indicate the 'reason for the suicide,' nor are suicide notes left that say: 'I am going to die by anomic suicide.' Suicide statistics have simply enumerated the incidence of the phenomenon called suicide. It is the same even when cross-tabulated by age, region, or married/unmarried status.

Durkheim's *On Suicide*, seen as a quantitative analysis, presents a 'narrative' for these disparate pieces of statistical data to be interpreted in a unified manner. In other words, it tries to explain the 'social causes' which give rise to the phenomenon of suicide by providing the type of suicide—'egoistic,' 'altruistic' and 'anomic' (in addition to these, there is a fourth, 'fatalistic suicide,' but this is not deemed important by Durkheim). These suicide types do not classify individual suicides, but constitute types of social causes of suicide (though Durkheim himself occasionally treats them as if they were types of individual suicide).

The success of *On Suicide*, one might say, lies in its triple-layered 'narrativity,' as I have described above.

Explanation and narrative

Explanation vs interpretation and understanding

In recent debates on meta-theory relating to sociology and social research, 'narrative/storytelling' and 'explanation' are often discussed contrastively. 'Explanation' is often supposed to be a method of sociological statement which is positivistic, and connected to a scientific view close to that of the natural sciences, while 'narrative,' on the other hand, is interpretive, and is considered the more appropriate as a method of statement about social phenomena. This distinction nearly overlaps that of the old-time 'explanation vs interpretation/ understanding' distinction. When the latter distinction used to be debated, the main task of sociology was thought to be the explanation or understanding of 'action.' Accordingly, 'understanding' meant elucidating action in line with the actor's subjective meaning-world. 'Explanation,' in contraposition with 'understanding,' was considered to be elucidation which employed a kind of arbitrary conceptual scheme of the observer's that ignored, and was unrelated to, the actor's subjective meaning-world.

Fundamental to such contraposition is whether 'the actor's meaning-world' or 'the observer's meaning-world' is privileged. Those who advocated 'interpretation' and 'understanding' over 'explanation' thought that the conceptual scheme used by the observer was inappropriate for apprehending the actor's meaning-world. (If one looks at qualitative research textbooks in current circulation, one can see that there are many people who think that way, even now). But, needless to say, even in 'interpretation' and 'understanding,' every statement will be expressed in the words of the sociologist who is the observer, and hence these ultimately will have to be rooted in the observer's meaning-world. Consequently, the real issue is not simply either the actor's meaning-world or the observer's meaning-world, but ought to be; how the observer's meaning-world could incorporate and position the actor's meaning-world in an appropriate way from the viewpoint of a sociological methodology. The reason for Alfred Schutz's criticism of Weber's Interpretive Sociology in his book, *The Phenomenology of the Social World* (Schutz [1932] 1967) was that Weber had not been sufficiently aware of the various problems associated with methods of inquiry into the meaning-world of the actor.

After that, action theory declined in sociology. In its place, the social-constructivist or constructionist view that the social world itself is something that has been constructed by people's meaning-worlds gathered ground. In other words, the view began to prevail that the social world itself was constructed as a meaning-world.

The distinction between 'explanation' and 'narrative' has this as its background. Here, too, there is a tendency for 'explanation' to be conceptualized as conforming to an observer's arbitrary schema of understanding, which ignores the constructionality of social phenomena as meaning-world which are the object of investigation. It is deemed that being empirical and scientific is bound to produce knowledge, which the observer self-righteously builds up, independently of the meaning structure inherent in the world being studied. 'Narrative' is different, for this view, in that it aims to describe, as faithfully as possible, the meaning structure of the social world. Being structured as a meaning-world, means that the very object of inquiry is made up of narratives of some kind. For that reason, 'narrative' is regarded as a more appropriate method of sociological statement than 'explanation.' This is fundamental to the position which distinguishes between the two.

What is 'narrative'?

The way of thinking which contrasts 'explanation' and 'narrative' considers that what has hitherto been taken as 'explanation' in sociology is different from 'narrative,' but, in fact, this is wrong, or, at least, is not a precise way of understanding. As we have already seen, Durkheim's *On Suicide* is full of all kinds of narratives.

A quite general definition of 'narrative' could probably be phrased as: 'a story which portrays various happenings (events) that occur over time as a particular realm which is meaningful and ordered, by those events being arranged and stated in a meaning-related way.' Novels, films, plays, historical sagas and suchlike are typical examples. Sometimes, critiques such as: 'This novel's story has collapsed' happen to be raised; this means that the link between the events is not well ordered. On the other hand, in the heyday of existentialism, a great fuss was once made over absurdist literature and absurdist theatre, but these represented a narrative ordered by the message that 'the world has no meaning (i.e. there is no God).'

The concept of 'narrative' can be formed in an even broader sense by removing the condition of 'temporality' from the above formulation. An academic paper, unlike a novel, which is not something with events arranged in temporal order, still often has narrativity in its form consisting of 'Introduction; Development; Turn; and Conclusion.' Of course, even in this case, one cannot say it is altogether divorced from temporality, as the task of reading a paper is carried out over a length of time. However, as it will be appreciated that it is possible to read a story even into a single picture, such as Michelangelo's 'Creation of Adam,' what is important is not the temporal arrangement, but some other kind of sequence. Noe Keiichi, for example, asserts that 'it is the forging of "relationships to a specific thematic subject in human life" which is the foundation for changing something incomprehensible into something acceptable' (Noe 2005: 316). In other words, while temporality has a deep association with 'narrative,' it is not essential.

When one thinks like this, one can say that a meaning-world which has been ordered in some form has the characteristic of a narrative. If this were true, then many scientific research theses would simultaneously constitute 'explanations' and 'narratives.' This is because scientific research is something which aims to elucidate the structure of the order hidden in the realm of the object of study.

Here, it would probably be a good idea to add an explanatory note about the concepts of 'meaning-world' and 'meaning' which I have used so far without particular explanation. 'Meaning' is a multifarious and subjective thing. People can discover a variety of meanings in all manner of things. This corresponds to what Noe calls the 'thematic subject.' 'Meaning' does not only refer to things such as the meaning of life or the meaning of history. 'Meaning' is basically a relational concept, and when an item called 'a' is related to 'A' in an ordered world composed of 'A, B, C...' for example, then an understanding that 'the meaning of "a" is "A" ' is generated. The 'meaning' of individual words is like that. An ordered world is a world which basically has been constructed by concepts. Of course, in the case of the natural world, first there are natural things, and an ordered world is constructed by their representations. We usually believe that there is order in the natural world itself, and that is not necessarily a problem, but that order is only ever represented at a conceptual level.

Accordingly, in natural science research, new knowledge is often obtained in the form: 'So that's what it meant!' The famous anecdote about Archimedes discovering the law of specific gravity, crying 'Eureka!' and leaping naked out of his bath proves that.

Thus, it can be seen that 'narratives' are not rare even in natural science. In actual fact, theories like the theory of evolution or the big bang hypothesis, as well as the periodic table of elements or the theory of continental drift, and so on, all have ample properties worthy of a 'narrative.' Each is a theory that gives coherent order to various things.

'Narrative' in scientific explanation

An 'explanation' is primarily an answer to a question in relation to certain given data or facts: 'Why does it exist as such?' There can be various answers to this. There are thin explanations and thick explanations, and there are simple ones and complex ones, too. Whatever the case, 'to explain' means basically 'to present an explicit answer to a question.' An 'explanation' is made up of a set consisting of a question and its answer. In addition, in order for an explanation to be accepted as such, it must be acknowledged as being a coherent answer to the question. This is based on the premise that a fixed, common understanding exists in relation to 'what kind of answer constitutes a coherent answer.' For example, in order to convincingly explain why $1/2 + 1/3$ equal $5/6$, rather than $2/5$, a basic knowledge of fractions and addition must be shared by both parties. In this manner, 'explanation' can be said to be the presentation of the answer to a question, with a presumption of a certain minimum level of common understanding.

Scientific theories, also, often have the characteristics of a narrative. It is not correct to think that scientific explanation and narrative are always going to be in opposition. However, just as it is not objectively determined as to in what we will find a meaning, neither is it basically determined as to in what we will find a narrative. It is similar to how some people will think that a certain novel is interesting, while others will think it uninteresting. Whether something is a narrative depends on whether all of its elements are arranged and connected in such a form as to project the image of an ordered meaning-world, and, in that case, it is fundamentally a subjective matter as to what kind of thing can constitute an ordered meaning-world.

Looking at it this way, it means that people who insist that scientific explanation is mere 'explanation,' and not 'narrative,' are simply protesting that 'the explanation is not a sufficiently meaningful explanation, as far as we are concerned.' Things that do not project the image of an ordered meaning-world in their own subjectivity are mere 'explanations,' not 'narratives,' that is to say, 'logically, they make sense, but somehow we are not totally convinced.'

By contrast, there are some researches in which 'arguments are unexpectedly convincing, though they do not make sense logically, or else cannot be said to make sense sufficiently.' These are cases in which the arguments that are developed do succeed in projecting an image of an ordered meaning-world for the reader, but that success is not necessarily dependent upon 'them making sense as scientific explanations,' and, at best, is assisted by 'them appearing to make sense.' Here, there could be room for debate as to 'whether they make sense as scientific explanations'—for example, there was once a long-running confrontation between Marxist economics and neo-classical economics as to which was the more 'scientific.' That was a case in which not even the minimum level of inter-subjectivity that would be needed for an explanation to be shared was established. (To say the truth, at the base of this confrontation was the fact that a 'narrative' which transcended a minimum 'explanation' had been posited by each as a condition for establishing its 'scientific explanation'). However, in many cases, researchers already have a certain level of shared understanding as to 'what kind of explanation is a valid explanation.' For example, even between Marxist economics and other schools of economics, there was a large common understanding about the basic explanatory schema relating to indicators of national economy and the supply-and-demand relationship of the market.

Even without relying upon it 'making sense as a scientific explanation,' if something can 'emerge as the image of an ordered meaning-world' for readers, it means that a 'narrative' has indeed come into existence there. Needless to say, regular novels and films have always been like that. For a certain thing to be a 'narrative,' there is no particular need for it 'to make sense as a scientific explanation.'

Here, let us call the system of a certain bunch of statements a tale (*setsuwa*) in general. A tale may be an 'explanation,' or 'narrative,' or neither. Consequently, we basically can establish the three categories in Figure 2.1, in relation to tales. Of these, we may probably give the name 'fiction' to 'narratives which are not explanations.'

It goes without saying; however, 'to make sense as a scientific explanation' is not the same as 'to be correct as a scientific explanation.' Naturally, we aim for 'correct explanation,' but we ultimately cannot know what constitutes correct explanation. What we can actually judge is whether it 'makes sense as a scientific explanation,' and that is something which can be judged in the light of the individuals' entire knowledge at that moment in time. In that case, we appeal to a certain minimum 'inter- subjectivity.' In other words, 'explanation' can be called an activity that builds up knowledge of the kind that can take on a shared nature, in respect to its 'making sense.'

Figure 2.1: Narrative and explanation

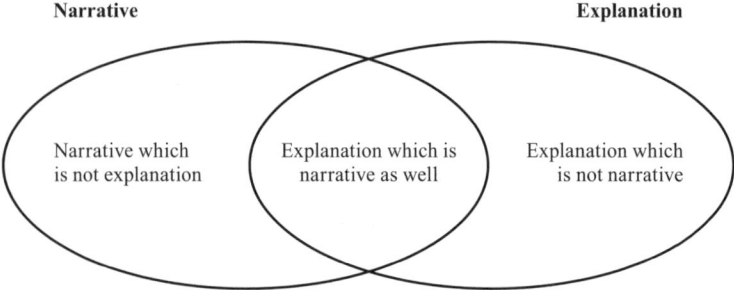

'Explanation' and 'narrative' in sociology

Reasons for narrativity

Here, once more, let us return to the confrontation between 'explanation' and 'narrative' in sociology. The following three types might be identified among discussions which emphasize 'narratives.' Firstly, there is the 'essential narrativity' theory, which asserts that sociological inquiry is essentially nothing but 'narrative,' and so is anything which has in the past been seen as 'scientific explanation.' Secondly, the 'negative narrativity' theory, which asserts that in sociology, as so-called scientific explanation is intrinsically impossible, sociology can but be narrative after all. Third and finally, the 'normative narrativity' theory, which asserts that in sociology, scientific explanation is an inappropriate or insufficient method of statement, and narrative is the statement method which sociology should adopt.

There are a number of important differences among the above. For example, normative narrativity theory, which is often held by people who emphasize qualitative research against quantitative research, maintains that it is possible for sociological tales not to be narratives, as in quantitative research. However, negative narrativity theory does not think so. Alternatively, in meta-methodological arguments in sociology, there is no small number of people who advocate essential narrativity theory's claim that even quantitative survey research is 'narrative,' after all.

Nevertheless, in spite of such differences, these theories all have a common factor in their judgment that 'scientific explanation' in sociology is impossible or inappropriate. This assessment is, in my view, definitely mistaken on the following points; that is, abandoning 'scientific explanation' would mean abandoning an orientation toward establishing correct knowledge that would be a shared asset. Though, there is not the space to discuss this in detail, it should be remarked, the activity called 'science' is, after all, a joint effort which tries to 'build up common knowledge which can be reasonably shared.' There can be different opinions as to what sort of methods and what kind of contents are 'reasonable,' and indeed there have been, and often, there also have existed mistaken understandings, but they do not waver in their determination to build up 'reasonable common knowledge.'

Among those debates which emphasize 'narrative,' there are some which consider that 'narrative is the most effective method for procuring reasonable common knowledge.' Certainly, 'narrative' is to some extent an effective method in the establishment of common knowledge and of communality which employs the latter as a medium. This will be immediately appreciated if one considers 'national narratives,' 'revolutionary narratives' and suchlike. However, in these narratives the concept of 'the validity of the knowledge' is obscure or is outright absent. There is a lack of problem-consciousness as to whether we should consider 'the validity of knowledge' as valuable, and if one is to consider it so, then how it is to be conceptualized, and what kind of guiding principle and procedures are to be determined for that purpose.

On the other hand, among arguments which advocate narratives there are several points of contention which can be concurred with.

1. Even in cases in which the aim is scientific exploration in sociology, it is desirable that the outcomes of the investigation should not remain at simple explanation, but are presented with some narrativity. Narrative and explanation can be made compatible rather than being in opposition and it is a good thing to add narrativity while establishing explanation as a minimum condition.

2. It cannot be denied that in sociology up till now, much of what has been seen as 'scientific explanation' does not, in actual fact, constitute a reasonable explanation, and instead was merely a narrative. It is well known that theories such as those of Comte, Spencer's views on evolution, and Marxism were like that. This may also be the case for Parsonian theory and Foucault's treatises on power. However, it is ubiquitous in the history of knowledge in general that theories which at some point have been seen as affording 'reasonable explanations in their own

way' is later found to be 'actually not reasonable,' and this is by no means a phenomenon peculiar to sociology.
3. Apart from the above, there is an even stronger point of contention which supports the narrativity of sociology. This asserts that the social world itself can be considered to be a sort of narrative. Certainly, as we have already seen, the social world is basically constructed by meaning, and, in many aspects, it is composed of a variety of 'narratives' which are intricately multi-layered. (Of course, this does not mean that everything is covered in narrative). 'National narratives,' 'revolutionary narratives,' 'spiritual narratives,' 'divine narratives' and so on are like that, and even on a micro level, so are 'family narratives' and 'company narratives.' It is probably indisputable that individuals and groups live through any number of 'narratives.'

Taking the last point into consideration, attention probably should be paid to the fact that there are two different types of 'narrative' in sociological research. These are firstly 'narratives' which the world in question generates about itself; and secondly, those 'narratives' which sociological researchers themselves produce in their own statements. This distinction overlaps that of first-order versus second-order social theory, or the emic/etic dichotomy.

Sociological inquiry as second-order theory sometimes aims to decipher the 'narratives' of the world it investigates, and at other times it does not. This is because the target world does not necessarily always have a 'narrative' of its own. However, at the same time, when explaining the phenomena of the world in question, it often happens that one discovers there is a 'narrative' of which one was hitherto unaware, and uses that to explain the target world. 'Class narratives' (Seiyama 1999) were discovered in just such a way.

Statistical indicators as first-order interpretations

As I have already noted, data in quantitative social research is quite removed from the discovery of 'laws,' and is not something easily 'able to be understood.' To analyze data means finding something understandable from among things which initially seem impossible to understand or to find a new way of understanding hitherto undiscovered.

In most cases of quantitative sociological data, it first appears in the form of a 'survey sheet.' Taken individually, each piece of data which is inscribed on a survey sheet is understandable. If, in answer to the question: 'How old are you now?' '49' is entered, then it is well understood that this respondent is forty-nine years of age. However, though such localized understandability may exist, it does not follow that the entire body of collected data can be immediately understood.

In order to make the whole body of quantitative data understandable, we usually transfer the entries on the survey sheets into a data file. Even when it is a text file, this file is nothing but a string of symbols in which the numerals from 0 to 9 and blank columns seem at first glance to be arranged completely at random. It would be hardly possible to read any kind of meaning from it in its present state.

When this string of symbols is processed by means of statistical software, a certain 'understandable' output becomes apparent, as in the case of simple tabulation and cross-tabulation, for instance. Statistical software plays the role of an Enigma cipher decoder. It generates statistically meaningful 'numeric values' such as frequency, percentage, mean, or variance of a certain 'variable,' from strings of symbols which deceptively appear to be lined up at random.

Such statistical indicators as these, have meaning in their own way. Knowing the statistical distribution addresses our intellectual interest. However, at this point we must pay heed to the following, namely that such statistical indicators are 'universally applicable.' In short, these indicators are by nature applicable to any kind of statistical data (naturally, some differences do exist according to whether the variables are numeric or categorical), and can be given figures as their concrete values. In consequence, statistical indicators constitute a 'common measuring instrument' like a ruler or a weighing machine, and a 'common yardstick' for the measurements thus obtained.

The values of statistical indicators which we obtain by using statistical software are numerical values resulting from having measured data with a universally-applicable yardstick. The values of mean and variance signify the characteristics of each piece of data measured with our common yardstick, as do the values of individuals' respective heights and weights. The numerical values resulting from the measurement of phenomena according to a common yardstick constitute numerical values which are meaningful to us, for the very reason that they were measured by a 'common yardstick.' Moreover, if we compare them with different data and different variables, this will satisfy an even greater intellectual interest, just as I can find out the difference between my weight a year ago and my present weight. In this sense, a bundle of numerical values which computes, for example, the incidence of suicide by calendar year appears as something meaningful to us, even by itself. In other words, it appears to us as 'something that has order.'

Usually, the first step in quantitative analysis is to derive such statistical indicators. Once this has progressed somewhat, one seeks statistical indicators with reference not only to a single variable, but to a combination of two or more variables. Computing suicide rates by year, region, sex and so on is one example. It is also possible to seek various kinds of quantitative or qualitative correlation coefficients (or association indices), although Durkheim did not do so.

Statistical indicators are universally applicable measuring instruments for viewing quantitative data as 'things which have order.' Those which were originally developed as such comprise the various statistical indicators widely used today. (One can also think of countless statistical indicators which nobody would use. They are not used because they do not show us anything significant to our intellectual interest).

Generally, something which gives order to data (or texts), or, to be more precise, 'something which we see as having order' or 'in which we find order,' is called an 'interpretation.' We could say this 'finds meaning,' but 'meaning' is something which has an interpenetrative relationship with some kind of ordered structure. We can probably call the task of computing statistical indicators from quantitative data 'first-order interpretation.' This gives a basic order to things which hitherto appeared only to be strings of random symbols. (For that matter, one might say that with qualitative data from interview surveys, records of observation, et cetera, in which the data itself is already documented, the 'first-order interpretation' is already completed. The data has already been given order in some form. Being able to read and understand it means that it is presented in a form that is able to be interpreted).

The fourteen tables in Durkheim's *On Suicide* in themselves exhibit such a first-order interpretation in relation to suicide. It is not difficult to imagine how much data-collection and calculation had been undertaken by various government organizations in each country, or what a sober and gigantic task it must have been for his nephew, Marcel Mauss, but this work has resulted in the computation of tables representing a first-order interpretation.

The importance of 'narrative' in quantitative research

Be that as it may, in quantitative research, the word 'interpretation' is usually used in a different sense from that of the above. For example, when one reads out cross-tabulated sex and individual income data, and finds that there is a tendency for men's income to be distributed at a higher level than women's, he or she may deduce from those results that 'the income discrepancy between men and women is large.' This is usually called 'interpretation.' In this case, 'interpretation' is meant to be a task that re-expresses calculated statistical indicators in 'language that could describe the structural traits of the world under scrutiny.' At this stage, we shift from the universal language of statistical indicators to the unique linguistic system used to describe the world in question. We can call this 'second-order interpretation.'

In many texts on survey methods, basically it is 'second-order interpretation' on this level which involves tasks called a 'hypothesis construction,' 'hypothesis verification by means of data,' and so on. Here, a 'hypothesis verification' is, for example, with setting up a 'hypothesis' such as 'men's individual income has a tendency to be higher than women's,' merely to check it with the data. A 'hypothesis,' in this sense, is about the structural traits of the world in question, and checking whether the data conforms to that hypothesis constitutes a second-order interpretation of the data.

As can be seen from the above example, such a second order interpretation, or hypothesis verification, is often trivial. This is so, even if one made good use of a high technique such as multivariate analysis. The judgment as to what is trivial and what is interesting is of course, mainly subjective. But, the following may be said generally. (1) Basically we are concerned with knowing something new about the world in question, and verifying something we already know is trivial. (2) It is more interesting to know a certain basic, or comprehensive structural trait of the world in question, rather than to know a single trait separately. (3) Consequently, what is more interesting for us in data analysis is to produce an explanatory scheme which would enable us to understand, in a unified way, the set of various statistical indicators obtained from first-order interpretation, and this may well be considered a 'narrative.'

An analysis of such, that is, an analysis which would explain data by a narrative may be called the 'third-order interpretation.' In fact,

Durkheim's *On Suicide* can be seen as a representative of such third-order interpretation among quantitative data analyses.

Explanation that is also narrative

As I have already stated, in contrast to quantitative data, qualitative data is 'self-interpretation-presenting,' in that it can be read and understood in its own terms. Frequently, it offers a self-narrative of the target world. This is one attribute of qualitative data which gives it vast advantages over quantitative data, and it is this very point which probably constitutes the major reason for today's relative surge of interest, among young researchers, in qualitative studies. This is the underside of the fact that, unlike as in Durkheim's day, recently it has become extremely difficult to contrive a 'narrative' out of quantitative data.

This is also linked to the downfall of grand theories, as we are now in an age when there would be little point in 'interpreting' research data according to Marxist doctrine, or in carrying out quantitative analysis in keeping with modernization theory. Other middling and small theories are not of much use, either. In such a situation, it is difficult to construct a 'narrative' out of quantitative data. That is why we seize upon qualitative data by which (it is thought) a 'narrative' could be obtained comparatively easily.

Of course, an easily obtained 'narrative' is not necessarily one worth our knowing. It does not follow that any 'narrative' will do. Valid research has, as its minimum objective, the explanation of all observed facts. It is the researcher's original explanation that makes the research worthy of the name. If the researcher could go even further and craft that explanation as a narrative, then it would probably become knowledge that is deeply interesting to many people. This transcends the differences between qualitative and quantitative studies, and applies equally to both.

3
Rethinking Case Studies: Research as a Power to Construct Lives

Taisuke Miyauchi

Introduction: what is a 'case study'?

In this article, the significance and method of 'case study research' and 'case study descriptions' will be explored. Prior to doing so, I will provide some background and discuss some of my thoughts and reflections underlying this piece.

I have written various works, including a variety of monographs, historical-sociological descriptions and policy debates. I have investigated specific topics and matters, such as the history of prawns, sago palms and dried bonito (Miyauchi 1989; Tsurumi and Miyauchi eds 1996; Fujibayashi and Miyauchi eds 2004), and recorded the lives of village people (Miyauchi 1998, 2000, 2003a). In academia these are called case studies. I myself have at times used the expression: 'From the case of...,' as subtitles for my articles. This shows a particular stance which uses the specific case study in order to discuss the whole issue. Nevertheless, this expression: 'From the case...,' does not sit well with my way of thinking. Do we deal with case studies only to discuss the whole picture? Is the case merely a starting point? What is the whole picture?

In the academic world, case studies are usually 'positioned' in either of two ways. The first and more common position and claim is that the case is a sample of the whole. It is not practical to investigate every small detail of the overall picture, so instead a typical or characteristic case is described and 'used' in the discussion regarding the whole. In this approach it is necessary to give an explanation of why that particular case was chosen. This is regarded as a sort of convention by the writer and reader and is given like an excuse, to be considered no further. However, sometimes there are people who read this more seriously and criticize the given reason for that case being chosen as insufficient or unconvincing.

The second position is that the essential quality of things can be seen in a case, and it is not a sample of the quantitative whole. This is a somewhat 'risky' expression, so only a few claim it openly.[1] It says that a case, which does not quantitatively represent the whole picture and is neither a typical nor average example, still displays some essential qualities. It is a claim that the overall picture and structure is presented, not quantitatively, but qualitatively in something minor. Although 'risky,' this is closer to the actual thoughts of many case study researchers. However, the question remains what are the 'essential nature' and the 'qualitative whole?'

Another area to reflect upon is the idea of the 'advanced case.' It is an expression not often used by sociologists but rather more so by local government staff and policy researchers. When something is 'more advanced' in some way (it may be a region, a local government, a company or an NPO (Non-profit organization)), this expression 'advanced case' is used in the sense of learning from that example.

In Sapporo City where I live, while talking with a local government officer in charge of the environmental policy, he asked me to 'tell him about advanced cases that I may know of.' My immediate thought was this was not a role for academic researchers. I thought that to 'know various cases' was more of a task for the consulting company or local government officials. It seemed to me that the role of scholars was not to pass on information about various cases, but to derive something from those cases. However, my thinking this way left me pondering, and I felt the need to pursue the meaning of 'case study' a little further.

Whether one is a researcher, local government officer or citizen, there cannot be a great deal of worth in just knowing many cases. Obviously, the meaning of each case must be understood. To know many cases, in the true sense, is not just to be a 'know-all.' So again, what is a 'case?'

Finally, I wish to think about the relationship between 'well-being' and case study research. In other words, what is the purpose of research? There is not much formal discussion on the purpose of case study research in particular. Sociology has been wary of clarifying an intent and thus setting a mold for the case study and this caution has been sensible. However, when sociological description is constructed, there is always a hidden background and purpose of why it was written. This may be uninteresting if shown clearly, or may not be possible to express in short, clear phrases, and therefore one tends to use more or less middling phrases such as 'to contribute to discussions in the academic world.' However, in most cases this is far from the actual intentions of the writer. There is always a reason for the researcher to have been attracted to the specific subject of the research. There is not only an attraction, of course, but also complex feelings and thoughts and the subject itself presents the researcher with a dilemma of some sort. An excellent ethnography suggestively shows these quandaries and, this in fact, draws the readers to the work. The 'well-being' of both the researcher and the researched becomes the main player behind the scenes of a strong and compelling case study research.

With such thoughts as the background, I would like to reflect once more on what case studies mean to us. I will reconsider the significance and method of case studies with consideration of the notion of 'well-being'. The connection between the issue of 'constructing life' and case studies will be discussed also. This discussion will begin with the 'case' of a man's life history, a man who has sought 'well-being' in life, just like any other person in the world.

Constructing life and case study research

Constructing life

This narrative is about the life history of a resident, P, of Malaita Island in the Solomon Islands where I have been carrying out research for a decade. P was born in 1959 in Anokelo Village on Malaita Island. His father had come down to the coastal area from an inland village with his family and relatives, in 1937, before P was born. Conversion to Christianity and increased access to consumer goods were some of the motivating factors behind the move. Immediately after relocating to the coast, the father went to work for two years at a coconut plantation, owned by an Australian, on another island. Soon afterwards war broke out (the invasion by the Japanese military during World War II) and the family moved again to an inland village, different to the one they were originally from. After the war, when an anti-colonial self-governance movement called the Maasina Rule began in the 1940s, many people came down to the coastal area in response to the call. P's father and family also returned and settled in the current Anokelo Village.

Here at Anokelo village, P was born. As a teenager, in 1975, he began to work along with his parents at an oil palm plantation on the neighboring island called Guadalcanal. The vast plantation was populated with workers from other islands. The plantation company even owned a construction division, in which P worked. He also became active in union activities, negotiating with the company for better wages and living conditions.

While working at the plantation, he married and had children. He was promoted and obtained wage rises. His children attended a primary school within the plantation. Pijin English (the common language in the Solomon Islands) was spoken at the school, where there were children from various regions. His children improved in their Pijin rather than their native Fataleka language.

P did not intend to work at the plantation forever. 'However hard you work at the plantation, you don't get big money. The reason I went to work there was to learn construction skills, and I intended to come back some day. The company asked me to stay but I returned, also because I thought that the children needed to learn about their own village.'

In the village the opportunity for cash income is greatly reduced but there is easy access to cultivable fields and natural resources. P's family returned to their village in 1991. Apart from growing crops for their own consumption, they worked hard at producing copra for the export market, and crops and processed food for the local market.

In 1996 P went by himself to the capital, Honiara, in Guadalcanal Island, to work in construction. He went there to earn school fees so that three of his children could attend secondary school. P began a life shuttling between his village and Honiara. Whenever he found a short-term construction job, he would go to Honiara to work. He chose a life where he earned money in the town and his family lived in the subsistence economy of the village.

P also considered another path, to buy land on Guadalcanal Island. This was a livelihood strategy which had gradually spread among the Malaitans since the 1980s. It involved purchasing land near Honiara and cultivating fields, as well as seeking a way of creating a cash income in Honiara. Like others, P too bought land twenty kilometers from Honiara.

This strategy, however, collapsed with the ethnic conflict which began in 1999. Armed groups of Guadalcanal islanders began to expel

Malaitans and other islanders. P was forced to abandon his acquired land. With the conflict there was less work in town and he went back to the village. After that, he planned a move to the inland area of Malaita Island and considered 'returning' to the land which his family group had supposedly originally owned. Anokelo Village, where the family presently lived, was not the land to which P and his family belonged, and with the conflict, this made them feel vulnerable. Also there were other reasons which compelled him to make this decision. Indeed, the coastal village was becoming overcrowded and areas suitable for slash-and-burn farming were running out. It became difficult to acquire natural resources in the vicinity, and even firewood, an everyday necessity, had become hard to obtain. The subsistence sector in the inland region was seen as more advantageous. With close relatives, P made this migration plan and set it into motion in 2000. In a small group they visited the site, building a simple dwelling and clearing a field. Later on, they went back from time to time, expanding the field.[2]

To summarize, P tried many ways to survive. His response was typical of the way of life in the Solomon Islands. People combine various resources to live. From a wide range of resources such as: access to land and natural resources (ownership and usufruct), an accumulated relationship with natural resources, various rights in the village, mutual aid systems, personal relationships, skills, school education, access to a monetary economy and wage labor, connections with town, political connections, and a variety of modern systems; these are combined at each turn to construct life. Each of these resources is insufficient or unstable on their own. By combining multiple resources, life could go on even if one failed. Or, if one improved over some period, the quality of life would improve also.

Watching the life of the Solomon Islanders, it occurred to me that such expressions as 'economic development is what people in developing countries hope for' or 'a life in harmony with nature is what they wish for' were unreasonable. The recently popular argument for community-based development also seemed problematic. I admit that I came to this research site with a sort of admiration for people living a subsistence life. However, when I actually entered the site, my attention was first drawn to the fact that their life was unexpectedly full of variety. There are those who have a clear inclination towards town life, and those who regard life in the village as preferable above all. In sum, one can see many different intentions and strategies employed by people, and while their available choices are not numerous and are limited, each individual and each household can support their life with ingenuity and attempt to improve their quality of life.

Here on the Solomon Islands, I wanted to consider the rather fundamental question of what was a desirable society. What I learnt there was that a happy society was a society where one could construct a life 'happily.' What did it mean to be able to construct a life 'happily?' From my observations in the Solomon Islands, I thought about these four provisional points. Firstly, that one would have choices. Of course, in any society it is not possible to have an infinite number of choices, but nevertheless, it is important to have a certain degree of freedom. Secondly, that one can construct their own life. It is not forced onto them by anyone, and one can take their own lead in the construction. Thirdly, it cannot be a good society if one can only construct life in painful situations. As an example from the circumstances in the Solomon Islands, a desirable life construction occurs in the midst of good human relationships centering on family and friends. Fourthly, that one's identity and dignity are maintained as life is constructed.

Residents' case study research and our case study research

P has been a friend of mine ever since I first began researching on the island, but he was not the one who first told me about the inland migration plan. That was A, who lives in a neighboring village. While I was talking with him the topic came up, that 'P's clan is thinking of moving to the *bush* (meaning inland in Pijin English). They already have a small shelter and field there, and go there sometimes.' Later I would hear a detailed story from P himself, but when I asked around, many villagers knew of this. B, a primary school principal living in a neighboring village to Anokelo, said:

> P and the others will probably not migrate completely. There's the problem of roads, and the difficulties of schooling and medical care. Even if they move, the foundation of their life will probably be their present village.[3]

B said that he was in fact thinking about an inland move himself. 'The land on which we live now isn't our land. I don't want to be involved in disputes, so I'm thinking of returning to our land. There are many who think that way.' Indeed, I gradually found that a lot of people and groups in this area were considering moving inland. By moving inland to where the land was said to 'belong' to their clan, troublesome conflicts about the land could be avoided. Other reasons to move included higher productivity in the inland fields and ease of obtaining wild plants and animals. However, the current situation is that people are hesitant to make the move because, as B says, there are no roads running inland, and no schools or hospitals.

The attempt by P's group had been an 'advanced case.' Therefore, people were watching their movements closely and analyzing them. Their individual situations may differ, but they were observing them to see whether they would succeed as a 'case study' for their own future life plan.

Why do people do 'case study research'?

People grasp things from various case studies to use as a reference for constructing their own life. 'Case studies' themselves are a kind of resource for their life. To learn about cases means to acquire wisdom for living and empowerment. Thinking in this way, there are a wide range of cases for villagers, not limited to those around them but including distant cases broadcast on radio, news of government and NGO activities, past as well as present cases and, in some instances, overseas cases (described by myself, for example). These are absorbed and used as references when constructing life. They are neither 'a case as a sample of the whole' nor 'a case for exploring an essential nature,' but rather a case which is a 'resource with which to construct life.'

The important thing is that people do not collect various cases to make up numbers, but interpret the cases while collecting and sorting them, and then reinterpret them as they are used. Cases are not resources from the start; they become a resource by going through a process in which they are selected, interpreted, and sorted.

Kōkichirō Miura (2004), based on his experience of research with residents in outcast villages in Japan, looked at the situation where people refused to partake in the research or felt hesitant to be questioned and analyzed. Miura thought that they were acting in such a way by means of a 'very social-science-like recognition.' As Miura says, irrespective of being a researcher or not, everyone has some form of 'social-science-like recognition.' However, while the 'recognition' of an academic scholar moves towards some systematic structure, people's 'social science-like recognition' moves towards a temporary, non-structured form. By combining various forms of recognition and methods for each situation, people attempt to improve and stabilize their life.

For the people, case study research is not for the purpose of obtaining a theory, nor for undertaking a systematic discussion, but for acquiring the wisdom and power with which to construct life. Let us assume that 'our' case study research may actually be the same, or that it should be the same. If we put aside for a moment the academic 'rules' like generalization and the 'whole,' maybe our 'case study research' will be connected to the people's 'case study research.'

Case study research as a resource

Looking at the whole life: as the research method

What needs to be done for our case studies to become a 'power' and have a connection to our/the people's construction of life? This question will be considered in several ways. First of all, let us think about what sort of research is desirable. In research methodology two things can be considered: firstly, the research should try to grasp the whole life as much as possible by looking at various levels; and secondly, it needs to proceed through trial and error.

As we know, the actual field is diverse and complex. It is of course possible to extract something by focusing the research on one aspect only, but this is often meaningless at the actual site. For example, from the research of the Solomon Islanders, it would be possible to depict them as 'living in harmony with nature,' but this would only represent a part of their life, even if an important part. Moreover, when one aims for a convergence with an ongoing discussion in an academic subject and extracts and uses a section of the site for this purpose, this approach is misleading for the purposes of a case study to construct life. To capture the totality of the actual site, steady and close observation is required. Naturally, at times it is important to hold an interview, or to step back and observe from a distance. There should be a variety of methods employed such as observing, listening and measuring. By undertaking this process, something can be 'seen' gradually. Conversely, it may be that as time goes by, what had been 'seen' in the beginning can no longer be grasped and understood. Therefore, it is necessary to take records from the beginning and to consider these records over the course of the research.

Furthermore, to see the entirety of the case, the fact is often noticed that apart from the site itself, there is something outside the site which also constitutes it. By grasping both the inside and outside, the case can gradually be highlighted. By combining different points of view such as near and distant, the 'case' comes alive as a 'case.' In other words, the research method will be a repetition of trial and error.

Deeper description as the method

A case study research paper has the typical pattern of: firstly, the aim of the research (including reviews of the literature); secondly, the description of the case; and finally, the discussion.

Many people will often hesitate when they try to write a paper in this format about case study research. For example, they will set an 'aim' and write a review of the literature, but will be unsure as to whether cases in the literature and their own case are really relevant. Other concerns may include whether case study descriptions and discussions can be clearly separated. Also, if the description of the case contains data which does not directly connect to the discussion that follows, how should this relationship be 'dealt with?'

Another dilemma arises from the flow between the case and discussions, or from case and theory. The meaning of the case, and the issues pursued by the case, is often embedded in the case itself. However, if the case is forcibly separated into case study descriptions without any discussion, the evocative powers of the case may be lost.

Describing a case is not simply to make a list of the facts. A 'case' is what is formed after one selects certain facts and restructures them. The act of restructuring implies an interpretation of what has been derived from each fact. After coding, the systematic restructuring of the produced code is the case study description. The 'analysis' based on the case is already implied in the way one systematically structures the code.

The reason why case study descriptions can become a form of power for the people is indeed, because they are thus 'observed' and structured. The case can become a force only when people communicate with the data.

Moreover, the case study description which we seek would be a 'deep description' where, as described above, the analysis and discussion is already implicit in the manner of structuring and is also contained in the description itself. To achieve 'deep description' it is also necessary to include three more features, the first of which is conceptualization. The task of restructuring a case is not easy. It is not enough to simply rearrange the data. It involves repeatedly talking to the data, finding the hidden meanings and restructuring it.

At that point, something which cannot be described in existing words will emerge and that point is the core for the deep description. If one can describe this in simple, attractive words, the whole description becomes smooth and focused. One word can often be more evocative than a lengthy description. Thus the act of creating a concept becomes a necessity in making the description powerful.

The second important feature is narrativity. For a 'deep description' an attractive plot is necessary for the sake of its readers. To say that an easy-to-understand and interesting plot is necessary does not simply refer to general writing skills. The task of restructuring the case and creating the concept is not only for the self-satisfaction of the researcher, it also should be convincing to and easy to understand for the reader. The task of writing is to communicate with the case, and at the same time, communicate with the reader.

The third feature is using the method of revelation—a favored method of sociology. Revelation refers to exposing some social concept or event, which people believe to be natural, by revealing that 'it is only an invented thing.' Revelation of the 'modern family,' of the 'nation-state,' of 'role sharing,' and so on; sociology has 'succeeded' in numerous revelations. However, revelation does not only exist for overthrowing something. It is necessary to show why that revelation is required at the specific site, and also to show (directly or indirectly) the existence of something that it is not (for instance something which is not the 'modern family,' something that is not the 'nation-state'). The case study description is the field where these things are possible.

Citizens' research: who is the bearer of the research?

Who then should carry out such case study descriptions? The Saitama NPO Center conducted the 'Research regarding the actual state of use of public nursing-care insurance' between December 2001 and January 2002 as a commissioned project from Saitama Prefecture.[4] Time had elapsed since the public nursing-care insurance system had begun in April 2000, and it was necessary to determine its actual state of operation and any issues that may have arisen since its inception. Prior to commencing the research project, Saitama NPO Center had implemented the 'Saitama public nursing-care insurance supporters' club project,' also commissioned by Saitama Prefecture. Through training courses, this project promoted 'nursing-care supporters' with a role to inform the public about the workings of and how to use nursing-care insurance.

When considering the scope of the research, the Center proposed a research project centered on interviews, as opposed to the idea of research based on a questionnaire only, as suggested by the Prefecture. The Center's proposal was accepted. 'Both Saitama Prefecture and we were thinking about doing research and from there it was decided that the research would go ahead. We had also talked with the supporters about not having heard directly from the users of nursing-care insurance.'[5]

The research consisted of posted questionnaires and interviews with the users of public nursing-care insurance, combined with questionnaires posted to nursing-care service providers. The main part of the research was the interviews. These were carried out by local groups who had been trained and formed through the supporters' club project. In each area, in pairs, the members of the group visited the users, exchanging small talk while conducting the interviews. 'We prepared a question sheet but didn't actually follow it for the interview. We decided that that was fine.'[6] Up to fifty–five of these local research groups were formed and the number of interviewers reached 410. Each group member visited around three to four households and there were a total of 764 interviewees. After the interviews, the interviewers wrote their own impressions on 'task summarizing forms' and submitted them to their area group. They then held meetings called 'task classification workshops' to analyze and discuss the research results. 'We often found that the answers on the question sheet indicated the family was happy and satisfied [with public nursing-care insurance], but on the respective 'task summarizing forms' it would be something completely different, and we'd realize that various issues needed to be addressed.'[7]

In addition, to record a result which highlighted the interviewers' experience of the research, interviewers were asked to write a 'letter to so and so, from the interviewer.' Two such letters are shown here as examples.

Letter no. 10: To the mother-in-law, the wife and the family
The rainy season is nearly over, and I hope you are all well. It has been seven months since we, the researchers, visited your home. To the mother-in-law, have you been able to use the day service as you wish? I remember you telling us that 'I feel happier at the day service than at home, as I can talk to the staff and friends.' To the son, please listen to your mother sometimes. It must be very hard for you to stand between your mother and your wife, but please try without wearing yourself

out. Your mother may speak harsh words but still, she is no longer young. I hope there'll come a day when you can all sit together at the table, maybe not every day, but even just once a month. To the wife, I want to ask of you, if possible, to say a few simple words or greeting to your mother-in-law even once a day, even if she ignores you. Living together creates many difficult issues, but please don't forget 'love,' for your own sake, for your children's sake and for the family's sake. Sorry about my one-sided comments.

I will listen if you need to complain,

From a positive-thinking woman.

Letter no. 14: To the interview partner
Dear Nakamura-san,

Back then, we paired up for the interview visits. I wonder how that old lady in S town is doing right now, but even more, I worry about the well-being of that old man.

I remember you were struggling to take notes.

We both brought back our notes to summarize them, and then sorted what we summarized. It's a fond memory now.

During this research we could only ask some fixed questions. I think there should be more projects like these, which provide the occasion to communicate with and visit more freely the users of the public nursing-care insurance.

Nakamura-san, I guess that you are at this moment working as a volunteer in the welfare field. Thank you for everything. Please take care and do your best.

From Kō-chan

(Saitama NPO Center 2002: 89, 91)

An organizer of the research said, 'I wanted to draw out the actual feeling [of the interview] that still remained. I thought that maybe the results of the research would be better conveyed by presenting these letters. I wanted a report on the research which was not just about the data.'[8]

Senryū poems were also written:

More worries over the quality of the care manager (by M. K.)

Knowing loneliness listening to the cheerful voice of the carer (by Getoko)

Rather than research, sunshine feels warmer when chatting (by Yukio)

'[The interviewers were] all very eager people who would go with a 'please let us listen!' attitude, so it was different to those passive administrative types of research. The advantage of this research is ultimately in that point.'[9]

The Saitama NPO Center's public nursing-care insurance citizens' research shows that case study research should be carried out by the people. Those involved in and those who wanted to be involved in local welfare carry out the research passionately. It was a study which not only showed the 'problem points' and 'issues' qualitatively and in detail in the research report, but also made them want to be close to the people involved. 'Some interviewers commented that research provides a systematic way to listen to each individual voice, and I really agree. This research increased the number of people you cared about.'[10] 'The best thing about this study was that people who led different lives met in the name of the research.'[11]

The encounters not only took place between interviewers and interviewees, but also between administrative officers and citizens, experts and laypersons, organizers and local activists, and between ordinary people. Those who met became further connected to each other through the 'case studies.' 'Letter 14' above, is addressed to the research partner of one pair who went together to the interviews.

The flexibility in the research method and the final report also has the characteristic of a citizens' research project. The above 'letters' and 'poems' were not for eccentricity, but were a method of case study description devised by those who considered that an unemotional research report would not convey the true feeling of the research findings. Consequently, when people themselves carry out case study research, the case is vividly portrayed and passed on. In this way, the research becomes a form of power.[12]

Conclusion

This article commenced from the simple question of what is a 'case' and what is 'case study research.' To consider this question, a seemingly indirect approach was taken; firstly reflecting on the issue and then discussing the Solomon Islanders' act of constructing their life. We learnt from the way the Solomon Islanders live and how they combine various elements as the resources with which to construct their life. We also learnt from their use of 'case study research' as one of their resources. To convey the importance of this, I sought a depiction of case study research that was not a sample of the whole.

I also proposed that there is a shared purpose of what case study research is to the people and to us. It should not be a means of producing a general theory or for systematic argument, but rather, the focus of case study research should be as the source of wisdom and as a force to construct life.

In order for case study research to have this quality, research needs to seek to understand the whole picture, and its description needs to be of a form where the case study description and discussion are not separate. Furthermore, as the work of the Saitama NPO Center shows, such case study research should be carried out by citizens themselves. To conclude, I propose that for the future, rich and deep case studies should be presented by more citizens.

4
Reflections on the Methodology of Seeing in *Kōgengaku* and the Study of Folklore

Makito Kawada

Introduction

The central focus of this paper is the exploration of two key questions: What is fieldwork in the social sciences; or, in a broader sense, what is the 'methodology of seeing' in social research? In particular, for those involved in anthropological fieldwork, the notion of 'participant observation' has long been emphasized as an essential and indispensable method. Within the concept of 'observation,' visual observation should be the core method of fieldwork; however, the know-how of this method, such as what subject should be observed and how, is rarely discussed. Ikuya Satō notes that while there is a fieldwork 'renaissance'—a recent recovery of fieldwork and ethnography—he describes the lack of attention to methodology, particularly in Japan, with the following words:

> The present situation in Japan, however, is not necessarily the same [as the situation in the USA and Europe, where research on the methodology of fieldwork and ethnography are very active]. In Japan, 'research' in sociology in many cases still points to the survey. In anthropology too, while some reflective research on ethnography has been published, there is not much to see in the way of close examination of various research methods, such as how to put together field notes, or the methodological discussion on how to consider the correlation between theory and information gained through these methods (Satō 1997: 43).

In reality, textbooks on fieldwork and research methodology explain interview methods quite elaborately and there is a great amount of detail on: how to ask questions, how to take notes in the field, how to rewrite them, how to classify and arrange cards, how to code and so on. This information is gathered mainly from the 'listen' part of the 'walk, look, and listen' phrase, often used to describe elements of fieldwork.

In contrast, visual information is difficult to express as written text,[1] as it cannot be converted entirely to language. Because of this, there is not as detailed and precise practical information available for observation research as compared to interview based research. However, if the phrases 'to see is to think,' 'deliberate carefully by observing through your eyes,' and 'use your legs as the lenses of your observation by visiting the scenes on foot' were seriously considered, then thinking in fieldwork could not be discussed without formulating a methodology for the sense of sight. Thus the question of what is the methodology of seeing could be replaced with the question of: What it means for sight to be directly connected to thought?

The fundamental principle—to see is to think—underpins modern science, which is based on observations and experiments. Seeing is essential, especially for procedures in rationalism and positivism, on which the natural sciences were established. In other words, saying that modern science exists, at the point where methodology is applied to seeing or sight, is not an overstatement. This is not only true for the natural sciences, but as is well known, the development of modern anthropology was deeply connected to the establishment of fieldwork as its core methodology. The figure central to this was of course Malinowski, whose fieldwork practice and method of participant observation were regarded as conterminous. One way of thinking about participant observation is to examine how Malinowski, whose methodology was established by the 'scientific' nature of observation, discussed and thought about the method himself.

However, rather than going down that path, I wish to focus, from a different angle, on the methodology of visual observation. The methodology of *Kōgengaku* (or the study of modern phenomenon or modernology), a neighboring field where the method of visual observation is most advanced, will be examined and compared to folklore study. Although folklore study uses very similar field research methods as cultural anthropology, the method of participant observation is not as emphasized, and its main research method comprises of writing down what one hears. Thus, what 'to see' means in this context will be discussed through comparisons with the neighboring field of *Kōgengaku*. There are a wide range of topics which need to be considered when exploring the 'way of seeing something visually,' including Malinowski's concept of observation and an examination of the 'scientific' concept when observation is regarded as a 'scientific' method. This article is an introduction to that task. But firstly, we will consider how the term participant observation is used in the current Japanese environment.

What is participant observation?

Try to locate the definition of 'participant observation' in the *Bunka jinruigaku jiten* (Cultural anthropology dictionary) and the first thing you will notice is that this term—the golden rule of anthropological fieldwork—does not appear in any headings. The term 'participant observation' or 'participant observation method' is only found in the context of explaining anthropological theories, academic history or general methodology. Does this mean that the concept is treated lightly, or is so natural that it is used casually in the context of discussing theories and method?

If one delves a little further into the text, one finds the term, firstly, under the heading of 'functionalism.' In the context of explaining its characteristics, there is the phrase: 'abandoning the reconstruction of human history based on analogism and instead going out to a specific local society to perform fieldwork, detailed description and analysis is carried out through participant observation' (*Bunka jinruigaku jiten* 1987: 196). Under the heading of 'social anthropology,' at the point where the revolution of functionalism is mentioned, it says that 'the characteristic method is a long-term fieldwork using local language, called participant observation' (1987: 340). In these contexts, the term participant observation is used with almost the same meaning as fieldwork, and is described as though the two terms are interchangeable. Participant observation considered in such a context seems to put more emphasis on the 'participation' than on the 'observation.'

Since the term participant observation seems to be used interchangeably with that of fieldwork, it may be useful to examine what they say about fieldwork itself. Here, participant observation is explained in the following way:

> In this research [Malinowski's Trobriand Island fieldwork] Malinowski focused on a research method called participant observation. Participant

observation is defined as living in a society that is the subject of the research, and collecting data on social life there in the process of socializing with the people...However...quite some time is required to sufficiently carry out this participant observation. The anthropologist is an alien who has suddenly appeared, and in many cases the people will experience various feelings such as fear, disdain and hostility. If the effort of the anthropologist, who attempts to melt into their lives, is accepted by the people, a trusting, friendly relationship will most likely be formed between the anthropologist and the people. This sort of relationship is called rapport (*Bunka jinruigaku jiten* 1987: 641).

What is written here is quite accurate and no one would object to the point that building a strong relationship of trust with the informant is essential for conducting fieldwork. However, the explanation of participant observation is such that it is described as a technique that at some stage seems to be transformed into the explanation of favorable attitudes for building a positive human relationship. Very complex and sensitive attention is required in the development of human relationships in the field. After this difficult task is accomplished, the method of participant observation can be used. It can be said that in such an argument, it is difficult to understand what the method of participant observation actually is.

One might also question another element of the argument—is it possible to clearly separate human relationships in the field and in the methodology that is used there? Participant observation is supposed to be a unique method in which the subjective participation and objective observation are woven together. However, this interconnection is severed in a scheme where first the relationships are built, and then participant observation is carried out.

As the term 'participant observation' consists of two separate words, the occurrence of some division in the concept may be unavoidable from a conceptual point of view, although in the act of field research they may be entwined during the process of its execution. Considering this point, there may be two possible arguments for the methodology of participant observation—one for 'participant (observation),' and another for '(participant) observation.' Currently, the notion of 'participant (observation)' is dominant in discussions,' and furthermore, there are not many productive arguments on the technicality of '(participant) observation.'[2]

Before discussing '(participant) observation' any further, the textbook meaning of participant observation will be considered by drawing upon the work of Satō. Ikuya Satō's *Fīrudowāku* (Fieldwork) (1992) is one of the most widely read texts on research methods and is extensively used at universities in Japan as a useful resource. In his book, there is one chapter allocated to the explanation of participant observation. Accordingly, participant observation in the broad sense involves five activities: firstly, participation in social life; secondly, direct observation of life in the target society; thirdly, hearing information about social life; fourthly, collection and analysis of reference materials and items; and finally interviews regarding the comments and attached meanings on events and affairs (Satō 1992: 129–35).[3] Participant observation, in the broad sense, is almost synonymous with fieldwork, and the above five elements comprise its main activities. In contrast, participant observation in the narrow sense, is focused on the first activity, and also involves the second and third.

From the term participant observation it is easy to guess that it is a combination of points one and two, and according to Satō's categorization, these two, together with the auditory interview or data collection through listening and hearing in point three, make up participant observation in the narrow, stricter sense. Here, participant observation cannot be considered restrictively as a purely visual method, and examination of its overlap with auditory methods is suggested in part. This may also imply that discussing '(participant) observation' must be undertaken at a different point than when discussing simple 'observation.'

In relation to this, Satō points out the transitions in the position and role of fieldworkers. He states that the fieldworker shifts, depending on the situation, between four states of full participation, participation as observer, observation as participant and full observation. Of these, he says that participant observation, in the strict sense, refers to the second state of participation as observer, where the fieldworker participates with recognition from the local residents of the research field, and 'that person is here as an observer.' Again, in these transitions, the theory of the 'participant,' in contrast to '(participant) observation,' refers to the fourth, complete observer stance, a hypothetical stance where there is no communication at all between the observer and the observed. In order for the local residents to recognize that the fieldworker is a participant in the role of an observer, the auditory method partially overlaps. This may be better described as a method of address, as it aims to make the other person aware of the worker. The prerequisite to this is mutual conversation through the exchange of auditory information, where for example, from the other's response to the fieldworker's self-introduction, the worker's positioning is re-adjusted.

From the question of why the visual method in participant observation is not often discussed, and what are the technical difficulties in visual observation, the previous discussion suggested that the focus is often on '(participant) observation,' positioned between 'participant (observation)' and 'observation.' It has been noted that in discussions about both the general significance of participant observation and the specificity of participant observation as a method, the focus has mostly been on 'participant (observation),' making it difficult to grasp sight as a method. However, '(participant) observation' has aspects not only related to sight but also to hearing, and is distinctive from pure 'observation.' This is the aporia in visual observation.

Wajirō Kon or sight of Kōgengaku

Whether it is possible to develop a discussion on '(participant) observation' as opposed to 'participant (observation),' depends on the extent of the ability to develop visual observation as a research method. From the discussion in the previous section, the need to examine the methodology of sight as a research method arises when exploring the notion of pure 'observation.' In addition, it comes to the fore when attempting to clarify the distance from the notion of participant (observation). By keeping these tensions in sight, to some degree, the limits of the reality of the sensory function of sight can be grasped. The 'construction of vision' in *Kōgengaku* will be discussed as the most radical attempt in visual observation.

The 'construction of sight' is a term used by Kenji Satō in the following comment:

> One of the essences of *Kōgengaku* is the unique 'construction of sight' by such schematization. This construction becomes the basis for 'thinking' about the 'present' that is difficult to see from the vague impression observed through the naked eye (Satō 1994: 103).

This comment contains a very important insight. That is, although facts and events that exist in front of one's eyes are certainly received through the visual sensory organs, this does not necessary mean that one is able to 'see' and there are things which are 'difficult to see.' For instance, this difficulty may become apparent when told to 'draw what you see' in sketching practices. Thus in the words of Satō, the visual sense deployed in participant observation '...does not reflect as it is' (Satō 1994: 102). It can be said, paradoxically, that because of this impossibility of describing what is seen as it is, the visual sense can be used as a specific method to observe the subject. The research method of *Kōgengaku* makes full use of this constructed vision.

Satō classifies the techniques for the 'construction of sight' in *Kōgengaku* into nine distinct categories, as listed in Table 4.1. Of these, the 'classification-and-statistics method' (a method to distinguish and count) is most characteristic of *Kōgengaku*. The result of the use of this method can be seen in the work 'A record of street custom in Ginza, Tokyo,' (Kon 1971: 53–108) which represents a typical report in *Kōgengaku*.

One reason for this is the simplicity of its methods. The conditions of the research were as follows:

> The research zone will be the stretch of street from *Kyōbashi* to *Shinbashi*; The scene of the research will only be on the sidewalk; The western side will mainly be researched; The researcher will walk at a pace of 20 minutes over the research zone, with only people approaching from the front to be examined and all others, such as those who stop, or pass the researcher from behind, to be excluded from the research; The classification mark, time and date, direction the researcher walked (north or south) and name of the research are to be entered on the research cards (Kon 1971: 57).

These are the only rules, and the method of observation is specifically indicated. Except for the vagueness of the third rule, which states 'mainly the western side,' the instructions are restrictive, and there would have been minimal confusion among researchers. However, this does not mean that as long as the same method is used, it can be done by anyone. This is because of the great detail in research content, and keeping in mind that data had to be collected at the same time as approaching subjects were observed, it is amazing that such a diverse research project could have been carried out. For example, in the case of male subjects, there are sixteen items as points of observation, with classifications made in each: the color of clothes, coat, collar, necktie, watch chain, gloves, shoes, condition of kimono, pattern on kimono and *haori* (Japanese half-coat), footwear, socks, beard, glasses, hat, things carried, and tobacco. In the case of female subjects there are

Table 4.1: Visual methods in Kōgengaku

Method & meaning	Survey results
1 *Classification-and-statistics method* Distinguish and count	• A record of street customs in Ginza, Tokyo • [Honjo–Fukagawa slum area street customs collection] • [Otaru City main street (*Hanazono-chō*) apparel survey]
2 *Bird's eye/Bug's eye method* Measure and imagine	• Inokashira Park suicide spot map
3 *Overlapping-sketch method* See and compare	• Heads of women • Miscellaneous street customs of the suburbs
4 *Notation method* Consider by expressing in symbols	• Melodies in the street • Bon-festival dance • [Street customs sociology in the department store]
5 *Thorough-listing method* Make a list of everything	• Children in poverty • [Honjo–Fukagawa slum area street customs collection]
6 *Breakage-decoding method* Discern symptoms	• Parts of western clothes subject to wear • Many chipped ceramic bowls
7 *Distribution-map method* Record positions on a map	• Inokashira Park suicide spot map • [Spring picnics in Inokashira Park] • [Distribution of various eating places around Waseda] • [Survey around Waseda, Keiō and Tokyo Universities]
8 *Movement-tailing method* Record movement on a map	• Dancehall in Yokohama • [Traffic map in a residence]
9 *Survey-all-possessions method* Thorough investigation of people in an area	• Survey of belongings of newly married couples • Survey of belongings of students in boarding houses

This Table has been constructed by the author based on Satō (1994: 104–119), though the survey results in brackets [ ] are supplemented from Kon (1971).

even more, with twenty-two items: the ratio of Western clothes and Japanese clothes, kimono, ratio of at-home wear and street clothes, pattern on kimono and *haori*, material of kimono and *haori*, markings on kimono, manner of overlapping collar, sash, sash clip, replaceable collar, footwear, color of scarf, socks, Western clothes, hairstyle, comb, makeup, glasses, color of handkerchief, gloves, handbag/things carried/umbrella, and way of walking.

The detail of these classifications was the result of and further maintained by the 'thorough listing method' (writing out a list of every detail) and 'survey all possessions method' (studying people at each location). These methods, called exhaustive surveys, advanced 'objectivity' and 'substantiation,' both of which are essential for the methodology of science at the largest scale. Considering the process of recording and then classifying every detail of the subject, it can be understood that these exhaustive surveys are closely related to the 'classification-and-statistics method.'

It is possible to deploy such methods on a much larger scale using visual recording equipment. For example, there is a photographic collection called *Chikyū kazoku* (A global family portrait). The concept behind this work was to select a middle-class family from each of thirty countries around the world, carry all household effects from their home into the yard outside or to an empty space, and photograph the whole family with their belongings. In the book there are separate sets of photographs for each of the families of the respective countries (Material World Project (Head: Peter Menzel) 1994).[4] For this project, after the selection of a family, a photographer would go and live with them for about a week. The photographer took a large portrait using a medium-format camera, photographs of daily life using a 35mm camera and took an average of four hours Hi-8 video per family (Material World Project 1994: 16). Thus, this project is very interesting in that it encompasses the notion of vision in visual anthropology and at the same time 'participant (observation).'[5] It could also be said to be a *Kōgengaku* project by using high-tech equipment.

Returning to *Kōgengaku*, its significance may be found in the point that such research, using high-tech visual equipment, has been undertaken utilizing observation by the naked eye as well as hand drawn sketches. In 'A record of street customs in Ginza, Tokyo' (Kon 1971: 53–108), using detailed categories to observe the cityscape, it could be said that the researchers had numerous filing boxes embedded in their heads. In the research, where the belongings of pedestrians passing in the opposite direction or the belongings of newly married couples were listed, it was as if the researchers became counting devices. Likewise, in *Kōgengaku* experiments, the researcher (human) as an instrument to count, collect and record, emerges. Developing the visual method promotes the development of the human being as a research tool.

Another thing, which can be noticed from the results of *Kōgengaku* research, is that there are many bird's eye view diagrams, such as maps, marked with dots representing buildings or people. This is the 'distribution-map method' (record positions on the map) and the 'movement-tailing method' (record movement on the map) outlined in Table 4.1. As they are aerial views, they are also the bird's eye perspective in the 'bird's eye/bug's eye method.' These map-based diagrams are still a familiar sight in present times, seen often in the street or in magazines, but they are rarely recognized as a characteristic method of visual observation of *Kōgengaku*. In the actual application of this method, for example, the survey of the Waseda area (Kon 1971: 309–342) probably used an existing map, while for the map of stores in the shopping arcade in the 'Miscellaneous street custom of suburbs' (Kon 1971: 134–158), or the compositional town map in the 'Otaru City main street (*Hanazono-chō*) apparel survey' (Kon 1971: 159–223), they devised a method and without using aerial photomaps, walked through the street, writing down the name of each shop, and later drawing up a diagram as if it was seen from above. Here the aerial view is a pseudo-vision, and what is actually seen is not an overall view from the sky but rather separate views of each shop. Satō comments on this as follows:

> I see a particular possibility in the point that combinations and accumulation of bug's eye views can, through diagrams, produce an imagination of the bird's eye view. In other words, we can schematize the 'fine details' or the 'overall circumstances,' which are not normally seen and therefore not measured, through the medium of actual measurements. Though we do not fly nor our bodies shrink, we can construct the perspective of the bird's eye or the experience of the bug's eye by manipulation of data. This is the process of dissimilation. This is because through the maximization and minimization of visual experiences, we can once again scrutinize everyday impressions (Satō 1994: 107).

As well as creating a line of sight to visualize what is not actually seen, the 'bird's eye/bug's eye method' (measure and imagine) acquires visual information which in reality cannot be obtained, even with equipment. For example, a microscope can only enlarge the view of things and a binocular can only be used to see distant things. The naked eye can make fine adjustments between close and remote views, but in everyday life this is usually done unconsciously. The method of visual observation in *Kōgengaku* makes us, in part, conscious of this function of the naked eye. Considering that bird's eye view diagrams are drawn from the supposition that human eyes are replaced by an aerial camera, these two themes—the creation of a new vision and the sight of a tool-like entity—are connected to each other.

Repercussion of 'expulsion'

As discussed in the previous section, *Kōgengaku*, equipped with its two themes—the sight of the tool-like entity and the creation of a new pseudo-vision—introduced the 'method to see through the eye' to the site of fieldwork in a radical form. This position of *Kōgengaku*, at a time when discussions on how to record observation and '(participant) observation' were scarce, deserves special mention. In consideration of the favored subject of *Kōgengaku*—the street customs of cities—if the visual observation method had been introduced in folklore study, the later development of folklore survey and research would have been quite different from its present state. However, such a possibility was rejected by the well-known episode, where Kon was expelled from the field of folklore study because of *Kōgengaku*.

According to chronological records,[6] Kon participated in the *Hakubōkai*, a study group established by Kunio Yanagita and others in 1917, with an objective to preserve old houses. The following year in 1918, the *Hakubōkai* conducted the joint-survey of a village, *Uchigō-mura* in *Sōshu*, with another group the *Kyōdokai*. Since then, Kon began to attend *Kyōdokai* meetings and visit rural residential houses for the surveys. As Kon's friendship with Yanagita grew, in 1923, the Great Kantō Earthquake occurred and thereafter Kon's major interest moved to recording the rebuilding process of the earthquake affected areas. In 1927, Kon held an exhibition called the 'Survey (*Kōgengaku*) exhibition' as an opening event for the Shinjuku Kinokuniya Bookshop, and this was the beginning of *Kōgengaku*. At this time the 'incident' is said to have happened. According to Kon's account of events, it was at this time when

> ...all because I launched *Kōgengaku*, I quite hurt the feelings of my teacher Kunio Yanagita, from whom I had learned for ten years. He

said, 'You are unpardonable,' and expelled me from the field of folklore study (Kon 1971: 482).

For that matter, Kon writes elsewhere that the joint-survey he started under the name of *Kōgengaku* was not the only cause of his expulsion. At first Kon had accompanied Yanagita on the rural area surveys, with Yanagita paying Kon's travel expenses. But later, Kon began to take part in the survey of rural residences under Tadaatsu Ishiguro, Agricultural Administration Division Manager in the Ministry of Agriculture and Forestry (Ministry of Agriculture and Commerce). Kon referred to this as 'an ungrateful act toward my teacher, Yanagita, in folklore study' (Kon 1987: 404), and he, at this stage, already felt guilt towards Yanagita. Kon declares that, as if this was not enough, his interest shifted from the rural villages to the city after the Great Kantō Earthquake. Furthermore he started a new academic movement called *Kōgengaku* and departed from folklore study. He saw these as the reasons for his expulsion.

This 'expulsion' was only unilaterally proclaimed by Kon, and there are actually several theories regarding its authenticity. For example, Tadao Umesao deduces that the banner of *Kōgengaku*, as opposed to folklore study, came as a bolt out of the blue for Yanagita. He also notes that on Kon's side there was academic rivalry between himself and Yanagita, and feels that the 'expulsion' was a logical conclusion by Yanagita (Umesao 1971: 509–11). In contrast, Noboru Kawazoe clearly states that 'there is no such fact' (Kawazoe 2004: 220). From this standpoint he contemplates how Kon perceived the rift as 'expulsion,' and examines the background of Yanagita's attempt to consider *Kōgengaku* as part of folklore study.[7] According to Kawazoe, rather than Yanagita having declared expulsion, this was an expression of Kon keeping his distance from Yanagita out of diffidence and reservation. In addition it showed that Kon realized that the viewpoint of modernism, such as in the '*Seikatsu byōrigaku* (Pathology of life),' was not compatible with Yanagita's fundamental view. Thus, saying that he was 'expelled' would have been the expression of Kon's consciousness, that he had 'shown such ungratefulness (as to warrant expulsion)' (Kawazoe 2004: 381–390).

For the purpose of this article, there is no need to explore the sensational elements of this 'expulsion' any further. Rather, the relevance is in Kawazoe's second point, that Yanagita thought *Kōgengaku* may be included in folklore study. In the first place, Yanagita mentioned *Kōgengaku* only on rare occasions, one of which was in the preface of 'Bunrui gyoson shūzoku jo (Classification of fishing village customs)' (Yanagita [1938] 1970). Here it is written:

> What we, as specialists, want to briefly clarify is that we try to find out the life of the past, which formed the basis for the present. Of this, it is especially those facts which go unnoticed by all, become buried, and will not emerge again. It is not everything, like the so-called *Kōgengaku* of Wajirō Kon and others (Yanagita [1938] 1970: 254).

Unlike *Kōgengaku* which deals with all and everything, the fundamental viewpoint of folklore study is to observe only those elements in which history (the history of changes in life) can be discerned, and therefore, from a methodological standpoint, *Kōgengaku* is more comprehensive. Kawazoe pointed out that Yanagita nevertheless wanted to think of *Kōgengaku* as folklore study because he felt a strong need for the 'two-dimensional' or 'horizontal' thinking through vision of *Kōgengaku*, as opposed to the linear thinking of folklore study, especially that of Kunio Yanagita, a 'man of words.' Yanagita designed the structure of folklore study in the five stages of: field work; classification; establishment of indices; comparison and conclusion. It may be said that these were to have become clarified and specified by taking in *Kōgengaku*.

Folklore study and *Kōgengaku* have generally been regarded as having contrasting trends, the former being past-oriented and the latter present (to future)-oriented. Even more so, this comparison of linear thinking and horizontal thinking is significant to the theme of the methodology of visual observation explored in this paper. The three-dimensional view of reality can be converted to a two-dimensional representation, and this, as Kawazoe points out, is advantageous when considering each data with a sense of continuity. But also, in direct contrast to this effect, it is also possible to individualize the data, or in other words to create data by extracting one area of the continuous scenery, as can be easily understood by imagining the conversion of sketches into cards. This notion of continuity and individualism, brought about by creating data from visual information through horizontal thinking, indicates a method which describes a certain event deeply and widely, most necessary in the stage of comparison in Yanagita's five-stage concept. In this sense then, as was written at the beginning of this section, if folklore study, from its close relationship to *Kōgengaku*, had worked on the visual observation method, its form would have been quite different to what it is today.

In general, the incident of 'expulsion,' seen as a turning point in the development of *Kōgengaku*, which split from folklore study and developed its own direction, is mostly discussed in terms of its effects on the field of *Kōgengaku*. However, the ripples would have been felt in the area of folklore study as well. Although folklore study did not proceed with the method of visual observation in the way of *Kōgengaku*, observation was not altogether discarded in folklore study, a theme explored below.

Folklore study or Kunio Yanagita's sight

Although Wajirō Kon's expulsion from folklore study may be a somewhat exaggerated fictional story, and Yanagita may not have considered there to have been an expulsion at all, there is no doubt that Yanagita was to some extent (perhaps quite strongly) conscious of *Kōgengaku*. In particular, it is worth noticing, as more than coincidence, that this corresponds to the early days in the establishment of folklore study methodology, such as in the later published 'Minkan denshō-ron (On folk traditions)'(Yanagita [1934] 1998b) and *'Kyōdo seikatsu no kenkyūhō* (Research method on country life)' (Yanagita [1935] 1998c).

There are not many documents in which Yanagita mentions *Kōgengaku* and in none of them does he describe his expulsion of Kon. However, he has writings which explain folklore study methodology from the differences when compared to *Kōgengaku*. One is the preface of the previously mentioned 'Bunrui gyoson shūzoku (Classification of fishing village customs)' (Yanagita [1938] 1970) and another is the 'Josei seikatsu-shi (History of women's life)' (Yanagita [1941] 2003). The latter was a serial published in the magazine *Fujin kōron* (Public opinion of women), in the form of questions and answers, where Yanagita would answer questions from readers. A part (or majority) of the questions were said to be 'decoys,' made up by Yanagita, or by the editor in consultation with Yanagita. One of them reads: 'I have understood why folklore study puts everyday life facts in front of us as the most important data. It seems to me then that folklore study is very close to *Kōgengaku*, talked about by Wajirō Kon and others, but is this right? Could you please explain the boundary between these two? (Ineko Ise).' Also by the same person: 'It seems the distinction between folklore study and the new *Kōgengaku* lies in their methods, especially in the handling or collection of data. What do you think?' (Yanagita [1941] 2003: 376–7).[8] Yanagita's answer to these questions can be summarized in three points. Firstly, changes in the material world which appeal to the eye belong to only one of the three categories of data. Secondly, present time should be considered with the passing of time as a big factor; and thirdly, instead of noticing common and obvious things, effort should be made to pick out the somewhat rarer things (Yanagita [1941] 2003: 377–8). From these ideas we can presume the past-oriented characteristics of folklore study. Furthermore, for folklorists, the visible material world is only partial and they regard trivial things at a glance as important.

What should be noted here is that these fabricated questions are asked as if the 'methodology of seeing,' a major feature of *Kōgengaku*, is already incorporated in the questions from general readers. There was wide recognition, a little short of commonsense, that *Kōgengaku* had a strong character of an academic discipline with an observation-centered methodology. This knowledge about *Kōgengaku*, was not limited to academic circles but was widespread, to some extent, in Japanese society at that time. In response, Yanagita emphasizes that folklore study is different from *Kōgengaku* in that it is equipped with a historical retrospective vision. It becomes clear that Yanagita fabricated or constructed these questions in an attempt to emphasize that the 'methodology of seeing' was employed in folklore study as well.

A few years before the 'Josei seikatsu-shi' was serialized in 1941, Yanagita proposed his famous 'three-part categorization of folklore data,' publishing books such as 'Minkan denshō-ron (On folk traditions)' ([1934] 1998b) and 'Kyōdo seikatsu no kenkyūhō (Research method on country life)' ([1935] 1998c) on folklore methodology. The three parts include culture, language arts and intent phenomena. There are some differences in the terms used in the three-part categorizations, as shown in Table 4.2. In 'Minkan denshō-ron,' published a year earlier, the names of these categories are further diversified. The first part is expressed as 'external form of life, collection through the eye, collection by travelers,' the second part, 'explanation of life, collection through the eye and ear, collection by lodgers,' and the third part, 'life awareness, collection by the mind, and collection by people from the same province.'[9] These were from the summarized description in the preface, but other expressions are also found, such as: 'record of life technology, body folklore, various ways of living, ethnography' for the first part; 'orally transmitted literature, oral folklore' for the second part; and 'folk belief, life concept' for the third part. There is a general impression that these three parts correspond to eye, ear, and mind, and the 'essence' of folklore study, which is considered most significant, is thought to be in part three, the clarification of the awareness or concept of life. However, collection through the eye appears in both parts one and two, and from this point also, the fact that the 'method to see through the eye' is not treated lightly (or the intention to place weight on visual collection) is seen. Furthermore, the title of an article, in which Yanagita states: 'We place importance on the facts seen by our eyes, and regard this as the primary material' (Yanagita [1934] 1998b: 60), is a so-called manifesto, *Wareware no hōhō* (Our method).'

Looking at Table 4.2, the differences between part one and parts two and three of 'Minkan denshō-ron' and 'Kyōdo seikatsu no kenkyūhō' can be seen in their 'Items' columns. The number of items in parts two and three has been reduced in 'Kyōdo seikatsu no kenkyūhō.' Also in part two, while there are two chapters 'Language arts' and 'Legends and tales' in 'Minkan denshō-ron,' in 'Kyōdo seikatsu no kenkyūhō' these have been integrated into a single chapter, 'Language arts.' Conversely, in part one of the latter, the items are further subdivided. These differences would be the variation in the nature of the two articles, the former aiming for an outline book-like content with the emphasis placed on a definitive explanation of the three-part categorization, while the latter is inclined towards a more practical methodology, offering explanations interspersed with case studies for each item. At the same time, the differences may also reflect a broad way of looking at facts, characteristic of sight. Whether it be 'dwelling,' 'clothes' or 'transportation,' each item suggests an individuality which can be compared to the sketch cards used in *Kōgengaku*, and a continuity worth the preparation for comparison. In other words, the beginning of the 'way of looking at something visually' can also be sufficiently recognized in folklore study.

Another article will be briefly mentioned here, the 'Meiji Taishō-shi sesō-hen (History of the Meiji and Taishō eras on their social trend)' ([1931] 1998a), in which Yanagita is said to have been conscious of *Kōgengaku*. This is not because this work focuses on cities rather than on rural communities. Looking at the chapter construction of this work, the reference to the senses in the chapters from 'Trend in the eyes,' 'Individual freedom for food,' 'House and its comfort' to 'Changes in the natural scenery' appear to correspond to the first part of the later three-part categorization. The next eight chapters, from 'Homeland and foreign-land' to 'Poverty and sickness,' do not necessary correspond to part two, but their topic is the macro-social issues that are beyond the individual, a theme which requires data

Table 4.2: Comparative table of the three-part categorization of folklore materials of Kunio Yanagita

	Minkan denshō ron (Yanagita [1934] 1998b)	**Kyōdo seikatsu no kenkyūhō** (Yanagita [1935] 1998c)
Part 1	*Life aspects* (Chapter 7) Outline Two ways of life New traffic Calendar and experience Roots of art Play and toys	*Tangible culture* Dwelling Clothes Food Method of acquiring materials Transportation Labor Village Ally Family and relatives Marriage Birth Calamity Funeral Annual events Shinto festivals Divination and incantation Dance Tournament Children's play and toys
Part 2	*Language arts* (Chapter 8) New word creation Proverb and parable Chants, riddles and children's talk Folksong Narrative Old tales *Legends and tales* (Chapter 9) Introduction to legends Rationalization of legends Issue of forms of legends Original form of myths Carrier of legends and tales Gossip	*Language arts* New word creation New phrase Proverb Riddles Chants Children's talk Song Narrative, fables and legend
Part 3	*Intent phenomena* Introduction Knowledge and skill Hobbies, love and hatred, and issues after death Observation of knowledge from the previous generation Magic and taboo Importance of intent phenomena research	*Intent Phenomena* Knowledge Life skills Life purpose

collection through the ear. The last three chapters, 'Mind longing for mates,' 'Ability to exceed the peer' and 'Goals for living condition improvements,' are issues of the mind and lifestyle knowledge, and correspond to part three. In short, the significance of the 'Meiji Taishō-shi sesō-hen,' three years before the 'Minkan denshō ron,' seems to have been a demonstration of the 'three-part categorization of folklore materials.'[10] In which case, seeing as Yanagita was trying to achieve the five stages of fieldwork, classification, establishment of indices, comparison, and conclusion with this three-part categorization, it can be said that he was aiming to reach the conclusion stage while holding a similar view to *Kōgengaku*. Yanagita, who conservatively stated: 'If the methods for fieldwork, data management, classification and comparison are correct (Yanagita [1931] 1998a: 16),' he would, no doubt, have been planning the next stage.

At this stage, I have no way of verifying the extent to which Yanagita considered *Kōgengaku* as a rival force, apart from employing a method of analysis and coming to a conclusion. However, even if a sense of rivalry had in fact existed in Yanagita (and not Kon), there was never a direct stand-off between the two. It was because Yanagita developed, after the manifesto, the so-called *Jūshutsu risshōhō* (a proof method using repeated appearances), which replaced the difference between eras with the difference between geographical regions, and implemented the sight to see the invisible past through visible matters.

Conclusion: what Yanagita saw or beyond his vision

Around 1888, before midday on a spring day, fourteen-year-old Yanagita was playing in the dirt at his brother's house in Fukawa, Kitasōma-gun, Shimousa. Just as he happened to dig up a glittering *Kaei-tsūhō* coin and was overcome by a strange feeling, he glanced up from where he was squatting and saw dozens of daytime stars in the clear blue sky. This was experienced by Yanagita, and discussed in his article titled 'Genkaku no jikken (Experiment of illusion)' (Yanagita [1956] 1999: 292–5). This episode is also quoted as 'a mysterious sign' in 'Kokyō 70 nen (Hometown, 70 years)' (Yanagita [1959] 1997: 44–45), and seems to have been one of his favourite tales.[11]

It would be too extreme to say from this one episode that Kunio Yanagita had supernatural abilities. However, he at least had the vision to notice so-called possibilities, to retain wonders and mysteries in their original form without hastily fitting them into a formula, turning them over in his memory for a long time, imagining what they may have been. There is a reason why the author cannot simply smile and call Yanagita a poet or an artist, and this is because of how he, pursuing the methodology of seeing, goes beyond that point at some stage and reaches something that is not visible. These unseen things include the past and issues of the mind, which this article did not explore. If the three-part categorization of folklore materials, or otherwise the complete methodology of folklore, is planned with this intent as its essence, then how does part one connect to part three?

Kunio Yanagita's visualizing of possibilities can be considered as the method to realize his research focus when he gave up intensive fieldwork (Seki 1993: 320). How this form of seeing developed into a more widely shared academic perspective, even though it derived from his unusual personal experiences, is unknown and would require further investigation. At that time, participant observation was, by contrast, the method always utilized for long-term fieldwork located in one place and undertaken in a concentrated form. Unfortunately (or fortunately), Yanagita had to give up his fieldwork. The reason he 'gave up' fieldwork was as a result of the lack of financial resources and time. In participant observation, what sort of vision can compensate for these shortfalls, so that there will be no need to 'give up?' The future issue is to ascertain the direction required for 'seeing' in participant observation, in order to reconsider this as a 'method to see through the eye.'

5
Drawing Sketches in the Field: Sketch Literacy for Social Research

Nobutaka Kamei

Introduction: human beings draw pictures

Based on my experiences in the field, this article discusses and analyzes the values and characteristics of sketching as an important methodological tool for social research. It acknowledges that this subject goes beyond the boundary of methodology and also relates to some fundamental issues concerning the social sciences. The paper touches on some of these issues, and in the final section briefly outlines some of the limitations and problems which arise from the use of drawing as a research method.

Pictures are the oldest form of description for human beings. *Homo sapiens*, with their excellent vision, highly manipulative fingers and brain, that enable the use of tools, led to the birth of pictures before the appearance of the oldest letters. According to archaeological evidence, pictures first appeared at least 35 000 years ago, and developed in various regions including Africa, India, Australia and Europe (Roberts 2000). Sumerian letters, which are the oldest letters, were only invented approximately 5,600 years ago (Comrie et al. eds 1996). Thus the history of letters is considerably short compared to that of pictures, and furthermore, those letters began as pictographs, a type of image.

Although there is a wide variation in method, material and subject, there has not been an ethnic group, historically, that has not drawn or shown any interest in pictures. Drawing pictures can be considered as a 'cultural universal' for human beings. As humans are animals who relate to pictures easily, this article is based on this premise and aims to place the human activity of drawing back into the social sciences.

Why should sketches be used in the social sciences?

The predominance of text

This paper recommends that a descriptive format of sketching be introduced into the social sciences. First of all, a summary of the reasons of why this is necessary and important will be outlined briefly. The social sciences in general are considered here, but examples will be primarily taken from the fields of anthropology and sociology with which the author is involved.

So far in the social sciences, text has been the prominent descriptive format for all processes, ranging from research, recording, analysis and expression. In the case of fieldwork, the interviewee's speech is recorded with a tape or video recorder, and transcribed in text format for documentation and publishing. In the case of survey questionnaires, the answers are either written on the survey sheets provided, or noted down in response to verbally answered questions. Whether it be qualitative or quantitative, most of the tasks relating to social research are conducted using text, and published in that format.

Of course, I am not refuting the importance of text in research; however, I am concerned that insistence on this format may limit the extent of research and expression, as well as reduce the flexibility of the social sciences. There are at least two reasons why the format should not be restricted to text.

The first concerns the foundation of social research. Although human society should be the most interesting subject for research, it seems that today, research of this area has become far too difficult to comprehend and fails to attract people's attention. One of the advantages of language is that a combination of concepts creates another concept. However, this advantage has often been detrimental and backfired, transforming social scientists into performers who prefer to manipulate concept after concept. In some cases, social scientists have even lost the energy to tackle the subject of the existent society. One way to release the extremely concept-oriented science of human society from the curse of concepts may be to introduce a form of social research which does not insist on text format.

The second reason for the use of sketches in research, concerns the pursuit of clarity and simplicity of expression. Even if an ambitious piece of social research were carried out, complicated language would put off many readers from the scientific knowledge. For instance we do not know the number of readers who stopped reading the first volume of *Capital* (Marx [1867] 1976), due to the extremely long narration on money and commodities, at its beginning. By inserting some figures, tables or illustrations in the text, we may have found that a large number of readers would have kept reading and could have appreciated the depth of Marx's work.

The technique of using diagrams effectively in writing a paper is a basic literacy skill required for scientists, whose essential role is to express ideas simply and guide the reader to comprehend the key concepts, argument and analysis. However, in the social sciences, this point has often been forgotten. There is still a tendency to regard an excellent piece of research as writing a long paper filled with big, hard-to-understand words. The education for social sciences also follows this trend and plays a large role in reproducing this tendency among young researchers.

As I have argued, in contrast to the concept-laden language and style of the social sciences, illustrations can express ideas more directly. For example, Figure 5.1 below is a sample of the cross-section of a sushi roll shown in a sushi restaurant. This is a brilliant presentation which caters for the customers' needs by showing the variety and amount of filling with one glance. Can the social sciences surpass this clear presentation by the sushi restaurant? The proposal in this paper arises from this kind of realization, my concern with the current situation and the means by which we express ideas and knowledge in our academic disciplines.

Tradition of sketching in the natural sciences

Unlike the social sciences, there are disciplines which have traditionally regarded drawing pictures as a method of science. These are the natural sciences, especially biology, geology and mineralogy, which retain a strong characteristic of natural history.

In these disciplines, where the structure of nature is studied and findings about its diversity are accumulated, detailed observations of the subject and accurate recording of its characteristics are required. Text may be used for recording, but sketching, where the observer reproduces characteristics visually, is considered important. Even today, where experiments in the biological sciences are flourishing,

Drawing Sketches in the Field

Figure 5.1: Cross-section sample of a sushi roll

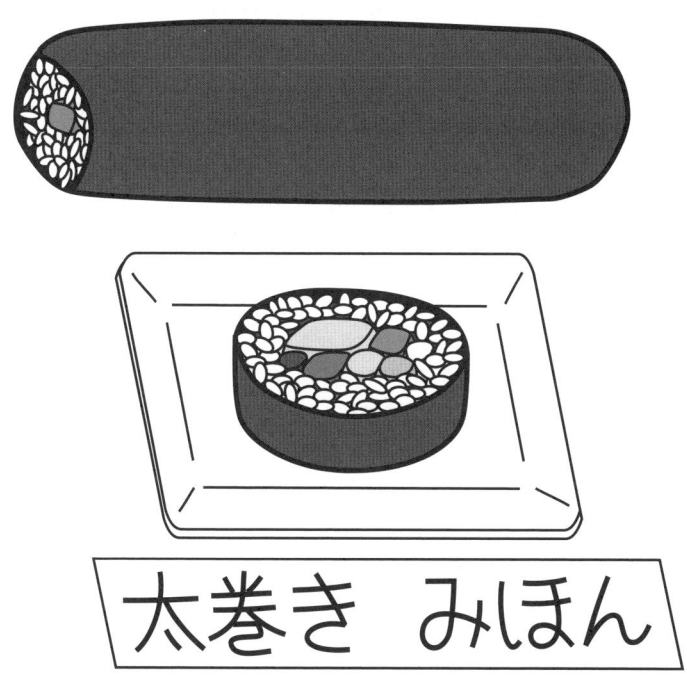

(Sample of a sushi roll)

Can the social sciences surpass the clear presentation by the sushi restaurant?

the sketching of life forms is always taught in practical sessions for biology, in university. I was fortunate to receive such an education.

I want to propose that we introduce this methodology, such as is used in biology, into the social sciences. This also implies that we take the viewpoint of natural history and learn from direct observation of human society.

Definition and characteristics of sketching

Sketching for the purpose of observation and research is not just about drawing pictures at random. There are a few points to note before applying it as a descriptive format for science. In this section, the definition and characteristics of sketching will be outlined. First, let me define what a sketch is from my own perspective:

A sketch is a picture and related text of a subject, which the researcher has observed directly and understood, and recorded the scientifically significant characteristics clearly and without omission.

There are three important points in this definition, firstly, understanding through direct observation of the subject. The researcher must observe the subject directly and thoroughly, before drawing the sketch. What was not seen must not be drawn. Secondly, the sketch needs to illustrate scientifically significant characteristics. Drawing should be undertaken with a process of selection and discarding information. For example, in the case of a biology sketch, shadow or gloss would not be included. To know which characteristics are important, fundamental knowledge of the academic discipline of the chosen field must be understood and mastered. Thirdly, a sketch should be clear and detailed without omission. This means that important points should be recorded and the visual execution of these elements must be clear. In principle, only continuous lines and dots should be used for drawing. Techniques such as broken or faded out lines or blacked out space, which can be interpreted in more than one way, should not be used. Outlines must be closed.

To help understand characteristics of the sketching method, some examples of: 'What is not a sketch?' will be presented here.

Characteristic 1: Sketching is not an art
Sketching is not an art which pursues beauty, but a record which places the utmost value on accuracy and clarity. It does not aim for a 'picture' which strikes people emotionally, but for a 'diagram' containing appropriate information.

Characteristic 2: Sketching does not require any special talent
Sketching does not require special talent such as creativeness or artistic sense. Artistic ambition can be a deterrent to sketching. What is required is patience to draw carefully and scientific ethics to draw what is seen as is.

Characteristic 3: Sketching does not require any special tools
Basically, if there is paper and writing tools, sketches can be drawn anywhere and at anytime. Field notebooks or grid notebooks may be convenient, but plain white paper is sufficient. As for writing tools, a common lead pencil or ballpoint pen is sufficient. No electrical appliances are used, so work can be done in a place without electricity.

Characteristic 4: Sketching does not consider the natural state as best

If necessary, the subject can be adjusted to better record its characteristics. In biology sketches, the object can be placed at an angle where the observer can see it better, a part of the tissue may be removed or a cross section may be taken. Sketching is different in purpose from landscape or still life, which try to replicate actual shapes and impressions.

Characteristic 5: Sketching does not exclude text

Sketches mainly consist of illustrations, but they are usually accompanied by words for information. For example, biology sketches require information about size, color, names of parts, time and date when recorded, place, scientific name and vernacular name. Thus, text must be used effectively.

Characteristic 6: Sketches cannot be drawn without training

Sketches portraying accurate and sufficient information cannot be drawn by beginners. Although artistic talent is not needed, specific training and experience is necessary. This is why sketch literacy education is a basic requirement.

The application of sketching in social research and what it can actually achieve is demonstrated below, with reference to my research history.

Sketching as a method of social research

Sketch education in university

I first received instruction on how to draw sketches in a biology practical class, which I enrolled in as a third year science student. Everyday, materials including plants and animals were presented. Students would single-mindedly draw them, one by one—dots on the back of a fern, a stem cross-section, crucian carp scales, a frog heart, and skulls of apes and ancient humans. I was impressed to find that by drawing sketches carefully and patiently, like taking records, I acquired a habit of looking at fine details, which also helped me to improve my memory of the information.

During a practical session, a student sitting opposite me said: 'This is so tedious; we should let a machine do it. I will invent such a machine!' I ignored these words, since this exercise was being undertaken to cultivate our eyes, and the student's thinking was off target. Since the human brain decides which features are important, no matter how technology advances, sketching needs to be carried out by hand.

The daily sessions of practical sketching were enjoyable. After the six month basic practical course, the majority of my friends took up practical classes in microbiology subjects, while I chose only macro biology subjects such as ecology, comparative anatomy and physical anthropology. These were the subjects related to natural history, where observation by the naked eye and sketching played a large role. I also practiced sketching geological formations of strata in field practical sessions for geology and mineralogy, which I was not enrolled in, but was granted permission to join casually.

My fundamental sketch literacy was most likely nurtured in this one year. Following this year, there was no opportunity to use sketching, and a few years passed without utilizing this skill. However, all of a sudden, I needed to make use of my skill and the importance of sketching became very apparent on the social research scene.

The encounter between social research and sketching

I went from a period of not using sketching to its regular use, while enrolled in the university doctorate course, when I undertook fieldwork in anthropology. I lived in a village with hunter-gatherer people, called the *Baka*, in the tropical rainforest of the Republic of Cameroon, Africa. During this period of fieldwork, I researched their traditional life and the way it was changing, with a particular interest in the children.[1]

Initially in the field, I believed that photography was the most accurate method of recording, and that everything should be photographed. My notebook was also filled with letters in those days. One day my camera broke. The extreme humidity in the tropical rainforest had caused the film to stick to an internal part of the camera, preventing the film wind-up mechanism from working correctly. When I forced the film to wind, the specific internal part of the camera cracked. As a result, I could not replace the film and I was no longer able to take any photographs.

It was the middle of the forest, with no camera shops to be seen. The car which had brought me to the village had long gone. I could not go to the capital city to buy a new camera, as it was approximately 900 kilometers away. The car would not come back to the site for another three months, to pick me up. How could I spend this precious time in the field without a recording medium? I felt that I was in big trouble.

However, this problem actually did me a favor. Without the camera and as an alternative to photography, I began making sketches by hand.

One day, the children brought back harvested cassava leaves to be used for the evening meal. Usually, I would have taken a photograph of the leaves and leave it at that, but I did not have my camera anymore. In the whim of the moment, I made a sketch of the leaf in my notebook. Instantly, the children gathered around excited: '*Nobou* (the locals' name for me) *e a de de* (drew a picture)!' '*Iyo. De na jaboka* (Hey, it's a cassava leaf).' I was surprised by their reaction. It was at that moment that I realized that sketching might be appealing. Since I was living in the field, I had plenty of time, so why not use this abundant time to draw sketches every day. So began the life of drawing the various elements of life in the village, which caught my eye.

Types of sketches for social research

Whenever I saw something unusual, I would say: 'Can I have a look?' and draw a sketch, completing the task in a few to ten minutes. It was not a difficult task with my once-trained eyes and hand. After adding information such as color and size and confirming both its vernacular name and its French name, the sketch would be complete.

As a sign of my gratitude, I would show the finished sketch to the children: 'Here!' The more detailed the sketch was, the louder the cheer, 'Wow!' Soon, children would come and surround me whenever I opened my notebook and squatted: 'What's this?' 'It's the head!' 'It's the tail!' Their chatting also became an important information source.

These sketches, which I drew daily amounted to 410 sketches in about seven months (Figure 5.2).[2] On average, this meant that I had made two sketches per day over some six months.

Coming from a background in biology, the subject which I drew the most was plants and animals (Figure 5.3a). I was particularly interested in food and in the plants which provided everyday food. Next, I drew the animals which were caught as prey, the fruit including the fruit trees, crops in the field, the surrounding trees, a pet dog having a nap, and insects.

After sketching the majority of plants and animals, then came material culture (Figure 5.3b). Residences such as houses and huts, their furniture such as chairs, cooking utensils such as a mortar, children's toys including miniature cars and guns, hunting goods; baskets, fishing tools, and musical instruments.

Figure 5.2: Subject and number of sketches (410 in total)

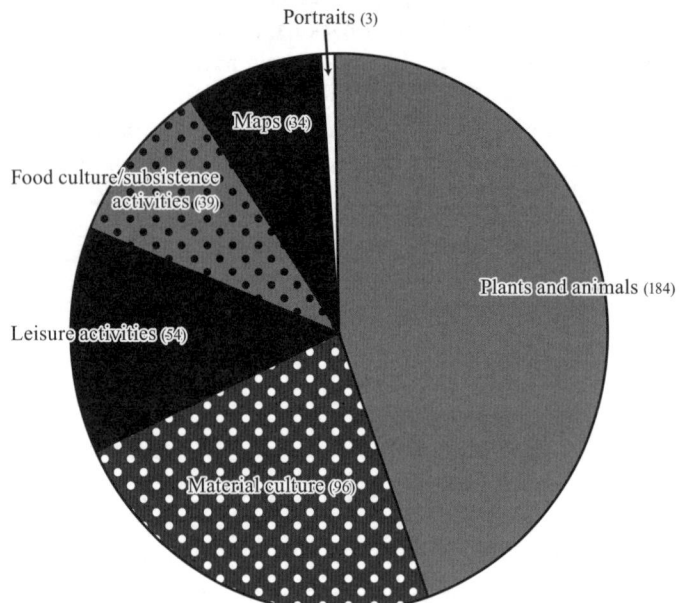

Furthermore, I liked sketching people's leisure activities (Figure 5.3c). I drew children's gatherings for play and dance, as well as dancers wearing costumes for the forest spirits' dance.

Besides this, I drew the way meals were presented. To observe and record the food culture, I also recorded the processes of cooking or hunting and gathering activities in a four-part comic style. In addition, I recorded the locations of villages, houses, roads and the river in a diagram. At times, I would make a map using accurate measures and even when I had no time, I would leave a rough sketch in my notebook. I was going to draw children's faces as well, but since there was a child who started crying because they could not stay still as a model, I did not do this very much. In this way, the subjects of my sketches covered many aspects of the culture of the Baka society. The accumulation of sketches became my utmost treasure. A few months later, the professor from my university dropped into my research area, and he lent me his high quality single-lens reflex camera. However, by then I was already completely absorbed in sketching, and I no longer depended on the camera as much. Sketching had become a fundamental method essential to my research.

Drawing Sketches in the Field

Figure 5.3: Fieldwork sketches in the tropical forest region of the Republic of Cameroon, August 1997–March 1998

a: Plants and animals (Left: a blue duiker; Right: a banana plant)

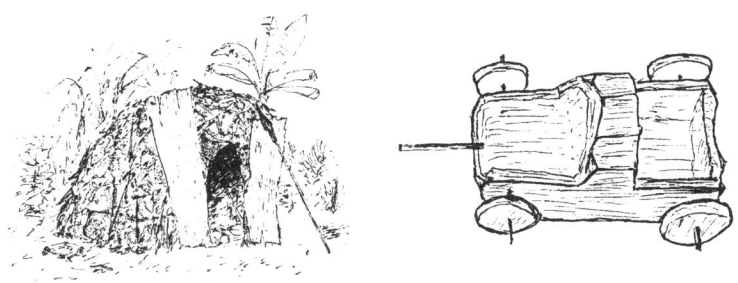

b: Material culture (Left: a traditional hut; Right: a miniature car carved from a finger of banana)

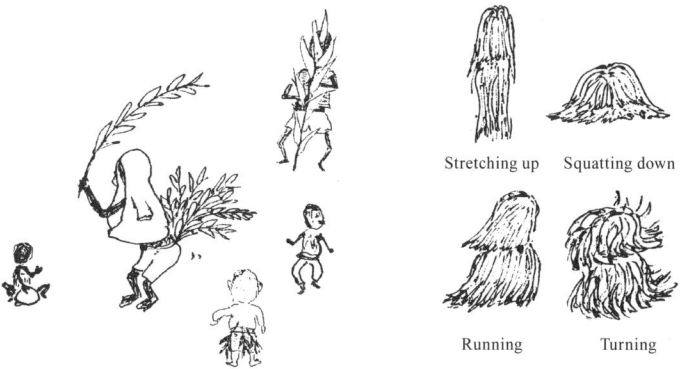

c: Leisure activities (Left: dancing children; Right: the dance of the forest spirit)

Advantages of sketching in social research

How did sketching benefit the social research? Reflecting on my actual field experiences, the advantages will be described in six points.

Advantage 1: Accurate understanding of the material

Sketches help to accurately understand a subject (Figure 5.4). Sketching requires thorough observation of the subject and subsequent reproduction by hand. Thus, the observer can understand the subject extremely well and have a clear memory of it.

This does not just concern the knowledge of plants and animals. The structure of traps to hunt animals, the way children knit costumes of the spirits, the material of fishing rods, and, how to build huts for playing in, are all topics for illustration. The reason I could understand these fine details was because I had made detailed sketches.

On one occasion this level of meticulousness put me in danger. One day, honey collected from the forest was delivered to me. It was a piece

Figure 5.4: Sketches help to accurately understand a subject (Advantage 1)

of beehive laden with honey, and it is eaten by biting into the beehive itself. It is the finest feast for hunter-gathering people and they had generously shared some of it with me. Being the first time I had been given honey, I began to sketch happily. My friend said 'You'd better eat it quickly.' While nodding 'Yeah, yeah,' I drew each of the hexagonal cells of the beehive and even drew a bee perched on top. I raised my face after I felt that the sketch was almost finished and was shocked. A large swarm of hundreds of bees, which had sensed the smell of honey, swirled around closing in on me. My friend made a fire to chase them away, and I ran to my tent taking the honey with me. The bees even flew into the tent and it was a great effort to get rid of them. The whole village was thrown into chaos.

It is a good learning experience to observe carefully when sketching; on the other hand, if you become lost in the detail of the sketch and forget the threat of nature, disastrous things can happen. Both these lessons can be learnt in the field.

Advantage 2: Accurate recording of information
Sketching allows accurate recording of a subject (Figure 5.5). The advantage of sketching is not only in encouraging careful observation, but it also leaves clear and useful data in the notebook.

Figure 5.5: Sketching allows accurate recording of a subject (Advantage 2)

For example, a sketch of a miniature car cut out from a banana or an air gun made by cutting a papaya stem; all of these were drawn carefully, with color, size, date and location written in. When I went fishing with the boys, I was sure to draw a diagram of the river with the width and direction of flow, also drawing in the positions of fallen trees and rocks. When I accompanied the girls to yam digging, I drew the shape of the holes that were dug, writing in their size, depth and angle. When there were people dancing, the movements of their limbs and costumes were recorded using sketches.

The subjects were all visual things and therefore they remained as visual sketches in the notebook. These data might not be used until several years later; if at that time there were only lines of text left, it would not be possible to recreate the original impression.

In these circumstances, photographs and videos may be thought of as good recording mediums; however, these technologies actually have many disadvantages. They capture the complete scenery, so the focus of interest is more diffuse, and checking important facts may not be possible later. Also, it is not possible to take a picture at 360 degrees and from all directions, so only a fragment of the scenery is recorded. This prevents a bird's eye view recording of the whole situation. Furthermore, it is not possible to write information noticed during observation, on film or tape, regarding its size, the number of objects, number of people, and the distance and so on.

The best characteristics of sketching are its flexibility when recording, and excellent reenactment ability. If a written description is required, the sketches can be interpreted to text when writing the paper. As will be discussed later, sketching is also extremely useful for the production of academic papers and at conference presentations.

Advantage 3: Formation of rapport
Sketching helps to create rapport (Figure 5.6); that is, the local people really love it when you sketch. They will be sure to burst into laughter if you draw something in front of them and show them the sketch. I wonder how many times this language-free method helped me to communicate, and how useful it was in reducing tension.

Of course, equipment such as digital cameras can display a picture straight away. This would also please the informants, and there are indeed situations where technical innovation contributes to the formation of rapport. However, sketching has something which generates an 'amusing' quality which is lacking in visual equipment. It may be the act of sketching which is amusing in itself, rather than

Figure 5.6: Sketching helps to create rapport (Advantage 3)

just the final image. The situation of a stranger from a faraway foreign country being attracted to something which is very ordinary to the local people, and sketching it passionately while asking them about every detail of these things; for them, this attitude seems to be very amusing. The more detailed the sketch, the funnier it is. The more the researcher is passionate, the more humorous it is. They usually laughed at me: 'Ha ha, look, he is drawing such a thing!'

Actually, taking a humble stance and conveying the message: 'Sorry I don't know anything' and being accepted by the people, your subject, is a highly refined tactic of fieldwork. It does not matter whether the response is a laugh of ridicule. If it generates their interest in you, you have moved one step forward in establishing rapport. Furthermore, if they are amused by what you have done, you have achieved a great deal.

Naturally, caution may be necessary for reproducing items or events of a religious nature, since some religions do not like the use of icons. I was nervous about their reaction when I drew a sketch of the forest spirit (a dancer playing the role), in which the hunter-gatherers believed. However, I did not need to worry, and they were thoroughly amused by my representation. Consequently, I drew many dances of spirits with ease. In such cases, it may be wise to draw some small related objects first, to see their reaction.

What is important is that in all of these processes, language is not required. In Cameroon villages where school education is not widespread, it is mainly the adult males who can speak French, one of the official languages. During the period when I was learning their language, sketching became a powerful communication tool, since it could also be easily understood by females and children. At times, I would draw sketches just for communication purposes.[3] Drawing is a universal form of expression which practically everybody can understand, irrespective of ethnicity, gender or age.

Advantage 4: Facilitation of material collection
Sketching makes the collection of samples smooth and easy (Figure 5.7). Members of the community may bring you material objects to draw, or else bring them to assist your memory while drawing.

The news: 'Nobou is said to draw sketches' became rather widespread talk. I would often overhear people talking about how 'today he drew that' and 'he drew this.' I would leave them to talk, since this was certainly good advertising.

In the evening, children would come and show me their catch: 'We caught a crab in the river today!' 'It's a shrimp.' I would borrow them

Figure 5.7: Sketching makes the collection of samples smooth and easy (Advantage 4)

Drawing Sketches in the Field 87

one by one with a 'thank you' and then proceed to draw sketches. When the children saw the complete sketches, they would smile at them and go home with the crab and the shrimp.

I enjoyed these occasions, most of all when they would come to show me various things; although, I also enjoyed it when they would give me food. Children would come because they enjoyed looking at my sketches, and at the same time I would have the opportunity to see many new things. On these occasions, I would ask the name of the object, hear the stories relating to it, and thus learned their language and knowledge of their culture gradually.

One morning, the village chief came with something long dangling from his hand.

'Look Nobou! It's a viper. I killed it in my house this morning.' The village chief himself had come to show me the corpse of the viper, its head nearly severed by a sharp blow from a sword. Of course, I humbly made a sketch for him.

In this way, the rapport between me and the locals grew. Through sketching, it also made material collection easier and contributed to a widening in my knowledge and outlook.

Advantage 5: Creation of a database

Sketches form a database (Figure 5.8). Sketching not only helps with the relationships with locals, it is also useful for the production of academic papers, as will be discussed below.

After several months in the forest I went into town. The due date for the research report, which was to be submitted to the Cameroon government, was fast approaching. At the time, it was an enormous task for me since I was having difficulty doing any systematic research, and I was agonizing over what to write.

Flipping through the pages of my notebook, there was not much text but there were many sketches. I photocopied the sketches and spread them out, wondering if these self-accumulated sketches were to be the outcome of my research. The various toys of the children playing in the forest were displayed before me. The image of children collecting plant materials from the forest, making innovative toys and playing with them came to my mind. 'That's it!' I thought. Choosing a keyword which came to me at that moment: 'Research on the material culture of the children of the Baka: Tools and toys' as the title, I compiled an English language report filled with many illustrations and submitted it to the Cameroon government (Kamei 1997).

Figure 5.8: Sketches form a database (Advantage 5)

The paper based on this report later became a chapter of a collection of academic papers in Japan (Kamei 2001c), and it eventually formed a section of my doctoral thesis (Kamei 2002c). It was also used for a presentation to the American Anthropological Association (Kamei 2002b), stirred up some laughter at the International Conference on Hunting and Gathering Societies (Kamei 2002a), and was included as a chapter of a book published in English (Kamei 2005). The accumulation of sketches had gradually become an attractive database, forming the source of these publications.

Advantage 6: Clarification of expression
Sketches make verbal and written expression clearer (Figure 5.9). If diagrams based on sketches are used in papers or presentations in conferences to report research results, the expression of ideas becomes very clear, and captures the attention of many readers and the audience.

In the forest, I saw a toy called 'miniature bananas.' Young girls would pick up unripe bananas a few centimeters long, thread them together and walk around carrying them on their shoulders. This was a type of play; imitating adult women carrying harvested big bananas. Before I reported this at a conference, I realized that I had not taken any photographs. Therefore, instead of having a photograph, I made

Figure 5.9: Sketches make verbal and written expression clearer (Advantage 6)

an illustration on the computer by recreating an image based on a rough sketch in the notebook. The audience commented favorably, saying it was easy to understand (Kamei 2001b).

The opportunity for me to present at international conferences gradually increased. Being a non-English native speaker, the only effective method to draw the audience's attention, without depending on language, was drawing. I made many illustrations based on sketches in my notebook and took them to various conferences (Kamei 2002a; 2002b), gaining the understanding of many people.

The theme of my doctoral thesis was the everyday life of the children of the hunter-gatherers (Kamei 2002c). While being told that the content was lacking, the public hearing day arrived, my only hope was the slides full of illustrations. After the session, the audience's reaction included comments centered on the illustrations, such as 'the picture of girls digging yams was funny,' and 'the depiction of tools was strangely realistic.' At least in terms of the level of expression, the presentation was well received.

In academic presentations, the utilization of illustrations should be pursued further. Some researchers are able to attract the audience by their way of speech, but there are not many people who can do this. Also, oratory skills are not universally shared and tend to be limited to one language. There must be many scenes of international conferences where English speakers enthusiastically give their papers, while the non-English speakers are getting bored.

Clear and simple visual expression has a universal power, which overcomes language differences and can be accepted by many people. Sketching as a form of visual expression has the potential to overcome language barriers and can exhibit its effectiveness as well.

Disadvantages of sketching in social research

While I have outlined all of the positive aspects of drawing as a research method for the social sciences, there are methodologically disadvantageous characteristics of sketching as well. Some of these aspects will be summarized here.

Disadvantage 1: Sketches take time
It takes time when sketching in the field, and in a sense, making records in text summarizes the information and saves time. However, sketching can be simplified and depending on its use, be less time consuming. For example, when I dropped by at a small church in Africa, all I drew was the position of the pews and well-known symbols for the gender of the people, instead of undertaking a very detailed sketch of the people themselves (Figure 5.10). This took only three minutes to draw.

Even for a detailed sketch, it takes ten minutes at most to complete. If it is possible to record valuable observation experiences realistically in that length of time, I believe that it is better to draw. Of course, this decision and point of view also depends on the purpose and values of the researcher.

Disadvantage 2: Sketches are hard to share with others
While extracting and documenting information observed in the field, sketching is an individual recording method which relies on craftsmanship. Although there are cases of fieldworkers, like myself, achieving some success in the area of drawing, there are probably no cases where social science researchers share their sketch data to undertake their research. If sketches are to be used in large-scale joint research projects, it may become necessary to specify a set of standards for sketching.

Figure 5.10: A simplified sketch. A sketch of a church in the Republic of Cameroon, March 2005

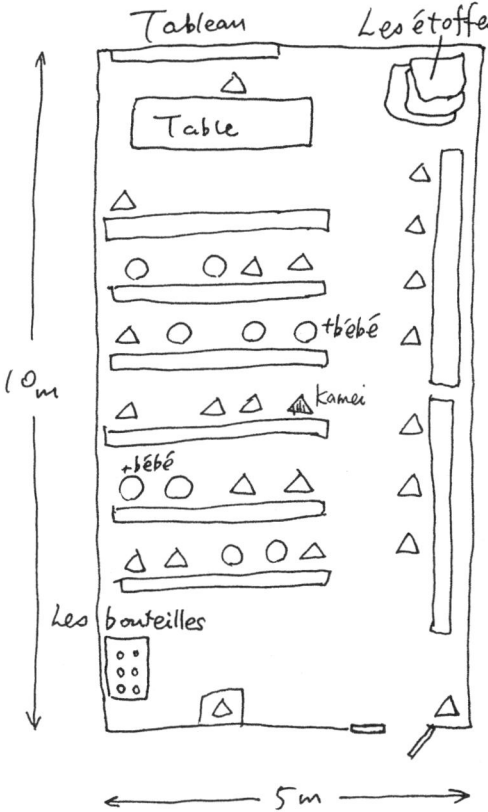

Sketches can be simplified depending on their use. © 2005, Nobutaka Kamei

Disadvantage 3: Sketches are not easily processed as data

The method of entering and saving data on a computer is suitable for text format, whereas sketches are recorded on a paper medium, so they cannot be as easily organized. Saving sketches as image data results in a significantly larger data size compared to text data. However, this problem can be overcome through technological innovation.

Disadvantage 4: Sketches may cause an information divide

Sketches are beneficial to those who can see but not beneficial to people with a visual disability. If a trend emerges where sketches by themselves are sufficient in relaying information, this will result in a new information divide. It is necessary to develop a system of education and research based on universal design, for example, by having a means to translate sketches into text forms. This is an issue which should be dealt with through visual educational materials, including videos and ethnographic films.

These disadvantages can be adequately covered by combining sketches with a range of mediums including text, sound, photography and video images. In this way, it is possible to lessen any ill effects that result from the introduction of sketches.

Recommendations for Sketching

Introduce sketching to basic literacy skills

In conclusion, I would like to make some recommendations relating to the use of sketching methodology as a research tool. First of all, to innovate the teaching of the social sciences, I would like to advocate a new education scheme which places the skill of sketching as a fundamental literacy skill for social research.

Social science is a science where the subject of human society is researched, but when it comes to actual university education, there is more emphasis on writing than investigation. Students often have an understanding that study at university means reading complicated books and writing long essays. Social science education should demonstrate the pleasure of investigating phenomena in society and conveying the research findings to other people in an easy to understand form.

I sometimes give students a sketching assignment in my lectures. The following is an actual example of this practice in the subject 'Cultural Anthropology B' at Seian University of Art and Design. The students were given the task of observing and sketching the traditional New Year food dishes and illustrating the changes in tradition by using diagrams. The students responded to this with assignments like those exemplified in Figure 5.11. As can be seen, these illustrations are just as good as the specimen outside the sushi restaurant, and do have the power to appeal to people.

Whenever I listen to unclear presentations at events such as conferences, I remember these excellent works by the students. Sketch literacy, where students are trained to express their ideas clearly by using illustrations, needs to be included in the undergraduate curriculum of the social science related faculties of the university.

Drawing Sketches in the Field 93

Figure 5.11: Literacy education using sketching

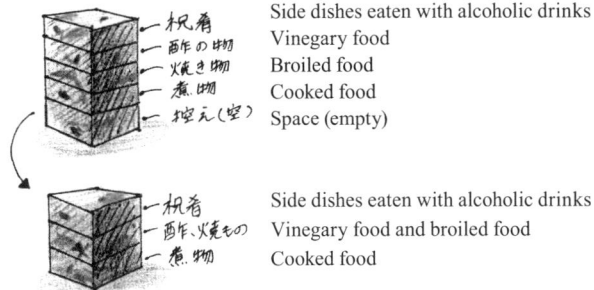

An explanatory diagram of changes in the traditional New Year dishes, *Osechi Ryōri* (Tsuboyama 2005). It shows the decrease of types and volume of dishes. ©2005, Hiroko Tsuboyama.

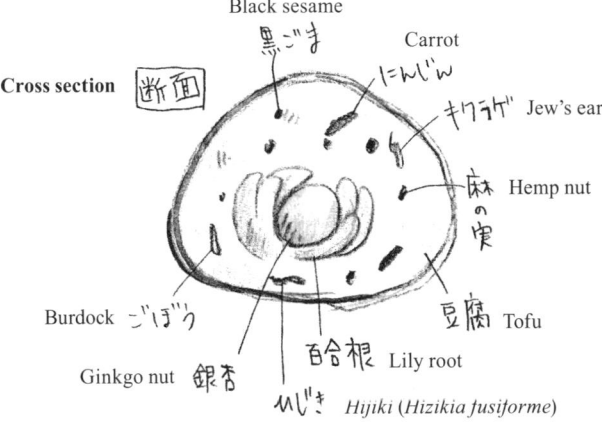

Internal structure of deep-fried tofu, *Ganmodoki* (Hara 2005). ©2005, Kimika Hara.

Source: From student assignments titled 'Collection and analysis of the traditional New Year dishes' submitted for 'Cultural Anthropology B' at Seian University of Art and Design in 2004. Sketch literacy education encourages accurate and clear expression.

Beyond text oriented literacy: innovation in descriptive format

What sort of meaning does the introduction of sketching, as a descriptive format, have for the development of the discipline of the social sciences? The characteristics of sketching will be highlighted here, in comparison to mathematics which is gaining significance in the discipline.

Mathematical sociology challenges sociology, which is traditionally expressed in written passages. Its aim is to pursue rationality and clarity by describing and analyzing social phenomena using mathematics. The task of establishing a logical format of description among professional researchers is necessary for the development of academic disciplines. However, using mathematics as a descriptive format can narrow the range of readers, as even though the rational ability in humans which produced mathematics is universal, the literacy to use mathematics is not.

The advantage of sketching lies in its accessibility. Pictures can convey what they portray in an instant. The simplified expression of social phenomena using illustrations is widespread in areas like journalism, such as in the use of satirical comics in newspapers from all over the world. The social sciences should seriously consider the introduction of drawing.[4]

The natural sciences, use the descriptive format of mathematics for recording and analyzing phenomena, and have constructed a system where researchers from around the world can hold 'narrow and deep' discussions. At the same time, they have a long tradition of natural history, and have been successful in seeking 'wide and shallow' understanding by using the descriptive format of sketching to record and express phenomena clearly.

In science, the descriptive formats of mathematics and sketching supplement each other, with neither being superior to the other. To actively promote generalization and wider application of knowledge, these two areas should be incorporated into the social sciences, which up until now have been limited to text-based description. It may be dangerous to regard the natural sciences as perfect, but a significant lesson can be learnt from this example of successful generalization and wider application of knowledge.

Collaboration with animation: innovation in the mode of expression

As the third recommendation, the potential of applying sketching will be considered, while examining the search for a method of expression which surpasses printed material. One of the projects in the twenty-first Century COE Program of Kwansei Gakuin University is the development of sociology which is expressed in the form of animation. The animated film produced for the project, called *Bōryoku no fūkei* (Landscape of Violence), is directed by Masahiro Ogino.

Figure 5.12: Animation-based sociology 'Boryoku no fūkei (Landscape of Violence)' (Ogino 2005)

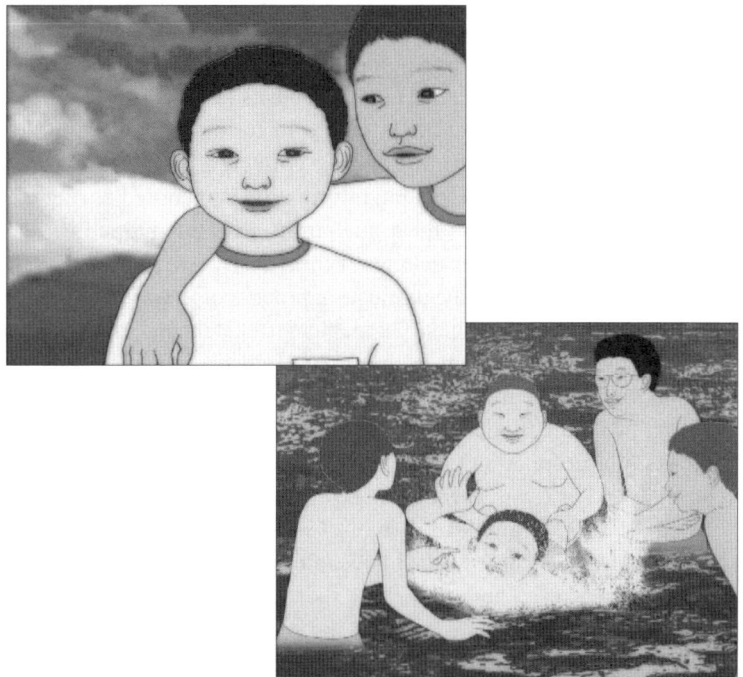

Animation is drawing attention as a new means of expressing social issues.

The expression of social issues through screen images has been attempted historically through the use of documentaries and dramas. However, in sociology, where ideas are pursued irrespective of the particularism of region, ethnicity or individual, the actual images which are used to show specific properties can become didactic and stereotypical. In contrast, visual expression through the fictional world of animation can convey the message of social issues and related paradigms in a highly purified form.

When summarizing the characteristics of animation based sociology, sociologically important characteristics are recorded clearly and without omission, while sociologically insignificant attributes are abstracted, resulting in a simple visual expression of social issues. The definition of animation-based sociology shares the same philosophy with the methodology of sketching discussed previously in this chapter (see the definition of sketching).

The possibility of collaboration between sketching and animation also increases through application. Sketches can be utilized in the preparatory investigation for the production of animation-based sociology. In the field, an infinite amount of information can be obtained, not just through words; including scenery, facial expressions, movement of people, and placement of objects and the angle of light. These factors, which have the potential to form the background of social phenomena, can be thoroughly collected by the researcher through the use of sketches. If the information is recorded during the investigation solely in text form, the ability to print and publish the information in forms other than text is practically lost.

For example, consider the production process of knowledge, where the observer uses all five senses in the field to sketch, and thus records, everything which appears to be important information, and produces an animation based on these sketches. There is the possibility for the creation of a new model of social science, which goes beyond the dimension of production technology and extends from investigation, recording and analysis, through to expression.

What if Karl Marx had drawn sketches of the landscape of workers in London, or if Michel Foucault had produced an animation portraying prison? There is no way that the social scientists of the twenty-first century would not work on such an ambitious task, one where both fieldwork and image processing technology could be fully utilized.

Break free from proper nouns: innovation in ethnography

Furthermore, the collaboration of sketching in social research and expression through animation could shake the foundation of ethnography in anthropology, where the major focus has been the inherent character of the region and the particularism of the local population.

In text-based ethnology, many proper nouns are scattered throughout the writings; the notion of culture is endemic and revered as holy. Historically, with the creation of an inviolable territory of 'uniqueness,' we saw the development of tourism and the offering of material objects to museums. However, in some political contexts, we also saw the condemnation of the anthropological discipline, and its actions and assumptions.

Visual anthropology, a later development, attempted to free itself of text, but the product was composed of real image clips which revealed many of the same conceptual attributes and problems. The particular communities and cases overflowed onto the screen and tied the audience to a particular space and time which shut out the sociological imagination as well as the capacity for generalization.

Let me propose an idea of a third type of ethnology, one which could be created through the process of sketching and animation. It could lead to an animation-based ethnology which excludes proper nouns and depicts only significant matters for scientific knowledge and analyses. Then what would we find on the screen? The sky? The ground? Tools? Food? Human behaviors? Facial expressions? Is it set in a forest? A village? A company? What do we want to draw there? What do we want to convey? In this case especially, an extremely sophisticated analysis and expression of human culture and behavior is required. The result may be something like a scientific TV program portraying communication, violence and peacemaking amongst a troop of the species of the great ape, *Homo sapiens*. Actually, social research by sketches observes human society through the lens of natural history. This seemingly reckless attempt may also be an interesting and productive contribution to the social sciences, which can be defined as 'research on human society by any means necessary and possible.'

Conclusion: literacy in the era of photo messages

I draw sketches in the field and I feel that this has become a very good occupation for me; however, sketching can sometimes be regarded as a minor occupation for a researcher. Nevertheless, I seriously think that everybody should draw, since it is a very good method for the social sciences. When I penned all of these thoughts together and considered the innovation of this research method, I unexpectedly glimpsed the deep darkness of the discipline. I feel I have touched upon the mechanics within the decision making process, where the fate of an academic discipline is decided by its descriptive format.

While I will leave the issues of a profound nature concerning science, for another time, my present concern is closer at hand. A short while ago, there was an announcement of the entrance exam results at my university. What were the happy applicants who passed the exam doing in front of the notice board? They were taking pictures of their applicant number on the board using their mobile phone, and sending the pictures to their friends by photo message. They were not using the phone function and they were not sending a text message. Nowadays, the mobile phone has become a tool to show each other images of what you have just seen. Prospective students are living in a dimension of visual conversations. University education must learn about this reality to some degree.

These successful applicants will soon come to my Anthropology class. Will the new students be willing to come to a class on ethnology, which is full of proper names and consists only of text? Amidst the compulsive feeling that they must fill paper with text, won't they resort to dishonest actions such as plagiarism? An essay of borrowed word after word devoid of any intellectual stimulus also makes me, the marker, miserable.

I believe that rather than repeating these incidents, owing to our obsession with a text-oriented style, there must be a way to share knowledge with people from the next generation by developing a research and educational style which consists of plenty of images. Professional researchers and educators can surely contribute some effort to realize this.

'Sketch literacy training for university students of social science!' This is a serious proposal, from an academic who was able to carry out social research happily by drawing sketches in the field.

Acknowledgements

This research is being carried out as a part of the Kwansei Gakuin University 21st Century Center of Excellence (COE) Program, *The study of social research for the enhancement of human well-being*. The fieldwork which formed the basis of this article was conducted with the Grant-In-Aid for International Scientific Research *'A study of multi-ethnic societies in the African evergreen forest'* (Adopted in 1996, No.08041080, Chief researcher: Dr. Hideaki Terashima [Professor, Kobe Gakuin University]) funded by the Ministry of Education, Science, Sports and Culture, Japan. I thank the Ministry of Scientific and Technical Research of the Republic of Cameroon, Kyoto University, Dr Hideaki Terashima (Kobe Gakuin University) and Dr Mitsuo Ichikawa (Kyoto University), for helping to realize this research. Dr Daisaku Tsuru (Toyama University), a forerunner in the field in drawing pictures, gave me encouragement by drawing comics. The Seian University of Art and Design Academic Committee, Ms Hiroko Tsuboyama and Ms Kimika Hara (both from Seian University of Art and Design), and Dr Masahiro Ogino (Kwansei Gakuin University) kindly gave permission to use the figures included. Lastly, the reason why I began to happily draw as part of my research is thanks to the children of the Baka hunter-gatherers, who always enjoyed my sketches. I look forward to taking this chapter to the children some day, and showing them the illustrations for another smile.

6
Opium and the Emperor: Anthropology, Colonialism and War during Imperial Japan

Kyung-soo Chun

Introduction: the sociology of Janus

If one word is chosen to express the crisis situation that human beings in our era confront, the word, in my view would be 'immorality.' I realize that the type of ethics taught in Chinese classics of Confucianism and in Aristotle's Nicomachean Ethics of ancient Greece no longer have any social influence. Moreover, the type of science that has degraded itself to the role of regulation, control and invasion, during the past two thousands years, has lost its position to argue about ethics. Also, I cannot help but question the intention with which social science was developed and, I regard as a major misfortune, the emergence of social science in a structural division, in which science is classified roughly into the sciences and humanities. Neither can I deny the fact that social science, which began with the intention of pioneering a new branch of learning for human understanding by scientifically analyzing human society, was also furnished with another face. This face is concerned with the regulation and control of human beings and society, just like Janus—the Roman god of gates and doors, beginnings and endings; represented with a double-faced head, each looking in opposite directions.

During the period of colonialism there was no room for ethics within a social science that justified its role as a political tool. Amid a crescendo of regulation and control in a war situation, an incident occurred in the USA immediately after the First World War. This incident raised ethical issues about social scientists and their behavior, which served the interests of their enemies (Boas 1919). This still remains a sensitive issue in social science today (Price 1998, 2002). If social scientific acts that have implications for government policies and military strategies are unrestrained by ethical standards, science, especially social science, is destined to accept a permanent role as a vehicle of political control. Since science is not guaranteed autonomy and as such is no longer qualified to argue the truth, the importance of ethics cannot be overstated. The credibility of social science for society is calculated on the basis of its sensitivity to ethical issues and its capacity to uphold ethics.

The issue of ethics and science was brought to light during the Second World War, where the inseparable relationship between a war and science was revealed and these relationships highlighted the need for a serious examination of scientific ethics. Kiyono, was one such anthropologist who overlooked ethics and claimed 'the nation requires anthropological knowledge...I only hope that anthropology takes the role in advances into the south' (Kiyono 1943: 2). This rhetoric of aggression was made by a part-time anthropologist who was an advocate of the Great East Asian Co-Prosperity Sphere.[1] Moreover there were many other instances. For example:

> In postwar Germany, W.E. Muhlmann warned autocratic countries of their exploitation of anthropology for political purposes in his paper, *Responsibility of Anthropologists*. His warning was sent out not only to Germany but also to all other countries participating in the all-out war (Proctor 1988: 169).

This paper aims to examine some of the ethical issues arising from the actions of anthropologists who undertook research during the period of colonialism and in a time of war. In particular, I would like to undertake a detailed analysis of the behavior of some Japanese anthropologists.

The fact that anthropologists' research activities were undertaken in close association with military operations cannot be overlooked. Anthropologists who conducted ethnographic field research 'assimilate themselves into the society under study...and act as an *insider* of that society' (Brymann 2001: x) (emphasis added). By contrast, the basic attitude of anthropologists who engaged in research activities, as an extension of military operations during the period of colonialism and in time of war, was far from that of the insider. Rather, they literally intended to keep a distance from the people in that society. In this regard, we need to pay attention to the activities of anthropologists who maintained distant relationships with the people under study, in order to see whether or not there may have been an association between their activities and the military.

When considering academic works Hattori reminds us that:

> In general, when evaluating a social scientific achievement, we should not regard it as a complete universe that has nothing to do with the context and trends of the times. Rather, we should evaluate it as what could be accomplished in the context of the times by picking up on the atmosphere of the times and by feeling the strained spirit of the times (Hattori 1974: 56).

The work of a researcher is located in time and thus has a historical background which can be the subject of evaluation. If the work being evaluated is a product of the times, for instance when the country was extremely autocratic, it must be closely examined in the context of the specificity of that period. Evaluation that disregards 'the strained spirit of the times,' will face questions about its ethical propriety.

Personal encounters and meta-ethnography

Bronislaw Malinowski was the greatest anthropologist from the United Kingdom, whose methodological work relating to 'the natives point of view,' discussed in *Argonauts of the Western Pacific* (1922), provided an air of freshness to the anthropological and social scientific worlds that were experiencing a thirst for methodological discussions. There seemed to be something in his work that captivated its readers. However, some would claim, the more captivating the work, the more it is considered to involve mystification. Clifford Geertz, cynically commented that the 'native's point of view' tends to be dramatized between the hope of self-transcendence and the fear of self-deception. He defined *fieldwork as personal encounters* while proposing that the I-witness style of ethnography, in the form of a diary, best reflects the reality of fieldwork (Geertz 1988: 84) (emphasis added). Geertz's proposition attempts to minimize the Malinowski-like way of mystification in participant observation. The common denominator between participant observation, based on viewpoints (Malinowski's proposition) and witnesses (Geertz's proposition), is a reciprocal arrangement comprising of personal encounters occurring between the anthropologist and the people in the particular society under study.

The ethnographic process of anthropologists, ranging from viewpoints to witnesses, is initiated by reciprocal personal encounters. The focus of this paper is a consideration of what kinds of actions are performed in such encounters, both by the anthropologist as well as the local inhabitants. Looking specifically at the actions of anthropologists raises some methodological questions regarding the type of personal encounters that are not part of the anthropological discipline and could be seen as a departure from science. The gist of these ideas is explored below.

There have been few anthropological studies that have preserved detailed records of the context in which the anthropologist entered the field and encountered its population. Given that the predominant perception of the field, in anthropological terms, is a kind of laboratory, Geertz thought that Malinowski depicted the field as an artificial domain under continual observation, in the fashion of Bentham's panopticon. Geertz's view seems to have resulted from the contrast between Malinowski's ethnography in the Trobriand Islands and the dramatic wrong-headedness reflected in his diary. Possibly because of this, Geertz used an expression 'dramatization of the fear of self-deception' to refer to Malinowski's ethnography (Geertz 1988: 84).

Approaching ethnography on the model of the panopticon involved a form of self-deception, because the observer's separation from the field situation inflicted a sacrifice on personal encounters. In view of the fact that a diary is private, the aim of the I-witness style ethnography in the form of a diary, proposed by Geertz, seems to suggest that descriptive studies, such as papers and books, should include private matters that have been previously hidden. During the production process of publications, invented for the public domain, the private domain is eliminated by publishers, editors or anthropologists themselves. The process and result of this elimination will ultimately cause damage to reality since the separation between the public and private, acts as an obstacle in the depiction of reality, and thus in the work process of ethnography itself.

The records, which reflected personal encounters have often been excluded from publication without explanation, because they were regarded as anthropologists' notes on their private lives. In this way, the context of personal encounters has been separated from ethnography. How should we explain this? In general, the act of publishing is accompanied by copyright, which is an author's right to the contents of their publications. In this way their creative activities are protected. If we question who the original owner of the contents of an ethnographic publication is, we would probably need to undertake a difficult and complex debate.

Skirting around the issue of who is the owner of the contents of an ethnographic publication for the present, knowledge is passed from an information source on to an ethnographer. Through the process of writing and publishing, the ownership of that knowledge is transferred from the information source to the ethnographer as the author of a publication. The information acquired from personal encounters is assimilated and transformed into a public format by the ethnographer. Thereby, knowledge of the information source becomes subject to the copyright of the ethnographer as author. During this process, details of personal encounters, in the form of notes about the ethnographer's private life are eliminated for various reasons, such as the style of the work or space limitations. That is to say, the act of eliminating these notes surrounding his or her personal encounters is thought to play an implicit and explicit role in the production of ethnography.

Interactions involved in the relationship between an information source, who provides local knowledge, and an ethnographer, who incorporates that knowledge into his or her ethnography, are often treated as episodes. Such episodes are generally used as a repertory to make a lecture or talk interesting, rather than as an important part of an academic paper or academic writing. Malinowski's diary (1967) is the best-known example of personal encounters that remain as inside stories which act as a background to an academic paper. Private matters seem to require a period of fermentation before their release into the public sphere and it took as long as fifty years for Malinowski's diary to appear in the public domain. As if opening Pandora's box, his diary caused a considerable stir in the anthropological discipline, activated debates about methodology and raised many ethical issues about fieldwork.

It is important to understand the thoughts, viewpoints and worldview of anthropologists because these act as a camera or lens in their work process in a similar way to photographs which come out differently depending on the camera or lens used. What enables us to understand these thoughts, viewpoints and worldviews is the record of their personal encounters in the form of their notes on their own private lives. In this way, anthropologists become the subject of ethnography concerning the context of the field in which they are involved. In other words, they become an ethnography of ethnography. Hidden parts between the lines of an ethnography, or inside stories behind a paper or book, released into the public domain in the form of a publication can be seen as the subject of 'meta-ethnography.' This has something in common with Geertz's I-witness style of ethnography that is in the form of a diary.

In this regard, I consider Malinowski's diary as a major meta-ethnography. Since the publication of his diary in 1967, there have been numerous papers and books published that have evaluated his work or reconsidered and appraised anthropological methods themselves. The influence of such papers and books called for the reinvention of ethnography, considered to be at the heart of anthropology. Ethnography had undoubtedly worn an indistinct veil of 'participant observation' until Malinowski's diary removed that veil and plunged a scalpel into the ethical issues facing anthropologists. The academic reaction to his diary demonstrates the interest in meta-ethnography. The debate on meta-ethnography has been significant by prompting discussion of anthropological field methods and ultimately of the ethics of fieldwork itself.

The contents of a meta-ethnography consist of stories generally categorized into personal encounters. These are not logical discussions, but are episodes corresponding to the notes of the private life of the anthropologist who comes into contact, during field research, with local people in the particular society under study. Although consisting of few logical discussions, the details of personal encounters reveal the author's worldview, view of life, personal interests and friendships. As it corresponds to stories behind the scenes, it can play an important role in reconstructing the context of the field. Hisakatsu Hijikata referred to himself as 'a layman who can hardly write an ethnological or anthropological paper' (Hijikata 1943: 7). His work *Ryūboku* (Driftwood) is the record, in the form of a diary, of his ten-year experience in Satawal Island of Palau. The work includes aspects that are easily categorized into Geertz's I-witness style of ethnography. The problem is how to interpret the compatibility of ethnography and meta-ethnography outlined in the records. For those who are accustomed to an academic style of ethnography, *Ryūboku* can be seen as a meta-ethnography in the form of a diary. However, in comparison to Malinowski's diary, Hijikata's work contains a considerable amount of formal analyses and ethnographic information.

Ethnography does not necessarily have a particular or typical style and there is no one road in its production. Ethnography can take any form such as a film, poem or cartoon. My attention is drawn to the possibility of considering *Ryūboku* as a meta-ethnography, in which the meta-ethnography exists in order to enrich the contents of an ethnography by providing inside stories that lie behind it. In other words, meta-ethnography is able to contextualize ethnography. Malinowski's ethnography is outstanding because of its contextualization (Chun 2001). His diary can play a role in providing a background to a great number of ethnographies about the Trobriand Islands that have been published previously. In this regard, Hijikata's *Ryūboku* should also be read for its context.

To prove meta-ethnography's capacity for contextualization is an attempt to provide a new perspective on ethnographic theory. Reflexive scrutiny between ethnography and meta-ethnography can serve as the basis on which the entire way of life is shown and this process can be seen as a form of ethnographic reflexivity. If meta-ethnography sheds light on the hidden side of ethnography, it enables an examination of the problem of power during the research process (for instance a hierarchy established between the researcher and the subjects of their research) and some of the fraudulent schemes that have traditionally been hidden from public scrutiny. Moreover ethical issues need to be included within the range of discussions about methodology. In other words, analysis of meta-ethnography is necessary for an in-depth discussion of the ethical issues involved in anthropological fieldwork.

Tobacco for the Trobrianders and opium for the Orochon

Malinowski and tobacco

Anthropologists, who visit a society, which is free from the domination of a monetary economy or one which does not place financial matters ahead of social matters, generally bring gifts for local people of that society. Because the gifts serve as a token of their friendship, anthropologists usually give careful consideration to the selection of the gifts before visiting the society. The gifts of anthropologists play a role in making their initial encounters with local people amiable. What kind of role do these gifts play in personal encounters and how are their effects estimated? This leads us to the theory of the gift and how it informs the relationship between researcher and subject.

In fieldwork methodology, gifts by anthropologists are rarely recommended. However, the function of gifts in data collection during field research cannot be ignored. Pharmaceutical products given to people as gifts will undoubtedly have some effect on their lives, as will cash paid to people in exchange for their contribution to interviews. The type and effect of gifts given by anthropologists are directly related to their words and actions. With this in mind, this paper analyzes some of the issues which arise in the private domain during field research, and surround gift giving by anthropologists. The paper aims to provide an opportunity to consider, from a methodological perspective, the specific issue of personal encounters in relation to the gifts of anthropologists. In order to do so, the actions of Seiichi Izumi, who gave opium to the Orochon in the north of Manchuria, are compared with those of Malinowski, who gave tobacco as a gift to the Trobriand Islanders.

According to his diaries during the periods from 1914 to 1915 and from 1917 to 1918, Malinowski mainly gave the islanders tobacco, but also gave some other substances such as betel-nut (hard nuts chewed like chewing gum). Tobacco is called *kuku* in Motu, a region of the Trobriand (Malinowski 1967: 309). In those days, tobacco was sold in a tin or can and was the shape of a square stick three inches long and one inch wide. A half stick of tobacco was a suitable quantity to fill a pipe [2] or to wrap in a piece of cigarette paper, and make a so-called rolly cigarette. The following illustrates the situations in which Malinowski gave tobacco as a gift to the islanders.

Each day, Malinowski provided a half stick of tobacco to *To'uluwa*, the paramount chief of Omarakana, sometimes with a cluster of betel-nuts (Malinowski 1965: I, 41). On one occasion, he presented several sticks of tobacco to *Kavaka*, a vital information provider in Mailu (Malinowski 1967: 30). Sometimes, he borrowed an *oro'u* (a large double canoe) in exchange for tobacco (Malinowski 1967: 59). One day he lost his temper in the middle of a negotiation with an islander who demanded twenty sticks of tobacco in return for lending an *oro'u* (Malinowski 1967: 65). On another occasion he gave some half-sticks of tobacco in exchange for viewing *bara* (i.e. a folk dance of Mailu) but the dancers left the scene quickly. This made him feel hatred towards the islanders to such an extent as to wish for their 'extinction' (Malinowski 1967: 69). On a different occasion, he got angry at *Pikana* who received six sticks of tobacco, and yet demanded more in exchange for his service to ride out in a boat from Mailu to the next island (Malinowski 1967: 70). Generally, he provided a half stick of tobacco to his interviewees and some interviews went very satisfactorily (Malinowski 1967: 71). One day, he entered a village carrying several sticks of tobacco with him to take photographs of *lugumi* (a canoe similar to an *oro'u*) (Malinowski 1967: 72). On another day, he gave three sticks of tobacco to *Bomera*, a policeman, and some boys who helped him set up a tent at a beach (Malinowski 1967: 150).

As illustrated above, Malinowski provided tobacco to the islanders according to his own consideration. He gave a different amount to people depending on the type of work they did for him. He was aware of the association between the amount and the relative effect of tobacco and appeared to have considered the effect of tobacco as a gift. For example, he regrettably reflected that two pounds in cash was found to be more effective in data collection than tobacco (Malinowski 1967: 69). Malinowski planned his future actions in Omarakana, especially in relation to the provision of tobacco, while somewhat excitedly thinking about his return to Kiriwina and Omarakana (Malinowski 1967: 290). He mentioned in his diary that Rich, probably another Caucasian, received a pig in exchange for tobacco in the village (Malinowski 1967: 52).

Together these descriptions show that Malinowski, who was well aware of the exchange value of tobacco, gave specific consideration to the association between the efficiency of data collection and the provision of gifts. In other words, his tobacco substantially contributed to the means of anthropological data collection in the Trobriands. This indicates that there was a mutual awareness of the exchange value of tobacco among researchers and the subjects of their research. It is therefore appropriate to understand that the provision of tobacco was a political process rather than a gift of human kindness. Tobacco, which illustrates the gift theory between Malinowski and the Trobriand Islanders, is thought to have played an important role in anthropological data collection. As discussed previously, gifts could also be betel-nut, confectionary or cash depending on the circumstantial conditions at the time. The gifts of anthropologists, which intervene in their reciprocal relations with the subjects of their research, can be analyzed on the basis of Mauss's gift theory (Mauss 1967).

Izumi and opium

Seiichi Izumi stated in his book:

> I traveled China with a friend to mark a turning point in my life upon reaching the age of twenty in 1936. However, we met with an accident on Mt. Halla of Chejudo Island in January of that year and I lost my friend as a result. This was the underlying reason behind my transfer of academic specialty from Japanese literature to cultural anthropology.

> I started my research on the Orochon who lead a wandering life in Daxinganling of Manchukuo (i.e. the northeast of China) in the summer of that year with the support of my academic adviser, Professor Takashi Akiba (Izumi 1969: 14).

After his transfer to anthropology, Izumi was recommended to read Malinowski's ethnography *Argonauts of the Western Pacific* (Malinowski 1922). This was recommended as his first ethnographic reading, by his advisor Professor Takashi Akiba, a sociology professor in the law and literature department at Keijō Imperial University (Keijō Teikoku Daigaku). The effect of the book can be seen in his use of the expression 'assimilate into their lives' in his first ethnographic report on the Orochon (Izumi 1937: 44).

Izumi conducted his data collection under the guidance of Yoshihito Yoshioka who was a secret agent behind the military operations of the Eastern Xinganling Troop (Kōan Higashi Keibi-gun) under the Kwantung Army. Izumi seemed to have had the delusion, during his research, that he had assimilated himself into Orochon society. In view of the fact; however, that his research activities were conducted as part of the military operations of the frontier troops, instructed to keep a distance from the Orochon, his physical and psychological relationship with them was by no means one of being assimilated into their society.

Izumi only engaged in his research activities for one month in July 1936. He left Mukden on the second of July, arrived at Buheto on the night of the third, and visited Chief General Sonezaki at the headquarters and received a telegram from his university on the fourth. He left Buheto at two pm on the seventh by horse-drawn carriage and arrived at a place name of Kantora after nine pm on that day. His visit to the Orochon started from the eighth. He packed all reference items to send on the nineteenth, caught a direct train for Buheto on the twenty-first, visited a shaman and went to Manzhouli for film development on the twenty-second. He visited the border after arriving at Manzhouli on the twenty-fourth and returned to Buheto on the twenty-seventh. He left Buheto on the twenty-ninth, stayed over night in Harbin on the thirtieth, visited a museum and met an ethnographer, Mr Posonov on the thirty-first, and arrived at Mukden on the first of August (Izumi 1937: 100–2). The actual time Izumi spent with the Orochon is accordingly estimated to be less than two weeks. The fieldwork was conducted only over six months, at the longest, after he entered the new field of specialty, anthropology.[3]

Surprisingly, opium was the gift he brought to the Orochon when visiting them in their residential area in Buheto in Daxinganling. As he writes:

> It is important for you to build rapport with them [subjects of your research] during research. Even though that is difficult, you must at least become closer to them to some extent, especially if you try to collect reference items from them. In order to do so, you need to bring some gift to them other than assimilating into their lives. As it would be a long journey, the gift should not be heavy or bulky. It has to be small, light and desirable. In this regard, opium seemed to be the perfect choice. By the courtesy of Sonezaki Chief General, I took approximately twelve *ryō* [A weight unit of the Japanese measuring system. Twelve *ryō* is 120 *momme*, approximately 450 grams] of opium with me and used approximately seven *ryō*. Despite the fact that opium can have harmful effects on them in the long view if it is distributed immoderately, it was unforgettable that they smiled like an innocent child when I gave them opium after hard labor or a long interview (Izumi 1937: 44–5).

In recognition of Izumi's work, the Orochon-related materials are currently kept in the museum at Seoul National University in Korea. It should not be forgotten, however, that they were collected from the Orochon in exchange for opium.

With the adoption of an opium monopoly system and a policy to gradually prohibit the use of opium, Manchukuo promulgated the Opium Control Law in November 1932 and enforced it in January 1933.[4] 'The Rehe operation in 1933 was an operation of the Kwantung Army to obtain opium' (Fujise 1992: 14) and 'the profits from the opium monopoly were an important revenue source of the Manchukuo government' (Fujise 1992: 18). In the monopoly system, the central office was set up in Shinking (capitol of the Manchukuo) and there were branch offices in rural areas. I am not able to question the legitimacy of Izumi's action to carry and provide opium as a subject of the Great Empire of Japan from a legal perspective.[5] However, in order to develop an anthropological method, I would like to pose the question of how we should evaluate the ethical issues involved in his actions where personal encounters were associated with gifts.

The use of opium has been reported by numerous researchers who studied the Orochon. Takashi Akiba, the first to visit the Orochon in 1935, stated that he 'largely relied on research of Mr Yoshihito

Yoshioka for the information on opium' (Akamatsu and Akiba 1941: 102). He also stated that 'opium has caused physiological and economical problems' (Imanishi and Ban 1948: 57), while providing the data from 'a household account book of the Reindeer Orochon during the period from October 1941 to June 1942, which was obtained from the Mohe Orochon' (Imanishi and Ban 1948: 54).[6] According to Hikoichi Ōyama, a professor at Manchuria National Foundation University (Manshū Kenkoku Daigaku), who left for Buheto on the nineteenth of December 1942, 'expenses for opium accounted for more than half the monthly income of approximately 120 yen of an average household composed of parents, two sons and a daughter' (Ōyama 1943: 2).

Among the supplies of thirty-five items of 5,534.38 yen worth, which Yōkō Akibayashi provided to the Orochon during the period from April to May 1937, the value of opium (140 *ryō*) was 642.25 yen (Nagata 1939: 93–4). The supplies provided at that time were more than usual as they included a large quantity of foodstuffs for the New Year holidays. The only items that cost more than opium were noodles (126 bags or 680.40 yen worth) and chestnuts (19,869 pieces or 1,192.16 yen worth). The fact that the value of opium was comparable to that of gunpowder shows us how large the amount of money spent on opium was. The value of opium accounted for 11.5 percent of the total value of the supplies. Given that the price of opium was 4.95 yen per one *ryō* in those days, the value of the twelve *ryō* of opium that Izumi brought was approximately 55.2 yen, of which he provided seven *ryō* or 35 yen worth to the Orochon.

He received twelve *ryō* of opium from a military chief of the Kwantung Army and used seven *ryō*. This means there should have been five *ryō* of opium left after he provided it to the Orochon, though nothing is mentioned about it. He did not keep any specific records about the process of providing opium. The problem is that Izumi provided opium to the Orochon even though he was aware of and concerned about its negative physiological effects. Tobacco favored by the Trobriand Islanders and opium favored by the Orochon may be considered in the same context, in that they were the gifts of anthropologists provided to local inhabitants. However, because of the historical context as well as the level of knowledge about the effects of the specific substances, Malinowski's consideration of providing tobacco is of a totally different nature to that of Izumi's concern about the physiological effects of opium.

Izumi's research was carried out in 1936 between the research conducted by Colonel Takao Matsumuro, the chief of the Qiqihar

Secret Military Agency (Chichiharu Tokumu Kikan) in 1934, and that of the research division of the General Staff Office (Sanbōshi) in 1938. Nagata notes that opium had taken its toll on the local inhabitants:

> The population of the Orochon decreased by approximately 1,100 in comparison with the figure of 4,111 collected by Shirokogoroff twenty years ago in 1929 and by 700 in comparison with the figure collected by the Qiqihar Secret Military Agency five years ago in 1934 (Nagata 1939: 16–19).

Izumi's concern about the problems of opium expressed in his report should be remembered in conjunction with Imanishi's indication of the association between the physiological problems of the Orochon and the use of opium. It is difficult to imagine that an anthropologist provided opium, which was used in a military operation, as a gift to locals during his field research. This leads me to wonder whether the anthropologist who received opium from the army and provided it to the local people, who were subjected to military operations, worked as an instrument of the army. There appears to be undeniable collusive ties between the Secret Military Agency, the General Staff Office and the anthropologist. Clarification about the extent and nature of these ties requires further analysis of additional information.

Nevertheless, this is not the end of the discussion about ethical issues in science. Unless we point out that 'immorality' is not restricted to the private domain of Izumi, we are unable to maintain our discussion about the association between ethics, anthropology, colonialism and war. Izumi, who was then a student of Keijō Imperial University, was given opium by Chief General Sonezaki of the Eastern Xinganling Troop under the Kwantung Army. He provided it to the Orochon in exchange for their cooperation in interviews, observation and collection of reference items to display at the folk material exhibition room in the University. If we explain his action as an unexpected personal indiscretion, we dismiss the possibility of collusion between military operations and anthropology during the period of colonialism and in the era of the war. Moreover, we demean ourselves by helping to conceal this tie. Unless we find out about Izumi's accomplices in the provision of opium to the Orochon and understand the historical background of his action, we fail to provide a full picture of the colonial system as it operated in a period of war.

According to Izumi, his paper was 'thoroughly revised' by his advisor, Professor Takashi Akiba.[7] This together with the fact that the responsibility for editing and publishing the paper rested with Kiyoto Furuno, the then editor of the Japanese Society of Ethnology (Nihon Minzoku Gakkai) based in Tokyo, means that both the advisor and the editor could be regarded as accomplices of Izumi's unethical action. In consideration of the above facts, we can grasp the historical background in which the advisor and the editor turned a blind eye to Izumi's action, but failed to recognize that their own action was also unethical. It should be pointed out that there was conformity in the academic world. There was also a mechanism of military-academic cooperation when the entire colonial regime, in the period of war, was operating in perfect coordination under the influence of the Imperial government.

Given the fact that Izumi was then a mere undergraduate who entered the field of anthropology just six months previously, it could be said that the academic world, in those days, was indifferent to and disregardful of ethical issues. How can we apply 'the strained spirit of the times' (Hattori 1974) in this case, which should be the basis for criticism of academic papers? It would not be an exaggeration to say that 'ethic-free' was the then spirit of the times in anthropology and this spirit produced the accomplices of 'immorality.' It was the strain of such a spirit that led Izumi to provide opium to the Orochon and mention it in his report. It is understandable that this spirit encouraged the cooperation of the advisor of the university and the editor of the academic society in the publication of Izumi's report, resulting in its transfer from the private into the public domain.

It is quite possible to say that the Orochon, an ethnic minority residing sparsely along the border, the anthropologist who visited them to observe their lives, and the secret military agent who guided the anthropologist, were all involved in a politically hierarchical relationship. The crucial point of the hierarchy was that the Orochon were the subject of the Kwantung Army's operations. The anthropologist was enmeshed in this hierarchy. In this regard, the position of the anthropologist, who provided opium to the Orochon as a gift, despite his fears about the potential of causing physiological problems, cannot simply be explained by a fraudulent scheme. In other words, the hierarchy was not what Izumi intended to establish but what was already in place under the strained spirit of the times. This further poses questions about a system that operated behind the context of anthropology in this period. It should be noted that the subjects of the fraudulent schemes of this system were not only the Orochon but also the anthropologists. After all, anthropologists who researched the

Orochon were entrapped by the fraudulent scheme of the Kwantung Army in compensation for their complicity in the hierarchy established by the army.

Izumi's report on the Orochon was published three separate times. It first appeared in *Minzokugaku kenkyū* (Ethnographic research) in 1937, then in his book published in 1969, *Fīrudowāku no kiroku—Bunkajinruigaku no jissen* (Record of a fieldwork—Practice of cultural anthropology), and again in another of his books published in 1972 after his death, *Izumi Seiichi chosaku-shū* (Collection of Seiichi Izumi) (Seiichi Izumi 1937, 1969 and 1972). When comparing these publications, it was found that the report published in 1969 is identical to that published in 1972. In other words, the 1972 version appears to have simply been reprinted from the 1969 version.[8] Therefore, you can only make a meaningful comparison between the versions of 1937 and 1969 to see whether there is any difference between these publications. As stated previously, it was in 1937 that Izumi wrote:

> By the courtesy of Sonezaki Chief General, I took approximately twelve *ryō* of opium (120 *momme*) with me and used approximately seven *ryō*. Despite the fact that opium can have harmful effects on them in the long view if it is distributed immoderately, it was unforgettable that they smiled like an innocent child when I gave them opium after hard labor or a long interview (Izumi 1937: 44–5).

However, this extract can only be found in the 1937 version. Some other parts of this version refer to opium but were systematically deleted in the reprint of 1969. In sum, the contents of the 1937 version were replaced with those of 1969. In this way, opium-related topics in the original record compiled by a student of Keijō Imperial University in 1937, at the height of state power, were deleted thirty years later by a Professor of cultural anthropology at the University of Tokyo. This action was undertaken by virtue of his position of authority, with an additional statement 'this is the research report that has been published in *Keijō nippō* (Keijō daily report) and *Minzokugaku kenkyū* (Ethnographic research) (Izumi 1969: 14). Apparently, Izumi's 'unforgettable' memory had turned into something that should be forgotten, by necessity, during this period. Parts of the record were thus deleted by means of editing.

It has been approximately thirty years since the deletion of sections of the original record, which described the provision of opium to the Orochon. There are few people now who mention the original record published approximately sixty years ago and the process of deletion

(Ogawa 1996: 61).⁹ Although Izumi's memory of providing opium to the Orochon was buried with him, the original record published in 1937 still exists, despite the attempt to eliminate it in 1969, and despite the fact that the collection compiled in 1972 after his death automatically lent a hand in renewing that attempt. As it turns out, the essential part of the history of anthropology is to conscientiously discover and analyze records rather than personal memories. The problem left behind for budding scholars is to make responsible remarks on ethical issues of science.

Hamlet and the Tiv and the Emperor and the Palau Islanders

Bohannan and Hamlet

Clifford Geertz referred to anthropological fieldwork as a learning process. More specifically, he recognized that the research process, in which anthropologists try to understand the culture of a given society, bears a resemblance to the learning process in which children of the society are growing up. Anthropologists, who work in a given society, chosen as the subject of their research because of its unknown culture, come to face an experience of losing their identity in the process of learning that culture. As cultures are relative in nature, this learning process involves both positions of the anthropologist, who see the culture of the society under study, and the local people, who see the culture of the anthropologist. In this sense, anthropological fieldwork relies on the interactive nature inherent in education that contains this learning process. In other words, there must be times when local people learn from the anthropologist, just as the anthropologist learns from the locals.

Referring to the loss of self-identity as part of the learning process of the field experience, Wengle remarks:

> Anthropologists are *constantly* deprived of their sense of self-identity in the process of field research. This is because, even for a shortest period, they experience a temporary loss of their significant others who help them maintain their sense of belonging as well as self-identity through which they interact with their local society (Wengle 1988: 153) (emphasis added).

For this reason, most anthropologists bring a large number of novels with them when undertaking a long-term stay in the field. In fact, there are several names of novels appearing in Malinowski's diary, which gives us a glimpse of the self-identity issue that he experienced as well as what it may be like for others who live alone in the field. Bohannan, to cope with her stay with the Tiv, brought some books by Shakespeare to read in her room, when time permitted. When the elders of the Tiv saw her reading books avidly, they became interested in their content. As a result, she told them the story of Hamlet and how his father was killed with poison. At that time, Bohannan, who had developed a good understanding of Tiv culture, was engaged in the ethnographic work of translating her understanding into English. However, she now found herself in the opposite situation where she had to translate her culture for the Tiv into their language. This process fostered Bohannan's deeper understanding of Tiv witchcraft.

Bohannan faced a new experience when she was narrating a scene involving the ghost of the murdered king. She found out that the Tiv did not have the concept of ghost. In this case, she and the Tiv reached the limit of their cultural understanding and shared the experience of being in a 'conceptual vacuum.' Bohannan initially tried to explain the ghost as the shadow of death but the Tiv could not understand this idea. In the end, she was able to make the Tiv understand the ghost in Hamlet as a witchcraft phenomenon comparable to their own cognitive system. Bohannan felt, that based on her power relationship with the Tiv elders, she adjusted Western culture to fit Tiv culture and became aware of the necessity to adapt Shakespeare's story. This example demonstrates that the process of cultural understanding inevitably possesses an element of misunderstanding. That is, understanding and misunderstanding always coexist in the process of cultural understanding.

Responding to this encounter, the Tiv elders were surprised that Bohannan dared to visit the Tiv given her lack of understanding of her own culture. They said: 'When you talk to us about your culture, we can better explain its meaning. On your return to your country, please tell your elders that the Tiv is not a wasteland where you have nothing to learn about but a place where the people who can give you wisdom are living' (Bohannan 1966). This illustrates the marginalized position of the anthropologist in the context of cultural relativity.

Ken'ichi Sugiura and the Emperor

The South Seas Agency (*Nanyō-chō*) was set up after the First World War in the Palau Islands, a trust territory acquired by the Imperial Japanese Army, to conduct a series of anthropological studies in its jurisdictional area. During this process Ken'ichi Sugiura gradually gained recognition as a regional specialist of the South Seas. He energetically wrote book reviews for *Jinruigaku zasshi* (Anthropological magazine) from 1934 to 1936 and for *Minzokugaku kenkyū* (Ethnographic research) from 1937 to 1939. It seems to me that in Japan's academic world of the day, Sugiura was the most knowledgeable about Western literature on anthropology. In other words, nobody was more familiar than he was with Western anthropological theories and ethnography.

The current paper deals with the case of Sugiura for two reasons. Firstly, in his day, he was the one best armed with theoretical knowledge compared to other anthropologists. By addressing his case, we can test his understanding of cultural relativity, thought to be a basic tenet of anthropology. Secondly, his case seems to belong to meta-ethnography in the domain of personal encounters; the main focus of this paper. He was engaged in data collection in the Yap Island in September 1938. His experiences, during this process, were somewhat reminiscent of Bohannan and her encounters with the Tiv of West Africa. The following episodes are described by Sugiura:

> I stayed in *Okao* for five days from the fifth of September [in 1938]. The head of *Okao*, *Momtum*, cooked meals himself for me everyday. He is proud of his education as a first student at a Japanese public school. He was able to communicate with me in broken Japanese…One evening *Momtum* respectfully took out a photo album of the Imperial Family from his *Wai*, a bag to store private possessions, and asked me to explain its contents. It was a supplement to a Japanese magazine in commemoration of the prince's birth (if my memory serves me correctly, the title of the magazine was *Shufu-no-tomo* [Friend of housewives]). I gave him a thorough explanation as I had been often offended in the previous summer at the Palau Islanders' lack of understanding of the significance of the Imperial Family even though they were well aware that they should respect the Imperial Family. I firstly explained to *Momtum*, that the Emperor is not merely a great powerful figure but a living god by referring to Yap myths. I was satisfied with his general understanding of my subsequent explanation about Japan's national policy. Although it was due to the august powers of the Emperor which were extended to barbarians in a remote region, it was gratifying that ethnography contributed to a better understanding of the majesty of the Imperial Family. Immediately after my explanation, *Momtum* gently explained what he had just heard to his wife and daughter. It was the first

time I saw an islander talking to his wife or daughter gently (Sugiura 1939: 126).

Unlike Bohannan, Sugiura did not have to worry about the loss of his significant others who helped him to maintain his sense of belonging and his self-identity through which he interacted with his local society. This was because he fully armed his sense of belonging with a Japanese ideology that centered on the Emperor, along with his self-identity as a subject of the Great Empire of Japan under the rule of the Emperor. The ideology embraced was: 'The Emperor is the absolute and holy living god' (Kōno 1942: 145). It was this ideology that helped Sugiura maintain his strong self-identity. He also indoctrinated the Yap Islanders into this ideology. In this way, the ethnographic process played a significant role in proselytizing some of the local people and this gave great satisfaction to Sugiura.

The personal encounter between Sugiura and Momtum included the process by which the invasive Japanese ideology of the Emperor was explained alongside Yap myths. This occurred within an established framework of a political and hierarchical relationship between the colonial ruler, its colony and subjects. There was no place for cultural relativity in such a relationship. Cultural relativity was also absent from the communication between the anthropologist and the village head when inculcating him with this Japanese ideology. As such, the existing political hierarchy provided no physical or psychological room for cultural relativity. Sugiura derived satisfaction from the fact that the village head was indoctrinated into Japanese ideology; and arguably, there was no difference between Sugiura's actions and that of a colonial administrator. If he was a genuine anthropologist or had the slightest awareness of cultural relativity, he should have encouraged the village head to express his own way of thinking, listened closely to his explanations and learnt about his way of understanding. Sugiura's approach was, however, the total opposite. No account was taken of the meaning of the Yap Islanders' myths; they were simply used by Sugiura as a means to indoctrinate the islanders. Through one-sided ideological dominance, the islanders were victim to the beliefs introduced by Sugiura as an anthropologist.

The words and actions of Sugiura, is in sharp contrast to that of Bohannan, who as an ethnographer enriched her learning process. Unlike Bohannan, Sugiura's words and actions can be seen as a form of ideological violence. In fact, the anthropologist who attempted to indoctrinate the islanders, could, in a sense, be thought to have ceased being a scholar. Sugiura, who felt great satisfaction with his performance of ideological violence, did not have a mirror to reflect his own words and actions. This shows us the limitations of the then intelligentsia. They were entangled in the fraudulent schemes of the Great Empire of Japan, under the strained spirit of the times when the Japanese ideology of the Emperor was dominant and the war machinery was in operation. Apparently, the extensive anthropological literature behind Sugiura's book reviews, written and published for his fellow and younger scholars, did not serve as a reflective mirror for him. The details of his proselytizing activities were outlined in *Minzokugaku kenkyū* (Ethnographic research), which is the journal of the Japanese Society of Ethnology (*Nihon Minzoku Gakkai*). This suggests that the Japanese Society of Ethnology did not have a filtering mechanism to address ethical issues in an official process of editing and also illustrates the interconnection between the private and public domains at the time. It is therefore, not an exaggeration to say that Sugiura's action of ideological violence was not an issue that remained solely in the private domain but was ultimately systematized into the public realm. There was no point at which the fraudulent schemes of the Great Empire of Japan were monitored and checked. After all, anthropology in the period of colonialism and in war was the product of these fraudulent operations.

Encounter as a 'preliminary approach'

Words and actions are always observed in a process that consists of stages, including a preliminary stage. Similarly, as with approaches to fieldwork, there is thought to be a 'preliminary approach.' In this section, I would like to discuss the preliminary approach as a process of reflecting on traditional approaches to fieldwork that have been discussed by anthropologists. Without such a reflection, all approaches have the potential of remaining at the stage of conjectures. Conjectures should be tested by the preliminary approach of reflection; only through this are they able to enter the process of becoming rational knowledge.

Anthropologists who try to work out fieldwork approaches will encounter people who are the subjects of their research. The preliminary approach depends on their encounter with these people who are the most essential partners for their research. All approaches that anthropologists have worked out previously will be tested in the initial encounter with them.

A graduate student of the anthropology department of the University of California at Berkeley visited Professor Alfred Kroeber to ask for his advice before leaving for an Indian village. In response to the student's question of how to undertake efficient field research, Kroeber only gave him a pencil and a notebook.[10] By his action, Kroeber probably wanted to say that there is no easy road to field research. Despite this, anthropological methodology advocates participant observation. As pointed out by Geertz, participant observation is an ambiguous term. The first means, which anthropologists mobilize when they enter the daily lives of local people, would not be participant observation but would include a range of activities required to satisfy the necessary preconditions for participant observation. This in itself is the issue of the preliminary approach. First of all, there should be a process by which anthropologists introduce themselves to local inhabitants in an agreeable way in order to facilitate communication. Other actions (for example participant observation, interviews and photography) will become feasible only after this process. I refer to this as the 'encountering stage.'

Scholars who became aware of the significance of the encountering stage consistently discuss the formation of rapport (Griaule 1957) or the formation of rapport with the maturity of organisms (Mauduit 1960); though none advised exactly what we have to do. Marcel Mauss pointed out the difficulty in establishing the observer-subject relationship (Mauss 1947) and expressed his sentiments that, although an intensive method enables observation, it is a kind of predicament (he described this by the French words 'debrouillage' or 'debrouillement') (Mauss 1947). He only discussed concrete techniques which he borrowed from his methodological books. In such a way, scholars have avoided discussing the issue of observation and learning during field research, in which ethnographers must act as a tool, or more specifically, their eyes, views, actions and words must serve as a tool. Where there is this kind of accumulated avoidance, there are conjectures.

Malinowski's work in the Trobriand Islands brought about a remarkable revolution in ethnographic methodology. One of his central contributions was to identify the method of participant observation which is said to derive from his long-term stay in the field. The opportunity for his work was created in a situation of exile. During the First World War, Malinowski, as a foreigner from an enemy country, had no choice but to live in the British Trobriands. In those days, his encounter with the Trobriand Islanders was sufficient to provide him with an unprecedented method of research. As Marcel Mauss pointed out, this encounter involved the issue of the observer-subject relationship.

It is this relationship based on rapport that can bring anthropology into existence and must be protected in any circumstance. In a court case against actions that served the interests of the enemy, an anthropologist tried to protect the confidentiality of his vital information providers even though there was a possibility of an unfavorable outcome due to his action. Such an action will suffice to illustrate the perfect image of the scholar:

> I am very sorry, Mr. Houston, but I cannot, I simply cannot be an informer on people who, in my judgment, have always been completely loyal to our country, and who do not believe in force and violence, who have never done anything illegal, and who are my friends (Melville Jacobs Collection, University of Washington Manuscript Collection—120–52, cited in Price 1998: 409).

Encounters between researchers and subjects of their research are the ethical basis of anthropology. As long as these encounters are maintained, they need to be protected by respectful rapport. It is not what we can misrepresent by calling it a predicament but is what we must judge rationally in the realm of ethics. Through discussion in the current paper, we seem to have found a possibility that such a judgment can be made in the experimental stage of ethical issues. It should be understood that ethical issues in anthropology are decided as early as the preliminary approach stage. Prior to commencing data collection, anthropologists will face ethical issues in their initial encounter with the subjects of their research. Needless to say, the words and actions of anthropologists who attach importance to this encounter will represent the ethical yardstick in anthropology.

Conclusion: anthropological ethics

In this paper, we discussed the actions of anthropologists who presented gifts to local inhabitants as well as their ideological exchanges with these people, as methodological processes. We examined their personal encounters with local people and made comparisons between the case of Malinowski, Bohannan, Izumi and Sugiura. The case of Malinowski, who gave tobacco to the Trobriand Islanders, was compared with that of Izumi who provided opium to the Orochon. While the case of Bohannan who gained a better understanding of witchcraft by narrating the story of Shakespeare's Hamlet to the Tiv, was compared with that of Sugiura who indoctrinated the Yap Islanders with the Japanese ideology of the Emperor. Some pharmacological analyses have shown that tobacco heightens the mortality rate to a greater extent than opium and in this sense, tobacco can be regarded as a more harmful gift than opium. However, during Malinowski's time people were not aware of the harm of tobacco, while, in Izumi's time, there was a general recognition of the political issues surrounding opium and its negative effects. In light of the ethical issues for anthropologists in the context of their personal encounters, the aim of this paper was to raise the subject of Izumi's action in providing opium to the Orochon, despite his concerns about its physiological problems.

One may raise a question about the method of comparing the selected cases in the current paper. As such, there may be problems in making comparisons between Malinowski, a trained anthropologist, and Izumi, a newcomer to anthropology, and between the studies of Sugiura and Bohannan conducted in 1930s and 1960s respectively. Nevertheless, even if there are problems in the comparison, it is believed that it is permissible to disregard these concerns, in order to discuss these key ethical issues. For example, it is possible to discuss ethical issues regarding murders that occurred in ancient times as well as those in the present, because ethical issues are oriented toward universality. Ethics, which goes beyond the cultural relativity of anthropology, is a metaphysical issue that transcends the particularities defined by time and space. Accordingly, the longevity of research seems to depend on the degree of its spatial and temporal validity in light of the universality of ethics.

Research on colonialism and anthropology is fairly advanced in Japan (Van Bremen and Shimizu 1999; Nakao 2000; Yamaji and Tanaka 2002). Most studies have reported systematic problems in the period of colonialism. These studies, from a macroscopic perspective, argue against the role of anthropology under colonial rule and administration. Unlike these existing macroscopic studies, this paper, attempted to analyze personal encounters from a microscopic point of view. These encounters explored anthropological methodology and posed ethical issues in anthropological research during periods of colonialism and war. Opium brought by Izumi physically dominated the Orochon while the ideology introduced by Sugiura psychologically dominated the Yap Islanders. These cases illustrate how science can develop a mode of domination over people and how a hegemonic relationship can be established. It seems that at the time, the academic system did not provide a protective function by identifying ethical standards and exercising control of behavior in the private domain. It may be more accurate to say that ethical issues were not of academic concern or interest. In such circumstances, the issue of fraudulent schemes can only be discussed at a systematic level.

In a Japanese journal, Sugiura wrote an introduction to an ethnographic conference (*Konferenz der Ethnologen*) which was held in Leningrad. This conference was assisted by the Soviet government and was conducted from the fifth to the eleventh of April in 1929. Given the fact that the conference was prepared by ethnographers in Leningrad and Moscow and also by the National Institute of Materialistic Cultural History, Sugiura pointed out that ethnography was used as the tool of the government.[11] He concluded the article with the following comment on the conference: 'I cannot help but think that ethnography was used as the tool of the government to speak in favor of the revolution' (Sugiura 1933: 17). What about the Japanese situation that developed through the Manchurian Incident and all of the colonial invasions since the end of the nineteenth century in which anthropology was used as the tool of the government to speak in favor of the war? Could Sugiura see the Russian Revolution but not the war of Japan? Or is it human nature to see other people's problems and failings, but never our own? Clyde Kluckhohn stated that anthropology is a 'mirror for man.' It can reflect who one really is. Apparently, Japanese anthropology associated with colonialism and in times of war, failed or refused to see the reflection of itself in that mirror. Nevertheless, even in that context Kano was able to write:

> The mission of ethnography is to investigate the basic structure of ethnic and tribal lives...and to provide background information about politics through observation from a different ethnic perspective. Anything else would lie outside its mission (Kano 1946: 1–2).

This comment was virtually an isolated exception in the colonial system during the period of war. The last voice, which Dr Tadao Kano left for his fellow scholars, who worked for the Great East Asian Co-Prosperity Sphere and were imbued with the Japanese ideology of the Emperor, was cut short by his unfortunate disappearance in North Borneo just after the defeat of Japan in the Second World War.

Whenever we discuss ethical issues of science, it is important for us to remember that Japanese anthropology during this period remains a tragic legacy of history.

The symbolism of the act of teaching involves a power relationship. As a general phenomenon, the teacher-learner relationship is replaced by the hierarchical relationship of superior and inferior. If a fieldwork situation, in which an anthropologist enters a field and learns its culture, is considered within the structure of the hierarchical relationship in teaching, he or she is thought to be in the inferior position, as in the case of Bohannan. However, in most fieldwork during the period of colonialism and in the wartime era, anthropologists who entered the field as a researcher dispatched by an external specialized agency, tended to be in a superior position—the opposite of what they should have been. This situation posed a serious problem, contrary to the philosophy of fieldwork and anthropological methodology. The implications of defining fieldwork as learning or research also apply to the entire anthropological enterprise. The objectivity of knowledge derived from a hierarchical relationship is also questionable.

The basis of science depends on the degree of objectivity in the research process. For instance, there is a constant process of trial and error in a chemical laboratory and many experiments are repeatedly conducted to identify and demonstrate the optimal procedure. Data collection is continued until expected data are obtained by carefully adjusting the values of the variables (for example the dose of necessary reagents and the amount of time). The process of attaining proven results is summarized through compiling a paper and working out an appropriate methodology. The most important point after this is to ensure that the same results can be reproduced when other researchers apply the same procedure. If this is achieved, it will be recognized as sound research. Consequently, we have to devote ourselves to the methodological issue of ensuring objectivity in the research process and spend the majority of our time working out an appropriate methodology.

The issue of objectivity in social scientific methodology remains unsolved because, it is difficult to gain the same level of objectivity in research involving human subjects compared to that of a chemical laboratory. For this reason, the current discussion cannot be brought to a neat conclusion. The issues of intervention in value judgment, freedom from value judgment, and reality recognition through intervention in value judgment have been relatively overlooked as a subject of discussion. Compared to the efforts to work out a specific methodology for research in human society, these issues concerning value judgments and the resultant ethical concerns have been neglected in the academic world despite the fact that they are open to methodological intervention.

In general, ethical issues of science are inadequately dealt with and tend to come at the end of methodological discussions in academic papers. The basis for the reinvention of anthropology can be achieved if we create an atmosphere in which ethical issues are thoroughly argued at the beginning of these discussions. The existence of anthropology as a positive science is justifiable by the fact that it is the subject of ethical experiments based on rational recognition and that its departure is verifiable by meta-ethnography as a product of field research and personal encounters. For the first time, this paper analyzed some of the ethical issues arising in anthropology during colonialism and war by using correct procedures for evaluation and criticism. These procedures provide us with a reflective mirror, which can also give us insight into an ethical foundation for anthropology.

Acknowledgement

I express my sincere gratitude to Dr Robert Winthrop who is my friend and an anthropologist who proof read the English version of this chapter.

7
Discovering the 'Sense of Co-Presence' in Urban Sociological Research

Michihiro Okuda

Field research on 'transnational' Asian newcomer migrants

Their motivation for coming to Japan

In March 2004 at the Kwansei Gakuin University's COE (Center of Excellence) symposium, I had the opportunity to report on the socalled Ikebukuro and Shinjuku fieldwork which, by that stage had been completed. This research, conducted with the help of undergraduate and postgraduate students at Rikkyo and Chuo Universities in Tokyo, was like one of the side branches of the main project of the COE (Okuda 2004a). The Ikebukuro and Shinjuku fieldwork in Tokyo is nothing but a simple case study in the history of social research, but I am pleased, as an urban sociologist, that our face-to-face interviews commenced in 1988, at the beginning of mass migration of Asian newcomers to Japan.

The style of face-to-face interviews remained unchanged for the following fifteen years, and the same set questions were asked to all participants: as to their motivation for coming to Japan; how they were getting on in Tokyo; what future plans they had made, and so on.

The earlier data from 1988 was published in *Ikebukuro no Ajia kei gaigokujin - shakaigakuteki jittai hokoku* (Asian migrants in Ikebukuro: a sociological report) (Okuda and Tajima eds 1991) and in *Shinjuku no Ajia kei gaigokujin - shakaigakuteki jittai hokoku* (Asian migrants in Shinjuku: a sociological report) (Okuda and Tajima eds

1993). At the time of these publications, the academic discussion in Japan was still concerned with issues such as 'the concentration of homogeneity and exclusion of heterogeneity in Japanese society' and questions like: 'Can Japan become a model for the rest of the world?' We were also troubled by such questions as: 'When will Ikebukuro and Shinjuku become slums and ghettos like Harlem in New York?'

Just before the exponentially growing bubble economy was about to burst, I was invited to an international symposium as a commentator on the future design for the Tokyo megalopolis, and I delivered the latest findings from our fieldwork study at Ikebukuro and Shinjuku. I recall that Nathan Glazer, one of the participants and co-author of *Beyond the Melting Pot* (1963), commented that 'the stories about such rigid societies as Japan and West Germany accepting migrant laborers are hard to comprehend.' In my view, by limiting his study of migrants in New York to those who were only of African, Puerto Rican, Jewish, Italian, Irish and other European extraction, he was totally oblivious to other newcomers, such as those from Asian and Hispanic origins (Glazer and Moynihan 1963; Harvard GSD Tokyo seminar 1989).

The inner-city in the megalopolis as the 'thirdspace'

When looking at the same greater Tokyo megalopolis under the twentieth century system, the inner-city is seen as a gray area lost between the ever polarizing city center and the suburbs. In our fieldwork in Ikebukuro and Shinjuku, we repositioned the inner-city as the 'thirdspace' of the twenty-first century Tokyo megalopolis, connecting the city center and the outer suburbs. We had conducted intensive face-to-face interviews with transnational Asian newcomers on their lives and lifestyles in Ikebukuro and Shinjuku, the 'thirdspace' where the elements of both the city center and the suburbs intermingle.

Fifteen years has passed since our first interviews in 1988. Those we spoke to then are now contemplating moving again, and the second generation who had been born and brought up in Ikebukuro or Shinjuku are reaching junior high school age. In a bid to restructure their lives again, they are contemplating either a move to the outer suburbs of Tokyo or moving overseas again which may mean returning home. On the ground level of the inner cities of the Asia Pacific transnational megalopolis, the formation of personal networks by the Asian newcomers and the inter-referencing activities of their career design are now becoming more visible. I refer to those inter-referencing activities as transnational inter-references or dynamic comparative methods.

A new definition of an urban community

Around 2001 in particular, as a result of the accumulated study of transmigrants and their descendants, sociologists in the USA attempted to conceptualize such notions as transnational community and transnationalism and urbanism 'from below' (Portes 1996; Korzeniewicz and Smith 1996; Levitt 2001; Smith and Guarnizo 1998; Bean and Stevens 2003). The same tendency can be observed among Japanese urban sociologists as well. The very dynamic nature of these transnational communities forms the background of my own definition of the urban community:

> They are a generative habitat for people to reside together, loosely connected, but with a shared sense of co-presence in urban conditions where all sorts of heterogeneities and diversity can exist (Okuda 2004b: iii).

The ground level of Ikebukuro and Shinjuku is a grassroots version of a complex city, where in a new reality, residents from all sorts of backgrounds intermingle, making notions such as 'ethnic communities' and 'foreign residents,' for example, seem obsolete. If we are to draw an additional line of loose connection, what sort of key word can be applied to this new reality, this intensely dense world which also includes trivial neighborhood conflicts? In the 2004 COE symposium, I employed the term, the 'sense of urban co-presence.' Drawn from the original anthropological term, this grasps the width and depth of the new reality much more clearly than the term I had used up till then, the 'manner of urban co-existence.'

This 'sense of urban co-presence' can be found in the words uttered by an old lady who lived in a small wooden rental apartment block in Ikebukuro where many newcomers resided. When we spoke to her in the first fieldwork interview about her neighbor, she concluded that: 'Just because a youngster from Fukien province has replaced another from Fukushima prefecture, that alone does not make me consider my new neighbor to be [a] stranger.' The same sense can be observed in another way, by another interviewee overhearing conversations across the street in a foreign language to 'note subconsciously the existence of a neighbor.' This sense resonates with what Elijah Anderson terms the 'Streetwise' (1990) and 'Codes of the street' (1999) which I will discuss later in this paper. Since we were aware that the traditional methods such as interviewing and analyzing interaction through dialogue were insufficient to grasp the full reality, our fieldwork employed the 'Participatory Action Research (PAR)' method.

Our fieldwork had a list of self-assessments such as foresightedness, representativeness, continuousness, and so on. Continuousness, rather than systemicity, for example, is like planting cuttings one after the other continuously into new soil. We used this system because, on the ground level of the urban community, the database for us to differentiate the local Japanese from the transnational Asian newcomers is no longer available.

Contextualizing our study in post war urban research

A new stage in the theories of community and ethnicity

It was not 'Japanese society' or the place from which this picture was drawn; the new middle class dominated outer suburbia of the megalopolis, nor the city center dominated by the Central Business District, that accommodated the new Asian migrant newcomers. What lies between the center and outer suburbs of the megalopolis is the inner-city. The inner-city has been seen in classic urban sociological research as a gray area sandwiched between the center and suburbia, and is mostly considered to be a stagnant pool or slums and ghettos occupied by early migrants.

All through the metropolis phase, where the modern city becomes polarized into the city center and outer suburbs, and the post-metropolis phase where the inner-city is reconstituted as the 'thirdspace' which connects the two, the 'real and imagined place' is gradually understood as the institutions are installed from below and the surrounding world is theorized (for example, see Soja 1996). My definition of the urban community is also based on the magnetic field of the inner-city of the megalopolis, or the 'thirdspace' that connects the outer suburbs and the center. Theorized as the 'thirdspace,' I consider the inner-city of the megalopolis as a model for 'being urban' and as a model of a city that is community generative.

According to urban sociological research, the inner-city of a megalopolis in the post-metropolis phase possesses two main characteristics: a global region and the notion of a transnational community.

A global region

The inner-city of a megalopolis does not belong to a bordered society of one particular nation state but is situated at the hub of transnational circuits for a migrating population and of 'culture, capital and ethnic networks.' Accordingly, for Asian newcomers from the 1970s onwards, inner-city areas of a megalopolis in the Pacific basin are seen as being of equal importance. For those non-Japanese residents of Asian origin in Ikebukuro, for example, the inner cities of the Tokyo and Osaka megalopolis offer a similar appeal. But Ikebukuro and Shinjuku just happen to be in Japan. These places may be their second or third preferred destinations, but it is not because they are in Japan.

The transnational community as a concept

A transnational community which crosses over the national boundaries can be defined also as transnationalism from below. The newcomers of Asian origin do not necessarily 'settle down' in the inner-city of the megalopolis like Ikebukuro and Shinjuku. They may, as a result of living in the same area for some time, be categorized as 'settled down,' but the boundary between 'settled down' and 'fluid' is blurred. One transnational resident of Chinese origin remarked that the place he/she happened to reside, for whatever reason, was the place for life and death, no matter what nation it belonged to. The parents of a family we came across during the course of our fieldwork were a couple of Taiwanese newcomers who had met in Shinjuku. When the older of their two children, the son, was approaching junior high school age, for schooling purposes, they considered moving to somewhere in the outer suburbs of Tokyo. But when they could not find a suitable property they decided to return to the outskirts of Taipei. Our interviewer, a female postgraduate student was devastated at the thought of them leaving Japan and went over to Taipei for further interviews. This was a rather intriguing case of an interviewer following the movements of transnational newcomers. What she found out was that the family did not go backwards in moving from Japan to Taiwan. Rather, from their Shinjuku residence, they had found the property they had looked for unsuccessfully in the outer Tokyo suburbs, but it just happened to be on the outskirts of Taipei. A sense of transnational community and double identity were clearly at work, which connects Shinjuku and the outer Taipei suburbs, bridging Japan and Taiwan.

The father of the family, who originally came to Japan in 1987, is now running an outbound tourist business to Japan. The elder son, who is of junior high school age, came first in the Japanese competency test in Taipei, and is planning to go to senior high school and university in Japan (and the USA). The younger daughter, who used to go to drawing classes in Shinjuku, wants to pursue her interest in art in Taipei. As a big fan of Japan and an enthusiast in children's education, the mother has brought back the lifestyle of a 'Japanese mother' with her. She learned from her neighbors in Shinjuku that mothers in Japan prepare breakfast for their children before sending them off to school. She has taken with her, to Taiwan, the parenting customs of Japan. Since most mothers go out to work, it is common in Tapei to see people tucking into dumplings or rice porridge in neighborhood eateries in the morning. The mother, considering it better for her children's health and way of life, has kept the Japanese mothers' tradition. She is also preparing to take the certification test to become an international tourist guide for Japanese tourists.

According to the political scientist, Takashi Inoguchi, who initiated a new international comparative study called 'Asia barometer,' a person's standard of living can be gauged from their answer to the question: 'Did you have breakfast?' (Inoguchi 2003: 18–23). But we have come to realize that transnational migrants manage to adapt and modify such routine customs as having breakfast. It could be termed as urbanism from below, an urban lifestyle management or urbanites' design.

In the light of the rising tide of the transnational community based on the 'thirdspace' of the inner-city of the megalopolis, the rise of urbanism 'from below' and transnationalism, it is worthwhile to critically evaluate the traditional sociological understanding and theories of urban local ethnic communities which have formed the basis of urban research and urban policy making.

For example, earlier settlements of migrants were described as 'the Italian slum in Boston' and 'the Black ghetto in New York,' and in this way categorized into ethnically and racially segregated closed local communities. These local ethnic communities, described as 'villages in the big city' and 'urban villages,' during the post World War II urban redevelopment, were treated by the authorities, with a slum clearance type of redesign from above. It is, however, well known that William Foote Whyte in his work *Street Corner Society* critically examined the categorization of the early Italian slums. This was achieved through his detailed sociological analysis of the breadth of the lives of the second generation street corner boys (Whyte [1943] (1993); [1993] 2000).[1] By the way, as Kenji Kosaka often points out, it was one of the oversights of the urban redevelopment authorities and urban sociologists, that they had not recognized many of the new findings mentioned in *Street Corner Society*, until their post world war slum clearance projects were resisted by the Italian communities themselves.

In much the same way, the reality of inner-city community in the megalopolis of the twenty-first century calls for a new way of seeing. The reality of the local ethnic communities in large cities needs to be reinterpreted. A clear line needs to be drawn to separate the earlier classic examples of migrants of the twentieth century from the influx of new migrants of Asian and Hispanic origins during the 1970s onwards. Our fieldwork studying newcomers from Asia in Ikebukuro and Shinjuku also dealt with the latter category of migrants.

With regards to the redevelopment and revitalization of old twentieth century style run-down ethnic districts, we must also note that new migrants, unlike their earlier counterparts, do not make their first home in the United States of America in the existing ethnic communities. They tend to choose where to live, not according to race or ethnicity, but by their means and way of life. For example, Hsiang-Shui Chen has written a book, *Chinatown No More*, based on his research into new Chinese (Taiwanese) migrants in New York (Chen 1992).

As the title indicates, middle class Chinese (Taiwanese) migrants found their first homes not in the existing Old Chinatown in the heart of New York, but in the outer suburbs, according to their income level and lifestyle. When I say outer suburbs, these are in reality inner suburbs just out of the center but they are 'suburban' residential areas nonetheless, where classes, races and ethnic groups are all intermingled. These 'suburban residential areas' are mostly inhabited by ethnic Chinese (Taiwanese), but they live side by side with the Koreans, Vietnamese and Hispanics. In other words, the ethnic zones just mingle together along the circuit of the streets.

Chinatown No More tells us that, although the middle class Taiwanese are the major group, residents of different ethnic and class backgrounds interconnect through political or religious community, friendship and other voluntary organizations. One such example is an organization called the Chinese-Korean Relations in Flushing. Interestingly, nearly half of *Chinatown No More* is dedicated to describing and analyzing these various organizations. Near Los Angeles on the West Coast, the birth of a suburban community dominated by migrants of Asian, Hispanic and African origins was described in a sociological report, entitled *The First Suburban Chinatown* (Fong 1994).

As far as the suburban way of life is concerned, what is described in the book resembles the 1960s outer suburbia which was predominantly inhabited by white middle class residents. I draw your attention to the title of the book, as it is a reference to the well-known classic, *The First Suburbs*, by socio-historian Henry Binford (Binford 1985). Binford's book details, socio-historically, the birth of an exclusively White Anglo Saxon Protestant, or WASP suburb, in Cambridge on the outskirts of Boston. Its title, *The First Suburbs*, metaphorically predicted the arrival of *The First Suburban Chinatown* thirty years later.

With the emergence of outer suburban Chinatowns, Koreatowns and others, what will be the future for their traditional counterparts in the middle of the city? Whether or not they are exclusive 'local ethnic communities' and 'villages in the city,' they cannot escape from the trend towards decline in the new century megalopolis. Traditional Chinatowns in Boston, New York, Philadelphia and elsewhere are surviving as symbols for their communities, with distinctive streetscapes and ethnic oriented businesses. To view a modern reincarnation of a classic local ethnic town as a microcosm, one has no option other than to visit the 'ethnic museums' which are being constructed on the former sites of old ethnic towns in the city center.

An ethnic museum not only displays vast amounts of materials such as interview transcripts, diaries, letters and photographs, but also utilizes various audio visual materials, organizes special events and displays and so on. It also depicts the history of early migration into the city where the museum stands, the life and work of early migrants, and the streetscapes and living conditions of the community.

I would not go so far as to say that 'one has to visit the local ethnic museum first and perceive an image in order to understand the significance of the local ethnic community.' However, apart from the definition of the 'village in the large city' and the issue of gauging reality, what sort of connections are there between the new transnational migrants and their offspring, who now reside in the newer ethnic communities in the outer suburbs and the old Chinatown, for example, in the city center. Basically, the connection between the old ethnic towns in the city center and the suburbs is severed. Except, for example, for the Chinese migrants in the suburbs, the old Chinatowns are places for: occasional dining, shopping, sightseeing, entertainment, business dealing and information swapping. For their children who were 'born and brought up in the suburbs,' the old ethnic towns remain as a symbolic place to remind them of their racial and ethnic identity and to nurture that identity.

How then, are the old Chinatown and old Chinese residential communities of New York, for example, seen by the country where those new transnational migrants and their families come from? According to urban sociological theory, the Chinatowns in North American cities were explained as 'enclaves in the city,' an alternative expression to 'villages, or islands in a city.' This expression itself has come to be understood differently in the days of globalization of information, capital and ethnic networks. Chinatown and surrounding areas of New York are now regarded by China as its 'enclaves' across and beyond the national border.

The new reality in Ikebukuro and Shinjuku is no different. As unconfirmed reports suggest, people connected to the official policy making networks in China and Korea, for example, are now assigned to these areas for community organization and intelligence gathering work.

Transnationalism from below and official policy making are clearly different, but as the territories extend to trans-border 'culture, capital, and ethnic networks' in the inner-city, there is no getting away from the 'impact from the side' working on various levels.

Between 'international comparison' and 'case study'

Inter-reference among the inner cities of a mega-city

The main theme of urban sociological research into 'the characteristics of the changing urban community,' which centers around the inner-city of the megalopolis where transnational migrants immigrate and emigrate, is also one of my answers to the sub theme of 'cultural diversity' which was explored at the COE symposium at the Kwansei Gakuin University. As stated already, the inner-city as the 'thirdspace' connecting the polarizing 'city center' and 'suburbia,' is where the urban revitalization policy has been tested through the proactive and positive urban lifestyle of transnational migrants. For example, as far as transnational migrants in the Pacific basin are concerned, that is newcomers of Asian origin; our main concern in urban sociological research is the process of their acceptance in the inner cities of Tokyo and Osaka megalopolis and their formation of 'transnational social fields.' This can be also observed in other inner cities, for example, in the cities of Australia and the West Coast of the USA. At the international symposium called 'Asian migration and settlement; focus on Japan,' held in 1999, and organized by Waseda University's Asia Pacific Studies Center, I presented findings from our research and, I remember, had meaningful exchanges on the common 'transnational social field' with sociologists from East Asia and Southeast Asia where newcomers of Asian origin immigrate and emigrate (Hirano et al. ed. 2000).[2] This symposium was clearly different in character from the previously mentioned one (Harvard GSD Tokyo seminar 1989). It was attended by urban sociologists, architects and city planners, and dealt with the model of the exponentially growing city of the twentieth century.

The dynamic comparative method

Try, for example, to explain 'the characteristics of the changing urban community' by cross-referencing amid the inner cities of transnational cities. Up until recently, the dominant method has been the static comparative study of nations and systems within the broad framework of the 'international comparative' study of the inner cities of a megalopolis. However, in our fieldwork in Ikebukuro and Shinjuku, to illuminate 'the characteristics of the changing urban community,' we employed the dynamic comparative method where the axes of time and space were cross-examined.

For example, in an attempt to decipher 'the characteristics of the changing urban community,' in Figure 7.1, the time axis describing the 'number of time periods' is set horizontally and the space axis describing the 'number of communities,' vertically. The first quadrant of multiple time and a single community is thus defined as the uni-trend analysis; the second quadrant of single time and a single community is defined as the case study; the third quadrant of single time and multiple communities is defined as the static comparative; and the fourth quadrant of multiple communities and multiple times is defined as the dynamic comparative. The method we employed, cross-

Figure 7.1: Typology of comparative analytic community study approaches (Swanson and Swanson 1977: 8)

		Number of time periods	
		One	Two or more
Number of communities	One	Case study	Uni-trend analysis
	Few/many	Static, comparative	Dynamic, comparative

referencing time and space transnationally, for dynamic comparative analysis of the inner-city corresponds to the fourth quadrant.

Apart from the static 'international comparative' on the national level, the static comparative study compares the static states of multiple communities at any given time. If it deals with a single community at any given time, it is a case study. The dynamic comparative method analyzes and cross-references multiple numbers of communities at a multiple number of times. The research method we employed in Ikebukuro and Shinjuku is a variation of the fourth quadrant, the dynamic comparative. We dealt with the inner cities of one particular megalopolis but we cross-referenced them dynamically in time and space, with more than one other transnational inner-city community.

What do you think your time in Japan will mean to you?

Aspirations in life and ingenuity

In our fieldwork in Ikebukuro and Shinjuku, we employed multiple research methods including participation and observation case study techniques. One method we employed throughout our fieldwork, from the first case study in 1988 until 2003, was face-to-face interviews using rather bulky set questionnaires. It was a time consuming method, as each interview took almost an hour to complete and we encountered all sorts of difficulties. Nevertheless, it did have the advantage of establishing communication between the interviewers and interviewees, and turned out to be a solid foundation for future work. Over the year, however, the use of the set questions was increasingly difficult.

The first fieldwork carried out in 1988 in Ikebukuro was relatively easy as the target subjects, new migrants of Asian origin, were living in a limited number of areas and blocks of apartments. The process was also helped by their willingness to talk to us and despite their imperfect language ability they enjoyed communicating with us. For this first field research, we had two sets of questions ready, one for the newcomers and the other for the local Japanese. The response from the local Japanese community leaders such as the precinct leaders, shop owners, local elders, preschool and primary school teachers and others, was all in a similar vein: 'To begin with, those *gaijins* (foreigners) are...,' which disappointed the students who were asking the questions. We stopped interviewing the local Japanese after our first fieldwork.

In 2001, a young sociologist revisited the fourth and fifth district of Higashi Ikebukuro (formerly the Hinodecho area), which was the heart of our first field research, and asked some of the same community leaders: 'If you had the opportunity, what advice would you like to offer those migrants of Asian origin whom you first encountered in 1988?' They were reported to have hesitantly answered that: 'It would be absurd of us to give any advice. It was we who were encouraged by them. We can do nothing but thank them. We are ashamed that we did not offer any help to them.' In this regard, we should have carried out a series of fresh interviews with the local Japanese in 2001. The responses we were given in 1988 were more like official answers. We now look back with regret that our research of 'new migrants of Asian origin and their interaction with the local Japanese' could have been better.

The questionnaires, for migrants, we used in 1988 consisted of twenty-five questions. They became the prototype of the 'Ikebukuro and Shinjuku questionnaires, 1988 to 2003.' Half of the questions had extra space for the interviewee to fill in whatever they wanted to write. The key four questions in the questionnaires were as follows:

Q1: What made you come to this country?
Q2: What did you have to endure?
Q3: What are the dreams you cherished?
Q4: What are some of the realities you encountered here?

These questions were derived from the interviews carried out with 136 first generation migrants in a North American urban community. Lasting individually for more than a few hours, these interviews provided detailed oral histories of the 136 interviewees who had differing ethnic backgrounds and racial heritage and had an age range from their twenties to over 100. Their oral histories and the research findings were published in a thick sociological monograph titled the *American Mosaic* (Morrison and Zabusky 1993).

In this publication, the first generation migrants are not depicted as 'migrant workers' or as the target of 'prejudice and discriminated against,' but are treated as members of their common communities, and they talk about their lives and plans and their difficulties and troubles, as well as their dreams. Following this approach we prepared our questionnaires using the four key questions we derived from *American Mosaic*. We also wanted to depart from the common preconception of transnational migrants in Japan, depicted as the 'migrant workers' and 'guest citizens,' being discriminated against and experiencing hardship. Our focus was on the migrant's dynamic and pro-active approach to their lives—their ingenuity.

The lives of these transnational migrants since the 1970s were sometimes seen in their local areas as an expression of the Confucian ethos. The migrants themselves sometimes seemed to have conformed to this perception as a precaution. In large cities in North America, the characteristics that the transnational migrants of Asian origin (especially those of Korean origin) exhibited, such as 'patience, willingness to undertake hard work, higher academic achievement and entrepreneurship' were not only seen as a manifestation of the Confucian values of 'diligence, education, achievement and frugality,' but were also sometimes interpreted as a reincarnation of the long lost 'Puritan ideals.' [3]

In our interviews in Ikebukuro and Shinjuku between 1988 and 2003, we always and without fail, concluded with the following question: 'In your life, what do you think your time in Japan will mean to you?' The intention of the question was not very easy for them to understand, but most of the interviewees showed interest and gave us lengthy answers, choosing their words more carefully. The transnational migrants of Asian origin at the time were perhaps more inclined to express themselves and their opinions through interviews. The majority of the answers to the question were concerned with more spiritual matters, such as the meaning of life, rather than with the more materialistic aspects of life.

Between quantity and quality

Between 1988 and 2003, we aimed to carry out at least 100 face-to-face interviews every calendar year and we achieved this even though we had some slow periods. We published the results and our analysis every year.[4]

To carry out one hundred usable interviews in a calendar year was the minimum required for quantitative data collection and analysis, but was also the maximum we could carry out under conditions where a data-base sampling process was not possible. Though the sample number was only one hundred, we had to codify many essentially individual responses to questions, then attach to the code as many attributes and as detailed a profile of the interviewees as possible without infringing on their privacy (for one example, see Okuda and Suzuki 2001).

This method of blending the details of the interview findings is termed the 'eclectic blending of quantitative and qualitative studies' according to Ryo Kawabata, a mathematical sociologist (Kawabata 1998: 266–267). The eclectic blending may imply a 'half measure' in both quantitative and qualitative studies, but the originality of our fieldwork lies in the very grasping of the reality between quantity and quality.

Among those undergraduate and postgraduate students who were involved in the face-to-face interviews, more than a few of them went on to carry out detailed participatory and observation case studies for their postgraduate work. They explored themes such as the identity of the second generation and their life aspiration, their criss-crossed personal network and the 'intermediate groups,' ethnic business and entrepreneurship, open community schools and children of foreign origin, the real estate market for transnational migrants, and so on, utilizing the personal bonds they had established with the interviewees. These case studies form the bulk of the content and the theme of their graduation theses.

On the other hand, from around 2000, it became increasingly difficult to find one hundred effective interviews, which is the very essence of our unique eclectic blending method. As mentioned above, at the time of our first fieldwork in Ikebukuro in 1988, to find our first interviewees we targeted the cheap rental apartment blocks in and around the Hinodecho area (now known as Higashi Ikebukuro fourth and fifth districts). This method could only be employed until 1992 or 1993 when the transnational newcomers drastically changed their locations and their mode of living. This was as a result of their fast assimilation as well as changes in the urban lifestyle in general. So by 2000, it became more and more difficult to complete one hundred effective interviews. We made it a rule to conduct our interviews at the interviewees' residence, but it was not easy to tell from outside whether a residence was inhabited by migrants or by Japanese people. Gradually, we had to expand our search for interviewees from residences to the streets, and around the streets to shops and fast food eateries. Unlike a residence, it was easy on the street to distinguish the target interviewees, although those we encountered on the street tended to be the young and single migrants who were there for shopping, entertainment, studying, business, sightseeing and other purposes. These were not necessarily our target. I called these young people we met on the street, the 'new newcomers' or the 'newest arrivals.' These 'new newcomers' seemed to include many people from various parts of Southeast Asia as well as, if they happened to be of Chinese origin, those from country areas who had come to Japan via large cities in China. Compared to the new migrants who we had spoken to in 1988, these more recent new arrivals had a much 'lighter air, an easier going attitude' and 'a sense of having fun and studying abroad.' But we also came across some who were inspired to come by older newcomers. These people said that: 'I saw off some friends from my district ten years ago who were going to Japan. When I heard the news from them in Japan, I wanted to change my life as well' (Okuda ed. 2001; 2002; 2003 and 2004).

In Shinjuku's established city center, one of our major areas for interviews, the rate of the registered foreign population in each precinct ranged from twelve or thirteen per cent to fifteen per cent, and the rate for Okubo 2 precinct, a street across from the Kabukicho area, exceeded thirty per cent.

According to *The Path of Neighborhood Change* by the Chicago urban sociologist, Richard Taub, a neighborhood can be called a black community when the black population compared with that of the white population exceeds thirty per cent (Taub et al. 1984). What about Ikebukuro and Shinjuku? It is possible to call a specific neighborhood a Korean town as a symbolic gesture, but it does not necessarily mean that any special local ethnic community system, as distinct from neighboring areas, is maintained. Our field research in Ikebukuro and Shinjuku focused on more than one area in the existing city center and its surroundings, and we carried out a 'research of all arbitrarily,' door-knocking the entire houses one by one. We could only learn about the interviewees' ethnic and national identity through face-to-face interviews.

For me, as well as the definition of an ethnic community, it was a kind of artificial exercise to differentiate the foreign residents from the local Japanese. Rather, a community that generously accommodates all sorts of diverse people, of different backgrounds, with different histories of migration, national and racial identity, is a true reflection of an urban community considered as transnationalism from below, or has the 'characteristics of a changing urban community.'

It is an irony in the post war history of sociology in Japan, that we, the urban sociologists, became the first to officially introduce the 'research of all arbitrarily' in a neighborhood, and were at the cutting edge of urban community fieldwork.

Grasping the complexity of reality

The inner-city of a megalopolis as a magnetic field

Here, let me go back again to the idea of the inner-city of a megalopolis as the 'thirdspace.' It may not need to be repeated, but our first fieldwork in Ikebukuro and Shinjuku was the starting point of our continuous research. Indeed the research began before 1988, under the title of 'the revitalization of degraded urban areas.' But 1988 was the watershed year, as it was the time when we encountered new transnational newcomers of Asian origin. Our annual research work was merely tracing the 'changing paths in the neighborhoods,' but when seen decades later as an overview, the aspect of 'social change' emerges.

Even now after sixteen years, the proactive and positive attitudes and lifestyle of the transnational migrants we detected in 1988, provides us with a frame of reference for research into newer transnational migrants of Asian origin, who are arriving from a wide range of regions in East, Southeast Asia and elsewhere. In the early days, the inner-city, itself a 'complex city,' had the old tradition of 'tolerance,' derived from years of accepting people from country areas without meddling in their 'privacy,' when it had to deal with the new migrants arriving from Asia.

We should not forget the fact, although seen here in a different social context, that the sense of regret people had come to feel from years of treating Japanese born Koreans with prejudice, may have prevented the Japanese from treating the new Asian migrants as total strangers. We must also note that the positive and proactive attitudes and disarming socializing skills of the initial transnational migrants of Asian origin, as mentioned above, did not work negatively against the next wave of newcomers. The same can be observed about the transnational newcomers from Asia since the 1970s in large cities in the USA and elsewhere. For example, it has been pointed out that 'the new transnational migrants from Korea are higher in such attributes as class, education, professional training and income, and so on, and they are not a cross section of their home population.'[5]

The class position and the aspirations of transnational migrants are not just seen in those of Korean origin but also in those of continental Chinese, Vietnamese and some of those of Indonesian origin. However, what are some of the hidden problems that the host nations have?

Children of transnational migrants and assimilation theory

One of the issues in sociology is the validity of assimilation theory, 'how migrants blend and assimilate into the host countries.' The migrant study centers at Princeton University and the University of California (San Diego and Davies) have been studying the process of assimilation, of, for example, those of Caribbean origin (including stowaways and refugees) in the large cities on the East Coast, and those of Asian and Hispanic origin in the cities of the West Coast. These centers are indeed the global hub of comprehensive transnational migration studies, but they seem to have already concluded that the understanding of the process and the goals of assimilation into the host cities of the USA have been achieved. The urgent issue at the moment in regards to assimilation theory, is the assimilation of the second generation who have been, for example, 'born and brought up in New York' and that of the one and a half generation whom the parents took with them when leaving their home countries. According to accepted assimilation theory, those 'born and brought up in New York' are supposed to exceed their parents' generation in language skills, lifestyle and aspiration, as well as in a sense of civility, and are therefore better placed to achieve their goals in life. According to general perception this may be the case. However, a comprehensive research project carried out at Princeton University under the supervision of Alejandro Portes, Ruben Rumbaut and others, (those who originated the new concepts of transnational community and transnationalism from below), arrived at more complex conclusions from their research which included case studies of the children of new migrants (see Rumbaut and Portes 2001a; Levitt 2001; Alba and Nee 2003).

Generally speaking, the children of migrants tend to reach the goal of assimilation much more easily than their parents' generation. However, this does not mean that their path of assimilation and blending is straight-forward. For example, according to accepted assimilation theory, transmigrants from the Caribbean, including stowaways and refugees, tend to follow the path of 'the Haitian—the American of Haitian origin—the American (or the Afro American).' However, it can be seen that the children of transnational migrants go the other way, starting from the 'American (or the Afro American)—the American of Haitian origin—the Haitian.' This reverse path is called the 'reactive ethnic theory' (Rumbaut and Portes 2001a: 254).

Traditionally, the classic cover of a research report on urban sociology and race and ethnicity studies has been decorated with pictures of migrants in the ghettos of large cities and children thronging at the street corners. Alternatively, the covers of post-1970s studies on transmigrants and their offspring are decorated with the portraits of smart looking boys wearing ties and glasses, standing alongside their smartly dressed parents. A Japanese urban sociologist (Hirota 2003: 350–351) who was involved in fieldwork research on transnational migrants in Boston and New York commented:

> Looking at *The Urban Villagers* by Gans and *The Transnational Villagers* by Levitt, both well-known classics of urban sociology, [I] remarked the following:
> As far as transnational migrants are concerned, though both books have 'villagers' in their titles, the two books are decisively different apart from the time period and the races they deal with...Gans' book depicts the villagers who settled down in large American cities, and the process of assimilation, during which their intensive relationships disappeared. Levitt's book, on the other hand, examines the villagers who migrated and settled down in American society without losing their complex relationships with their fellow migrants from the same district. Both books have pictures of the children of migrants on their covers, but that of Levitt shows those children neatly attired wearing ties and carefree smiles, and giving the impression that they would rise in society in the future.

But, as large-scale research concerning the children of transmigrants progressed, a new reality of the paradoxical assimilation theory was revealed. This new reality does not immediately deny the existence of a path for the children of transmigrants to become 'Americans' as a part of a system. However, acceptance of 'Americans' as a part of a system and the ethnic identity of being 'Haitian' are not necessarily mutually exclusive.

Ruben Rumbaut and Alejandro Portes (2001b), who advocated the paradoxical assimilation theory, put forward the key concept of 'legacies' to unlock the theory.[6] 'Legacies' means 'heritage' and 'negative inheritance' (Rumbaut and Portes 2001b: 254). The first generation of transnational migrants imposed discipline, education and a moral code in order to fit into the dominant society of the host nation. That has brought about some success stories, although this was achieved, in some respects, at the cost of losing their own ethnic identity. It should be said that this notion of ethnic identity refers to their way of life and meaning of life, the structural identity for their reason for existence, rather than ideas about their ancestral race and blood identities.

The issue of structural identities can be pointed out in relation to not just those transmigrants of Caribbean origin, but of Asian and Hispanic origins as well. The overseas Chinese merchants, who have provided a model for Taiwanese and continental Chinese migrants, are mostly of the Han ethnic group. But since the reforms and opening of mainland China during the 1980s, Chinese minorities, especially the Islamic Uyghurs, started migrating to Beijing, Shanghai, Guangzhou and other large cities, taking up residence based on their personal networks, and then, from there, routinely crossing the borders en masse.[7]

When the transnational Uyghurs from Xinjiang arrived, with their proactive and positive attitude as well as their high degree of sophistication and entrepreneurship, in large cities in the USA, the old picture of Chinatown and the local Chinese society being dominated by the Han group, inevitably had to change. In particular, the Islamic ethnic identity, which praises 'maturity and sophistication,' certainly adds another dimension to the ideas posited in the 'reactive ethnic theory.'

The individual response to institutionalization 'from above'

A general comparison of trends in Japan and the USA is not possible as the systems of permanent residency and citizenship are quite different. Yet, based on our field research in Ikebukuro and Shinjuku, more and more migrants, after having lived in the country for years, are taking up permanent residency and citizenship in Japan. Of course, they may just see this as a very useful pathway for further transmigration.

The first transmigrants officially accepted for residency in Japan were from Central and South America, but were of Japanese ancestral origin. According to research undertaken in the Tsurumi district of Yokohama city, the housing, employment opportunities, schools and other conditions were generally good, but the gap between the institutions and their life opportunities was huge. When their offspring, or the one and a half generation, were of adult age, we could see a wide range of opinions with regard to ethnic identity and their future life plans. For example, there was a tendency to identify themselves as 'Brazilians' and 'Okinawans' in relation to the Japanese part of their origin, as most were descendents of migrants who originally came from Okinawa (Hirota 2003).

I have so far analyzed the proactive and positive attitude of the transnational migrant newcomers of Asian origin, with reference to our field research and compared this with the latest research on transmigrants in large cities in the USA. By examining the same field of the inner-city areas of the megalopolis, I have so far displayed the method of understanding the transnational communities, transnationalism 'from below,' urbanism and other key issues.

It is worthwhile to note the way the transnational migrants design their lives while they constantly search for the meaning of life according to the paths their lives take, and ascertain their position in their networks and the state of the megalopolis of various countries including their own, from their current situation. To our concluding question: 'In your life, what do you think your time in Japan will mean to you?' it is easy to understand why those transnational newcomers make such earnest answers, reflecting their lives so far. Their children were in primary school, and coupled with feelings of uncertainty over their status, residency and nationality, some of them were motivated to migrate again for reasons which included the children's education. They might choose to migrate either back home or to other countries, or to the outer suburbs of the city, if they felt that their status would be settled in the not-too-distant future.

At Okubo primary school in Shinjuku in the late afternoons, we heard many exotic names being called, illustrating the high percentage of new migrants in the area. There were some straightforward responses from the second generation such as 'because we are living in Japan, it is natural to use Japanese textbooks and behave like the Japanese' (Okuda and Suzuki 2001: 191). However, it can be argued that their parents' generation is not necessarily a role model for the second generation when identifying race and ethnicity. Their intentionally and consciously internalized racial and ethnic awareness is their achieved status, rather than their ascribed status. The context is different, but it is an era in which titles like *Tatta hitori no Kureoru* (A lone Creole) (Ueno 2003), *Ichininsho de kataru kenri* (The right to speak in the first person) (Osada 1984), *Tojisha shuken* (Sovereign rights of the person concerned) (Nakanishi and Ueno 2003) and others of a similar vein are being published.

A new definition for the urban community

Having worked at studying the processes of large-scale suburbanization in the large cities for a quarter of a century, and focusing now on the inner-city of a megalopolis which includes parts of existing city centers as well as suburbs, I have arrived at the following definition of urban community:

> It is a generative habitat for people to reside together with loose connections but with a shared sense of co-presence in urban conditions where all sorts of heterogeneities and diversity exist (Okuda 2004b: iii).

This definition relates denotatively to the transnational community, transnationalism 'from below' and other concepts, and connotatively to the grassroots versions of the complex city, the space altering 'from function to modality,' loose connections and other concepts.

It should be noted again that this definition of the urban community of the twenty-first century, although in a different context, resonates with the sub-theme 'the construction of a society that promotes cultural diversity' of the twenty-first century COE program in the study of 'social research improving human happiness' by Kwansei Gakuin University. In this context, 'the study' should not just deal with the static comparative, using the existing world system and national image as its main theme, but it should also deal with the development of more case studies using dynamic comparative methods, focusing, for example, on transnational individuals and families, their way of life and their urban lifestyle in the inner cities of the megalopolis.

Models and recognition of heterogeneity

Looking at the field of our research and reflecting on my definition of the urban community, it is no longer possible to clearly differentiate the 'foreigners' from the 'Japanese.' This is also the case judging from the population of the neighborhoods and the state of the residential areas. Research has already been conducted on the topic of: 'How do we identify people as Japanese when they are not of Japanese appearance,' dealing with the local Japanese themselves.

We hear it being said about the inner cities of large North American cities that 'on the other side of the street, even in a reasonably tight knit neighborhood, one can encounter people of a different class, of different ethnic and racial backgrounds, education, urban lifestyle, living conditions and sometimes, identifying with a different kind of rap music.' The same could be said, in varying degrees, about Ikebukuro and Shinjuku, the field of our research.

Even without resorting to the previously mentioned notions, 'space (from function to modality),' 'changing cities = acceleration of mutation,' 'the power of chaos' and so on, I wonder where the critical point lies in their connotativeness for heterogeneity and diversity in Ikebukuro and Shinjuku. Of course the critical point cannot be pinpointed as it can be affected by new institutional measures from above, as well as by the mobilization of public opinion. My concern is to find out what relationship structures exist there, supporting this fluid reality with width and complexity, in a neighborhood that incorporates heterogeneity and diversity of all kinds. It is possible to explain the new reality, resorting to particular cases which illustrate the previously mentioned 'loose connections' (Wuthnow 1998). However, our concern here is to examine this widely used concept in order to explain the new reality, the 'manner of urban co-existence,' and the common code of the residents.

'Sense of urban co-presence' as a concept

From 'urban co-existence' to the 'sense of co-presence'

I myself used the term 'living together, co-existence' as a theme for our first field research in Ikebukuro in an attempt to find out about the 'new reality of living together as experienced by the foreigners of Asian origin and the local Japanese.' This expression, 'living together,' was later picked up and widely used as a new concept by urban sociologists and sociologists in general. I myself have since refined the concept, like the 'manner of urban co-existence' mentioned above (see Okuda 1996: 233–278).[8]

In the 1970s when a community model was presented based on the new middle class residents in the sprawling large-scale suburbia, it was suggested that this model's inherent weakness was the lack of consideration for those who had dropped out of the new middle class value system. The 'manner of urban co-existence' as a means of control, conceals problems arising from the new middle class values and the dropouts from those values. The inherent problems with the new middle class values continued to exist well into the 1990s, when the 'civil public world,' the 'changing space of co-existence,' 'citizenship and the revitalization of the local community' became refocused.

Focusing on the urban world which has connotations of heterogeneity and diversity of various kinds, and on the local actuality of the inner-city of the megalopolis, I decided to shift from 'the manner of urban co-existence' to the 'sense of urban co-presence.' In 2004 I incorporated that term in my new definition of the urban community. The 'sense of urban co-presence' was originally coined by Daiji Kimura, an anthropologist, during his participatory action research in Central Africa. It was applied to a different context, but the term describes the new reality from below, of 'how people co-habitate within a system of infinitely extending relations' (Kimura 2003).

This sense of co-presence, free from specific value notions such as co-existence and behind such terms as 'communality,' conveys much more clearly to us the complex state of the inner-city communities of large cities that extend across borders. There is no prior definition of the sense of co-presence; instead, here are some descriptive quotes from Kimura:

> People exist side by side with people. I experienced myself how diverse it could be from living together with people in Africa during my fieldwork. To describe their attitudes, manners and so on in living together, I would like to use the term the 'sense of co-presence' (Kimura 2003: ii).

> Characteristic of their [the locals] beliefs is that the space for establishing relationships is very elastic. Under their sort of conditions, there is no way of setting up trivial 'rules for persons and space' (Kimura 2003: 88).

> I call an imaginary line drawn about 150 to 200 meters away from the house of the informant, the greeting border. You could say that those inside the line don't feel the need to greet each other because 'they have met.' It is clear that this line is drawn much further away from home than that of the Japanese (Kimura 2003: 107).

> 'The sense of co-presence conveyed via loud voices.' 'Separated in terms of space, but sharing the sense of togetherness.' 'A feeling of co-presence or a sense of co-presence' (Kimura 2003: 155).

> These examples indicate that the Baka Pygmy people don't feel very concerned about us looking at them or that they know how to ignore people looking at them. When they are looked at the Baka people don't seem to focus their attention in any direction…Our line of sight and theirs, or our voices and theirs, co-present without their direction

> obviously connecting. This must be a characteristic of Baka interaction (Kimura 2003: 206).

> When I was researching their pattern of speech, [I] came to recognize the existence of 'layers of meaning piled up just like roof tiles,' which was an important outcome...I can see a broad expanse of possibilities with conversation as mutual interaction (Kimura 2003: 209).

> What made me feel 'interested' during my fieldwork was the pattern of mutual interaction being woven by the local people (Kimura 2003: 305).

> As I began to understand the structure of mutual interaction, I came to realize that the sense of co-presence was a highly sophisticated cultural structure (Kimura 2003: 305).

When interpreting the state of the inner-city of a megalopolis by using the sense of co-presence, the path towards grasping the reality of, for example, loose connections and fragmented community, becomes more visible. We could explain, by means of this sense of co-presence, how people of heterogeneous and diverse origins interact by relying on loose connections, using the street as a channel rather than a separator. If the 'manner of urban co-existence,' discussed previously, is the key term for the post metropolis stage, this 'sense of co-presence' could be the key term for the next stage.

Towards the compilation of an urban ethnography

Daiji Kimura, the anthropologist who came up with the concept of the 'sense of co-presence,' has compiled the findings from his many years of fieldwork into the book *Kyozai kankaku: Afurika no futatsu no shakai ni okeru gengoteki sougokoui kara* (The sense of co-presence: the linguistic interactions of two African societies) (Kimura 2003). Published recently, it is an uncompleted ethnography but it examines various interpretations of the 'sense of co-presence' and lends its validity to urban sociological work. For my part, there is still a task to be done. That is, for me to compile a small urban ethnography, like *Ikebukuro noto* (The Ikebukuro notes) or *Shinjuku noto* (The Shinjuku notes), drawing upon the concept of the 'sense of urban co-presence.' It may end up, in reality, to be just a matter of putting together the fieldwork reports we have published nearly every year since 1988 into one volume and publishing *Ajia no Shinjuku/Ikebukuro: genchi mensetsu chosa kiroku korekushon* (Shinjuku and Ikebukuro in Asia: A collection of research based on face-to-face interviews in the field).

The field we are dealing with, the inner-city of a megalopolis where 'so-called non-Japanese looking Japanese' live shoulder to shoulder with transnational migrants is like an 'area of brackish water' where the sea water and fresh water mingle together. How does this heterogeneous and diverse group of people co-habitate in this 'area of brackish water?'

I have made it a rule when carrying out fieldwork on transnational migrants in the inner-city of the megalopolis, 'to reflect the complexities as they are' and 'to let the world speak for itself.' When I compile my short *Ikebukuro noto* or *Shinjuku noto*, as well as sticking to those principles, I intend to use the following books about urban ethnography as my models. They are W. F. Whyte's *Street Corner Society: the Social Structure of an Italian Slum* ([1943] 1993) [9] and Elijah Anderson's *Streetwise: Race, Class and Change in an Urban Community* (1990). The former is characterized as the 'urban ethnography of the twentieth century' while the latter is that of 'the twenty-first century.' Both of them are wonderful examples of participatory action research carried out in the inner cities of large cities.

A new reading 'Street corner society' and 'Streetwise'

Twentieth century urban ethnography

In the mid to late 1930s, at the time when *Street Corner Society* was written, the inner-city of Boston, where Whyte carried out his fieldwork, was considered to be an Italian slum or ghetto, as far as theory and policy making were concerned. Whyte comprehended, from below, the reality of juvenile delinquent groups who roamed around the streets and reconstructed their worldviews, while challenging the notion that the inner-city of large cities were slums and ghettos.

Street Corner Society ([1943] 1993) has been reprinted over the years, not just in the USA but also in other countries. When released, the new prints have been read as 'new books.' Yet it took scholars and policy makers fifty years from the time the first edition was issued to adjust their view of the inner cities and to realize that they are not slums and ghettos. To mark the fiftieth anniversary of its first publication, the 'fiftieth commemorative extended revised edition' was published in Japan with a fresh translation. The author contributed a forward to the Japanese edition which became his last published note (Whyte [1993] 2000). A modest and pleasant-countenanced man, Whyte succinctly writes:

> Could a single case study lead to generalizable conclusions? I wanted to show that this was possible. [10]

Twenty-first century urban ethnography

Half a century after the publication of *Street Corner Society* (1943), Anderson's *Streetwise* was published (1990). This, considered to be the urban ethnography of the twenty-first century, also focuses on the inner cities of the megalopolis, but it no longer needs to dismiss them as ghettos. Instead, it attempts to locate them as the 'thirdspace' in the post metropolis era. In practice, it is with the revitalized communities, which are positioned beyond the mere revitalization of the run-down neighborhoods of large cities, that Anderson is mainly concerned. The area in which he did his fieldwork for the book still remains anonymous at the time of writing this paper in 2004. But it is widely assumed to be one of the revitalized inner-city areas of Philadelphia, around the old city center. Anderson, himself a resident of his area of fieldwork, as well as a Professor of Sociology at the University of Pennsylvania, took part in, observed, wrote about and analyzed detailed accounts of various incidents in the area. Anderson, an Afro-American who in the past had been solely an informant to sociological studies, exhibits a sharp insight into people's relationships in the revitalized community and an ability to grasp what is happening from within, while switching between the roles of observer and observed.

As for the diverse world of people living in the revitalized community, Anderson writes:

> When my wife Nancy and I moved to the village in 1975, I had not planned to study the area; but this changed as I encountered the local community and discovered what seemed an ideal urban laboratory.
>
> I found the village one of the most culturally and ethnically diverse areas of the city, where wealthy people and poor people, gays, hippies, students, Jews, WASPs, Italian-Americans, Irish-Americans, newly arrived Southeast Asians, Ethiopians, Zambians, Pakistanis, Iranians, and others lived together in relative community. First I came to know the setting informally, simply experiencing its everyday life, making contacts almost by accident, and learning cultural rules from these experiences as any newcomer might (Anderson 1990: ix).

In order to grasp and describe the multi-layered reality of the revitalized community, Anderson, a permanent resident as well as a participatory observer, used the so-called 'Afro community,' across the street from the revitalized community, as a reference point. He observed and recorded various incidents as they happened in the neighborhood. The following is my summary of some examples from his monograph:

In front of a convenience store, where teenage black girls hang around after school, one day an elderly black woman, their mentor, was bashed and robbed by a group of the girls. Anderson ran to her rescue and spoke to the girls who had assaulted her. The assault of an elderly leader of the neighborhood was a 'prelude' to the changes to come in the revitalized community (Anderson 1990: 227).

Anderson had his car stolen. He rode around the neighborhood in a police car looking for his car. Right outside his work, at a bus stop, he happened to see a white colleague of his. Noticing the white policeman at the wheel and Anderson in the back, his colleague quickly looked away at the newspaper he held in his hand. How should Anderson interpret his colleague's change of eye contact? (Anderson 1990: 204–205).

Anderson was chatting over the back fence with a white architect and her husband, who asked him to look after their house because they were going to be away in California for a couple of weeks. The couple was known for their liberal attitude, but nonchalantly remarked 'there is nothing to be stolen, even if they [the blacks] broke in' and kept on chatting (Anderson 1990: 216).

When he was walking down the road, he heard a man yelling 'Nigger, what are you doing here? Get out of here right now!' Surprised, Anderson turned around and found a man with a dog. The man apologized and said 'Sorry, sorry, I was not talking to you. Nigger is the name of this dog' (Anderson 1990: 46).

Late at night, while hurrying home, Anderson came across a group of kids spread out across the street playing with a ball. He sat on the porch of a house, and observed them. Realizing it was past midnight, he asked one of the kids if their mother knew that they were playing there. Anderson was surprised to see some of the kids were as young as two or three years old. When it was past one o'clock they all hurried home. An older boy seemed to have been assigned to look after the younger ones. Anderson learned that the kids' play group had a self appointed 'division of roles' (Anderson 1990: 156–157).

Street life as a circuit

Ironically for Anderson, sometimes his historical roots as a black man and those of the black community overshadowed his research. For his research, the black community across the street from the revitalized community acted as a reference point. The street in this sense had a dual role, one as a 'divider' and the other as a 'connector.'

By the way, understanding the street in a wider context and treating it as the object of observation and participatory research, Anderson wrote *Code of the Street* (1999) as a follow-up to *Streetwise* (1990). Various individuals walk and hang around the street acting in a dual role 'anonymously,' away from their positions in the neighborhood, be that the revitalized community or the black community. This ability of many people co-present 'anonymously' is, to use Anderson's analogy, like the way skillful drivers maneuver and steer smoothly around pedestrians and other obstacles on the road. The dogmatic drivers, sticking strictly to the rules, would 'crash' into unexpected pedestrians and obstacles. This 'crash' should be seen as a 'cost' of street life, rather than as an 'incident.' To be a skilful driver, one is required to be adaptable to the conditions, be able to 'detour,' 'let go,' 'slide' and be 'indifferent' at any one time. It is the maneuverability and ingenuity of the skilful driver to which the mature sense of streetwise behavior corresponds.

If you follow the accepted manners of a racially diverse society and a revitalized community to the letter, there is a danger that comments and related behavior like 'all the blacks in this community are good neighbors and friends,' can be taken as a paradox, as opposed to the 'discriminatory' comments and behavior Anderson actually encountered. By the way, Anderson describes himself and others as blacks. Hence, here I also avoid the use of the more accepted terminology of 'Afro-Americans.'

Code of the Street (1999), like *Streetwise* (1990), is an urban ethnography and the last of a trilogy, which began with *A Place on the Corner* (Anderson 1978). *Code of the Street* is more organized in terms of methodology than *Streetwise*, and takes a more detached look at the world of 'co-presence' in the inner-city.

The street that lies between the revitalized community and the black community in the inner-city of a large city plays the role of an additional line drawn in the inner-city, and it also provides a place for people to walk around and hang around anonymously. How can we define the sophisticated behavioral code of these people? Anderson nominates three key concepts: decency, violence, and the moral life of the inner-city. Decency incorporates kindness, generosity and pleasantness, while violence, he explains, should not be used by or against anybody. To describe the moral life of the inner-city using twenty-first century terminology, one can interpret it as spiritual life or spirituality.

Along with the frontier explored previously in *Streetwise*, *Code of the Street* resonates with the well-being of the people, the sense of co-presence in a diversified world I have mentioned above.

Aftermath of fieldwork in Ikebukuro and Shinjuku

Transnational areas as a circuit: an attempt to 'study the inter areas'

So far, I have attempted to find the connection between the COE project set up to study 'social research improving human happiness' by Kwansei Gakuin University, and the reinterpretation and new findings of our research project in Ikebukuro and Shinjuku which has continued since 1988. The project required all participating sociologists to question themselves about the range of its impact. For me, if you will allow me to repeat myself, the sub theme of the COE project, 'the construction of a society that promotes cultural diversity' was precisely the subject matter required for the Ikebukuro and Shinjuku research.

For my research field for urban sociology, I have focused on the inner-city of large cities. As I have already mentioned, like the sociologists of the early Chicago school who have influenced the paradigm of urban sociology in Japan, the inner-city or inner area of large cities have been considered as ghettos or slums, a place of segregation inhabited by domestic and international migrant laborers. The view that the inner-city of a megalopolis must be an ethnic slum was dominant even among Japanese urban sociologists. But some reassessment is taking place that such a view was, even in the context of those days, contrary to the sociological reality.

Under the twentieth century system of urbanization and exponentially growing industrialization, the inner-city was a degraded area, a 'gray area' buried in a no man's land between the polarizing city center and outer suburbia. Under the twenty-first century system where rundown areas are being given a chance to be revitalized, a paradigm shift has occurred with regard to the inner-city. It is now considered to be the 'thirdspace' that connects both ends of the city, the center and suburbia.

I have attempted to revise my definition of the inner area of the megalopolis from that which was used for the twentieth century system, to one that will fit into the reality of the twenty-first century system, of the post metropolis state, where the inner-city is the 'thirdspace' with multiple layers of breadth and expansiveness. The inner-city of large cities as the 'thirdspace' is considered to be the way to come to terms with the reality of the so-called complex city of the twenty-first century. The complex city is my definition and its grassroots version is the urban community. It is not necessary to repeat the definition of the urban community that relates to the sub theme of the COE project. According to the *Shinpen Tokyo ken no shakai chizu 1975–90* (New edition, A social map of the Tokyo area, 1975–1990) edited by Susumu Kurasawa and Tatsuto Asakawa, the process of development from the city center to the outskirts did not go together with a ribbon like ecological order, but, as the model analysis shows, it was more like a mosaic pattern (Kurasawa and Asakawa eds 2004).

The inner-city of the complex city was the magnetic field for our research in Ikebukuro and Shinjuku. As the general view of the megalopolis' inner-city and foreign laborers was being revised, I was fortunate, as a sociologist, to be involved in face-to-face fieldwork in 1988, the first year that transnational migrants of Asian origin were officially accepted. I have concentrated on carrying out fieldwork comprising an on-going series of face-to-face interviews and annual publication of the findings in order to examine the proactive way of life and the aspirations of the transnational newcomers of Asian origin who move and live around the Asia Pacific region. For us, world wide comparative studies based on particular nation states and ethnic structures were out of our range. Rather, we developed the dynamic comparative method where we interrelated the ways of life and urban lifestyles of individuals and families of transnational migrants of Asian origin, in the magnetic field of the inner cities of large cities. Our method was similar to that of a case study, but our method of dynamic comparative was clearly different from the static comparative which compares individuals and districts according to national and ethnic boundaries.

As a result of our accumulated new findings and interpretations of the grassroots version of the complex city through the dynamic comparative method, the horizon for my main concern, 'the characteristics of the emerging urban community' has gradually opened up (Okuda

2004b). It may sound like self-vindication, but our research was the result of a small person to person effort, even though, it's results may have captured the new tide of the twenty-first century, the ground level reality of the megalopolis' inner-city through transnational inter-referencing. We mobilized a team of elite undergraduate and postgraduate students to carry out the interviews, and some moved on to work on individual participatory action research. [11]

One of the books Whyte wrote in his twilight years was *Learning from the Field: A Guide from Experience* (Whyte and Whyte 1984). In our early days, this book was our main reference material. Both Whyte and Anderson had their most significant research experiences during their postgraduate days. Just as Whyte took Kathleen King Whyte to help him to carry out fieldwork research in later years, I enlisted volunteer undergraduate and postgraduate students I met at two universities. Our research is like a small branch of the main stem which is comprised of an increasing number of big budget international comparative studies. That does not matter much, and small research like ours, dealing with the same field in the big cities, is able to view the transnational characteristics from below, as horizontally aligned 'neighborhoods of the world.'

Learning from the field: pivotal survey research centers

The training ground for fieldwork at any university's department of sociology is its survey research center. Indeed before World War II, at Tokyo University, the University of Chicago and elsewhere, the survey research center played a pivotal role in the development of fieldwork.

Between the 1920s and the 1940s, Tokyo University had its survey research center set up underneath the Social Studies center building facing Gotenyama hill. Along with Teijirō Toda (1887–1955), fresh from his studies abroad at the University of Chicago, the center had many sociologists studying topics which included the family, community, cities, social issues, ethnicity and many more. It was almost like a 'second Social Studies center.' I heard this said several times by Tomio Yonebayashi (1905–1968) who was an assistant at the center, and this was confirmed by some other sources as well (Yonebayashi 1960; Furuno 1967; Kitano 1967; Makino Tatsumi sensei tuitoroku kanko kai ed. 1977). The room was full of sociologists, who would all later, after the war, make their names as first class sociologists in their fields. The senior researchers included Tatsumi Makino, Seiichi Kitano, Takashi Koyama, Hiroshi Oikawa, Ken Okada, Eiichi Isomura and others, engaging in heated discussions after coming back from their fieldwork. It reminded me of the center at the University of Chicago. Their sociological monographs were based on various areas of field research and indeed the '*Shakai Chosa*,' Japan's first publication on social research by Teijirō Toda, was clearly a collaborative work with Yonebayashi and others (Toda 1933).

I studied at the postgraduate school of Brandeis University, on the outskirts of Boston in 1962. The university was known as a Jewish new research institute university. At the time, Everett Hughes of the Chicago school had been invited as the Head of the Department of Sociology in an attempt to revive the early Chicago school in a contemporary context. On numerous occasions I was told, both during our seminars and in private, about Robert Park and the sociological thinking and training in social research methods of the early tradition of the Chicago school. The survey research center was still present as a symbolic center at the Harper Memorial Library. Here, I would just like to quote a paragraph from the memoir of E.W. Burges, Park's excellent collaborator:[12]

> Our office arrangement was most fortunate for me, because Dr. Park had a most creative mind. He lived and slept research. I never knew when I would get home for dinner, because we would spend whole afternoons discussing both theoretical and practical aspects of sociology and social research (Burgess and Bogue eds 1964: 1–14).

What is now required is a plan to construct an archive for social research into the pursuit of happiness for human beings. With a survey research center under its wing, it would serve as a symbolic facility. This facility should be accompanied by a specialist postgraduate institute which is open to domestic and international universities as well as other research organizations.

8
Through the Eyes of a Good Deed Investigator

Yukihiko Shigenobu

Seventeen investigators explore the scorched city

Modern Japan talks about the *bidan* stories of good deeds

From the end of October until December 1923, seventeen investigators searched for stories of good deeds carried out in the ruined city of Tokyo. Tokyo had been devastated, firstly by the Great Kanto Earthquake which took place on the first of September in 1923, and subsequently by the fire caused by the earthquake. The investigators were selected by the Tokyo government and were dedicated to finding stories about the good deeds that people had undertaken during and after this major event. The search for and documentation of these deeds was the investigator's field work; researching the acts of decency and collecting the memories of someone's good deeds at the time of the great disaster.

Based on research by the investigators, the Tokyo government published *Good Deeds of the Taishō Earthquake* on the first of September in 1924, to mark the first anniversary of the Great Kanto Earthquake (Tokyo-fu hen 1924). The book had a cloth binding and was enclosed in a box; the price was six yen. The total number of pages was 774, and Katsuo Usami, the then Governor of Tokyo appeared in the introduction of the book. The book included 215 cases of good deeds and the contents were categorized into the following themes: stories of life-saving (58 cases), fire-prevention (32 cases), duty and commitment (53 cases), love (34 cases) and rescue operation (38 cases).

One hundred and fifty-four stories or one third of the documents submitted by the investigators were not published due to the limited space in the book. The addresses and names of the people and brief descriptions of the cases which were omitted were listed at the end of the editor's note. Including this brief list, the book contained, in total, 369 *bidan* stories or stories of good deeds (Tokyo-fu hen 1924).

In Japan, stories of good deeds are called *bidan*. The word *bidan* is difficult to translate into other languages. If translated literally, it means 'a beautiful story,' and if translated based on the meaning, it refers to 'a story of good deed.' The word *bidan* or 'story of good deed' had been used in the modern print media to convey those stories which spoke of the positive values of righteousness, goodness, virtue, and beauty; values required at the time by society. The variations in *bidan* stories such as filial devotion, success stories and tales of patriotic militarism, were issued as *bidan* collections. Tales of filial devotion reinforce the values of the modern Imperial system, and the success stories could be seen to reinforce capitalism, while tales of patriotic militarism reproduce the stories of heroism of soldiers and the self-sacrifice on the home front. Various *bidan* stories reinforcing these perspectives permeated society via the print media of the time. These *bidan* stories helped people to construct particular images of society and its people by depicting the values of righteousness, goodness and beauty.

Good Deeds of the Taishō Earthquake (Tokyo-fu hen 1924) is one of the numerous *bidan* stories which was the product of modern Japan. At the time of the Great Kanto Earthquake, many bidan stories had been relayed through the printed media, immediately following and until one year after the disaster. At first, the stories appeared in newspapers and later in magazines, in inexpensive books and documents issued by public institutions. Through these media, *bidan* stories born of the greatest disaster were placed on record in modern Japan.

Ryūichi Narita, a historian, analyzed the rhetoric of *bidan* stories (Narita [1996] 2003) and discussed the issue of how the disaster of the Great Kanto Earthquake was told and historicized. Firstly, the whole image of the disaster was created according to press reports and special edition magazines. The individual experiences of the victims gradually built up to become a major component of the entire story of the disaster. Narita noticed the stories of sorrow and good deeds as concrete examples of the rhetoric. He also observed how individual experience would be regarded as our own experience in the overall picture. He indicated that the characteristics of the *bidan* stories of the earthquake were as follows: firstly, the names of the people involved were included so that each act was considered to be unique to the individual. Secondly, the stories contained not only the acts of people, but also the characters and nature of the people. And thirdly, the stories were related to the public recognition of good deeds. Narita noted that the stories published in *Good Deeds of the Taishō Earthquake* (Tokyo-fu hen 1924) were not just anecdotes, but were graphic examples of the public recognition and the awards won.[1] He mentioned that: 'When government institutions address '*bidan* stories' it meant that they acknowledged the good deeds and the characteristics of them, and officially recognized them.' He further stated: 'This trend leads to [a] rather monochromatic view of people's acts, which may have various significances, and influenced the formalized conceptualization of them. [The] general public was even obliged to accept a monolithic value by recognizing 'good deeds' (Narita [1996] 2003: 223–224). *Bidan* stories published after the Great Kanto Earthquake historicized the event and the experiences of individuals, and constructed admirable models for good deeds.

Memoirs from an investigator collecting the stories

Although there were many *bidan* stories that had been published in modern Japan, most of them had no clear source as to how they were collected, selected and compiled. The same was true for the numerous *bidan* stories published at the time of the Great Kanto Earthquake.

In relation to the government publication *Good Deeds of the Taishō Earthquake* (Tokyo-fu hen 1924), an account of one investigator actually involved in the research was published. Written by Sōsen Endō, it was called *Memoir of a Good Deed Investigator* and was in total one hundred and twenty-one pages (Endō 1924). The memoir was circulated one month before the Tokyo government publication (Tokyo-fu hen 1924) on the first anniversary of the Great Kanto Earthquake. Endō was one of the seventeen investigators who were actually involved in the research conducted for the Tokyo government, and his memoir was based on the experiences during this research. Endō was born in Sakura-City, in Chiba, in 1886 and his real name was Shichibei. At the time of the research, he was in his late thirties. After he graduated from Chiba Teacher's School, he became a teacher and continued working in Chiba and Tokyo. He was also involved in editing a magazine for education, called Imperial Education (Kami 1988). At the time of the Great Kanto Earthquake, he was teaching in Tokyo and was selected as an investigator. His memoir was originally published in serial form, from February to June 1924, in the Imperial Education magazine, with the original title. In the introduction to his memoir, he revealed his motives for writing it, and stated:

> To be appointed as an investigator though unexpectedly, for researching on good deeds in the Great Earthquake, which is Tokyo government's worthy achievement, was one of the most memorable experiences that ever happened in my life. I did my best to fulfill the mission, walking around all over in the ruined city day after day, after the earthquake, shivering in a cold wind...the stories I gathered this way, were reported to the Tokyo government, and they will be published soon. Unfortunately, I cannot publicize these stories privately, as it is not necessary and not possible, either. One thing I am very sorry about is that, this process, how I collected the stories, the feelings I had from these experiences, and others will be lost and wasted. I suffered a great deal for the loss (Endō 1924: 1).

This memoir was written after the government investigation, and it presented opposing points of view to the official standpoint. In the introduction to his memoir two different viewpoints are perceived, one is the official position as an investigator appointed by the government; and the other is the view as an individual, who was actually engaged in the research. Endō's rumination: 'I cannot publicize these stories privately, as it is not necessary and not possible either,' reveals that he had expected that there may be a gap in the perspective of the Tokyo government publication and his own memoir. This subtle difference between the formal investigation and the investigator as a subjective performer, clearly describes his sentiment and response to the actual investigation. This memoir is a valuable source of material in which to explore how *bidan* stories were compiled, based on the research by an investigator that still included a subjective point of view.

In this document, which portrays the experience through the eyes of an investigator, I explored how the information was collected and the method used to collect this information. I also examined how this influenced the cultural trend of admiring good deeds, as well as the process of selecting the stories. Moreover, I looked into the cases which had been investigated but omitted, and examined how the scene of the investigation depicted the outline of these stories. We also glimpse one investigator's soul-searching: how he questioned the definition of good deeds; his self examination on the meaning of facts in regard to investigations; and how he struggled to position his subjective judgment in the investigation. In examining this memoir, we came to be aware of the historical practices of various investigations as a part of modern history in Japan.

In this paper, we will further examine why the society needed to visualize good deeds in *bidan* stories after the earthquake. By doing so, we may reveal the political climate which wanted to diminish the trauma and impact of the massacre and assault on Korean people at the time. Moreover, I would like also to briefly consider the historical events which link to the records of *bidan* stories and try to connect these stories and their production to their historical context. For instance, we will see the way in which responses to disaster prevention against natural calamities later link to air defense systems during a period of war.

The scene of investigation

Investigation of good deeds of the Great Kanto Earthquake

The explanatory notes of *Good Deeds of the Taishō Earthquake* briefly comment on the principles and the method of investigation. The investigators were directed to undertake the following:
1. Should look for the materials from the organizations such as: each country council, ward offices, Metropolitan Police and police stations, Martial Law Head Quarters, Army personnel, military police, town and village offices, town council, primary and secondary schools
2. Should research and investigate on authenticity of the newspaper articles
3. Should invite public participation for information by advertising in [the] newspaper (Tokyo-fu hen 1924, *Hanrei* (explanatory note): 2).

While the document outlines some of its selection and investigative processes, such as: 'We selected 17 principals and teachers in primary schools in Tokyo and the near suburbs, entrusted the investigations with them, and they worked together with the officers according to the methods we mentioned above' (Tokyo-fu hen 1924, *Hanrei* (explanatory note): 2), it also leaves many aspects out. In this government account there were many stories of good deeds relating to organizations and groups, and I believe that this was due to some process of control over the source of the materials. For instance, we could not find the advertisements which were supposed to be in the newspapers. Moreover, the names of the investigators who were allocated to each region and dedicated to collect the appropriate materials were not in the government publication either. Furthermore, we still haven't found the public documents which include details about the specific organization which conducted the investigation, the process of the investigation, or the procedures for compiling the document.

However, in one of the ten agendas of the meeting of the ward heads for the earthquake disaster countermeasure, held on the twenty-second of October, we found a record related to the 'Investigation on good deeds of the earthquakes' (Tokyo-fu hen 1925: 6). The meeting was one of fourteen which were held to discuss rescue operations, supervision, administration and communication in the communities in wards, towns and villages. Ward heads for Ebara, Toyotama, Kita Toshima, Minami Adachi, and Minami Katsushika attended the meeting as well as the governor of Tokyo-fu. Considering the date of the meeting, we concluded that the agenda was related to the major investigation for the *Good Deeds of the Taishō Earthquake* (Tokyo-fu hen 1924).

We also found an article from the Asahi Newspaper dated the twenty-sixth of December 1923, which reported calling off the investigation:

> *17 teachers formed good deeds investigators. Investigation on the good deeds on earthquake was called off yesterday*
> The investigation on good deeds of the earthquake, led by the Supervisor of Social Education, and conducted by 17 primary school teachers, was called off yesterday. The investigation covered various areas, and the number of the total cases reached was 480. The volume is more than 10 times larger compared to the investigations conducted by the Education Ministry, and the Honganji-Temple. The document will be published as an incredibly long great book. Secretary of the Supervisor of Social Education, Mr Matsubara and others are currently editing the document, and the book will be titled appropriately soon (Tokyo Asahi, 26 December 1923).

According to this newspaper article, we found out that the investigation was led by the Supervisor of Social Education. Seventeen primary school teachers were actually engaged in the investigation, which was also confirmed in the government publication (Tokyo-fu hen 1924,

Hanrei (explanatory notes): 2). The investigation was completed on the twenty-fifth of December.

Consistent with the record of the ward-head meeting, the period of two months from the end of October until the twenty-fifth of December was probably the actual duration of the investigation. We could see already at that time that they planned a large book to document all of the good deeds. The investigation conducted by the Ministry of Education, as reported in a newspaper article, probably referred to another investigation undertaken by the Youth Association to collect information for youth education (Houchi Newspaper, 24 September 1923).

While the number of *bidan* stories included in the *Good Deeds of the Taishō Earthquake* was 369, including the brief list of the cases omitted (Tokyo-fu hen 1924); according to the newspaper article, the number of the *bidan* stories was actually 480. It seemed that about 100 *bidan* stories were possibly excluded as inappropriate, but how were those cases in the book selected as appropriate and accepted as *bidan* stories?

Judgment by the investigators

According to the explanatory note of the *Good Deeds of the Taishō Earthquake* there were eight criteria employed for selecting good deeds:

1. Sacrifice oneself for the sake of work ethics and commitment
2. Examples of beauty in humanity in the disaster
3. Examples of handling the situation calmly at the time of disaster
4. Examples of contributing and devoting oneself for the community and society
5. Examples of preventing the disaster by helping each other in the neighborhood
6. Examples of devoting oneself and hard work with gratitude in disaster
7. Good deeds by trained organizations
8. Facts of preventing danger by everyday thorough preparation, or by learning lessons from our forerunners (Tokyo-fu hen 1924, *Hanrei* (explanatory notes: 2).

Note that in those lists, apart from Item 7, the words 'facts' and 'examples' were used. This indicates that at the time when *bidan* stories were in newspapers and special editions of magazines the investigation was focusing on facts rather than just on stories and tales. This orientation toward facts also defined the scene of the investigation.

These eight criteria, listed above, were also raised as a point of discussion in the Investigation Committee meeting (Endō 1924: 4–6). According to Endō, the subject of what defines good deeds was raised as a question at the meeting. He recounted that one committee member broached questions about the criteria of the deeds and asked for more specific details about these criteria. The committee member also sought clarification as to what extent there would be selection and exclusion of good deeds even if the deeds satisfied the eight requirements. The Tokyo government struggled to answer these questions and could not provide a definitive answer. Endō noted: 'It is impossible to ask such a request. We are unable to list details of each deed and the concrete criteria for them.' So in the meeting he responded with his own idea: 'It is better to list the general idea of good deeds first, and there is no way other than each investigator should decide himself and judge if they are appropriate deeds according to his own conscience.' However, the person who requested the details of the criteria for the good deeds objected to Endō's opinion. He argued: 'If good deeds are selected according to each person's judgment, there is no fairness in that method...So, better not judge by our own subjective mind, and conduct [the] investigation and take records' (Endō 1924: 4–6).

In his memoir Endō declared that the idea of excluding the subjective view was absurd. He further stated: 'If we view an act as good where our own moral conceptions and judgments towards good deeds were already involved...[then]...Of course it is not good to exaggerate the deeds and make the stories up, but rejecting a subjective point of view of the investigator is not approved' (Endō 1924: 6).

From the investigator's point of view, he had doubt as to what constituted standardized criteria for good deeds. Endō stated that there was no other way but for the criteria to be ultimately left to each investigator's conscience and was aware that these criteria would depend ultimately on each investigator's subjective view. This attitude directly challenged the government's stance, where every investigation was theoretically conducted according to a homogeneous logic and decision making process. In keeping with the official position, neither the names of the investigators or the specific localities investigated by them, were identified in the government report *Good Deeds of the Taishō Earthquake* (Tokyo-fu hen 1924).

By commenting on the discussion about the criteria for defining good deeds, Endō's memoir highlighted the importance of each investigator's judgment. This was in contrast to the monochromic view of good deeds which the government attempted to establish by setting up the criteria for them.

Police, schools, and passed on stories

How did these investigators collect information and conduct a concrete investigation, in their search for good deeds. In neither of the two sources—the *Good Deeds of the Taishō Earthquake* (Tokyo-fu hen 1924) nor the *Memoir of a Good Deed Investigator* (Endō 1924)—were there clear records that stated which area was allocated to Endō to investigate. However, most of the cases in the memoir were from the Fukagawa-ku area. In the main document of *Good Deeds of the Taishō Earthquake* the number of case examples in the Fukagawa-ku area was nineteen, and if we include two brief descriptions from the omitted cases in the editor's note, the total number of cases was twenty-one (Tokyo-fu hen 1924). Among these, eleven cases also appear in Endō's *Memoir* (Endō 1924). From this, we can assume that Endō conducted his investigations mainly in the Fukagawa-ku area.

According to his memoir, the first case Endō wanted to investigate was about two Koreans and was reported in the Hochi newspaper. Endō visited the owner of a cheap hotel, in a barrack style residence in Kazuya-chō, Fukagawa-ku, 'one day at the end of October,' and interviewed the owner (Endō 1924: 14). Even though newspapers were the main vehicle to promulgate images of the earthquake, this was the only case example which had been based on an article from a newspaper that appeared in Endō's memoir. At the time of the disaster, the public organizations such as administrative institutions—the army and the police—conducted rescue activities and collected and stored information sequentially. Rather than use newspapers as his primary source, Endō acquired and utilized the information from these public organizations. For example, for many cases, he browsed information collected during the rescue operation at each police station and found evidence of good deeds in the materials. When he visited the Modoribashi Police Station, he found one case of a good deed among the reports by the police sergeant to the police commissioner. The information he collected there was used in the story of RS [encoded by Shigenobu] who was one of the staff of an organization that operated settlement house work at Sarueura in Fukagawa-ku. The report stated that RS was 'calm and contemplative, takes proper action by judging the situation well, and ensured the safety for many in neighborhoods.' Based on this information, Endō started interviewing the officer and asked specifically about the process of the rescue and evacuation operation taking place (Endō 1924: 7–12). At the same time, he was researching the history and philosophy of the organization (Endō 1924: 27–31). This case also appeared in the 'Life saving' section in *Good Deeds of the Taishō Earthquake* by the Tokyo government (Tokyo-fu hen 1924: 70–73).

Another example of using material from the police station was the case of HT [encoded by Shigenobu], whose nickname was Ōtora (Big tiger). In his memoir, Endō noted that this story was based on a document from the Modoribashi Police Station. The story about Ōtora is included in the 'Rescue operation' section of the *Good Deeds of the Taishō Earthquake*, titled 'Outstanding Act of Ōtora-kun' (Tokyo-fu hen 1924: 52–53). Ōtora had been a carpenter since he was a boy, and had lived in Honjo and Fukagawa for twenty years. At the time of the earthquake, he was in Tomikawa-chō running an agency for laborers and had a large following. He was a gambler and engaged in unlawful activities at times, but he cleaned up his act and stopped gambling. When the earthquake occurred he organized a private rescue squad with his twenty followers and in the story he and his squad saved people who were trapped under the rubble. Since the content of the police report was not quoted directly in Endō's memoir and there were no statements that suggested that Endō had met Ōtora personally, we have to assume that the information about the case was collected from the police report.

In addition to collecting information from police offices, other pubic organizations such as schools were a key data source. As Endō was a primary school teacher, he used to collect information from school children in his daily life. In addition, the burnt-out sites of schools had become the location where many people lived in temporary accommodation after the earthquake; it was on these sites that barracks had been built to house local residents (Tokyo-fu hen 1925: 4, 9–10). Considering that fact, schools should have been the main source of information in the community.[2] Outlined below is one example of a case which came from a school.

The story 'Protecting a child from furious fire' was about a fourteen year-old boy who was asked to protect a child while his neighbor brought out the furniture and other personal belongings from their house. But the fire was getting stronger and the boy carried the child on his back so that he could escape from the fire. One day later, the boy returned the child to the neighbor. Endō recounted:

> It was the 22nd of November. While I was visiting Rokkenbori Primary School in Fukagawa, and talking about *bidan* stories, one teacher who was standing by my side mentioned, "I am not sure if this is true or not, but I heard a story that the boy called H [encoded by Shigenobu] rescued a 2 year-old child next door, at the devastated site of the *Hifukusho-ato*."[3] I asked the teacher his full name, but she said she didn't know. She didn't know where he lived, either. However, the story and the character were very impressive, I started searching for the clue of the case, and I came to know that the boy graduated from Rokkenbori School in March this year. He was 14 years old, and his name was HY [encoded by Shigenobu] (Endō 1924: 56).

Endō did not know the boy's address, but finally thought of asking his address from a year six girl who was attending the class at the time. After some time, one teacher came to him with a boy. The teacher said that the boy knew the child that Endō was looking for (Endō 1924: 57). Endō was guided by the boy and visited the child in a barrack and interviewed him.

School children were often the source of information in communities and teachers collected data and knowledge that they heard from the children. This incident illustrates the way in which information collected and stored at schools were an important resource for Endo's investigation. We could see how Endō put the puzzle together and finally found the boy. He utilized officially collected information, such as the knowledge available from public organizations (police and schools), as well as drawing on unofficial information from around the scene, which seemed at times to practically include rumors. In particular, we should note the fact that the stories passed on, the so-called rumors, were important sources of information for Endō, as we have seen in previous cases. For instance, Endō commented:

> I was investigating the act of OT [encoded by Shigenobu] around Ettiyūjima. He is running a business of renting ships and rafts near Aioi Bridge. He is a man of duty and obligation. I wanted to investigate him because I heard of his heroic act during the severe fire caused by the earthquake (Endō 1924: 20).

And in another remark he noted: 'I noticed the work of the Benefit Club, because I heard that the club protected Koreans, and that this is the primary motive for me to decide approaching N [encoded by Shigenobu]' (Endō 1924: 22). With the first case, the source of his investigation was a rumor, and with the second, after hearing the rumor he visited the police and checked the record, confirming the fact that N had saved nineteen Korean lives and had protected them. After the confirmation, he went ahead and interviewed N. The first story appeared in the 'Rescue operation' section of *Good Deeds of the Taishō Earthquake*, titled 'Rafts, ships and obligation' (Tokyo-fu hen 1924: 59–63). The second was included in the 'Duty and commitment' section, titled: 'The benefit club leader who protected Koreans' (Tokyo-fu hen 1924: 333–337).

Rejected stories

Even if he acquired information about a case and researched it, this did not mean that the information turned out to be reportable data. Especially with the rumors, they often became unreported incidents after the research or investigation was completed. For example, Endō heard a story from a woman at one barrack in Ettiyūjima, that while she was evacuating with her daughter she injured her leg and almost could not make it. Then a young man appeared, put her on his back and escaped to safety until the next morning of the second of September. The young man just said that he was in the house of Matsudaira, Kōjimachi, and left. The woman told Endō: 'If your job is to investigate these cases, would you find the young man and let us know?' Endō was searching for the house of Matsudaira in Kōjimachi, but there was no such person who had been in this house. After all of this searching, as he could not find the young man, this became one of the cases which was excluded from the document because of the strict policy for the government investigation (Endō 1924: 45–51). On the other hand, Endō stated that 'although this case was rejected, the act itself was special and virtuous, and there was no reason to draw back' (Endō 1924: 51). He chose the word 'rejected' here, and we can note his criticism of and discomfort towards the 'strict government examination.'

Endō criticized the strict method for investigation as lacking sensitivity. It was similar to the national census which collects detailed data including the person's address, date of birth, occupation and so on. At the same time, he did support the principles of the government investigation, and recognized that 'if the materials do not include these details under strict rules, the government will not accept them.' He then referred to '*Konjaku Monogatari*—Tales of Ages Ago,' and thought that we were more attracted by those essays and private records than historiography, which has every detail of data and facts (Endō 1924: 107).

Konjaku Monogatari is folklore from the middle-ages. It has stories based on morals and the gossip of common people in Kyoto during this era. In his comments on the strict rules of the government investigation in which he was engaged, Endō compared the national census, which aims to provide precise quantitative data about the Japanese nation, to the *Konjaku Monogatari* which is based on rumors and historical anecdotal evidence. Even if he did not accept the requirements fully, Endō tried to understand the quality of the facts and details required by the first national census in 1920, which was still fresh in his memory. In Japanese society at that time, there was greater social mobility. Family registers alone could not cope with the level of movement and social change occurring in the rapidly changing society, so a national census was commenced to try to keep track of the population. Modern Japan conducted and formalized the census with the strict policy that everyone should be included in it, with a sense of national pride.[4] Endō, who was involved in the investigation of good deeds, struggled between the strict policy which he looked to as a model for government investigation, and his own individual orientation.

As discussed previously, in reference to the eight criteria for selecting good deeds, we pointed out that the investigations were orientated towards facts and actual examples, rather than stories and tales, and investigators including Endō were required to confirm the authenticity of the events. Endō mentioned another example of a deed, which was excluded from the facts, by calling it a 'legend.' The case involved a rumor raised by a teacher colleague. Endō heard a story from a principal that someone had saved a boy who was wearing only *juban* (underwear) and hung his wooden sandals around his neck with a strap. The principal overheard the story in a train (Endō 1924: 51–53). The principal who told Endō the story didn't know the name of the boy, but he remembered the *happi* coat which had *Chūgen* letters on it, worn by the man who was telling the story. The man looked like a young owner of a timber shop in Kiba, or Bantō, some kind of mercantile clerk. Endō felt that somehow he could find the man and he searched for the *happi* coat with *Chūgen* letters. Not only did he walk in the town of Kiba, but he also stood on streets in Shitamachi (the old town) in Tokyo, and kept an eye on the letters on the clothes of laborers. But in the end he could not find the letters *Chūgen*. He mentioned that the story of 'A boy hanging his wooden sandal on his neck' became a 'legend.' That Endō was searching for the boy with a *happi* coat, as a clue, was interesting, but the fact that it ended up as a legend, told us clearly that the act of investigation involved sorting out the information between rumor and fact.

The great earthquake hit Tokyo at a time when the city was developing into a modern metropolis. The investigator's job was to find specific individuals in this giant metropolis, with anonymity, as well as struggle with the rumors. Carrying out that sort of duty was rather like the investigations of a detective. The good deeds investigators had to search for specific people and locate their whereabouts in the big city. In addition they had to find the cases, in which the person was involved, from the pieces of information, rather than undertake a type of social research which is based on surveys and public questionnaires. During *Taishō* and the beginning of the *Showa* era, the scene of practice of detectives and their culture, as depicted in the detective novels of that period, contributed to the mass interest in 'detective investigations' (Nagai 2000). Endō himself used the word 'investigation' in his memoir and this probably reflects the cultural outlook of the time.

Endō was having a hard time dealing with the rumors, and this included *bidan* stories published soon after the earthquake in newspapers and magazines. One of his teacher colleagues handed him a story written by a child. It said: 'I heard this story from my neighbor.' It was a story of a young man who had saved three children from a fire, and sacrificed himself. Endō felt like investigating this case and he visited the child's school the next day. The child's teacher brought him the boy who wrote the story, and the boy recounted that he had heard the story from a next door butcher. Endō visited the butcher and inquired about the story, but the butcher said that he didn't remember telling that story (Endō 1924: 63–65). Then Endō visited the child's house and asked his parents about the story. They murmured 'Well...' and looked at each other. Then the mother said: 'Oh, now I remember, I read the story in a book.' She showed Endō a book, with a cover of bad taste, titled *Stories of Sorrow and Good Deeds of the Great Earthquake*, published soon after the Earthquake (Iizuka 1923). Endō and the mother looked in the book thoroughly from one page to the next, but they could not find the story after all (Endō 1924: 63–65).

There was no such story in the book. According to the date of publication, the book was printed on the twenty-eighth of September 1923, and issued on the thirtieth of September in the same year. The second edition was issued on the second of October 1923 (Iizuka

1923). This book must have been compiled and published soon after the great earthquake during the chaos and in its aftermath. Most of the stories in the book were based on articles from newspapers. Endō collected these types of stories as much as possible during the investigation, but in these quickly constructed books, there was almost nothing to which he could refer. He criticized the fact that these stories were nothing more than rumors and lacking in authenticity (Endō 1924: 63–65).

At the time when Endō was engaged in the investigation, there had already been a lot of *bidan* stories about the earthquake which permeated the society via the print media, particularly through newspapers, magazines and also through books. People often said: 'I read the story in so and so a book,' and numerous *bidan* stories were cited and repeated and were spread as folklore. 'They are almost rumors without any authenticity' Endō commented (Endō 1924: 65), and we can imagine his frustration at being tossed about with these stories being repeatedly told without any clear source or verification as to their validity.

While Endō felt uncomfortable about being restricted by the strict criteria and rules of the government investigation, he also kept some distance from tales based on rumor, and he attempted to keep his investigation objective, in line with the facts. We see in Endō's attitude that he decided whether the stories were facts or just rumors on the basis of being an investigator; rather than from the point of view of the government judging what the facts were.

'Criticality' in the investigation of good deeds

Investigators of good deeds had to deal with issues relating to the definition of good deeds, and they also had to tackle issues involved in the investigation itself, during the process of making deeds that were invisible, become visible. These issues were related to the critical nature of the investigation itself.

For instance one person offered his house and tenement in the back of his house, rescued 5,000 people and provided accommodation for them. But the government authority did not give him credit for his deed. The reason was that he was said to be motivated by publicity seeking and the act was not seen as the genuine act of a good person (Endō 1924: 13). We could see that the Tokyo government wanted to exclude acts of self-promotion—they were not classified as good deeds. While there were not any written criteria defining what constituted self-promotion, this issue related to the question of what constituted a good deed. Endō questioned himself: 'In a situation like this, we have to distinguish between a good deed and a good person.' He cited a proverb: 'You can't make a silk purse out of a sow's ear,' and correlated it with the concept of 'a good person and a good deed.' He noted that a good person may not do bad things; however, we cannot reach a definite conclusion that a bad person never does good things (Endō 1924: 13). In this instance, Endō criticized the government's judgment for their conclusion that this man's act was motivated by self-promotion.

The same problem of differentiation also arose in relation to a story about a school principal that had escaped with a picture of the Emperor, and who safely placed it back in the location where it had originally belonged. According to Endō, the first impression of the principal was not a very good one, and his attitude was quite arrogant. Endō reflected: 'I am a gentle person, but I couldn't help feeling rebellious toward him' (Endō 1924: 42). Endō continued and noted that it was the principal's own responsibility to place the image of the Emperor back, and if he had failed to do so, he would have been remiss in his duty. Making his act known to the public was beyond acceptability, even if the act was worth praising. Notwithstanding this comment, Endō concluded that this was a good deed for us after all (Endō 1924: 42).

The following excerpt shows Endō's persistently critical attitude in seeking to distinguish a good deed from a good person. His thought process reminds us of his judgment 'what makes a good deed and a good man should be left to an investigator's conscience' (Endō 1924: 42). The act of investigation cannot avoid scrutinizing the deed and the person for signs of particular sentiments including the desire for publicity and hunger for fame. The Tokyo government had a policy to exclude these desires and left the difficult task of defining this issue with the investigators.

Both the sentiments of desire for publicity and self promotion were related to the context of how the deed was carried out. The investigators task was to try to objectively see a deed as a fact. Therefore, even if deeds were the same, some of them may not be recognized as good deeds because of the motivations of the people concerned and their different circumstances; as a result, their deeds may be excluded as not constituting facts.

We will further see how Endō judged the cases during the actual investigation and then excluded them by defining them as not being good deeds. For example, one school reported that there were two cases of good deeds among their students, so he visited the school. One girl's name was Y, and according to the report: 'She had very little food but she shared it with people who were starving' (Endō 1924: 65). The other case was about a girl K, and the report said that: 'She helped the sick people who could not evacuate themselves, and gave mattresses and quilts, when she had very little of them herself' (Endō 1924: 65). Endō interviewed the girl Y, and she said: 'My father cooked rice for rice balls, and his mistress had enough, so I gave the rest to others' (Endō 1924: 66). Endō was disappointed to hear what she said. The more accurate story about K was as follows, when K was evacuating, she saw her teacher carrying an old lady on his back, so she gave them some sheets and pillows. In the end, Endō thought that neither of the stories had much impact or basis as a good deed, compared to the original reports kept at the school.

While you could not call the reports from the school false, there was a gap between the description by others of the action carried out, and the actual account by the people involved in the cases themselves. In the report, the act which was supposed to be good and the object of an award, said that the girl shared a meal, of which she had very little herself. The way the report described the case contributed to make the story sound like a *bidan* story. The investigators perceived the gap and drew a boundary around the deed. Endō stated that: 'Good deeds are precious however small they may be' (Endō 1924: 66), but he had to consider if the deeds were up to the standard of those already included in *Good Deeds of the Taishō Earthquake* (Tokyo-fu hen 1924). These two stories were not included in that publication.

Reflecting on this, Endō claimed that the 'good deeds in these stories did not have much impact' (Endō 1924: 66) and their significance is a matter of degree. In today's terms, this debate relates to the critical issue about what constitutes a fact and the way facts are depicted. Furthermore, Endō was in a bind. This bind not only concerned the problems relating to perception, judgment and approval of what makes a good deed and what makes a good person, but was also connected to some of the dilemmas raised when carrying out the investigation itself. For instance, Endō had heard that a woman had found a baby at the site of the fire and was looking after the baby in one of the barracks. He visited the woman and interviewed her, asking her questions such as: where she lived, the size of her family, how old the baby was and so on. The woman answered and while this child had become hers, he was not her own child. The woman thought Endō was an investigator from the family register. Endō was not an official with an interest in the child's background or status so he let her tell the story. However, when he finished the interview and returned to the barrack office, the woman came to see him and started pleading: 'Please do not publish the story in the newspaper and other media. The child lost his parents and I am going to raise him as my own, and if this is revealed somehow it might affect his success in his career' (Endō 1924: 53–54). This case was not included in *Good Deeds of the Taishō Earthquake* either (Tokyo-fu hen 1924).

The results of the investigations of good deeds reveal hidden stories to the public by providing them with details of people's proper names, amongst other things. In other words, this process involves retelling individual experiences as experiences with public values attached to them. Concern and anxiety of preserving the records about what they said, revealed a potentially violating aspect of the investigation. For instance, it is interesting that the woman thought Endō was an investigator of the family register. The first national survey was conducted in 1920 on the fifteenth of November and was a census of the entire population. It was conducted with the same method used in the first survey, by the Temporary Rescue Operation Administration Office led by the Department of the Interior, undertaken for countermeasure against fire after the earthquake. Memories of these surveys might have been still fresh in the mind of the woman, and that may have been the reason why she thought Endō was an investigator from the family register.[5] We could surmise that for the people who were investigated, the census taking to calculate the death toll after the earthquake and the investigation of good deeds were experienced as almost the same.

While the case above illustrated the potentially harmful effects to the individuals concerned through making public their good deed, there were also cases where the participant themselves thought their act was not worthy of being documented. The following example was a case where the doer of the act refused her deed to be categorized as good. Endō heard a rumor that one school teacher carried her old mother on her back and escaped to Ōmori. He interviewed the school teacher, but the teacher pleaded with Endō not to publish the case. She said: 'The act I did is natural and it is not a significantly good deed as such. It is just a normal thing that I, the child, carried my mother and escaped from danger. Please do not publish this.' Endō thought: 'As the condition was not normal, to do a normal thing is supernormal, and my intention to announce this act as good was very strong' (Endō 1924: 104). But the teacher wrote a letter to Endō and asked him not to include her case, and instead she was willing to introduce him to a better story of a good deed. After all of this, the case the teacher told him was included in the 'Love' section in *Good Deeds of the Taishō Earthquake*, titled, 'Thirty people under galvanized iron' (Tokyo-fu hen 1924: 634–638). In the story Endō mentioned this case as follows:

> A teacher in Aikawa Primary School was one of the thirty people in that story, and she was carrying her mother on her back. She came across the violence against the Korean people, and she left the place and escaped to her relation's house for the safety of her mother. This story was inserted elsewhere (Tokyo-fu hen 1924: 637).

Endō mentions that the story was inserted 'elsewhere;' however, he did not include it in the *Good Deeds of the Taishō Earthquake* (1924), but he did refer to it in his *Memoir of a Good Deed Investigator* (Endō 1924:103–105). Although investigators were invisible to the government, this remark on the teacher's deed in the *Good Deeds of the Taishō Earthquake* (1924: 637), showed Endō's strong determination to insert the story as a good deed even, though he was asked to omit the account by the doer of the act.

There certainly was a critical process involved where, during their investigations, investigators had to consider and make decisions about what was a good deed and who was a good doer. Furthermore, there was a critical consideration about the potentially violating effects of the investigation that may occur through the act of publicizing an individual's act as a good deed. Thus, investigators had to always question their own perception and attitudes relating to all aspects of the investigation.

Investigation of good deeds and mobilization

Although Endō struggled and suffered with the given structure and the rules of the investigation, he did not have any doubts about collecting *bidan* stories and publicizing them (Endō 1924). He engaged himself actively, and he recounted that this experience was the most memorable event in his life. In his memoir, we can see Endō's motivation to involve himself actively in the investigation, demonstrating that it was not a mechanical involvement. This may be the key to understanding what Endō actually did get involved with, in the context of the historical period, through the investigation.

In his memoir we can see that the massacre of the Korean people clearly left him with a traumatic impression. In the introduction to this memoir, there is a speech by a social education director, Mr Matsubara recounting a story which is supposed to be told by a Korean man. This speech was made at the First Conference of the investigation of the Good Deed Committee. Mr Matsubara heard the story from Mr Usami, the then Governor of Tokyo, and Mr Usami picked up this story while he was in Korea. The story is as follows:

> When the surging floodwater occurred, Korean people ran for their lives. Chinese picked up the flood wood drawing in the floodwater. Only Japanese save the lives of others. No wonder Japan is developing (Endō 1924: 1).

This is a typical ethnic joke and behind this joke lies discrimination; but it is a perverse joke because it supposed to be told by a Korean. Endō conceived of the story as:

> Our Governor Usami has seen a lot of impressive incidents which reveal our national character. Among the incidents, the behavior of the Japanese that betrayed the Koreans was seen; however, during that period, the true good nature of the Japanese people must have been observed behind the scene (Endō 1924: 2).

The description of 'the behavior of the Japanese that betrayed the Koreans' definitely points to the massacre of Koreans. Endō used the adversative conjunction, 'however' and then he talked of the 'true good nature of the Japanese people,' and further stated: 'I mean this word 'good deeds' tells us something about our good nature' (Endō 1924: 2). The concept of good deeds was definitely at the opposite end to the massacre of the Koreans. Without doubt, Endō hoped to wipe away the disgrace and shame of the Japanese and tried to make reparation during the investigation of good deeds.

At the same time, I wonder what the intention of the government might have been that was controlling and ruling the entire picture of the investigation of good deeds. At least Endō assumed that Usami, the then Governor of Tokyo and the chief of the investigation, shared his intention. In the section on 'Duty and commitment' in *Good Deeds of the Taishō Earthquake* there were four stories about protecting Koreans during the massacre (Tokyo-fu hen 1924: 333–337, 429–434). One of the stories was about the Director of a benefit club, who risked his life to save a Korean. Endō investigated this story, as well as another case which was about the Sugamo Police Station which safeguarded Koreans. Another case was about saving a Chinese who was mistaken as a Korean. In the 'Love' section, there were six other stories about protecting Koreans, including the town mayor who was committed to do so (1924: 547–567).

If you recall, the first case that Endō selected to investigate which he had read in the newspaper, was the case about a Korean who guarded his master's children and belongings. Endō remarked: 'Good deeds have nothing to do with races, regardless of Japanese or Koreans or whatever. There are bad Japanese, and there are good Koreans and bad Koreans.' He further stated: 'It was the fact that some neighborhood watch group persecuted innocent Koreans, on the other hand, there must be some Japanese who protected good Koreans' (Endō 1924: 19). By investigating the good deeds of Koreans he was opposed to the vicious rumors about Koreans, and by investigating the good deeds of the Japanese who protected Koreans, he was trying to face the guilt of the massacre committed by the Japanese.

As Ryūichi Narita indicated, there was the rhetoric of *bidan* stories. In other words, *bidan* stories were used effectively to exclude the people who were involved in the massacre from 'us,' and it had the effect to place 'the act of the massacre' behind the scenes. The rhetoric served as a basis to place good deeds on the center stage (Narita [1996] 2003: 231). However, Endō commented that: 'The worst scandal that happened after the earthquake was the massacre of Korean people' (Endō 1924: 16). And at a later point reflected: 'I wonder which class of Japanese made a low point in the history of the Taishō Earthquake. We were terribly traumatized' (Endō 1924: 21). We do not question that Endō was putting himself aside here, but in his comments we can assume his shock and confusion when facing the fact of the massacre of Koreans, an event that was definitely a low point in Japanese history.

On the twentieth of October 1923 the Daily Tokyo published an article titled: 'Massacre of Koreans in each region in Japan' (Daily Tokyo, 20 October 1923). The newspaper's headline was 'Prohibited news were released' and a whole page was filled with articles about the massacre of Korean people in each region of Kanto district. The fact was that the massacre was not just a rumor, but had been carried out by groups of people. Endō started his investigation of good deeds with cases related to Korean people, and I wonder if his target for the investigation was affected by the fact of the massacre. The investigation involved the process of constituting national character, creating the image of 'the nation' which is doing good and righteous things, during the unusual time of an earthquake.

Katsuo Usami, the then Governor of Tokyo, defined 'good deeds' in the preface of *Good Deeds of the Taishō Earthquake,* as follows:

> Acting from a sense of duty and commitment for one's occupation, sacrificing oneself and devoting to the benefit of the public, acting and responding calmly and handling situations properly, helping the neighborhood and minimizing disaster, avoiding danger for themselves and others by learning from the experiences of forerunner's, or by doing thorough preparation for a disaster everyday, using the skills of trained groups...(Tokyo-fu hen 1924: 2).

And the list of *bidan* stories went on: 'sense of duty and commitment,' 'remaining calm,' 'helping each other in the neighborhood,' 'being thorough in making preparation,' and 'using the skills of trained groups'—these key words were also seen in the eight criteria for the investigation of good deeds.

Let us compare these criteria to that of the investigation for good deeds conducted by the Youth Association in the Education Ministry. Their criteria were:

1. Special cases showing royalty to the Emperor
2. Cases about love between parent and child
3. Cases about commitment for one's occupation and other commitment
4. Cases about sacrificing oneself to society and the public
5. Cases about love of siblings
6. Cases about love between husband and wife
7. Cases about love between master and servant
8. Cases about humanity
9. Cases about rescuing others during the earthquake, and other cases which can be models for the future generation (Hochi newspaper, 24 September 1923).

Among these criteria, 'commitment for one's occupation,' and 'sacrifice of oneself for others,' was also seen in the criteria of the Tokyo government publication (Tokyo-fu hen 1924, *Hanrei* (explanatory notes)). But there were other criteria as well; some based on love, or the spirit of royalty to the Emperor (at the top of the list), or friendship, or love between husband and wife, and then there were *bidan* stories about the love between master and servant and humanity itself—all of these possibilities were on the list.

On the other hand, the spirit behind the *Good Deeds of the Taishō Earthquake* (1924), including the introduction and the eight criteria for good deeds, were related to individuals who could act rationally and calmly based on their own decisions, not those acting like a herd of cattle and listening to rumors, in times of disaster. The models for these individuals were: 'the sense of duty and commitment,' to 'act calmly,' 'helping each other in the community,' 'thorough preparation,' and the 'power of the trained group.'

Good Deeds of the Taishō Earthquake was published for the first anniversary of the earthquake, during the post-quake reconstruction, and had the purpose to 'hand down the information to the generations so that they can make use of the information at the time of emergency, preparing for the disaster, and bring the spirit of sacrificing oneself for others after the earthquake' (Tokyo-fu hen 1924: 3).

We know that fifteen to twenty years after the earthquake, Tokyo had to face another emergency, the air raid of the Second World War. The Japanese people were asked once again to have the sprit of sacrificing themselves, but this time for war. After the earthquake, the following titles of articles were seen in the newspapers:

> 'Only one aircraft is enough / to destroy our entire capital city / Concerned about defense against attack from the sky / The army submitted a strategy' (Daily Tokyo, 1 November, 1923). 'If we are attacked from the sky / it will be far more destructive than the earthquake / Even the entire uptown will be destroyed' (Daily Tokyo, 26 December, 1923).

The military knew the power of aircraft during the First World War, which was a total war, and tried to employ the concept of anti-air-raid for reconstruction of the capital. An 'Imperial script about Capital Reconstruction' was released by the Emperor on the twelfth of September 1923 and decreed that the reconstruction of Tokyo was a national priority. On the tenth of November of the same year, the Emperor issued an 'Imperial script about Building a National Spirit.' Both of the documents were released soon after the earthquake; it was not a coincidence—they were related each other. The latter document was celebrated on the tenth year anniversary of the earthquake in 1933. Furthermore, according to Harada Katsumasa, after the earthquake, countermeasures for natural disasters and strategies for defense against the air force were the key issues competing with one another. *Dōin-taisei*, which means 'mobilization,' was strengthened as a result, and communities and networking in each region in Japan was reestablished (Harada 1997).[6]

The government publication *Good Deeds of the Taishō Earthquake* (Tokyo-fu hen 1924) was showing, hypothetically, ideal models of the morals for national mobilization at the time of emergency. The items listed as the criteria of good deeds, and the concepts outlined in the document—duty and commitment, calmness, helping each other, obligation and appreciation, offering oneself and hard work, power of the trained group, everyday practice of thorough preparation—represented the essential characteristics of the era of national mobilization. By the time of the Second World War, these slogans were controlling the nation and constituted the heart of national mobilization. For example the concept of gratitude and appreciation towards the Emperor's army was advocated, and the spirit of diligence and patriotism in which everyone undertook their own duty was promoted. Standing strong or resolved against the enemy and attitudes that one should remain calm regardless of rumors were also required. The spirit of helping each other in communities was strengthened as a result of the introduction of the so-called *tonarigumi* system, which was a network of neighborhood organizations. On top of that, saving daily was encouraged (Nagahama [1937] 1988). These national slogans of mobilization resonated with the criteria outlined in the Tokyo government's publication *Good Deeds of the Taishō Earthquake* (Tokyo-fu hen 1924).

This investigation of good deeds and the subsequent publication by the Tokyo government formed a stream moving towards the era of national mobilization, a period in which the words 'home front' emerged as a slogan. There is clearly a link between the investigation of good deeds that we have discussed in detail, and the *bidan* stories about the 'home front' compiled much later during the era of national mobilization.[7]

Conclusion

The investigation of *Good Deeds of the Taishō Earthquake* by the Tokyo government (Tokyo-fu hen 1924) set the standard for good deeds, and by doing so aimed to collect and compile particular examples and facts of *bidan* stories, which were not just beautiful tales.

The investigators, whose names were not even listed in the government document, were supposed to have collected the facts, according to a certain standard, at least in principal, without being influenced by their subjectivity. However, as has been illustrated, in the actual scene of the investigation, there were numerous methods utlized to determine a fact. There were so many ways to investigate the existing records and articles and numerous ways to practice fieldwork and undertake interviews. During the process of investigation, depending on how the stories were told, and under which circumstances, the values and meanings of good deeds could be changed. The potential for inconsistency and distortion of specific values and meanings was always at issue during the investigation. Collected facts were put into concrete form by the investigators. In their exploration of public records and in interviewing people, they selected the cases by contemplating the concept of what constitutes a good deed. Sōsen Endō, one of the investigators, was trying to be conscious about all of these issues through writing his *Memoir of a Good Deed Investigator* (Endō 1924). About eighty years ago, this investigator of good deeds was facing the same concerns that we face today in fieldwork. One of them, which is often unclear, is related to the problem of how to connect research and analysis with facts. Another is how to deal with the potentially violating effects of research that can be caused in the process of investigation itself.

Investigators never behaved like robots, working in a routine and mechanical way, as the government assumed and expected. We cannot simply judge whether an investigator tried to resimulate the cases, had a critical viewpoint towards a seemingly uniform approach to the good deeds investigation, or if it was just the expression of an individual who internalized the basic concept of the investigation.

Sōsen Endō was traumatized by the massacre of the Koreans. He walked in the post-quake ruins in Tokyo as one of the seventeen investigators and during this time he asked himself a question about what makes a good deed. As an investigator, Endō was at the crossroads of history. The system of national mobilization, at the time of emergency, was developing rapidly, and in that sense, he would possibly be in the historical stream of national mobilization, which started in the restoration after the earthquake.

9
How Does the Village Express Local Knowledge
Akira Furukawa

Introduction

'*Gōshū Chinai-mura 'Kiroku'* ('Records' of Chinai Village, Gōshū)', (hereinafter referred to as '*Kiroku*'), is a village diary which is still being kept in a small village in the Chinai District of Makino-chō, Shiga Prefecture, an area located on the west shore of Lake Biwa.[1] Notes on a slip of paper put between the pages of a volume, which contain records from the end of the Edo period, say that Mr Toshinao Yoneyama visited the village in 1967 and read the *Kiroku*.

Regarding the repair of records (written by Nakagawa Tajū in August 1978)
August 1978: As the festivals of a shrine dedicated to Kannon, known as Karasaki Okunoin and located in the precincts of An'yōji Temple, have declined in recent years, volunteers from *Chinai Rōjin Kurabu* (Chinai Senior Citizens' Club) gathered and investigated ancient events of the Kannon shrine in an effort to revive those festivals, and they found that this thin volume is the oldest record book.

There are older records but they are fragmentary and none seem to have been organized in chronological order. This book thus seems to be the first volume of the records. As the cover has been torn off, we decided to create a new cover.

Since the records contained in the book agree with the research records found in NHK Books No.65, *Nippon no mura no hyakunen* (One hundred years of Japanese villages), published by Japan Broadcast Publishing Co. Ltd. (written by Mr Toshinao Yoneyama,

Assistant Professor of Kōnan University), part of this book is extracted and recorded below for future reference.

The *Kiroku* is currently kept by the head of the district, and it seems to have been always kept by the village chief serving at the time when a given article was written. The oldest *Kiroku* was written in 1745 and the record keeping diary system has been kept continuously to this day. The *Kiroku* consists of the following volumes: fourteen volumes which were produced from 1745 to 1973 and are retained in the village archives; thirty volumes which were produced from 1974 to 2003 and are retained in the community center; and one volume being kept by the current head of the district. These volumes have been recognized by their respective writers as the same type of documents, and every time a volume became too bulky a note was written saying that the volume was closed and a new one would be started. For example, the volume commenced in the sixth year of the Ansei era (1859) begins as follows:

> Since the former record book was used for a long time and became too bulky, we decided to start a new record book in the 6th year of Ansei. I hereby pass on to my successor that the former record book should be referred to for older events (Furukawa and Itō 1992b).

Though the contents have been changing gradually, the *Kiroku* mainly describes events in the village. This means that the *Kiroku* is a 'diary of the village itself,' which has kept records of events occurring in the village, as one and the same series of documents, for at least 250 years.

Read carefully, these records reveal that the village has always been the subject of investigation, from both the inside and the outside, since the age of the shogunate system and this system of record keeping has continued to this day. Thus the history of the village can be described as a history of investigations. Moreover, I wish to propose that the history of the village viewed through this history of investigations—where the village is both the subject of investigation and the investigator—will reveal how its people have lived their lives.

The investigations can be classified roughly into two categories. One consists of those which the ruler conducted either directly or indirectly through the village. In this case the ruler needed to know the village in order to rule it. A national census is one example of this type of investigation. For instance:

20 November [1920]: The national census was conducted in Shiga prefecture also, and three census takers were appointed for Ōaza Chinai (Furukawa and Itō 1989b: 133).[2]

The other category consists of investigations conducted out of the village's own necessity to know itself. Examples of this include a survey of the number of grasshoppers in the area—seen as pests—and an examination of wind and flood damage, a topic discussed at greater length later in this paper. For example:

September [1937]: Rice farming was severely damaged by a major outbreak of grasshoppers. We thus considered various means of extermination and, as a result, decided that all households in Chinai should bring 2 *shō* (3.6 litres) of dried grasshoppers per household to the assembly hall by the end of September. Grasshoppers so collected amounted to 2 *koku* 6 *to* 1 *shō* and 4 *gō* (470 litres) in total. As the farmer's cooperative decided to purchase these grasshoppers at the rate of 10 *sen* for 1.8 litres, we sent them to the farmer's cooperative on 5 October and received 26 *yen* and 14 *sen* as the price on 20 February of the following year. We distributed the money on 27 February to each of those who had brought grasshoppers (Furukawa and Itō 1992b: 234).

As has been discussed, most of the descriptions in the *Kiroku* are extensive records of investigations into events that occurred in the village. This paper will examine more closely, those documents which recorded the investigations of floods, undertaken by the village. These floods occurred mainly during the period from the end of the Edo period to the Meiji era. By citing sections of these documents, wherever appropriate, the paper will explore how the village, as the intermediate structure between families or individuals and the state, reacted to and dealt with, the process through which Japan was transformed from the nation, under the shogunate system through the Meiji Restoration, to a modern nation state. In addition, through this discussion, the paper intends to consider the meaning of the 'investigations' from the viewpoint of the village.[3]

The village's quiet life and 'investigations'

Just like a family, a village is a unit, which aims for permanent existence and continuity. It is of course also possible to discuss functional aspects of a village or a family, but these factors can never be independent variables on which the continuing permanent existence of the village depends. It is significant that Kizaemon Aruga ([1948] 1969: 176) understood a village as an association of families and saw that a village had no choice but to exist as this association, in the sense that the permanent existence of the village was required for families' permanent existence and vice versa.

The fact that a village is a unit whose ultimate aim is to sustain itself means that the environment in and outside a village is maintained for the sole purpose of its 'continuity.' This is what a quiet life is for a village. Uchiyama Takashi has pointed out that:

> In order for 'me' as a unique human being to live a quiet life, my 'village' and 'nature' as our communal space-time must live their quiet lives and mutual relationships among these parties in this space-time must exist in peace (Uchiyama 1998: 52–53).

In other words, living a quiet life is simply natural for a village and also represents its zero point in the sense that anything more than that is an excess and anything less than that is a shortage. A shortage is a misfortune itself, but an excess is also regarded as an omen of misfortune, and a village at large works to achieve the zero point. Therefore, everything about the village has needed to be known and everything known has had to be recorded. Each village has developed its know-how for these activities; in Chinai Village, investigations described below were conducted and the *Kiroku* was kept.

In this paper, partly because the materials are limited to the 'village' diary, I will not discuss 'the individual villager as a unique human being.' Rather I will consider, based on the manner of the investigations of the village, how the quiet life of the village and village families have been maintained.[4]

Let me describe briefly an outline of the historical and structural location of Chinai Village (currently Chinai District). Chinai District was an independent village throughout the age of the shogunate system, but it was merged into Dai-1-ku, Takashima-gun, Dai-6-Daiku (the first District, Takashima County, the sixth Ward), Inugami Prefecture by the imposition of the *daiku-shōku* (ward-district) system in 1872. After another reorganization through the enforcement of the *gun* (county) system in 1879, it was put under the jurisdiction of Shinbo-mura Hoka 6-ka Mura Kochō Yakuba (Shinbo Village and Other 6 Villages' Heads Office) by the imposition of the *rengō kochō* (joint heads) system in 1885. Further, Chinai Village was consolidated with five other villages into Momose-mura through the *chō-son* (town-village) system introduced in 1898, followed by the consolidation into Makino-chō as a result of the town-village consolidation enforced in 1955. Although Chinai 'village' has been subject to these changes in the administrative framework, it seems to have existed continuously as an autonomous unit, as evidenced by the existence of its *Kiroku*. It has been confirmed that, at least in many villages in Shiga Prefecture, their organization and administrative framework as a village, from before the Meiji era, has not been completely broken down, but has been kept to this day, to some extent, despite the expansion of changing administrative sections. A village, whose framework has been kept, although it is no longer a village in administrative terms, will hereafter be referred to as '*mura.*'

In Chinai Village, the Shintō organization *Moroto* (*Miyaza*) overlapped with the village's dominant political organization *Osabun* until the Taishō era. In other words, Shintō affairs and political affairs intersected with each other. These Shintō and political affairs; however, were separated from each other due to pressures from both inside and outside the village, and the former control of the *Osabun* gradually transformed itself. Under the control of the *Osabun*, Shintō and political affairs were directly administered by the village. The village bylaw contained provisions on Shintō affairs, and both Shintō and political affairs were conducted as *muragoto* (village affairs). Under the impact of modernization; however, village affairs were gradually divided into 'family affairs' and 'administration,' while at the same time their functions were reduced, and in some contexts ended up virtually disappearing.

Neighborhood associations and districts function as the smallest units of administrative organization, and basically the central government is directly connected to each household. This has lead to the proposition which argues that the externalization of household affairs has increased the personal nature of social affairs. However, this theoretical explanation of current urbanization and modernization in Japanese society as a whole, is not always sufficiently persuasive, as evidenced by communities like Chinai District where the community has remained relatively significant. Rather, in recent years we have seen cases where 'village affairs,' 'household affairs' and 'personal affairs,' function through each other for the maintenance of the community. Nevertheless, as this is not the main concern of this paper, I will not discuss this interesting idea in detail here, it is an area for future consideration.[5]

Floods and village investigations

Of all the articles contained in the *Kiroku* of Chinai Village that have been discovered so far, the oldest ones are '*Enkyō 2-nen ushi 8-gatsu meisaichō* (Compendium of Chinai Village 1745)' and '*Kenchi-chō utsushi* (Copy of cadastral survey).' It is inferred that the preceding record book had become too bulky, so on the occasion of starting a new one, they recorded a then current compendium of the village in the new book.

Let us have a look at the articles on floods in the following records. In 1803 the Tokugawa government conducted '*Seta kawasuji go-kenbun* (Survey of Seta River)' and checked the yields of villages around the shores of Lake Biwa. In 1805 Inou Tadataka, who had been assigned by the Tokugawa government to conduct (and had been conducting), topographical surveys all over Japan, undertook a large-scale survey.

> 13 September 1805: The survey magistrate Mr Inou Tadataka and three others from Edo visited the village on a tour from the east of Lake Biwa. Two seniors from Chinai Village paid a visit to their abode. They surveyed various places, mainly village roads along Lake Biwa (Furukawa and Itō 1992b: 105).

As if the village reacted to the topographical surveys being conducted by the Tokugawa government and others, Chinai Village, which suffered flood damage almost every year, generated its own detailed data on this subject. Based on this data, the village continuously filed complaints with the local magistrate's office about the extent of the flood damage. We can learn that in 1807 the village suffered flood damage because of heavy rains, despite their construction of an embankment, and that they obtained rice aid which had been stored by the *daimyo* in preparation for the disaster.

> 23 May 1807: On this day the rain became heavier at night, and the Chinai River's bank on the Chinai Village's side collapsed over more than 90 metres. That was somehow repaired, but it continued to rain heavily on the first, second and third of June, which caused Lake Biwa to flood into many rice fields, spoiling the rice...Regarding this flood, the village was granted 50 sacks (3,000 kg) of rice by the lord (Furukawa and Itō 1992b: 106).

During this period, the village frequently investigated defective sites around the pipes and the river and kept detailed records of these inspections. For example, in 1,815 collapsed sites were recorded:

> 27 June 1815: Collapsed sites are detailed below:
> 1. Hattanda, Momose River: 5 metres out of 49 metres in length completely collapsed
> 2. Mizutakekurumazutsumi, Chinai River: Part of 27 metres in length half-collapsed. (Furukawa and Itō 1992b: 63).

They then filed documents, describing these collapsed sites, with the local government and requested aid, in response to which the local magistrate's office conducted an inspection and provided the village with rice aid in accordance with the scale of the collapsed sites.

Part of the *Kiroku* written during the age of the shogunate system contains extensive descriptions of exchanges of information between the village and the local magistrate's office obtained from these investigations and inspections of defective sites. In these exchanges, the village conveyed its viewpoint by delivering official letters titled '*Osorenagara kakitsuke wo motte negaiage tatematsurite sōrō* (A petition hereby most humbly filed).' The *Kiroku* contains copies of these letters as well as records of the investigations undertaken by the village.

Not surprisingly, however, these local activities of the village, undertaken in response to the flood caused by Lake Biwa, were only makeshift measures. It was also necessary to collect similar data that had been accumulated in neighboring villages and take action on a larger scale. How these activities were carried out can be read in an article written in 1831.

The flooding which had been damaging the village was caused by the shallow nature of the Seta River, the only river flowing from Lake Biwa. Accordingly, a petition requesting dredging of the river was repeatedly filed for many years by four generations of Tarobē of the Fukamizo Village. The delight upon the long-awaited acceptance of the petition and the implementation of an inspection by the Tokugawa government is described in the article (Furukawa and Itō 1994a: 179–80).

The *Kiroku* reads that in March of the following year (1832), the villages involved provided drawings and plans and progressed towards carrying out the dredging works. In June, a detailed lakeshore survey was conducted. Piling and other measures were also undertaken, as changes were expected to occur on the lakeshore as a result of the proposed dredging which would lower the water level of the lake.[6]

However, in November of the same year, an intriguing article was written titled '*Ōtsu Ishihara Kiyozaemon-sama ikken no koto* (The incident of Mr Ishihara Kiyozaemon of Ōtsu).' It describes the incident where Mr Ishihara Kiyozaemon conducted the aforementioned inspection and on that occasion included certain lands in the calculation of the recognized yield of the village. This was despite the fact that these lands had not been previously included in this calculation. Chinai Village raised an objection, and it was accepted. When the village raised this objection, they made use of the records of investigations which had been conducted many times by the village, as well as utilizing copies of their letters which had been delivered to the local magistrate's office in order to authorize these records (Furukawa and Itō 1994a: 187).

The fact that the village conducted their own investigations and maintained detailed records; that they, under pressure, authorized these records in the form of letters titled '*Osorenagara kakitsuke wo motte negaiage tatematsurite sōrō* (A petition hereby most humbly filed)'; and that they retained these letters in the village archives as their data, all helped to support the village's claim and allegations.

In many cases, a letter was duplicated and one copy was retained by the village probably out of fear that their data might be taken away by the local magistrate's office or the Tokugawa government. It was rare, however, that these letters were copied to documents like the *Kiroku* of Chinai Village, together with descriptions of the background of these letters. These documents remain to this day. In other words, the *Kiroku* of Chinai Village not only describes events which occurred in the village but also serves as an index of the official documents delivered by the village and a list of the investigations they conducted. This is why every time a record book was closed and a new one was commenced, the beginning of the new book has a note, together with a compendium of the village, to the effect that the record book had been renewed and that the former record book should be referred to for older events. Later, flood damages were recorded in March 1860, May 1866 and June 1867, before the start of the Meiji era.

Disasters and measures undertaken by the village

Even after the start of the Meiji era, as far as the *Kiroku* reads, nothing seems to have happened; no change in the manner of description is noted and it seems as though the shogunate system continued unchanged in this village. The first article written in the Meiji era was on the replacement of guardians of the village shrine (the post was rotated among villagers).

> 5 June 1868: As the younger brother of Gendayū, the current guardian of the village shrine, passed away, *Kumigashira* (magnates of the village) held a meeting and drew lots to decide the next shrine guardian, which fell on Shichizaemon. The magnates then got dressed in full costume and brought the new shrine guardian items necessary for him to take over the post (Furukawa and Itō 1988a: 47).[7]

In 1871 an article titled '*Otonosama owakare* (Departure of the lord)' of the local magistrate's office was recorded, marking the end of the shogunate system in the village (Furukawa and Itō 1988a: 54). An article written in 1873 titled '*Shiga-ken kan'in mura ni on-mawari shikashite on-shirabe no utsushi* (A copy of records of investigation around the village conducted by administrative officials from the Shiga prefectural government) shows that the administrative officials conducted their first investigation of the village. In 1875 another investigation was conducted for Land Tax Reform (Furukawa and Itō 1988a: 55). In 1876 a new record book of the *Kiroku* was commenced, which begins with the following record of political reform:

> As this record book faces a major reform of the Japanese Empire, many of the affairs in the village still remain the same as they have been under the old system, which has caused much confusion. In addition, as the preceding volume of the *Kiroku* is becoming too bulky, we decided to start a new record book. Please refer to the former volume for events in the past (Furukawa and Itō 1988a: 59).

This is followed by a detailed transcription from older records of data generated during the age of the shogunate system, followed further by lengthy records of land tax data as the Land Tax Reform conducted in 1875 'completely abolished the traditional method of tax payment in rice and demanded that three per cent of land price should be paid as land tax depending on the land value assessed by investigation' (Furukawa and Itō 1988a: 60).

At the same time, Chinai Village left its first description of the change from the shogunate system to the Meiji government as a description of the changing administrative units and rulers. Upon the start of the new administrative unit, matters to be handed over were written down as follows:

> March 1872: Household registers subject to handover and persons registered:
> 1. Number of households: 103 households. (Including 3 temples).
> 2. Total number of persons: 521 persons. (Including 251 males, including 1 permanently disabled and 3 priests).
>
> The End (Furukawa and Itō 1988a: 62).

As seen in the phrase 'household registers subject to handover,' the village was 'handed over' from the Tokugawa government to the Meiji government. This was followed by a series of investigations of paddies and fields, mountain forests, rivers, riverbeds, roads, public hygiene and the like, by Shiga Prefecture and other administrative bodies. Although no longer in the form of letters, data from these investigations are detailed in the *Kiroku*. Along with this succession of investigations, the village received a series of notifications from the government (Furukawa and Itō 1988a: 63).

As early as 1870, the allocation of river improvement expenses between the government and the village community was determined. Accordingly, all expenses for improvement of Chinai River and Momose River, the major rivers marking the southern and northern boundaries, respectively, of Chinai Village (Ōaza Chinai), were to be borne by the government, while improvement of small rivers flowing within the village were to be borne by the community. The fact that the allocation of river improvement expenses was determined earlier than the handover of household registers and the issuance of land certificates, probably shows that the improvement of rivers and pipes, mentioned frequently in both the official letters and the *Kiroku*, was the subject of utmost importance for a rural community at that time.

For farming villages around Lake Biwa where they suffered flood damage and severe storms almost every year, this allocation of expenses between the government and communities was critical not only to the villages' economy, but also to its life. For example, the issue of improvement of the Suta Creek, mentioned in an article written in 1939, was one of the problems initiated by the allocation, and only to be exposed nearly some seventy years later (Furukawa and Itō 1991: 171).

Let us go back to the articles on flood damage. Even after the start of the Meiji era, the dredging of the Seta River failed to control water levels sufficiently, leaving Chinai Village vulnerable to flood damage. A complaint about collapsed embankments, resulting from a typhoon in September 1870, was still filed with the local magistrate's office. The complaint was accompanied by a detailed list of collapsed sites found by the investigation. The situation was described as follows:

> 18 September: A storm raised the lake water level by about two metres, and most of the rice fields were covered with water (Furukawa and Itō 1988a: 50–1).

The next flood damage in the Meiji era was recorded in 1880 and was of a small scale. This was followed by a major flood which occurred in 1885.

> It rained continuously during May 1885, and there was still a lot of rain during June. On 30 June Lake Biwa overflowed due to heavy rain and 80 per cent of the rice fields were flooded. The number of submerged houses rose to 73 (the Nakagawa family's document) (Furukawa and Itō 1988a: 75).

This major flood damage, where the majority of the village's one hundred-odd houses were flooded, was dealt with by the village community as follows:

> The 7th [of May 1885]: The water of Lake Biwa gradually rose, and the poor did not have enough food even to last the day and asked for help. After deliberation, seniors of the village decided to loan the village's *shasoumai* (rice stored in preparation for disaster) until autumn (Furukawa and Ito 1988a: 82).

> September [1885]: Villagers' daily lives had become very difficult because of the flood damage. Accordingly, the village community decided to give special permission to villagers other than seniors to use the common forests which are usually not available for them except on special days (Furukawa and Itō 1988a: 83).

We can see that, at the village community's discretion, '*shasoumai*' was used to aid the needy and in September they gave permission to the villagers to use brushwood and undergrowth in the common lands, despite the fact that they were usually not available at that time of year. Meanwhile, the central government dispatched investigation commissions one after another and provided financial support.

The damage caused by this flood, however, was so serious that it could not possibly be covered by these conventional measures taken by the village or by support from the government alone. In other words, the village's quiet life was under threat. Chinai Village community broke down its conventional system and proceeded to take measures against disasters and, as their first priority, to aid the poor. These measures included the establishment of the 'the fishing system specifically for the poor,' which was a totally new system for allocating village property.[8]

> *Yana* trap fishing in Chinai River had been available for all Chinai villagers, whether rich or poor and its proceeds had been called *murakasegi* (village income) and had been distributed equally to all villagers who participated in it. Meanwhile, due to the flood damage in June 1885, the village had the misfortune of having most of the villagers' houses flooded. In particular, the difficulty experienced by the poor was beyond description. Their misery was such that any conventional help from the village would still have resulted in starvation. Accordingly, Gengo Nakagawa and Goyomo Torii, the village representatives at that time, consulted with each other with much heartache and agony and, as a result, assembled the villagers and proposed to them that starting from the latter period of the year the traditional *murakasegi* should be abolished and a system should be established under which only the poor without assets can engage in fishing and obtain proceeds from it, in order to provide them with a means of survival. Their proposal received unanimous approval of the villagers. This resulted in the enforcement of the fishing system for the poor, which continues to this day. As the proceeds are still regarded as part of the village's property; however, they decided to appoint two representatives by village election to be in charge of accounts and other affairs. In addition, fishing people have been saving deposits (as prescribed in Article 3, Paragraph 2 of the Chinai Village Code of Savings Association) from their fishing proceeds, as rental charges for fishing equipment and other property, in accordance with the number of non-fishing people with assets (at least 36 *sen* per person per year) (*Chinai Gyogyō Kumiai enkaku-shi* (The history of Chinai Fishermen's Association) nd: 31).

The requirements of the fishing system for the poor were that the traditional *murakasegi* should be abolished; fishing should be made available exclusively for the poor who did not have assets; and fishing proceeds should be distributed among these fishing people to provide them with a means of survival. Chinai River, which flows along the northern boundary of Chinai Village (the boundary with Nishihama Village), has runs of *ayu* fish (*Plecoglossus altivelis*) and trout. *Yana* is a type of fish trap installed about one hundred meters upstream of the river's mouth. Proceeds from *yana* had been distributed equally to all villagers as *muragaksegi*. The village community intended to overcome their fellow villagers' plight by making this village income available exclusively for the poor who did not have any assets. Moreover, this measure was intended to be established as a system that would continue into the future.

Does this, then, represent alms from those with assets to those without? Whether or not we view this drastic change in the village's system, as a program to give alms to the poor, will make a significant difference in our view of what the normal system of the village should be. Thus, we need to give this point more detailed consideration.

Article 3 of the 'Chinai Village Code of Savings Association,' mentioned at the end of the last excerpt says, 'the amount to be saved shall be deposited each year in accordance with the following minimum requirements,' and specifies amounts to be saved. Paragraph 2 of the same article stipulates the amounts to be saved by different categories of members:

1. *Yana* fishermen: At least two per cent of their annual fishing proceeds
2. Other fishermen: At least thirty-six *sen* per year
3. Those falling under both of the preceding two items: The total sum of the amounts specified in the preceding two items (*Chinai Gyogyō Kumiai enkaku-shi* (The history of Chinai Fishermen's Association) nd: 44).

Despite this list, *yana* fishermen were required, in reality, to save two percent of their catch of a year, plus thirty-six sen, the amount required for 'other fishermen.' Who on earth are the 'other fishermen?' Let us take a look at Article 2 of the Code of Association.

> Article 2: The Association shall be established for the purpose of protecting aquatic resources and regulating fishing operations. To achieve this purpose, *any and all persons who live in Chinai Village shall join the Association*. In January of each year, members who shall be permitted to fish shall be determined by dividing members into active members and non-active members (*Chinai Gyogyō Kumiai enkaku-shi* (The history of Chinai Fishermen's Association) nd: 44).

These provisions mean that it is mandatory for 'any and all' residents of Chinai Village to join the Association as fishermen. These fishermen will then be divided into 'non-active' and 'active members,' and those who have been categorized as non-active can become active members at any time if the economic circumstances of their lives have become difficult. Whether a person is a 'non-active' or 'active' member will be determined in January of each year.

Although it might have been impossible, it was assumed that any villager could become poor at any time. If they did, then they would be 'provided with a means of survival' by being granted the 'right' to this 'income.' The fact that life security in the village was provided for as a villager's right is extremely significant. It means that under this system in Chinai Village, even if certain villagers were described as poor, it was nothing more than a description of their temporary condition, and a system had been established under which these people would be entitled, by right, to support from the village at any time.

At the same time, it can be understood that the various stabilizing systems in the village, developed under the shogunate system, started to change into activities which aimed to ensure the village's permanent existence and quiet life. Because the village was now placed within the modern nation, it had to determine its position relative to that nation.

The nation and the investigation of the village

Let us go back to the discussion on flood damage. After suffering minor flood damage several more times, at the end of 1895 a representative of the Emperor visited Chinai Village for an inspection. From then on, a representative of the Emperor visited the village for an inspection every time the village suffered major flood damage. The term 'Emperor' was used for the first time in the following context in the *Kiroku*:

> Chamberlain Kataoka, a representative of the Emperor, inspected the collapsed sites of the embankment and the miserable state of the houses (Furukawa and Itō 1988b: 80).

The following year (1896) was another year in which a new record book of the *Kiroku* was commenced. The new record book begins as follows: 'As there is no more space to enter records in record book No.3, we decided to set up record book No. 4' (Furukawa and Itō 1988b: 81).

In July of that year, Chinai Village suffered the most disastrous flood damage that it had ever experienced.

> It rained continuously from the middle of July 1896, and around 10 August Chinai River overflowed and started to flood residential lands. By 30 August most of the residential lands in Chinai Village had been flooded. In addition, a stormy southeast wind caused damage to houses, resulting in two completely destroyed, six half-destroyed, and ten seriously damaged houses. The heavy rain on 6 and 7 September caused river flooding everywhere in the village, and [although many houses held out somehow] on 11 September the water level of Lake Biwa rose by as much as 3.6 meters, leaving most houses flooded two metres above the floor, with some houses deeply flooded above the roof. Not a single house seemed to have survived the rain without some flooding. A stormy southeast wind blew from around 4:00 p.m. that day. People attempted to somehow save their property from their flooded houses, but the current was so powerful that many had no choice but to simply escape. It was just like war; some attempted to save their property by rowing a boat up to their house, while women and children were heard crying…Although some houses did survive being swept away, very few people remained in their house. Paddies and fields which were about to be harvested were devastated. What little rice plants that had happened to survive were found unacceptable because they had been under water. Wheat was successfully harvested, but pulses were infested with insects and produced no crop. There was no vegetable crop at all (Furukawa and Itō 1988b: 83).

In the next article, 'names of villagers who received wind and flood relief money from the Emperor and amounts received' are listed with their full names, and also accompanied by a detailed description of the damage. By the time the 'flood damage inspection by the head of [the] county [was conducted] on the 17th,' the village had had a nearly perfect grasp of the extent of the damage (Furukawa and Itō 1988b: 84–5). Similarly, after flood damage was suffered in 1899, fourteen damaged sites were listed in the *Kiroku* with a description of the extent of the damage, followed by an article reporting that difficult restoration work had been completed. Also because there was a succession of floods, this restoration work, financed by 'grants for planning' from the prefecture government, took more than half a year to be finished (Furukawa and Itō 1988b: 80).

In 1889—between the flood damage in 1885 and that of 1896—the *chō-son* (town-village) system was imposed, whereby Chinai Village was consolidated with five other villages into Momose Village. In other words, Chinai Village ceased to exist as such. In March of the following year; however, Chinai Village community revised their own village bylaw and established '*Momose-mura Ōaza Chinai Jūmin Moushiawase Kisoku* (the Bylaw by Agreement among the Residents of Ōaza Chinai, Momose Village).' Their intention was described in the preamble of the bylaw as follows:

> The town-village system was enforced in April 1889. The residents have the right and obligation to comply with the bylaws and regulations promulgated by the public office, and it is only fair for them as citizens to work for public projects. Unlike urban communities; however, rural village communities are under different, individual circumstances. Accordingly, we have established this bylaw by agreement among the residents themselves, which shall be enforced for six years starting this year (Furukawa and Itō 1994b: 180).

This was a declaration that because Chinai Village had its own good reasons to do so, it would maintain its autonomy as Chinai Village. This village had had no bylaws before then. The self constructed bylaw described an excellent functional system for conducting '*muragoto* (village affairs)' of various events which had been detailed previously in the *Kiroku*.[9] The bylaw was revised in 1897 and 1902 and gradually became more extensive. The 1917 version of the bylaw included more than one hundred articles (Furukawa and Itō 1994b).

The functional system of the village, as described in these versions of bylaws, shows the fact that a village under the shogunate system was able to intentionally transform itself, through these bylaws and their revisions, into a village located within a modern nation state. The type of activities undertaken by the village in order to intentionally create their 'own' village, while at the same time being incorporated into the larger administrative framework through the town-village consolidation, are illustrated by, for example, the creation and operation of the 'fishing system for the poor,' discussed earlier. These activities aimed to both create and ensure the permanent existence and quiet life of the village. They were based on their experience of the past, or, I would venture to say, were based upon the body of accumulated knowledge about the village and the villagers, which had accrued over time through their numerous investigations. This is why

Chinai Village, even if called Ōaza Chinai, had to be chosen instead of Momose Village.

Continuity of the village and its relationship with the state

Before going back to the discussion of flood damage, let us review some of the changes in the village's administrative structure by examining the bylaws. In 1902 the bylaw underwent another revision. In the 1897 version of the bylaw, *Osabun*, who had been the village's magnates since the age of the shogunate system, and *Morotō*, who had been Shintō ritual participants and members of *Miyaza*, had positions in the administration of the village. In fact, *Osabun* and *Morotō* consisted of almost entirely overlapping members. For instance:
1. Osabun shall be at least twenty-five years old, shall own his own home, and shall own land valued at 400 yen or more.
2. Any charge collected from Shintō ritual participants pursuant to the *Morotō* rules shall be included in consulting expenses (Furukawa and Itō 1994b: 183).

However, the revision in 1902 resulted in the abolition of both *Osabun* and *Morotō*:

> All deliberations and decisions under this bylaw have conventionally been made by reading *Osabun* as *Kumigashira*, but the resolution passed at the general meeting of Chinai Village on 26 April 1902 abolished *Kumigashira* (Furukawa and Itō 1994b: 187).

This meant that the village, which had been under the shogunate system where political affairs and Shintō affairs were inseparable and overlapped with each other, transformed itself into a more modern autonomous district. This response also represented a continuation of the subtle capacity of the village to retain some elements of autonomy, even while being incorporated more strongly into the state.

On the other hand, these movements of the village can be seen also as an indication of the struggle between the forces attempting to maintain self-government and those aiming at state control. The state established various systems and structures necessary for a nation state, including the Diet, tax collection system, education, military forces, religious ceremonies and production systems. It also strongly promoted national standardization of people as its citizens in terms of their space, time, manners and customs, and physical aspects; and intended to position the village as the smallest unit of the nation's administrative organization. However, the village showed no intentional movements to strongly oppose the force of national standardization.[10]

New methods for reorganizing the village's living and functional systems in accordance with national standardization can be found everywhere in both the bylaws and the *Kiroku*. Nevertheless, despite the state's intentions, these documents clearly show the village's orientation for independence. This must be because the village was sensitive enough to understand that its permanent existence and quiet life could be assured only through the body of knowledge accumulated by the village itself. It could not be achieved by administration through the bureaucracy provided by the state, which only vaguely understood the village. In this context, the *Kiroku* served as a visible index of this body of knowledge.

Let us now go back to the discussion on flood damage. The article on the rainfall of 23 September 1912 is somewhat different from the other articles written before then. It says:

> At 8:00 p.m. on 23 September 1912, Chinai River gradually rose due to rainfall, and eight officers of the village were sent to protect the sites which had collapsed from previous floods. On the other hand, the head of the district and some others went to the prefectural office and negotiated about works needed on the sites...The rain became so heavy that it was difficult to prevent flooding by the officers' effort only. From the evening all residents were mobilized and carried old straw bags and ropes and worked to protect the sites with the straw bags...From around 3:00 a.m. on the following day (the 24th) Lake Biwa started to rise, and the fire brigade of Momose Village came to help and worked on flood prevention. The wind fell around 6:00 a.m., and all people who had been exhausted from all-night work were withdrawn from the sites to the assembly hall and were provided with breakfast. Still worried, *Nengyōji* (an officer) was sent to watch the sites and, sure enough, a collapsed site was found. Villagers worked on the site with the help of people from the adjacent village, but as it was not sufficient, staff members were sent from the prefectural office, the county office and the police station to carry out embankment work (Furukawa and Itō 1989a: 69).

Although the investigation of damage was conducted promptly by the village, disaster prevention activities, which had always been conducted by 'all district residents' led by *Nengyōji*, were joined by 'the prefectural office, the county office and the police station' which had sent their staff members to the village to help deal with the problem. It may seem that measures against disasters were finally being placed under administrative control. But later articles in the *Kiroku* still described the circumstances within the village where *Moroto*—the Shintō organization (religion), and *Nengyōji*—an intermediate position between the Shintō section and the political section, and the head and councillors of the district in charge of agricultural affairs (production and living), conduct activities in different situations.

If it rains continuously in Chinai, first *Nengyōji* is dispatched (as of 1939, 'embankment protection officials and *Nengyōji*') to conduct an investigation of the sites which have been collapsed in the past. If any site collapses later, first the village administration, including *Nengyōji*, conducts an on-site investigation and decides whether the problem should be dealt with by the village or a petition should be filed for the problem to be dealt with.

For example, there is no description as to who did what for 'damage to trees and field crops,' but 'half-destruction of the roofs of the shrine' was repaired by mobilizing 'all *Morotō* members for the time being' (Furukawa and Itō 1989a: 123). Some problems were dealt with by villagers who served as hands; 'sites damaged due to collapsed embankment' were repaired by 'youth association members from Momose Village who were on duty for emergent repairs;' and other problems were dealt with by all residents in the district (Furukawa and Itō 1989a: 123). By contrast, in those incidents where the embankments along Momose River or Chinai River had collapsed, on-site investigations were conducted by the chief of the Public Works Section of the prefectural government and repairs were made at government expense (Furukawa and Itō 1989b: 169).

No matter what authority ultimately controlled the village, the village kept its style of administration, in which everything was investigated, recorded and understood by the village, for at least 260 years during which the 'village diary' has been kept. The village community does not exactly resist the authority of the nation aggressively; in fact, they comply with the formalities by delivering letters to the local magistrate's office or by filing petitions with the Department of Interior through the prefectural governor. In either case, the response is based on data generated by the village itself. In many cases these are digital data expressed in figures. But upon closer examination of the investigation items it becomes clear these data are supported by a massive body of analogue experiential knowledge (life knowledge and everyday knowledge) which has been thus far accumulated and exists behind the digital data. Although we tend to intuitively regard local experiential knowledge as analogue data, digital and analogue data cannot be clearly distinguished from one another.

Chinai Village has not existed as a static entity but has kept transforming itself into a village which has consistently adapted to each of the different epochs. As seen in the documents, the villagers have dealt with flood damage, not by maintaining the village as something unchangeable, but by changing the borders of the village at will. These borders sometimes went beyond the boundaries of Chinai. For instance, they claimed as their domain, the new Momose Village which had been created as a result of the town-village consolidation, and they even claimed the entirety of Lake Biwa.

As the theory of the nation state suggests,[11] there are homogenizing forces at work as part of its construction and maintenance. While it is true that Chinai villagers have experienced many facets of nationally-standardized time and space, it is doubtful whether the village has been totally homogenized and standardized through these processes. The village was able to keep, at least until the pre-war period of the Shōwa era, its means to negotiate fairly with the state. It was able to do so by knowing itself, investigating and recording in meticulous detail, and accumulating and handing down information, by itself.

If the ability of the village to conduct investigations (the ability to collect information); to hand down information (the ability to record and hand down information); and to connect information with activities (the ability to process information and put this into practice), are referred to collectively as the village's investigation ability, I am strongly inclined to think that it is exactly this capacity that has supported its continued existence. There have been various arguments that emphasize Japanese villages' strong ability to continue to exist within the modern nation state. Is it not the villages' investigation ability, discussed thus far, that constitutes one major force that has enabled their continued existence? And furthermore '*mura*' as the village's own core, seen in the case of Chinai Village, has supported their investigation ability, and sometimes their information has been shared among different *mura* cores, enabling them to act as if they were a large collective entity.[12]

10
Discovering Happiness through Environmental Research Conducted by Local Residents
Yukiko Kada

'The ordinary life-world is fairly solid, tinged with immovable objectivity...[and]...has the prerogative to reject doubts' (Murakami 1979: 17–18). We do not usually ask ourselves questions such as: Why do we call this square shaped object in front of us a 'desk'? Whether it is called a 'bench' or a 'table,' the name is merely a 'symbol.' We do not question the name. At the same time, ordinariness has a deeply rooted 'nonverbal domain.' The size and material of a desk and even its position in a room, of say, a government office, 'tacitly symbolizes' the social role or status of the person who sits at the desk. It even conceals connotations like 'it is the desk that does the job,' for example, without explicitly saying so.

Moreover, as Polanyi noted: 'We can know more than we can tell' (Polanyi 1983: 4). He analyzed what tacit knowledge meant to physical acts, in particular. While Polanyi's concept of tacit knowledge is premised on an 'individualist' schema, Bourdieu looked at a system that generates collectively recognized customs, attitudes and conduct from social acts practiced over a long period. He called this 'habitus' (Bourdieu [1980] 1990: 52–65).

Many of us understand that 'desk' is a 'symbol' and 'representation' based on our everyday life experience, but rarely become aware of what sort of things are represented in a statement such as: 'This river is clean.' A casual statement such as this, however, has not-so-trivial and strong symbolic connections embedded within it. We have been led to believe that references to rivers, waters, mountains and the earth, regarded as part of the 'natural domain,' are representations of verifiable facts. Furthermore, environmental issues such as water pollution, now recognized as a social problem, are tacitly believed to be verifiable issues in themselves. These beliefs are in turn connected to the outlook on nature, reflected in the concept of the 'environment' in environmental sociology. I would like to look at all of this in more detail, using the water environment of Lake Biwa as an example.

The shadow of positivism in decontextualized discourses

In the mid-1970s, Lake Biwa was faced with a so-called water pollution problem. In 1977 it experienced its first red tide outbreak and it was feared that Lake Biwa might turn into a 'dead lake.' The theory that the pollution was caused by various organic matters such as phosphorus and nitrogen pouring in from the surrounding tributaries was put forward and a range of policy measures were introduced to control contamination from these substances. Among such measures, the Eutrophication Prevention Ordinance was introduced in 1980 and attracted public attention. It became known as the 'soap ordinance' that restricted the sale and use of 'phosphorous synthetic detergent.' In 1979 a citizens' movement developed in response to the growing concern about the issue of pollution in Lake Biwa. This movement culminated in the introduction of the soap ordinance, and was regarded as an environmental conservation movement of women. These were women, who until then, had few opportunities to have a say on social issues, and through their movement they contributed to what is now called the empowerment of women. While positive in many ways, this movement had contradictory effects and helped to create the perception that 'Lake Biwa's water is polluted,' an explanation that was taken out of its social context and widely circulated. In the end, what prevailed was a 'reductionist view of nature' that regarded phosphorus and nitrogen as the villains causing the water pollution.

In terms of the classical theory of 'value-free science,' it is the proper duty of water scientists to deal with the physical cycle of matters such as phosphorus and nitrogen; however, they cannot define what water pollution is. They can 'positively' define the scientific mechanism of a natural physical cycle but a decision circuit as to what level of water quality should be recognized as pollution rests on a social judgment.

Logical bases required for science are 'representativeness,' 'reliability (reproducibility)' and 'validity.' The issue of representativeness can be addressed temporarily with the concept of 'mean value.' In the real-life situation where it is impossible to measure the quality of all water in Lake Biwa all of the time, the lake is divided into uniformly sized grids, and water quality data for each section, measured over a certain period of time, are 'averaged' to ensure representativeness. Reliability is ensured by the enhancement of measuring accuracy so that repeated measurement of the samples of homogeneous quality should produce identical results.

In contrast, the establishment of validity involves a substantially more difficult process. The question here is whether it is appropriate to measure the levels of 'phosphorus' and 'nitrogen' in order to determine the 'water quality of Lake Biwa' in the first place. Lake water contains numerous substances. What is the reason to only select phosphorus and nitrogen from an endless number of these substances? Is it purely a chemical issue? Does the water quality issue not belong to the biological sphere inhabited by microorganisms and fish? Why are these creatures not analyzed as part of water quality analysis? One question leads to another. Even a mere 'definition of water quality' permits various judgments in such ambiguous chemical and biological contexts. How can the perception that 'Lake Biwa's water is polluted' be defined based on this?

Pollution risk: public policy and local residents

When the environmental pollution issue became a global topic in the 1970s and the early 1980s, cultural anthropologist Mary Douglas and her colleague argued that 'the risks involved in pollution are culturally defined' (Douglas and Wildavsky 1982). With the Lele society of Africa and the modern North American society in mind, Douglas pointed out that each society had its own set of values for the evaluation of social risks which were not exactly the same as technically definable pollution risks. She reported that such variances from technically measurable risks such as the death toll and mortality rate could be explained by factors such as lightening and infertility in the Lele and smoking and traffic accidents in the case of North Americans.

Phosphorus and nitrogen that are used as pollution indicators for the water quality of Lake Biwa are very ubiquitous elements and essential components of living organisms, including humans. They are non-toxic in themselves and totally different from harmful substances such as organic mercury, which caused Minamata disease. Fish cannot survive in water lacking phosphorus or nitrogen; they are essential elements for the ecosystem. Using these elements as the measure of 'pollution' is merely for the convenience of bureaucracy and science. In Japanese society today, 'social rules' are made so that 'pollution' is defined by the level of certain substances in excess of administratively determined 'environmental standards.'

In other words, pollution is a socially constructed concept and therefore positivist data can only provide information for decision making but cannot reveal the logic behind its definition. The problem here is that the concept of pollution has all the appearances of positivism because of this disregard for its social component. This can be explained by the invisibility of the specified pollution indicators. In normal living conditions, phosphorus and nitrogen are invisible to the eye. The level of invisible objects can only be calculated via a process of scientific instrumental measurement. Therefore, this creates a perception that any dealing with phosphorus or nitrogen levels in itself falls within the territory of science, and produces this societal perception that 'pollution is defined by science.' From there, a 'situational definition' is made by manipulating scientific knowledge administratively (Wakita 1995).

In such a situational definition dependence on 'outside experts in their white coats' tends to prevail. That is, people are inclined to rely on science or government bodies rather than on their own knowledge or experience when deciding, for example, whether the waterway in front of their house is clean or polluted. The 'white coat' here is merely a symbol that represents 'science.' Thus, a blind trust in the authority of scientific knowledge and an over-reliance on this form of knowledge in making decisions became widespread in the consciousness of local residents. This type of scientism reinforces the effectiveness of policy measures based on 'modern technologism' (Torigoe and Kada 1984), such as a sewerage policy to 'prevent water pollution by removing pollutants.' It lays the groundwork for a cognitive system which is very convenient for bureaucratic control and those who are trying to politically manipulate society with large-scale public work projects. In short, as long as we are dealing with measurable substances such as nitrogen and phosphorus, the existence of science and technology to 'control' them has a meaning. It provides a logical and political background for control theory.

The scientific judgment made by the bureaucracy about Lake Biwa's environmental issue was circulated with authority during the 1970s and 1980s. Based on a decontextualized and symbolized control-oriented discourse that 'Lake Biwa's water is polluted,' people became the 'subjects to be educated' by scientific knowledge, at schools and in communities. This control-oriented discourse and people's belief in it is not conducive to the creation of independent action to 'understand one's local environment and do something to improve it.'

In order to counter this way of thinking and understanding, we decided to formulate a social research method which would bring the context of everyday living into the scientific paradigm with which to consider how Lake Biwa and its water should be. We realized that the deeply and widely ingrained 'standardized knowledge system' could be unraveled only by trying to 'stay close' and 'shift the ground.' We used Miyamoto Tsuneichi's (1984) method of *kikigaki* (recording of interviews) and *kyōdo seikatsu no kenkyūhō* (folk life research method) by Kunio Yanagita (1935) as key elements of the research approach. Tadao Umesao's (1969) *chiteki seisan no gijutsu* (the art of intellectual production) was also utilized as well as the methods of Kada and Ōnishi (1992) for the sharing of scientific information.

Revelations from everyday life

We began our local environmental research of the Lake Biwa catchment area from a 'bird's eye' and an 'insect's eye' perspective, to use somewhat simple expressions from the early 1980s. From a bird's eye perspective, detailed local data for each of the 1,600 small communities were collected using the geographical information system being developed at the time and cross-referenced with 120 tributary areas around Lake Biwa to calculate pollution loads of phosphorus and nitrogen for each river. We used the results to consider whether an accumulation of scientific data could explain the pollution of Lake Biwa. This was the device used to 'stay close' to the situation in which the environment was defined in reductionist terms. It used the perspective of control theory. That was how the database called the Shiga Prefecture Regional Environmental Atlas was built.

At the same time, we began an interview based survey to find out how Lake Biwa and associated water areas were perceived and evaluated from the perspective of everyday life, by asking questions such as: 'How do you describe a waterside which is desirable for you?' It is called an insect's eye research and it is a device to 'shift the ground.' It also can be called a communicational 'empathic perspective' which focuses on questions to ascertain the perception of local residents.

What our bird's eye research has revealed is that the seemingly positivist pollution load calculation actually contains many 'arbitrary assumptions.' It contains socially constructed factors from the beginning. For example, an 'average value' from the representative sample has to be used as a unit data for everything from the amount of human waste to the amount of excretion by a livestock animal and the amount of industrial waste from a factory. Relationships between phenomena are also based on many rules and parameters. Therefore, a resultant water quality simulation model is just a 'temporary model for expediency' and is full of assumptions. It cannot prove the circulatory process of materials in the tributaries scientifically because even a slight change in assumptions can alter the result. In fact, our Lake Biwa water quality model, which was constructed with the most meticulously collected data that was possible in the 1980s, for which we devoted so much time and energy, is now faced with the need for major remodeling due to unexpected changes in the composition of planktons, and so on, later on.

On the other hand, what did our insect's eye research tell us? Its results can be summarized into the following four points. Firstly, people's perception of the environment was so loosely and expansively defined that it did not fit into the positivist and materialistic view of water quality criteria as proposed by the bureaucracy. The depth and expansiveness of perception is perhaps created by the local people's judgment that is based on their 'five senses.' For example, what people thought undesirable was visible 'rubbish' such as empty cans, cigarette butts and plastic bags scattered on the water's edge. In addition they were concerned about the state of water or beaches that they perceived with their five senses, as 'smelly,' 'slimy,' 'turbid' and those that had 'muddy sludge at the bottom' (Kada 1989). The materials perceived as 'rubbish' also included essentially natural materials such as 'aquatic plants' and 'reeds.' In this sense, we realized that rubbish is something that is constructed and defined socially and cannot be defined absolutely.

Secondly, we discovered the semantic structure of materials when we consider our life as a system. This is deeply connected to 'everyday-life experience.' Natural materials such as aquatic plants and reeds are now classified as rubbish but used to be perceived as the necessities for life and production. People used to scramble to collect aquatic plants which were useful materials for fertilizer production. Reeds were not totally wild since they were harvested and partly cultivated by people who used them to make household items. In other words, the meaning of 'rubbish' is not intrinsic to a material. A material becomes 'rubbish' when it is defined as 'unnecessary' in the context of its relationship with the life system of people. What is hidden underneath these changing perceptions is people's outlook on everyday life.

The third point was their assessment of aquatic life. When people talked about water pollution, they often referred to the level of prevalence of living creatures. They said: 'There used to be so many fireflies flying into my face here' or 'there used to be a myriad of small fish (like Japanese bitterling) here.' The creatures most commonly mentioned included firefly and some fish species such as bitterling, roach and killifish.

The fourth point was the context of everyday-life activity based on one's experiences on the waterfront. People say that 'water has become dirty' even though the water is clear and drinkable. Why? They say: 'Children used to play here but not any more,' or 'we used to get drinking water from here but can't do that now,' or 'we used to wash our clothes here but can't do it any more.' In other words, the water, which has 'lost its relevance' to their everyday-life activity in light of their personal experience, was perceived as 'polluted.' With the introduction of city water, washing machines and computer games, to keep children at home, the weakening of water's direct relevance to their daily life was expressed as 'water pollution' in terms of action theory.

This action based assessment of water pollution, built on personal experiences on the time axis, points to the limitations inherent in the current water pollution countermeasures, such as sewerage policy, undertaken by the bureaucracy at huge public financial cost. No matter how well a sewerage system is built and nitrogen and phosphorus are removed, the waterfront may not return to a desirable state for people as long as it has no relevance to their life activity. Children's perception, in particular, was deeply rooted in their 'relevance' to water. This raises a doubt about the proposed solution; imposing 'controls' on the influx of harmful substances may not enhance the value of the water area to the locals.

As a hypothesis, although somewhat schematic, we have summarized the environmental perception gap between scientists and local residents in Figure 10.1. Scientific knowledge emphasizes numbers and scientific causal relationships, aiming for the discovery of

Figure 10.1: Environmental awareness of residents and scientists

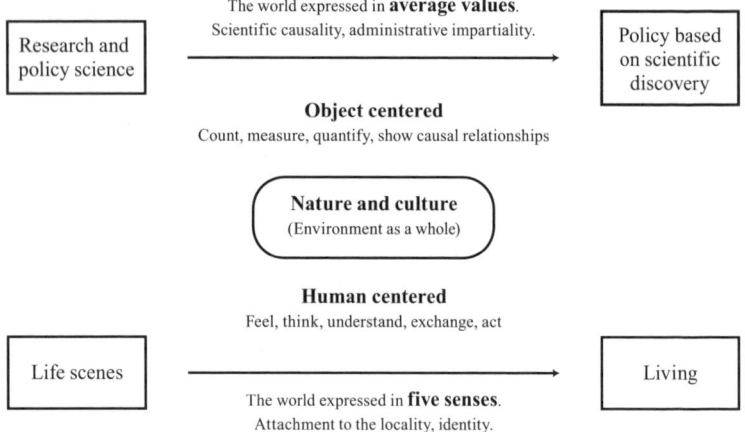

Source: Kada (1992b: 7)

phenomena and the offering of policy recommendations. This is penetrated by the 'control' principle to reduce the level of substances that define pollution. On the other hand, life knowledge developed at everyday life scenes tends to place more importance on experience-based perception formed by one's five senses and sensitivity, and this leads to the meaning of 'living' (Kada ed. 1992). It contains a structure of empathy with the water area and its creatures.

With this perception gap in mind, we devised an environmental study to be conducted by the local residents themselves so they could examine the state of their waterfront, recognize and understand its changes and restore their association with the water. This was for the purpose of verifying our hypothetical 'empathic structure.' I would like to discuss this process briefly here in relation to positivism and constructionism in sociological research and theory. We selected 'rubbish,' 'firefly,' 'water use' and 'play on the waterside' as our study themes, since they were most frequently referred to by the respondents in our field research.

From awareness to action

In 1989, we became involved in a research project with the residents of Gamō town on the east coast of Lake Biwa in response to their claim that the local waterways were polluted and were full of rubbish. We started from an exploratory study of waterways, which the residents called 'drains' from houses, together with elementary school children and senior citizens. It was a joint environmental study by different generations of people. It was not designed to be a 'rubbish cleanup' campaign but a waterway survey to observe and identify 'what materials were present in the waterways in what state.' Using their five senses, participants were encouraged to record the description of the smell and color of the water, sludge and fish, make detailed sketches of the materials in waterways and think about why they had ended up there. As a result, the participating children discovered that even sludge-filled waterways had living creatures in it, such as dragonfly nymphs and crayfish, and that some of the rubbish in the waterways was the packaging from their favorite snacks or empty cans from their fathers' favorite coffee.

We also discovered in a casual conversation with Akie Nishibori, a woman then in her sixties, that these waterways used to be called *mizokko* and they were where people washed their rice bowls and clothes. Mrs Nishibori did not deliberately use this expression; until then, at the government sponsored meetings, she had been calling them 'drains.' When she walked around the area and reminisced about life in the old days, the word *mizokko* (waterways) just popped out of her mouth. She herself was surprised to find that she had been calling them 'drains.' In fact, Mrs Nishibori was one of the leaders of the soap campaign, locally well known as a 'soap lady.' She had been calling the waterways 'drains' for a long time. In the social context of the soap campaign, she had been transformed, from someone who called them *mizokko* (waterways) to someone who called them 'drains,' without even noticing it. The idea of control was concealed in the expression.

When she began strolling along the waterways with us, however, and answering our questions about how the laundry and dishes were done in the old days, she remembered the expression *mizokko,* together with deeply rooted memories of her lifestyle that were so closely connected to the waterways. We can perhaps call it a kind of habitus shift. The drain is an administrative term to describe a waste water channel. Such an administrative term is based on the value system of control theory, within a reductionist view of nature mentioned earlier. By reviving the real meaning of the waterways—*mizokko*—at the scenes of everyday life which had deep empathy with the water, a complete relationship with people and water can be restored.

Using Kojiro Miyahara's expression, 'drains' is an 'impersonal word' and *mizokko* is a 'personal word' (Miyahara 2000). When

Mrs Nishibori recalled the personal word *mizokko*, the children's perception of the waterways also changed. The meaning that the waterways had to the lives of their parents and grandparents was revived, and revealed its relevance to the children themselves.

I describe this change in the psyche as the 'personalization of the environment' (Kada 2001). The waterways they used to ignore and perceive as dirty, as taught at school or by the bureaucracy, suddenly became familiar and friendly. The *mizokko* is a habitat for crayfish, dragonfly nymphs and other creatures. It has many items in it that had been thrown away by the children themselves. The children thought: 'Let us pick out these items ourselves.' Thus, a *mizokko* cleanup campaign was started. These children's action arose spontaneously from their thinking, rather than as a result of being initiated by adults.

The process of this change in the children's awareness and the emergence of action were named *tanken, hakken, hottoken* (explore, discover, action) by Mr Tadashi Isaka of Gamōhigashi Elementary School. It is a process of survey, discovery and thinking, and taking action (Isaka and Gamō Yakōgen Kurabu 2001). It shows the shift from awareness to action, where field research induced a deepening of thought and developed into action. As part of this process, the symbolic nature of linguistic expressions such as 'rubbish' and 'drains' was also questioned. Those materials washed up on the shore were defined as 'rubbish' in their relationship with people. For the children, reductionism represented by the word 'drains' was replaced by a more real, interactive relationship with the water and its environs when the word *mizokko* came back to life via Aunty Nishibori's reminiscence, during their walkabout together.

Here, my hypothetical schema shown in Figure 10.1 above was also destroyed by the dynamics in the field. I felt the thrill of witnessing the destruction and creation of a concept. About this time, I started to sense the possibility of 'empathy' rather than 'control.'

Humanization of fireflies

Many people expressed their association with the waterside through 'living organisms' as described in the previous section. One of the more frequently referred to organisms was the firefly, which was considered, at the time, to be the symbol of 'clean water.' The firefly could be a kind of 'reference organism' when people talked about changes in the waterside. Therefore, a series of questions were raised, including: to what extent the firefly population had decreased, if it indeed had decreased as the residents said; in which areas had the decrease occurred; what was the original habitat for the firefly like; and how did it relate to the lives of the locals?

In response to our appeal, almost 3,000 people living near Lake Biwa participated in a survey of waterways and rivers within the Shiga Prefecture over three years from 1989, amassing a total of about 50 000 survey days. As a result, we found that the firefly, previously believed to have vanished, was still surviving tenaciously in the waterways near built-up towns and overflow ditches of cultivated rice fields. People began to doubt the accuracy of hearsay information that the fireflies had disappeared and they also became skeptical about the widely held view that 'the firefly can only live in clean water.' Our distribution study also found that more fireflies lived near human settlements where waterways contained 'some levels of nutrients,' which means 'polluted,' rather than living in more pristine waters in the mountains (Yūma 1992). Another finding was the rather obvious fact that water flow was more important for firefly survival than water quality. Due to the advancement of land improvement in the catchment area, the flow of water stopped during the winter off-season of rice growing. It was found that the firefly population was significantly affected by this loss of 'permanent water.' We also realized that the importance of 'getting to know the environment around oneself,' lay in the discovery, by the local residents themselves, of the limitations of hearsay information and the multiple meanings of the environment.

At the same time, I, as the research coordinator, discovered that the firefly was a rather 'human' species deeply involved in the past personal relationships of the residents. The firefly triggered the memory in one person of going firefly catching with a childhood friend who later died during the war. In the night we found some fireflies, he said that it was as if his friend had come back. Another person remembered her father who used to bring many fireflies home for the children after patrolling his rice fields. Many people talked about their memories of weaving straw into a firefly basket, making a broom of empty mustard seed pods, and going firefly catching while singing a firefly song. They stated: 'As I wove firefly baskets, my mind was already in the world of the fireflies.' We realized that the firefly was a 'humanized insect' reflecting human relationships that were deeply rooted in people's everyday life (Kada 1992; Mizu to Bunka Kenkyūkai 2000). The new meaning of living organisms and the waterside, defined in the context of human relationships, was reinforced from this perspective.

Because the firefly is a human-like creature, people's motives for their participation in the firefly survey were naturally tinged with humanness. I kept asking the participants in conversations, at presentations and in questionnaires, to write why they had decided to participate in the survey. I found that there were two philosophically different types of people involved. One was those who had what I called the 'association-type' motive—the seekers of scientific knowledge who viewed the firefly objectively and sought to know its habitat as well as other scientific information. They had the association-type motive to gain 'knowledge about the habitat of the firefly.' The other included the 'community-type' people who related to the firefly as part of their social connections with people (Mizu to Bunka Kenkyūkai 2000). In simple terms, the former tends to be more interested in scientific knowledge for control and the latter is more empathy-oriented and is inclined to value connections between people and between the firefly and people.

What is important for the association-type people is finding out about the living conditions of the firefly, for instance: 'The firefly appears at the temperature of 20°C.' While the community-type people make comments like: 'Going out to observe the firefly with the whole family is the happiest moment for us.'

However, it gradually became clear to me that this classification by motives was merely an expedient measure. The initial motives of the participants gradually changed or evolved in the process of conducting their own research and exchanging findings with others. Figure 10.2 shows the motive evolution process for each type.

In each group, some keen researchers pursued their interest or involvement further. For example, among the scientific knowledge seekers there was Mr Masahiro Kumode of Santō Town. He accumulated his own data over many years, matching the biological data of the firefly with environmental data such as water and air temperatures, and wrote a scientific paper on forecasting the appearance of the firefly in conjunction with the landing season of the larvae. On the other hand, the community type people tended to place more emphasis on family and community relationships. Ms Noriko Arai of Ōtsu City was a typical example. She expanded the firefly observation activity to launch the Firefly Concert, which has been held annually during the firefly season, and involved more local children in the river conservation activity which still continues today.

Figure 10.3 is a schematic depiction of how the ecology of the firefly and the social relationships among people were developed through the

Figure 10.2: Relationship between the firefly and me (Dynamic model)

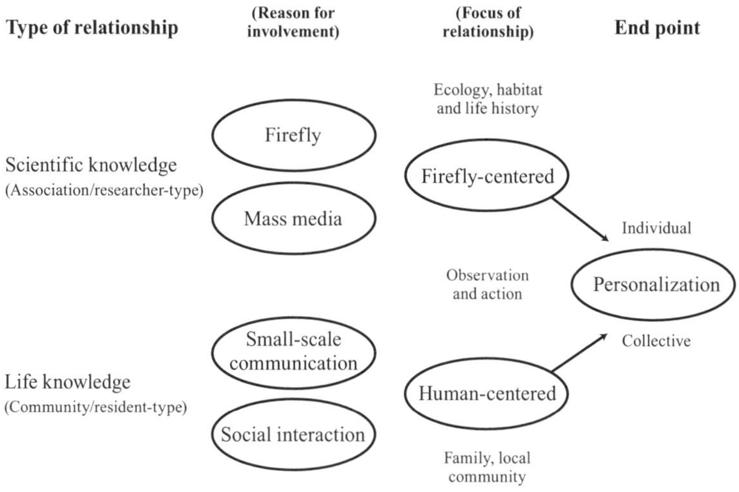

Type of relationship	(Reason for involvement)	(Focus of relationship)	End point
Scientific knowledge (Association/researcher-type)	Firefly / Mass media	Firefly-centered (Ecology, habitat and life history)	Individual → Personalization
Life knowledge (Community/resident-type)	Small-scale communication / Social interaction	Human-centered (Family, local community) — Observation and action	Collective → Personalization

Source: Kada (2000: 206)

medium of the firefly. These two worlds gave rise to new values in the field. For example, Mr Kumode had a tendency to seek scientific knowledge from the start, but what motivated him to forecast the commencement of the firefly season with the larvae landing was his desire, as a community member, to organize the town's firefly festival to exactly coincide with the appearance of the fireflies. He called the larvae landing observation gathering: 'Firefly larvae support gathering,' and this emotive expression helped to expand the circle of empathy among the locals. Here we can see that scientific control theory is resonating with life-empathy theory. The initially hypothesized dichotomy between science and life, and control and empathy, was resolved and sublimated.

Since then, both groups of people have been observing the firefly activity every season and the firefly observation is being 'personalized' now that it has become a sort of 'habit' for them. The firefly study, which began as a three-year project, is still going strong after more than fifteen years (as of 2004), with its study network being maintained and the annual report being published by a residents' group called *Mizu to Bunka Kenkyūkai* (Water and Culture Study Group). Many people appear to have discovered happiness in the firefly study. Their comments describing their feelings of happiness have been compiled into a book and published (Mizu to Bunka Kenkyūka 2000).

Figure 10.3: Relationship between the firefly and me (Static model)

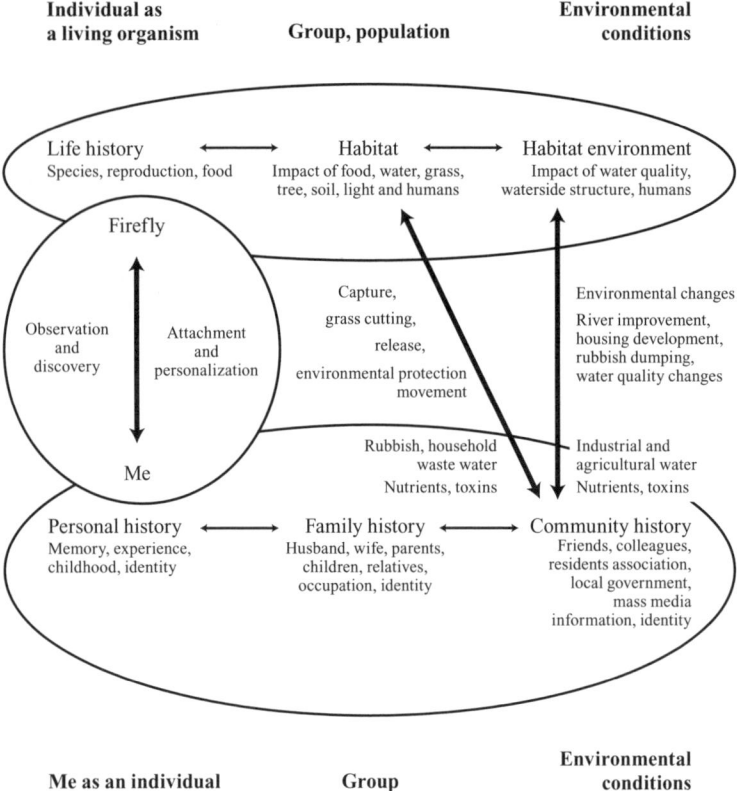

Source: Kada (2000: 212)

From 1992 to 1995, a 'water utilization' study of 600 communities in Shiga Prefecture was conducted by approximately fifty volunteers who had been participants in the firefly study. The results were presented in the form of an exhibition *Shōwa 30-nendaino mizu riyō—Tomie-ke tenji* (Water utilization in the 30s of the *Shōwa* era—The Tomie household exhibition) at Biwako Museum where everyday life scenes of the time were faithfully recreated. It has become a popular exhibit at the museum, which was opened in 1996 and in March 2005 it welcomed its five millionth visitor. It has become a regular place for elementary school students to learn about people's lifestyle in the old days. Some people bring their grandchildren to the exhibition and talk, with a radiant look on their face, about their own childhood. At the same time, some women decline to see the exhibition since they 'suffered hardships as a young wife in this type of home and do not want to be reminded of the experience' (Kada and Furukawa 2000). The database of 12 000 photographs collected in this study is available to the public via Biwako Museum's website.

During the same period of the water utilization study (1992–1995), we conducted a three intergenerational questionnaire survey of approximately 6,000 people regarding children's play. We asked elementary school students how they played on the waterside by using self-administered questionnaires and by interviewing their parent's and grandparent's generations using similar questionnaire items (Kada and Yūma 2000). The questionnaire contents are also open to the public on PC's at Biwako Museum.

Selecting 'water utilization' and 'play' as the study subject, has prompted people to re-acquaint themselves with the waterfront and to start some movements to personalize their local environment in various areas.

Environment as distilled in the memory of the land

As I continued to conduct these interviews in various places, assist the environmental study projects by the residents, and make plans for the Biwako Museum, I still felt some dissatisfaction, a feeling of 'scratching an itchy spot over one's shoe.' In addition to sociological studies which explore the relationships between people, environmental sociological studies require a contextual frame of the land, which is the relationship between people and nature. Thus, the history of the environment must be connected to the history of the land and the memories of people's relationships with the land. The records and memories accumulated over a period of 10 000 to 20 000 years of human habitation in the Japanese islands were preserved relatively well until 1955, the thirties of the *Shōwa* era. Until this period, the memories of the lifestyle were securely passed on, as typified by the opening line of the tale of *Momotarō*: 'The old man went to the woods to gather firewood and the old woman went to the river to wash clothes.' Now the situation is dramatically changing within a single generation (Kada 2000).

The rivers and the waterside dropped out of these memories and were never talked about. I felt that it was my role to create the setting for the recovery and dissemination of the memories of people's relationship with the water—just like Mrs Akie Nishibori of Gamō

Town who had responded to the local firefly study and recalled the personal word *mizokko*.

The epistemological problems of an environmental sociological study cannot be overcome by survey research, which is categorical in nature. But can it be supplemented by life context-finding interviews alone? The answer is 'no.' The problem of interpreting the meaning of linguistic nuance in the methodology of interviewing has been the subject of debate for years (Sakurai 2002: 30). As Polanyi's analysis of 'tacit knowledge' suggests, one does not verbalize everything one knows or experiences. Moreover, one does not remember every detail of one's life. One's memory is selective and one's account is even more context sensitive. With what Sakurai calls Edward Bruner's 'three modes of life,' there is a gap between a 'life as lived' and a 'life as experienced,' and the former, and a 'life as told' (Sakurai 2002: 31). A life as lived includes the behaviour appearing as external action and is observable from the outside. By contrast, a life as experienced refers to the narrator's image, sense, emotion, desire, idea or meaning.

In order to provide better insights into the relational logic contained in the multiple structure of 'the relationship between people' plus 'the relationship between people and nature,' a methodological device is required to find out about nonverbal 'knowledge in the tacit space,' so to speak. The collective memories of communities and local societies are stored in the land. Our next challenge was to incorporate habitus, Bourdieu's practical structure, into our research methodology.

One technique we devised was to show photographs while conducting interviews. We called it the 'photo material presentation-interview' and tried to find photographs of everyday life scenes from 1955, the thirties of the *Shōwa* era, before Lake Biwa went through dramatic environmental changes. We would visit the actual sites, find the people in the photographs and sketch out the actual life scenes and lifestyle activity from the experiences and memories of these people. We collected tens of thousands of photographs taken around Lake Biwa. Of these photographs, we selected about one hundred and in the middle of the 1990s began visiting the photographed sites.

'Pollution' perception buried in interpersonal relationships

Let us pick a few examples from these photographs. The first one is the waterside in Okishima, an island in Lake Biwa, in 1955, the thirties of the *Shōwa* era. Photograph 10.1.1 shows an early morning scene on the lakeside on the fifth of August 1956 (the thirty-first year of *Shōwa*). We

Discovering Happiness through Environmental Research

Photograph 10.1.1: Morning on the Lake Biwa foreshore on 5 August 1956.

began visiting Okishima in 1993, and took this photograph with us. We soon found the people in the photograph. The woman washing a pot in the middle of the pier is Mrs Yoshiko Chatani and the girls standing on her right with tea towels on their shoulders are her daughters, Aiko and Kimiko. In 1993, Yoshiko and Aiko were still living in Okishima. While looking at the photograph we interviewed them about how they used the lake water in those days. The following is the account given spontaneously by Yoshiko while looking at the image.

> The first thing in the morning, I had to go (to the beach) with a rice cooker to get clean water. [For] washed rice grains, it had to be clean. [We washed it] twice with a bucket, in four water jugs. [We also] had to go fishing, so we all got up at around three o'clock in the morning and did it. [I] got up before [the rest of the family], cooked breakfast and when you saw a faint light over the lake, we all went to catch fish.
>
> After dark, we also went to the beach to wash things. We got bath water from the beach too, about seven times with a wooden bucket. We did rice rinsing and pickles washing at the bottom [of the pier], so as not to dirty the water at the end [of the pier]. For some people came later to get water…
>
> We washed diapers in a bucket first at home, [and] then took them to the beach to rinse. Not on the pier, at the jetty, at the jetty past the harbor. There were more fish around the pier. They loved eating leftover rice. They even tried to eat pooh from the diapers.

> We used ashes (to do the dishes), straw ashes. We would bring some ashes on the rim of a pot or the lid and used a net scrubber. We made a scrubber from fishing nets. A rice tub had to be scrubbed with a palm fiber scourer. Palm fibers were used for rice tubs and other wooden tubs. Hard to clean things like a rice tub, were washed with polishing powder called *ishiko*. We did all our washing on the beach. We didn't have water at home.
>
> Water jugs were used only to keep water for drinking, cooking side dishes and steaming rice. We drank water as it was, without filtering. The lake was a lot clearer in the old days. It was beautiful.

This pier was used by six or seven families living nearby. The island had these piers located about fifty meters apart; they had been built and used jointly by the locals. At the time of typhoons, they brought the piers up onto the beach to avoid damage and carried out day-to-day maintenance. From what Yoshiko told us, it became clear that the pier was only several meters long but the beach end and the lake end of it were used for subtly different purposes. In particular, we found that they tried not to contaminate the water on the lake end, keeping in mind the people who came later to get drinking water. Also they washed dirty things like diapers on a faraway jetty rather than on their pier, and they drank the lake water without filtering. They could drink the unfiltered lake water because of a tacit 'social arrangement' by which you would not pollute the water there and the other users would not pollute it either. This social arrangement supported their confidence that the lake water was drinkable.

In other words, it is possible to interpret that 'pollution' is not a matter of the physical characteristics or quality of the water but is 'defined within the relationships between people' as well as the aforementioned actions of the locals. 'Confidence' or similar expressions were never mentioned; however, this value must have been present in their belief system, hidden in these life scenes. Could we gather such information by simply asking in a questionnaire: 'Did you have confidence in the water quality?'

Pollution and relationships between people and living things

Yoshiko continued while looking at Photograph 10.1.1 and said:

> When I washed rice grains off the pot, small fish quickly came. Small fish scrambled to eat rice grains. I could see it. The water was clear.

> There were many corbicula clams on the beach. I went down to the beach to wash my face in the morning, grabbed some clams and put them in a miso soup.

Aiko, one of the girls in the photograph also recalled:

> We used to catch small fish with a scoop net from the pier. Many small fish were hiding beneath the pier and even children could catch them easily. Small fish were cooked in a sweet and salty sauce and served as a side dish.
>
> The beach was full of corbicula shells, called the shell beach, and crunched underfoot when we walked.
>
> There were many small fish and corbicula clams…Food scraps from the pots became their feed, so what went around came around.

Here, she talked of the existence of a 'circulatory process of materials' by which waste products such as rice grains washed away in people's daily life, became food for fish in the water and the fish that grew up eating such food were caught by children who ate them as food. Corbicula clams were also easily caught and eaten in miso soup. Behind the act of eating, there was a hidden 'relationship of confidence' in living things. The locals of course did not call it the 'circulatory process of materials.' Mrs Aiko Okumura described it as 'what went around came around.'

Actually, I had been conducting my own water utilization study in Okishima since the early 1980s even before I obtained this photograph. I did find out in interviews that the people were drinking the unfiltered lake water and that they took their dirty washing, like diapers, to a separate area. The interview format allowed me to collect pieces of information that were verbally memorized and expressed. However, when I visited Okishima with the photograph, the following additional information and scenes emerged for the first time from the people's stories. Firstly, the photograph helped storytellers remember the spatial configuration of the place and recount 'subtle differences in how the place was used.' Secondly, a social arrangement based on 'confidence in your neighbors' action' was hidden in the feeling of 'drinking the lake water.' And finally, there was an underlying material circulation process by which fish ate human waste products and people ate these fish.

Borrowing Atsushi Sakurai's words (2002), this photograph contained 'life as lived,' in which people were doing washing-up and where 'behavior appeared as external action.' But 'life as experienced' was added to it in the form of a feeling, desire, idea or meaning. In particular, a relationship between people and place is embedded in 'the phenomenological world'—'the memory of an event' in the background of the visible, observable material world. 'The meaning memory' was extracted and recounted as the cognitive framework, expressed as the relationship of mutual confidence between people.

I would like to provide a supplementary explanation on the significance of this photograph. Mr Takashi Maeno actually 'sealed' the photographs he took of Okishima in 1955, the thirties of the *Shōwa* era, and had not published them. Mr Maeno was a well-known local amateur photographer and his works had won many awards at competitions. But he hesitated to publish them because he took them without getting permission from the people of Okishima. In 1993 I went to Okishima with Mr Maeno and his photographs and asked the president of the residents' association to organize a viewing by the people who were in these photographs. Photograph 10.1.1 was one of the images which prompted Mrs Chatani's recollection. At the viewing, the people of Okishima said: 'We certainly used to live like this but we don't have a single photograph. The only photographs we took in those days were school photographs.' Many of the people thanked Mr Maeno for taking and keeping these photographs. Mr Maeno was pleased and said: 'I feel as if a thorn stuck deep in my throat for many years has finally come off.'

Photograph 10.1.2 shows the same people standing at the same spot as in photograph 10.1.1. As the city water service was introduced to Okishima in 1961 (the thirty-sixth year of *Shōwa*) and the sewerage system was built in 1983 (the fifty-eighth year of *Shōwa*), household waste which would pollute Lake Biwa was physically intercepted at the sewerage treatment plant and the attempt to improve the living environment by controlling water quality was completed.

The problem was that people did not think the sewerage system had cleaned up the lake water. Mr Ichiji Ogawa of Okishima said: 'In the old days, we took all human waste to the field and fertilized crops. Now it's washed out from toilets through the sewer and flows into Lake Biwa. Even though it goes through the treatment plant, it can't be clean.'

Washing on the lakeside pier and a washed-up pram

Now fishing sheds have been built on the waterfront of Okishima and the beaches are quite 'far away.' But the memory of how this

Discovering Happiness through Environmental Research 223

Photograph 10.1.2: Okishima (same place and angle as photograph 10.1.1). Mrs Yoshiko Chatani (left) and her daughter Aiko, among those seen in photograph 10.1.1. 12 August 1997.

space was used is still very much alive. For example, people bring out washbowls to wash vegetables and cook them on the beach when they cook a large amount of food for funerals and festivals. The 'memory of the place' has been inherited.

Photograph 10.2.1 shows another washing-up scene on the lakeside of Nakajō, Makino Town (now Takashima City), on the western side of Lake Biwa around 1955 (the thirtieth year of *Shōwa*). A young woman, perhaps a mother, is washing clothes on a small pier over the lake, with a bucket on her side. A baby, perhaps one or two years old, is leaning out of her pram, watching the woman. It is just a casual scene, but Mr Maeno who took this photograph said: 'When I was walking on the beach, I came across the mother and her baby. It gave me such a warm feeling that I pressed the shutter button.'

It actually took me several years to locate the woman in this photograph. There is no background scenery in the photograph and it was difficult to pinpoint the precise location. Finally in the summer of 1996, I found her when I walked along the lakeside with this photograph in my hand. She was Mrs Kimi Nakano. She looked at the photograph and exclaimed, 'It's me!' and told me the following story:

> This pram was a rich family's pram. It was a high quality pram made of rattan. We couldn't have bought it. One morning after a night of a strong wind, it was washed up on the beach. I thought perhaps it was a gift from God or Buddha and thankfully used it to raise my eight children.

Photograph 10.2.1: A mother doing the laundry and a baby in a pram, around 1955.

For Kimi, the lake was the place which brought her blessings and good luck and she raised her children using the pram, given by this luck.

Social changes seen in photographs of old and new

Photograph 10.2.2 shows Mrs Kimi Nakano in 1997 sitting in the same place as in photograph 10.2.1. These days people use a washing machine to do the laundry at home but they still come to the beach to dry their washing. Here, the memory of the place has been inherited.

This attempt to extract the memories of past lifestyle using old photographs has created a new movement by local residents' associations and schools. One of the schools, Imazu Junior High School in Imazu Town (now Takashima City), mobilized all grade three students in 2003 and 2004, (about 150 students each year), to undertake a general learning project called 'Revive Photos.' Using old photographs, taken by a local amateur photographer (Mr Kanji Ishiida had left nearly 30 000 prints of old photographs), or found in their own family albums, they visited the places and interviewed the people related to the photographs to study various changes in the environment and lifestyle.

Let us present a few examples. One study was prompted by the fact that Ms Kaori Kuwata, a great grandchild of Mrs Kimi Nakano, happened to be a student at Imazu Junior High School. Kaori spent

Discovering Happiness through Environmental Research

Photograph 10.2.2: Mrs Kimi Nakano, who was doing the laundry in photograph 10.2.1. Almost at the same spot, 7 June 1997.

two months drawing up a family tree showing how many offspring were produced by Kimi's eight children. Kaori's grandmother was one of them, who grew up in that pram. The family tree ended up with the names of 120 people. Although it is almost unimaginable for Kaori's generation to do the laundry in the lake, the drawing of her family tree seems to have made the great grandmother's lifestyle feel closer to herself rather than as some remote event.

Inspired by the photograph of Mrs Kimi Nakano's washing-up, one group sought old photographs of the piers in Imazu and studied them. Ms Mika Arai and Miyako Ebata of the group were given photographs 10.3.1 and 10.4.1 by their local acquaintances and visited the same spots to take photographs 10.3.2 and 10.4.2 in order to study changes in the lakeside. Both pairs of photographs show the waterside of Lake Biwa near Imazu. In Imazu, the piers were called *ashigeta*. The interviews of many elderly residents, using the photographs, found the following information:

The piers were used to do household chores on the lakeside.

Lake Biwa's water was used for domestic purposes.

There were many fish including *funa* and *ayu*.

The lake water was crystal clear and people could see rocks at the bottom.

Photograph 10.3.1: Piers on Imazu beach, possibly taken around 1960. Probably early spring as some snow is seen on the mountain in the background.

Photograph 10.3.2: The same place as in photograph 10.3.1, no pier remains, December 2004.

Discovering Happiness through Environmental Research 227

Photograph 10.4.1: A family photograph on the pier with some guests from Tokyo, around 1940.

Photograph 10.4.2: The same place as in photograph 10.4.1. There is no sign of people on the beach and some buildings have been built, December 2004.

Sand on the foreshore was fine.

Children swam in the lake.

The beach was visited by many people and was lively.

The two students made a couple of recommendations; firstly, to make Lake Biwa more relevant to people's lives; and secondly, to restore the piers at Lake Biwa in order to re-establish their relevance. It goes without saying that they would like to see some improvement in the water quality, but they also hope to revive the 'relationship between people and the lake' in order to improve the environment. Here, we can see the significance of environmental awareness based on empathy.

The study of missed opportunity

With regard to the main theme of this project, 'social research for the enhancement of human well-being,' the project leader Kenji Kosaka suggests that the 'increase of well-being' and the 'decrease of ill-being' may become the research arenas. Kosaka hypothesizes four quadrants for the sociological study of well-being. The four domains are created by the combination of two axes: 'citizen' or 'sociology' on the researcher axis, and the 'realization of well-being' or the 'reduction of ill-being' on the subject axis. The four domains include: 'pursuit of well-being as a citizen,' 'reduction of ill-being as a citizen,' 'pursuit of well-being as sociology' and 'reduction of ill-being as sociology.'

What Kosaka expects of sociology here is the study of 'missed opportunity' to reduce current and future ill-being by revisiting past ill-being (Kosaka 2004: 29). It aims 'to recognize the past cases of ill-being and enable them to have the same effect as hope in the pursuit of well-being.' He suggests a direction for the study of missed opportunity, using the Vietnam War and Minamata disease as examples. Its purpose is to scoop out the source of inappropriate decisions in view of avoiding or reducing ill-being rather than to make an objective assessment by following the development of these ill-being examples and finding out turning points (Kosaka 2004: 34).

The 'source' is a meta-methodological basis rather than a specific method. Kosaka emphasizes the following three points:

1. Non-obviousness: to convey a principle that is not obvious or natural to anyone

2. Tri-level schema of 'structure-action-image:' to recognize that an action is not driven by a structure but defined through the medium of an image; and
   3. Non-homogeneity: to focus on the synchronicity of heterogeneous things and the synchronicity of non-synchronized things.

I now think that our approach to study change in the life environment of Lake Biwa with the residents, from the viewpoint of the residents' life, as explained in the previous sections, is precisely the study of missed opportunity that Kosaka proposes.

The Lake Biwa issue was contemporaneous with the outbreak of Minamata disease. In 1955, the 30s of the *Shōwa* era, Minamata suffered a massive pollution problem caused by the effluent containing organic mercury from Chisso Corporation's factory. At the same time a comprehensive development of Lake Biwa occurred so that it could become a major supplier of water for the downstream cities of Osaka and Kobe. Lake Biwa region was also going through a transition in its economic structure, changing from an agricultural based prefecture to an industry based one (Kada 2002). The pollution problem in Lake Biwa was constructed as and made into a 'social problem' by experts and government bodies, on the basis of a reductionist theory of pollution—the main subject of this paper. The soap campaign and the government's sewerage policy were both born out of a control theory paradigm based on materialism. Of course, excessive nutrients and toxic substances need to be controlled so that they do not flow out into the tributaries. However, the limitations of this type of assessment lay in the belief that the water pollution problem could be resolved by these measures alone.

As I mentioned earlier, the completion of the sewerage system did not bring back people's confidence in or attachment to the waterfront. It is in fact the other way around. Neither the government nor the experts have envisaged a structure of empathy where people are involved with the lake and the creatures that inhabit it. This deficiency has created a social structure which has enabled a massive public works investment in the catchment-wide sewerage system (Kada 2003).

This is where Kosaka's tri-level schema of 'structure-image-action,' which defines action theory that creates an environmental policy, becomes relevant. The 'image' in this schema is the domain of 'verbalization.' It has a bearing on the world of linguistic image in which the 'drain' is transformed into *mizokko*, and also on visual images of three-dimensional life scenes on the lakeside, as we saw in the second half of this paper.

Now, among the current generation of children—those junior high school students of Imazu Town (now Takashima City), for example—who take the city water and sewerage system for granted, a seed of independent thinking to try to connect non-homogeneous 'past' and 'present' with 'future,' appears to be growing. This thinking is in the form of a desire to restore the era when people did their laundry on the piers and the lakeside was bustling with everyday life activity.

How can we restore the piers? We need to find a practical solution for that. In reality, although the locals used to build piers as they wished, in the 30s of *Shōwa*, the lake is now under full administrative control of the Shiga Prefecture government and the Ministry of Land, Infrastructure and Transport. Anyone who would like to build a pier there must go through an administrative process to obtain 'permission to occupy publicly owned land.' When Lake Biwa and nearby rivers were classified as Class 1 Rivers following the amendment of the River Law in 1964 (the thirty-fourth year of *Shōwa*), the lake was legally taken away from the residents.

How to overcome the difficulty of self-learning

When we look back, 'research,' which is a methodology recognized by the academic industry, is a social device to separate oneself, who conducts the research, from others who are the subject of research, and put oneself in a dominant position. By contrast, the ideology and social trend of self-learning as a device for research by residents themselves, was developed in Japan through the study of regions from the Meiji era and through Kunio Yanagita's folklore study methodology advanced around the 1930s to the 1940s. Our research into the history of life environment also derives from the same perspective.

Miyauchi (2003) rearranged a genealogy of citizens' research along the lines of 'civic study' and pointed out the following three social demands:
1. A demand from the civic sector itself, such as NPO's
2. A demand from the citizen participation-type policy process
3. A demand from the empowerment of citizens.

He pronounced that citizens' research 'is the research with a new paradigm, not a simplified version of research by professional researchers' because of its freedom to select methodology, its desire for practical persuasiveness, and the 'closeness' of the problem solver and the researcher.

By the way, I have been using the word 'self' to imply 'people who are close to the scene' of some event or social phenomenon without actually asking what it is. However, it must be the most fundamental question in terms of 'self-learning resident research.' As Motoji Matsuda aptly pointed out, the heterogeneity of the researcher and the research subject cannot be resolved in the name of 'research as concerted action,' as argued by Kamon Nitagai (Matsuda 2003). By reflecting upon research into an already existing matter, one is faced with an aporia of awareness which is different from that of an ordinary citizen. What do we make of this difference between the two positions? Matsuda sees a possible direction to break the impasse reached by fieldwork theory in Takashi Nakano's concerted action theory which considers it possible to 'make an exchange between the two (the researcher and the research subject) while allowing the heterogeneity.' He sees a potential to build up creative and heuristic co-operativity between selves in the life-world beyond exclusive and closed-off self-consciousness categorized by race, sex or age. It has its roots in the modern revival of the Motoori school of the Japanese classics pursued by Hiroyuki Torigoe and a potential process to approach society 'by heart and with everyday life sensitivity' without separating senses and reason (Torigoe 2002).

The process of integrating senses and reason has been turned into a sort of practical method in the 'study of local neighborhoods' advocated by Tetsurō Yoshimoto and others. In Minamata City where Minamata disease patients suffered a disgraceful ordeal and local communities were pushed to the brink of collapse, Yoshimoto had a feeling of real disappointment that 'although many experts came to Minamata for research, all research results were taken out of Minamata and the most important local communities were left with nothing.' He came to the realization that 'only those who research can get to know' (Yoshimoto 2001). He began formulating the 'study of local neighborhood' from the early 1990s. In his local neighborhood study, Yoshimoto focuses on 'food' and 'waste.' The pollution problem brought on to the scenes of everyday living by eating the fish contaminated by waste products is picked out of the life domain as the central theme. Kosaka's concept of missed opportunity is embedded in Yoshimoto's methodological consciousness and the 'difficulty of self-learning' is already presupposed in the local neighborhood study methodology. In other words, because 'one does not know one's self, or it is difficult to know one's self,' the local neighborhood study has developed a methodology for 'people of the land and people of the wind jointly' to do research from the beginning, which is now being adopted by various local governments as an important local government policy methodology.

Yoshimoto is attempting to approach a tacit life mentality via positivism which focuses thoroughly on the material existence of people's life memories and practices utilized in relation to land and water. We can see a link between Yoshimoto's method and the ideology of the new Japanese classics. What is hidden in the background is the Jōmon worldview which regards fish and birds as their fellow beings existing empathically in their life-world, despite or because of their suffering of a very modern pathological manifestation around the periphery of Japan's capitalism, called Minamata disease. The world according to Jōmon culture is expressed in the thinking of Minamata patients, Eiko Sugimoto (Kurihara ed. 2000: 129–146) and Masato Ogata (Ogata and Tsuji 1996) and in the deep literary world of Michiko Ishimure (Ishimure 1969).

Lake Biwa and Minamata are synchronous as well as heterogeneous. I recently have begun to think intuitively that I may be able to see the cognitive and practical depth of the Lake Biwa issue in this comparison; a subject for my future research.

My discussion has been based on a relatively simple premise which explored the dichotomy between control and empathy. But after all, well-being as the aggregate of person-to-person and person-to-nature relationships exists dynamically, only at the point where both are in a precarious state of balance. As I continue my involvement in environmental studies by residents, I am a versatile presence who is conscious of my position and role in searching for methodologies of environmental sociology while I find joy and happiness in new encounters with various fields because of their heterogeneity.

11
A Film's 'Power of Enlightenment' or Effect: An Exploration of the Film *Freaks*

Hiroaki Yoshii

Introduction

'Films and documentaries change the lives of their audience.' 'It is a bit of an exaggeration, they are just movies.' 'They are fictions, the world of fantasies, and even documentaries are stories edited for certain purposes, aren't they?' 'We should just casually enjoy them.' These are common statements that we regularly hear about film, their influence and their purpose. In this paper I would like to analyze in more detail, and from an angle more closely aligned with film as my subject, the meaning of the statement that films change the lives of their audience, and influence the viewer's outlook on the world, their values, and their commonsense knowledge about life.

Why do I hold this view? I could illustrate the veracity of these claims in some detail by just thinking about how films have influenced my life so far, but more than anything, the memory of an experience from several years ago vividly comes to mind. It demonstrates the view that one film can actually change the life of a viewer and also transform his relationship with his close friends and others.

There was a student in my seminar at a private university where I used to work who wrote a very good graduation thesis on film for which he read books, reviewed them, grappled with images and expressed his own thoughts in his own words. Why did he choose a film for his focus of analysis? When we talked, he told me about what had happened when he was a high school student. He said he was not a very 'good' student and many things had happened and he was suspended and ordered to stay home. Then, his class teacher came to his home and left a videotape for him to watch as he had plenty of spare time.

It was a film called New Cinema Paradiso (*Nuovo Cinema Paradiso*), directed by Giuseppe Tornatore in 1989. It is an excellent film about a relationship between a boy named Toto and a projectionist called Alfredo at a small film theater in Sicily, Italy, from the post-second World War period to the 1950s. In those days, films were censored by the church and kiss scenes could not be shown. A priest would view a film in advance and ring a hand held bell at inappropriate scenes, which had to be cut. The censored film is shown to the audience. When the mood is building up to a kiss scene, the image abruptly switches and the audience stomp their feet and boo. It is a very humorous scene. The boy sees the projectionist as a father figure and a warm relationship develops between them. The boy grows up, experiences his first love, and later succeeds in the film industry in Rome. He receives a memento of the projectionist who died. The memento is a film made up of all the kiss scenes that were cut from the censored films. In the final scene, he watches the film, crying. It is an indescribably gentle and warm final scene in which his love of films, love for the projectionist, feelings for the first girl he fell in love with, nostalgia for his own childhood when he grew up being loved by various people including the projectionist, and the meaning of life are all overlapped with the images of censored kiss scenes. Together with its beautiful music, it is one of my favorite films. The student said that his life changed when he watched this film during his suspension from school. He casually began watching the film and was captivated by its world and perhaps watched it many times. He said that he became a film lover after this and his life and behavior definitely started to change.

In his thesis he discussed *GO* (2001) directed by Isao Yukisada, in terms of his own relationship with his Korean friend(s) from his high school days. It was a comparative study of the original novel and the film, the story, and his experience. It was not the type of thesis that arranged knowledge neatly and explained theory in an orderly fashion. It was a suffocatingly realistic thesis filled with various residues from his life experience.

He encountered a particular film at a specific time of his life which became a turning point for him to steadily change the meaning of his life. Films do have such power. What is this power? And how does it exert such influences upon us? Or does the power emerge from the mutual reflection between films and the lives of their viewers?

When we speak of films, of course, there are many different types, from entertainment to documentaries and experimental images. Normally, I should classify them according to certain rules before discussing the potential of analyzing films. It would require more work and time, so I will leave it as a future task for the moment. In this essay, I would like to use my intuitive sense to further explore the topic of film and its power and influence.

Films have moments in which they exert their power and effect upon viewers to completely overturn the device for defining their personal characters. I am referring here to the device by which people usually lead their lives but are rarely aware of doing so; including their outlook on life and the world, their values and commonsense. The power films exert upon me in these moments is beyond the scope of the myriad of analytical discourses in sociology which aspire to achieve the same effect. I would like to discuss tentatively, what these moments, power and effects are, and how we can interpret them. By exploring this process, it may provide me with some clues in the future, as to the analysis of the sociological act of interpreting films.

The film viewing experience

By the way, what kind of activity is film viewing, and for what purpose do we watch a film? Generally, we watch films for enjoyment, to kill time, develop a relationship with someone precious, or escape from troubles of daily life even temporarily, amongst other things. Of course there are many other motives. Here, however, let us think about a film viewing experience not from the perspective of the purpose or motivation, but from the viewpoint of how we view a film. What happens to us while viewing a film, or what does a film or an image do to us in an encounter with it. These are the type of questions I would like to pose.

The theatre lights slowly dim and I sit in the dark for two hours to watch a film. I may be distracted by other people in the cinema but I focus my attention on the film and get absorbed into its world for its duration. Scenes have been created by the very latest computer graphic and other imaging technologies—a hail of bullets appears to be stationary and a male actor weaves through them. While I think to myself that what I am watching is not realistic and is impossible to believe, I find myself enjoying the story development as well as looking at the astonishing images. I see and feel the young protagonist's sense of helplessness, frustration and disappointment.

Angered by his own stupidity of believing that he knew the realities of his counterpart's life, he smashes his guitar and throws it into a river. Hearing the very beautiful melody of an old popular folk song, I find myself unexpectedly shedding tears. I can think of many other images when sitting in the dark, faced with a movie and being emotionally moved by it.

What kind of act is 'being moved by a film?' Is it amazement of seeing something that is usually unimaginable? Perhaps it recreates my past experience or event and evokes a sudden nostalgia in me? The appeal of films may lie in their ability to unfold an event, whether known or unknown, past or future, possible or impossible, in front of our eyes as a fiction. That is when my heart is moved.

When the heart is moved, something occasionally causes a dramatic upheaval in my inner landscape and fundamentally changes aspects of it. It is something I call 'practical knowledge,' which I use almost subconsciously to conduct my daily activity in this life-world. Using this practical knowledge, from time to time and place to place, I 'appropriately' understand and 'appropriately' deal with various phenomena and events in the world. Men, women, heterosexual love, homosexual love, children, family, grandfather, grandmother, relatives, neighbors, children's friends, colleagues, partner's friends, partner's job, cooking, cleaning, housework, holidays, elementary school PTA, son's school entrance exam, and so on. Just randomly mentioning things around me makes me realize that there is an endless stream of practical knowledge in my life. This knowledge is used in daily life and fine-tuned from time to time, but its fundamental state does not change drastically unless it experiences a profound, specific shock. Usually, however, the lack of change does not necessarily mean that the content and structure of the knowledge itself is desirable and pleasant in leading our everyday lives. It contains inadequacy, inappropriateness and various distortions which can hinder us in our understanding of other people and events. It can also limit our comprehension of different points of view, or the range of realities that are not understandable to us and seem distant from our thoughts and behavior which is based on our understanding. The sense of distance or lack of understanding may be due to a range of reasons, including that I have no past experience with a certain problem or reality and do not know how to understand it, and therefore may be completely missing that part of practical knowledge.

Films, while presenting themselves as fiction, significantly influence our practical knowledge of people, events and issues. The action and speed of the images of a man flying around skyscrapers on a piece of string may amaze me but would hardly make an impact on my practical knowledge. When we feel 'some kind of power' in the protagonist's words, casual gestures or dialogues, or the way people, issues and realities are depicted, or the way language is used, the relevant part of our (or at least my) practical knowledge cracks and shatters with a crash. And as I continue to savor the images, a new aspect of practical knowledge is gradually created in me.

I would like to further consider the effect achieved in my interactions with various images when I am faced with a film and its power, and with what I refer to as the 'power of enlightenment' of a film viewing experience. While films are a form of entertainment, it is not an ordinary type of entertainment. I would like now to discuss a particular film as an example of the idea of a film's power of enlightenment.

An attempt to analyze *Freaks*

Freaks as the best exploitation film

Freaks was directed by Tod Browning and released in North America in 1932 and it has recently been released on DVD in Japan. I had known of the existence of this film for a long time and I remember finding and hiring a copy, encased in an old faded cover that I found in a corner of a rental video shop in Hiroshima. I had a memory of its strangely powerful final scene of the revenge of the freaks. But somehow I had no memory of the Duck Woman, who used to be a beautiful trapeze artist but was disfigured in their revenge, until I saw the film again on DVD. According to the note on the DVD package, the film was released in Japan in 1932 but taken off two weeks later due to public controversy. I don't think it has been shown in Japan since then except on some special occasions.

Why did the film cause such a controversy and then the cancellation of screening? Perhaps it was because the film dealt directly with the existence of handicapped people and their feelings and as such exploited them. In the 1930s when the film was made, disability was not seen as a 'social issue' as it is now. At that time there were no services for people with disabilities, including services for their rights and welfare. During the period in which the film was made there was a tendency to 'enjoy the exploitation of the handicapped and mock and laugh at someone's disability.' This view was very much alive as 'commonsense.' Many of the disabled actors in the film *Freaks* were real performers working at circus shows and appeared in support roles in many movies. They occupied a place that satisfied the need of such 'commonsense.' However, *Freaks* was the 'best exploitation film' of its kind and it more than enough satisfied this form of 'commonsense.' For example, Kiichirō Yanagishita rates *Freaks* as the 'best exploitation film' and states:

> This film pays no attention at all to the love story of 'normal' people who are supposed to be closer to the audience. Browning's eyes are focusing on the disfigured people who are friends of Hans…even the main revenge drama is merely a container in which he places the freaks. Browning's aim was to gather as many freaks as possible who were as extraordinary as possible. According to his wishes, talent scouts traveled all over America and recruited many of the leading sideshow freaks. As the result, Freaks looked like a catalogue of sideshow stars at the time. Each of them could fill up a tent on his or her own. Among them were beautiful Siamese twin sisters Violet and Daisy Hilton, 'half boy' Johnny Eck, 'the living torso' Prince Rardion, 'bearded lady' Olga Roderick, and three Pinheads. The main character of Hans, a dwarf, was played by Harry Earles, who was already a regular in Browning's films including 'The Unholy Three,' and his sister Daisy played Hans' lover who was abandoned by him (Yanagishita 2003: 83).

While Yanagishita detects a feeling of empathy that Browning held for the disabled, he points out Browning's discriminatory perspective as well. Yanagishita comments the '…horribleness of the freaks was particularly emphasized in the climatic scene of attack on Hercules and Cleopatra. Not only limbless people but also those who were supposed to be able to walk normally came crawling in the mud. The figures lit up by flashes of lightening in the storm looked nothing but monsters. It is indeed impossible to insist that there is no discriminatory intention in his direction of this scene' (Yanagishita 2003: 85–86), and argues that Browning, after all, directed this film for the maximum exploitative effect.

> Fundamentally, the act of making a show of disfigured people is deeply discriminatory by itself. Tod Browning couldn't possibly be unaware of this. Exploitation shows attract people's eyes because they are discriminatory. 'Freaks' became the ultimate exploitation film because Browning knew everything about how to present the disfigured in the

most shocking way. They say that Browning loved the freaks he gathered by himself and looked very much at home when he was mixing with them. However, whether or not Browning had a sense of discrimination against them (he was probably more sympathetic than discriminatory—it shows in some of the scenes which conscientiously captured the performances of these people) and whether or not the film itself is discriminatory are completely different matters…Browning only directed the film in this way to achieve the maximum exploitative effect (Yanagishita 2003: 86).

As Yanagishita points out, this film puts on view, a huge array of handicapped actors who display their unusual appearances. As I write this essay, I am reminded of an experience from my childhood, at a festival in Osaka in the garden of Shitennōji temple. Among many festival stalls, there was a show tent, a peep show. Enticed by the promoter's sales pitch and overcome by my urge to 'peep' at something unusual, I was lured into the tent even though I thought 'it couldn't be real.' Nevertheless there was an urge to 'peep' at something unusual. When this urge is satisfied in one moment within a confined space, concealed by some kind of shield, we can go past the moment and return to our normal life while feeling a little embarrassed by our desire to satisfy such an urge. How then do we feel when we are confronted by full-frontal, detailed and a prolonged depiction of the unusual? Perhaps our initial reaction would be a laugh, and then amazement. After that our urge to 'peep' would be fulfilled, and if that continued over a long period, the fulfillment would eventually exceed its capacity. We would say: 'That's enough; I can't take it any more.' We would ruminate on the image of ourselves, feel embarrassed, anxious, and annoyed by the prolongation of such a state, and end up getting angry at the 'abnormality' of the film.

Yanagishita is critical of the films' discriminatory impact, and argues that it is the result of Browning's direction to 'achieve the maximum exploitative effect.' He states that whether or not Browning had a sense of discrimination against the handicapped and whether or not the film itself is discriminatory are completely different matters. I agree with his argument; however, can we simply determine the film's discriminatory perspective as 'discriminatory' and criticize it? Can we seal off this film as an exploitative and sensationalist film just because it has a discriminatory perspective? These questions arose repeatedly as I watched *Freaks*.

It is far too early to say that we have enough practical knowledge and know-how to deal with people with disabilities in the way that they deserve to be dealt with as 'people.' However, the commonsense view prevalent at the time of the film's release to 'enjoy the exploitation of the handicapped and mock and laugh at someone's disability,' is certainly changing now. New knowledge surrounding the issue of disability is being developed, influencing the media and taking root in our daily life. When we see *Freaks* from our present standpoint, its depiction of disability and its perspective is 'discriminatory.' But what kind of power does the 'discriminatory perspective' exert upon us as viewers? Usually, *Freaks* would not be regarded as a film that enlightens people on the disability issue. However, I would like to try to identify the 'power of enlightenment' in the 'discriminatory perspective' employed by the film.

An unaffected portrayal of the disabled

Let me introduce the storyline of *Freaks*. A lengthy introduction appears leading up to the opening scene of the film.

> Before proceeding with the showing of the following HIGHLY UNUSUAL ATTRACTION, a few words should be said about the amazing subject matter, BELIEVE IT OR NOT...STRANGE AS IT SEEMS. In ancient times anything that deviated from the normal was considered an omen of ill-luck or representative of evil. Gods of misfortune and adversity were invariably cast in the form of monstrosities, and deeds of injustice and hardship have been attributed to the many crippled and deformed tyrants of Europe and Asia. HISTORY, RELIGION, FOLKLORE, and LITERATURE. In the tales of misshapen misfits who have altered the world's course, GOLIATH, CALABAN, FRANKENSTEIN, GLOUCESTER, TOM THUMB and KAISER WILHELM are just a few; whose fame is worldwide.
>
> The accident of abnormal birth was considered a disgrace and malformed children were placed out in the elements to die. If, perchance, one of these freaks of nature survived, he was always regarded with suspicion. Society shunned him because of his deformity, and a family so hampered was always ashamed of the curse put upon it.
>
> Occasionally, one of these unfortunates was taken to court to be jeered at or ridiculed for the amusement of the nobles. Others were left to eke out a living by begging, stealing or starving.
>
> For the love of beauty is a deep-seated urge which dates back to the beginning of civilization, the revulsion with which we view the abnormal, the malformed and the mutilated is the result of long

conditioning by our forefathers. The majority of freaks, themselves, are endowed with normal thoughts and emotions. Their lot is truly a heart-breaking one. They are forced into the most unnatural of lives. Therefore, they have built up among themselves a code of ethics to protect them from the barbs of normal people. Their rules are rigidly adhered to and the hurt of one is the hurt of all; the joy of one is the joy of all. The story about to be revealed is a story based on the effect of this code upon their lives.

Never again will such a story be filmed, as modern science and teratology is rapidly eliminating such blunders of nature from the world. With humility for the many injustices done to such people, (they have no power to control their lot) we present the most startling horror story of the ABNORMAL and UNWANTED (Extract from DVD subtitles).

The introduction finishes and the title *FREAKS* appears. The title is torn up by hands from behind and the story begins.

> Barker: We didn't lie to you, folks. We told you we had living, breathing, monstrosities. You'll laugh at them, shudder at them, and yet, but for the accident of birth, you might be even as they are. They did not ask to be brought into the world, but into the world they came. Their code is a law unto themselves. Offend one, and you offend them all.
>
> And now, folks, if you'll just step this way, you are about to witness the most amazing, the most astounding, living monstrosity of all time.
>
> *[A woman looks at the figure in the cage, screams, and steps backward covering her face with her hands].*
>
> Friends, she was once a beautiful woman. A royal prince shot himself for [the] love of her. She was known as the peacock of the air...

Here, the scene switches to the image of a woman Cleopatra, 'Cleo' for short, on a trapeze. Hans and Frieda, both dwarfs, look up to watch her. Hans praises Cleo's beauty. Frieda becomes jealous about his remarks. Hans and Frieda reconfirm their feelings for each other.

Hans is the film's main character. He is engaged to Frieda but has a liking for Cleo who is the symbol of beauty at the circus company. Cleo becomes aware of his feelings for her and takes advantage of him for money and expensive gifts. Cleo is having an affair with Hercules who flaunts his physique while toying with Hans' sincere affections for her. Frieda becomes concerned about Hans and asks Cleo to stop flirting with him. Cleo brushes off Frieda's plea. Not only that, when Frieda lets slip that Cleo is just after his inheritance, Cleo realizes the existence of an inheritance due to Hans, and conspires together with Hercules to marry Hans before killing him with poison.

At Hans and Cleo's wedding party, all the handicapped members of the circus gather and celebrate Hans' marriage. When they offer Cleo a drink to become one of them, she changes her attitude altogether, abuses them and drives them away. Then Cleo and Hercules insult Hans by treating him like a child. Hans realizes Cleo's deceit and finds out their conspiracy to murder him. Hans plots revenge together with his friends and feigns ignorance while waiting for his chance. His friends quietly keep watch on Cleo and Hercules to put pressure on them. One stormy night when the circus is about to move, they carry out revenge. Hercules is stabbed in the chest with a knife thrown by a dwarf master knife thrower and murdered by the handicapped people edging toward him. Cleo runs away screaming, into the woods. Hans and others go after her relentlessly. (Fade out).

> The same promoter appears.
>
> Barker: How she got that way will never be known. Some say a jealous lover. Others, that it was the code of the freaks. Others, the storm. Believe it or not, there she is.
>
> A close-up of the quacking 'Duck Woman.' She has Cleo's face.
>
> Another change of scene.
>
> Hans has received his inheritance and now lives in a mansion. Phroso the clown and his wife Venus visit with Frieda in tow. 'Why did you come here?' says Hans.
>
> Frieda: Please Hans don't be angry. Venus and Phroso have been so kind by me.
>
> Hans: Please, go away...I can't see no-one.
>
> Frieda: But Hans, you tried to stop them. It was only the poison you wanted. It wasn't your fault. Don't...don't worry, Hans. Come to me, my lieber. Don't cry. Don't, Hans. Don't cry.
>
> Frieda gently embraces Hans, 'I love you. I love you.'
>
> End title.

The lengthy introduction at the beginning of the film makes clear how we should see this revenge drama of the handicapped and the story that develops from it. It explains that the malformed have developed their own code of ethics amid the history of persecution and ostracism, and that this unusual and absurd story was born as an outcome of this code. Immediately after the introduction, the promoter tells us: 'Their code is a law unto themselves. Offend one, and you offend them all.' If we accept this explanation we would be able to interpret the scene, for example, in which Cleo's conspiracy is uncovered after the wedding. The freaks hiding, watch Cleo and Hercules intensely, and silently pressure them. This represents a collective action, based on their understanding that the insult hurled at Hans was an 'insult to all.'

Yet, when I try to appreciate this film 'here and now,' the viewpoint of those times expressed at the start of the film, does not sit well with me. There is the horrible scene in a stormy night when the handicapped characters crawl under a horse carriage, slowly closing in on the target of their vengeance. I feel that the indescribable power of this image does not come from 'a unique code of ethics of the malformed' but grows out of their heart felt anger at betrayal as 'people.' Why is this? The handicapped people and their everyday life at the circus company, is depicted meticulously and in detail, and very naturally in the film. This is, perhaps, an expression of Browning's 'sympathy' for the disabled, as observed by Yanagishita and is far removed from the 'explanation' of the absurd drama. For instance, in the world of the circus, people with various disabilities live as performers. The film depicts all sorts of activities and conversations in their everyday life and there is no absurdity or horror there.

In one scene, for example, Phroso the clown talks to the Siamese twin sisters who are joined at the waist. He congratulates the older sister Daisy who is getting married and chats with the younger sister Violet in a friendly manner. The older sister's fiancé sees them and becomes jealous.

> Phroso: Well, well, well! Tomorrow night's the big night, hey ladies? *(Toward Daisy)*
>
> Violet: Yes, my sister's getting married.
>
> Daisy: And I'm thrilled to death.
>
> Violet: She thrills at anything.
>
> Phroso: Oh, Roscoe's a good kid.
>
> Daisy: She's only joking. She'll like him lots after she knows him better.
>
> Phroso: Oh, that reminds me. Close your eyes, Violet. Go ahead, close them. What did I do? *(When Violet closes her eyes, Phroso pinches Daisy's arm. Daisy laughs.)*

Violet: You pinched Daisy's arm.

(Roscoe watches the exchange between the three anxiously.)

Roscoe: Oh, D-Daisy. *(He stutters).*

Violet: Her master's voice is calling.

Roscoe: Getting fresh, ay? Well, I don't like it one b-b-b-

Violet: Well, come on. Come on. You'll have to hurry. We haven't much time.

Roscoe: So you were flirting with that cheap clown, were you? *(Toward Daisy)*

Daisy: No, I wasn't.

Violet: All he was doing was a trick with me.

Roscoe: You shut up. I'm m-marrying your sister, n-not you. *(To Violet, then turn to Daisy)* I saw him getting familiar with you.

Violet: Oh come on, Daisy.

Roscoe: Oh no you d-don't. She's gonna stay right here!

Violet: No she isn't! I gotta go. *(The sisters leave Roscoe behind).*

Roscoe: Oh, phooey! You're always using that for an excu- for an excu- for an ali-b-b-bi.

This scene is quite funny. Two sisters joined at the waist, each one has her own personality and behaves like a 'person.' The exchange between them and Phroso conveys this to the viewers. Although they have different personalities, they understand each other through their connected bodies. Phroso makes Violet close her eyes, pinches Daisy's arm and asks Violet what he did. Phroso's joke is amplified by the jealousy in Roscoe's words. Even though Daisy is ordered by her fiancé to 'stay right here,' she has no choice but to leave if her sister wants to leave, as their bodies are joined. She has no choice because she is a Siamese twin. The silliness of ordering them around like that is highlighted by Roscoe's muttering: 'You're always using that for an excuse.' I found myself laughing at this scene.

Let me tell you about another scene. Phroso the clown and Venus are talking closely. Johnny, who has no legs and walks nimbly on two hands, comes in, saying: 'Did you try that gag I told you about?' 'Yeah, I did, and it was a wow. Get up here, Johnny and I'll show it you,' says Phroso and tries to put his costume on. Johnny walks up three steps and faces Phroso. Phroso talks to Johnny as a fellow comic performer. It is symbolized by the two figures talking to each other at the same eye level. Then, an intellectually disabled girl comes in and whispers something in Phroso's ear. 'Come on!' Phroso shouts with excitement and runs out with the girl. Johnny follows. 'Come on, Venus, the bearded lady's baby's born!' In a room, the bearded lady is lying in her bed, surrounded by joyful looking handicapped children. An armless girl lifts one end of the blanket with her foot. Phroso peers down the baby and says to the girl: 'Oh, ain't it beautiful! What is it?' 'A girl.' 'Oh boy, that's great—and it's gonna have a beard', says Phroso happily.

In another scene, a woman called Frances who does not have hands is wearing a white dress, and Angelino a dwarf man, are about to have some wine. Angelino pours wine in their glasses.

> Frances: Cleopatra ain't one of us. Why. We're just filthy things to her. She'd spit on Hans if he wasn't giving her presents.
>
> Angelino: Let her try it. Let her try doing anything to one of us.
>
> Frances: You're right. She don't know us. But she'll find out.

As they talk, the man hands a wine glass over to the woman's toes. He lifts his glass up to toast. The woman bends over to drink her wine.

Switching to another scene in which another man, Rollo, and Human Worm (a limbless man wrapped in a sweater) are talking. Rollo says: 'I kinda peeked out the corner of my eye and caught Madame Tetrallini giving us the once over. I guess she knows she's got a good act—one of the best in the business. It isn't only our act that gets them. We've got personality.' While listening to Rollo, the limbless man holds a match and a cigarette in his mouth, strikes the match, places the lighted match on a box and deftly lights the cigarette. The camera stays close on his face while he lights his cigarette. Rollo continues: 'We know how to sell the stuff. Same way in the last town. Never heard such applause in your life. Let me tell you something that everybody around here don't know. We're only killing time with this circus. We've got bigger time to follow. And we can do it too. Well, catch our act tomorrow night. We've got something new.' 'Anything I can do in the act, bro?' says Human Worm with a cigarette in his mouth.

In another scene, the girl who lifted the Bearded Lady's blanket using her foot is talking with another handicapped person over a meal. Close-ups of her having a meal. She uses her foot to hold a folk, eat food on her plate and hold a beer glass.

A series of such scenes portray, perhaps unintentionally by the director, the disabled people smoking, drinking, eating and involved in other usual daily activities. In those days, when people didn't have any fixed perception of disability, in the eyes of the viewers they may have appeared like amazing acts by deformed people. But now, these scenes feel lively and refreshing in that they portray the everyday lives of people with disabilities, in a natural way. These scenes have none of those standardized and rigid perceptions spread by the media such as 'sympathy and pity' toward the handicapped or 'praise' for those who are striving despite their disabilities. Because the handicapped were the object of curiosity rather than sympathy, pity or praise, these scenes of everyday life may have been shot simply with curious eyes rather than with 'consideration' for their disabilities. In those eyes, there was clearly a discriminatory connotation; however, the resultant images depict each of them as a 'person' living with disabilities rather than bundling them together as the 'handicapped' and thus stereotyping them. When I'm faced with these images 'here and now,' I feel the power of real 'people' who are living their lives, not the discriminatory connotation they are supposed to contain.

Depiction of deep-seated discrimination, ostracism and dread

For the analysis of *Freaks*' power to enlighten us 'here and now,' the wedding feast scene is essential. Or rather, it is the finest scene that very realistically depicts the way a person ostracizes, shuns, hates and dreads people with a deformity. I shall try to transcribe the details below as accurately as possible.

The wedding feast

The handicapped members of the circus have gathered around tables in a cheerful mood. One of them is dancing on the table. Cleo and Hercules are smiling and drinking wine. They exchange glances and put poison in the wine under the table. She pours the poisoned wine into Hans' glass and says: 'Oh, come on, my little precious, let's drink. Be happy! Drink!'

Roscoe (the husband of Daisy, a Siamese twin sister) tells the dancing woman: 'Hey, K-Koo, give somebody else a chance! All right, professor.' The professor stands up and says: 'A waltz, please.' He draws a long saber and inserts it into his mouth. People watch him with amazement and admiration. Frieda sits beside them with a gloomy look on her face. Angelino shouts: 'Show him up. Volcano!' Another man swallows and licks a flame. The three sisters clap their hands with excitement.

Cleo is drunk and says to Hans with a loud laugh: 'Our wedding night! What a thrill!' 'Never before did I think I should be so lucky,' says Hans happily. Cleo bursts into laughter, 'Lucky! I'm the lucky one, my little Hans.' 'My Cleo's happy…happy,' says Hans. 'Happy?' Cleo bursts into laughter again. Hercules sitting next to her also laughs loudly. Frieda looks on sadly. 'I'm so happy I even could kiss you, you big homely brute!' says Cleo to Hercules and they embrace and kiss each other. Hans watches them in shock and sobers up at once.

Madame Tetrallini (the three sisters' mother) tries to comfort Frieda. Cleo laughs at Hans, 'Ah, my little green-eyed monster.' A close-up of Frieda's sad face, tears well up. Cleo laughs, 'My husband is jealous! He loves me!' Frieda stands up and runs out of the room. Madame Tetrallini looks on the scene disdainfully, then hurls an epithet at Cleo and runs after Frieda. 'Come, my little lover. Drink to the happiness of your loving wife,' Cleo pours poisoned wine in Hans' glass. Hans looks down with a stone-like expression on his face.

Angelino orders silence 'Attention! Attention! We'll make her one of us. A loving cup! A loving cup!' Josephine-Joseph bangs the table with a folk rhythmically and starts singing; 'We accept her—one of us—gooble, gobble—we accept her—One of us—gooble, gobble…' All the guests start singing along. Angelino fills a large cup with wine. A close-up image of each of them chanting: 'We accept her—one of us—gooble, gobble—we accept her—one of us—gooble, gobble…'

Hercules and Cleo laugh out loud. Hercules says: 'They're going to make you one of them, my peacock!' Hearing this Cleo's drunken face sobers up instantly and turns into a stony expression. Cleo's eyes are on the dwarf man with a big cup on the table, feeding each guest wine from the cup. Cleo's face hardens and grimaces at the sight of it. The party warms up even more.

The camera pans to a close-up of Cleo who has a mixture of hatred and dread on her face as she tries to get up from her seat. It is not the same Cleo who was drunk and laughing loud just then. After giving champagne to everyone, Angelino approaches Cleo at last with a large cup in his hands. Cleo stands up, stony faced, and stares at him.

Angelino drinks from the cup and offers it to Cleo. She takes it in her hand with an awful expression on her face, looks at Angelino and the cup alternately. She frowns with one hand on her hip, not knowing what to do. The guests cheer and chant. There is a close-up of Cleo who glares and shouts: 'You!…Dirty!…Slimy!…Freaks! Freaks! Freaks!…Get out of here!' She throws the cup at Angelino. Cheering stops, everyone falls silent and stares at Cleo. 'Get out! You heard her! Get out!' Hercules shouts, laughing. The guests get up and leave one by one.

'You filth! Make me one of you, will you!' says Cleo to Hans. The freaks watch with an indescribable expression on their faces. Cleo shouts at Hans angrily: 'Well, what are you going to do? What are you a man or a baby!' 'Please! Please! You make me ashamed' says Hans. 'Ashamed! You! Holy Christmas! What must I do? Must I play games with you? Must Mamma take you on a horsey-back ride?' Cleo to Hans. Hercules stands up, 'Ha, ha, that's it! Horsey-back ride! Come, come, my little fly speck. Momma is going to take you on a horsey-back ride.' He goes behind Hans, lifts him up on to Cleo's shoulders. Hercules and Cleo dance around the table, laughing and carrying Hans on Cleo's shoulders. The freaks watch them in silence. (Fade Out).

It is at the wedding feast scene that the freaks discover Cleo's conspiracy and it becomes the turning point in the film which triggers the revenge drama. Apart from Frieda who feels sad for Hans being deceived, the scene is full of joy and happiness. Hans is over the moon, believing that Cleo is really marrying him. Cleo is thrilled that her plot, of marrying Hans to then murder him and claim his inheritance, is being realized. Hans' fellow circus performers joyfully celebrate his marriage. Although each one is feeling a different type of happiness or pleasure, the scene is filled with a joyous mood.

However, I have just said that Hans' colleagues were celebrating his marriage, but is it that simple? Not only Frieda, but also his colleagues must know that Cleo cannot be serious about Hans. Some of them spoke about their distrust for Cleo. In that case, the joyous mood, in this scene, is not how it seems on the surface. It is charged with contradictory feelings. Does Cleo genuinely love Hans? Is she just playing on his feelings? What is her real intention? There are suspicions and a feeling of distrust. At the same time, there is a faint expectation that Cleo will become Hans' partner and a member of their world. These conflicting feelings become visible through the images of the joyful freaks. In other words, they want to celebrate, feel and act happy, but cannot cast aside a doubt about whether they should do so or not. Their chanting: 'We'll make her one of us. A loving cup! A loving cup!' is said in the hope of erasing their suspicion once and for all. It clearly reveals their dark feelings and thoughts behind their happy appearances.

Cleo has no intention, whatsoever, of becoming one of the freaks. She doesn't want to drink from the loving cup, she doesn't even touch it. Faced with their forthright demand to join them, Cleo realizes where she is for the first time and panics, unable to feign love for Hans. She sobers up and her face hardens quickly. Her facial expression becomes more stony and twisted at the sight of the cheering freaks offering a large cup of wine. There is a close-up of Cleo trying to get up, and on her face is a mixed expression of hatred and dread. This is followed by a close-up of her, with her big eyes wide open, shouting 'You!...Dirty!...Slimy!...Freaks! Freaks! Freaks!...Get out of here!'

These images successfully depict the intense expression of ostracism and discrimination directed toward the handicapped and at the same time the terror and dread she feels about the thought of becoming one of them. This brilliant scene depicts, speaks and acts discrimination, ostracism, rejection and terror in the most precise manner. I was greatly impressed by the power of this scene. It is Cleo, shouting 'Slimy! Freaks!' who looms as an ugly figure in the eyes of the viewers.

The power of enlightenment of *Freaks*

So what is the power of enlightenment imbued by the film *Freaks*? As I said earlier, this film is not dealing with 'disability issues.' It is what Yanagishita called an exploitation film which 'looked like a catalogue of sideshow stars at the time.' The film presented handicapped people as freaks for 'curiosity' and the audience might be amazed, horrified and entertained. It portrays people, like Phroso the clown and his lover Venus, who regard the other people with disabilities as their fellow circus performers, and tries to treat them as equals. While, also portraying those characters that dislike the other people's existence, and ridiculing, mocking, and shunning them. The film highlights the contrast between these types of people, but does not necessarily criticize the latter. In a way, both types of people appear matter-of-factly and the story progresses. It has no direct message about the injustice of discrimination or persecution, and if we look only at the surface of the film's images, it may be discriminatory.

However, I am not convinced by such criticisms. Who are the 'freaks' here? Are the unusual looking people the 'freaks?' Those armless, legless, limbless people and two people sharing one body.

They certainly look unusual. The film takes a very close look at their everyday life, but its images convey their vitality to live their lives as 'people,' rather than portray them simply boxed in a category of the 'handicapped' or 'freaks.' So who are the freaks? This question arises as I keep watching the film.

In one scene, Hans, whose sincere love was played upon and who was nearly killed by poison, finally finds out what Cleo is as she spits out, 'dirty...slimy...freaks.' This muttering gives us the answer to the above question. They are not the freaks. It is Cleo and Hercules who do not regard the handicapped as 'people,' and nonchalantly discriminate, ostracize and even try to murder them—they are the real freaks (monsters). Viewed in this light, another mystery in the film starts to make sense. Why has Cleo become the Duck Woman? This may be offensive to ducks and to all animals, but Cleo didn't see the handicapped person as a 'person' and tried to kill him. These are the acts of a 'non-person,' a truly ugly figure. In retribution for her ugly deeds, she was literally turned into a 'non-person' in the shape of a duck. When one does not consider the handicapped as 'people' and tries to discriminate, ostracize and exterminate them, one is no longer a 'person.' But nor are they animal either. They become a 'freak.' This parable is written between the lines of this exploitation film *Freaks*.

In poorly made films or documentaries that aim to be enlightening, the discriminatory or ostracizing characters tend to be somewhat restrained or overly caricatured. The viewers feel that such restraint or characterization is artificial and can even be amusing. This is despite the fact that we know we mustn't find it funny, and nor should we avoid the 'serious meaning' of the films or documentaries because 'we know they are films which want to enlighten us after all.'

On the other hand, when I am confronted by the wedding feast scene, previously discussed, I find myself catching my breath in horror at the ugly sight of Cleo who ostracizes Hans and his friends and discriminates against them in an outburst of terror by calling them 'Slimy! Freaks!' There is no time to distance myself from the scene and I cannot help but stare and wonder about what the nature of its power is. It is important to see discrimination and ostracism in action if we want to understand how it works, depicting discriminatory acts in a direct manner and expressing hatred and dread, as it is. Such frankness appeals to me as a viewer, and makes me ruminate on the many meanings flowing out of the image 'here and now.' I believe that this power makes the film *Freaks* 'the best exploitation film,' not just another exploitation film.

The potential of sociology to analyze films

I am interested in the idea of film as a political product (Hase and Nakamura eds 2003) and the importance of interpreting film in the context of the times in which they were produced. Although this view argues that films reflect their historical background, the approach could turn towards the analysis of the various powers that each image has. As I wrote in the beginning of this paper, I believe that films have moments in which they exert their power and effect upon viewers. This power, when achieved, has the potential to completely overturn the device for defining personal character, by which people usually lead their lives but are rarely aware of doing so. This notion of practical knowledge includes outlook on life and the world, values and common sense. In such moments, the film's power may move me, or it may disturb my 'stability' in an indescribable way. But I am not reacting only at an emotional level. Various parts of my commonsense (practical knowledge) that I use in my everyday life are definitely changing. I want to propose that *Freaks,* exerts on its viewers, the power to change the categorization of the disabled. It also has the power to clearly and accurately present to us the way a person discriminates against and ostracizes another person without being constrained by the rigid concept of 'justice' such as 'welfare' and 'human rights.' The power of the images shakes up and overturns the categorization 'here and now.' We may wake up to the problems of the categorization we used to use innocently, or we may deepen our doubt about the categorization we are already concerned about.

In the moment of our encounter with the images and narratives, the people and events in the images, what are we doing and what are the images doing to us? I think we could develop a new field of sociology along this line of thinking to decipher films as social expressions. While saying this, I am already thinking about a particular scene in another film, *Hush!* (2001) directed by Ryōsuke Hashiguchi. Wanting to have her own child, a woman asks a gay man for 'help.' She is confronted by the wife of the gay man's brother in one scene. I will not go into details here, but there are many scenes which depict intensely discriminatory narratives and events in which characters ostracize and express hate. It is not just the wife's repulsion about the woman's preposterous request. The wife's words and actions suggest the oppression she suffers in her married life, her family life, and the overpowering authority of existing family values. The signs of such authority are explained simply but resonantly in other scenes.

The moment her discriminatory words and actions burst out of the screen, I am trapped into that moment and overwhelmed by it. And in the next moment, I am trying to ruminate on the meaning of these overwhelming images.

Films sometimes approve, ridicule, mock or instantly overturn our commonsense categorization. I have commenced an exploration of this theme in this paper, and I would like to decipher further the sociological meanings of the interactions 'here and now' between films and myself.

12
Lessons on Human Rights Derived from an Epistolary Style: the Sociography of Structural Discrimination

Kōkichirō Miura

First letter: a letter as a medium

Epistolary style

Why would I try to write this thesis for an academic journal in the form of a letter that is in an epistolary style?

I believe that the letter format possesses two seemingly completely opposite qualities simultaneously. One is highly personal and private, as with a love letter addressed to a particular individual. The other is public and open, as with a letter to the editor or an open letter to the general public.[1]

What I am trying to achieve through this thesis is to incorporate, or restore, in the so-called 'academic paper' writing, various motives underlying these two qualities that prompt us when we write a letter.

You will understand the reason if you think about all the rules an academic paper format imposes on us today.

Firstly, this format assumes that its readers are a group of specific academics who share a certain level of specialist knowledge and a common paradigm. Accordingly, it does not require special attention or effort to use easy-to-understand expressions as in the case of writing for large numbers of the general public. It tends to be full of difficult jargon or uncommon and special terminology.

Secondly, the academic paper format requires a positivist and/or (social) scientific writing style. It imposes stylistic restrictions from the outset on the expression of the author's feelings or reflection on his/her own experience. In that sense, it is no exaggeration to say that we, the researchers, are locked in the role of a positivist 'neutral third party' or a 'coolheaded observer' from the beginning.

I have so far resorted to the form of a letter to counter this situation. It started when I searched for an appropriate writing style for my report on the interview-survey of the residents of *hisabetsu buraku* (outcast villages in Japan). I was looking for a style that would enable me to convey exactly what I thought, what surprised me, how I felt and what moved me, as a person listening to their stories, rather than simply summarizing what I heard and what data I collected. I chose an epistolary style because it satisfied the dual objectives of writing to the survey interviewees while writing to a larger number of people beyond a particular group of academics (Miura 1997).

In writing this thesis in the epistolary style, I would like to state first that I have another unfinished dream of writing a research paper satisfying a certain academic standard while adopting a letter style open to a wide range of readers.

Some people may wonder why I used such a formal word as 'lessons' in the title. It seems to me that 'lessons' given in front of several hundred students who are not fully equipped with specialized knowledge of sociology are far closer to a 'letter' than an 'academic paper' is.

What is 'structural discrimination'?

At the core of the main subject of this thesis—the 'structural discrimination' concept—is a very radical attempt to reexamine from the ground up the conventional dichotomy between the minority (those who are discriminated against) and the majority (those who discriminate against others) assumed by sociology.

Accordingly, it is distinct from 'discrimination as a result' suggested by the 'structural discrimination' concept put forward in the USA, (for example, the fact that more minorities live in the areas of environmental degradation near industrial waste processing facilities is in itself discrimination against them), or the so-called 'social structural discrimination' (an approach for the examination of the state of discrimination experienced by those who belong to the lower strata in the social structure).

Structural discrimination proposed in this study is based on the concept of 'discrimination understood from a relational standard' derived from fundamental criticisms of the conventional concepts of discrimination that have 'occurred by circumstances' or 'occurred psychologically.'[2] A characteristic of 'relational' discrimination is that we sometimes contribute to or cause discrimination regardless of whether we have any prejudice or discriminatory idea as individuals when we are placed in certain types of relational situations.

In this sense, 'structural discrimination' tries to understand discriminatory phenomenon not from a so-called substantial (or subjective) standard, but from a relational standard. In contrast with discrimination that has occurred by circumstances or psychologically understood from a substantial point of view, it is in a way 'unintentional discrimination' resulting from the nature of social relations between those who discriminate and those who are discriminated against.

Once the paradigm for the understanding of discriminatory phenomenon has undergone this shift, the limitations of the conventional dichotomy between the majority and the minority become obvious. It is because the dichotomy necessarily demands substantiation and perpetuation of the two concepts on the opposite ends of a spectrum.

Our strategic position on this point was to focus on complex relationships such as 'a minority within a minority,' 'a majority supporting a minority,' 'a majority cooperating with a minority' and 'a majority yet a minority.'

I will focus on particular kinds of relationships at the scenes of support and care in particular.

One example is the independent living movement of severely handicapped people who aspire to move out of their family homes or nursing homes to lead their own lives in society. There is a memorable episode in *Sei no gihō* (The technique of life), a book following the lives of those who are involved in this movement (Asaka et al. 1995).

In a city, various obstacles are waiting for a wheelchair. A stairway with no nearby elevator is one of them. The helper pushing the wheelchair calls out to passers-by for assistance. 'Excuse me, could anyone please help me lifting this up?' The person sitting in the wheelchair protests: 'I don't like the way you say it. I'm the one who wants to go up the stairs, not my wheelchair. I don't like it when you say "this" because I feel like I am being treated as an object.'

Now, if you were the helper, how would you feel about this remark? It may be natural for you to feel offended, thinking: 'Why do you have to be so fussy about such a trivial thing—I didn't mean it.'

But the person in the wheelchair had a good reason for feeling that way. Imagine, for example, a similar situation in which someone is stranded at the bottom of a stairway. You decide to help, and who will you talk to first, the handicapped person or the helper? Generally, the person would start talking to the helper over the handicapped person's head in the overwhelming majority of cases.

The main actor here was supposed to be the handicapped person, not the helper. In reality, the handicapped person has been forced to take a supporting role. Perhaps what was behind the remark: 'I don't like it when you say "this" because I feel like I am being treated as an object,' was the handicapped person's ample experience of being forced out of the leading role. That is why they venture to live independently in spite of various risks.

What concerns me here is the perception gap between the handicapped person and the helper (able-bodied person) on this point. Moreover, the helper and other able-bodied people are all well-intentioned. Yes, they point to the wheelchair unintentionally and talk over the handicapped person's head unintentionally.

As in this example, these people are well-intentioned, not narrow-minded or exclusionists, and show understanding of the handicapped people, but commit something that may not be a violation of human rights, but is infinitely close to it. I believe that the word 'structural discrimination' will start making sense as we attempt to look at this issue from a relational standard of the parties involved, not by heavy-handed criticisms of paternalism.[3]

Toward sociography of relationship

Various spaces that have to be called 'relational gaps,' yet to be defined (socially or sociologically), will emerge from the reexamination of the social relationship between the helper and the helped. We will badly need *a method of in-depth social description based on detailed field research* in order to add this concept to our perception.

Field research may sound a little technical, but I believe all living persons are virtually field researchers of the life-world, not just those who are professional field researchers (Yoshii and Miura eds 2004).

In fact, the 'in-depth social descriptions' we are going to look at below were made by those who were directly involved in each case, whether as the helper or the helped.

In the course of their daily work or in the process of building their own daily life, they have patiently observed various social relationships involving themselves. Not only that, some of them have expressed their thoughts in seventeen syllables of *senryū* (5-7-5 syllabic poem), or published as a memoir, as you will see later. These acts are, in our eyes, the examples of *social research that are unintentionally conducted* in modern society and the examples of 'in-depth social description' based on such research.

Strangely enough, we still do not have an appropriate name for this method of social description.

I would like to propose a new name—'sociography'[4]—to describe *a method of in-depth social description of social relationships*.

Of course, whether or not we can present this term as a clear concept will depend on the amount of sociographical works we will accumulate on 'relational gaps' in the above context.

I would like to restrict myself to pointing out the following two features of the sociography of relationships, in contrast with the conventional ethnography at this stage.

Firstly, sociography literally means a 'style of description' (graphy) 'about/relating to society' (socio). In this sense, it is important that the basic subject of the description is the *various standards of social relationships* that underlie social groups, organizations, networks and systems. It does not necessarily aim at a 'general' description of 'culture' which is the purpose of ethnography. This may sound extreme but even a single *senryū* poem can be considered a fine piece of sociography as long as it closely describes some sort of 'relational gap' from the sociographic point of view.[5]

Secondly, sociography attaches great importance to *participation* and *practice*. If ethnography has been conducted mainly from the 'outsider's perspective' of explorers, travelers, missionaries, colonial administrators, journalists and academics, sociography aims to fully reflect the 'insider's perspective' more than anything. Of course the writer of a sociography does not have to be a participant but researchers will be required to become more involved than ever before when writing a sociography. In this context, an aspiration for practical application, such as how to rearrange the conventional relationships of 'those who discriminate/those who are discriminated against,' is another feature of sociography.

Second letter: with a heavy heart of a perpetrator

The root cause of the discrimination incident

Do you remember an incident which was called the '*fukushi senryū* (welfare poem)' incident that was widely covered by the Japanese media?

Yes, I am talking about the series of events in which poems written by case workers at welfare offices triggered a storm of protests from organizations for the disabled and the publication of the welfare journal which published these poems was suspended.

The following headlines jumped out of newspapers from that period:

> Discriminatory poems in welfare journal—Deriding welfare recipients (Yomiuri Shimbun, 15 June 1993, p. 30).

> 'A client's death, just laugh and tidy up?'—Disability organizations protest (Asahi Shimbun, 15 June 1993, p. 31).

> Poems deride the handicapped—Case workers' journal—The handicapped demands withdrawal (Mainichi Shimbun, 15 June 1993, p. 30).

This incident was shocking because these poems were written by case workers, (welfare field workers, to be more accurate), who were responsible for the eligibility assessment for welfare benefits and for providing advice or support to the recipients until they became independent.

How would you feel about the following poems for example?

> On returning from holiday, I smile at the news of death of my client.

> Call an ambulance? Do it by yourself, stupid.

> No money? What about it? Don't come here (welfare office).

> Please stay in hospital forever, you alcoholic.

The following criticisms by disability organizations are understandable:

> We were shocked to find out that case workers were actually feeling that way as we thought they were sincere people. We don't understand why the publisher wanted to do this (Asahi Shimbun, 15 June 1993, p. 31).

> It is unforgivable that the workers who are supposed to protect the socially disadvantaged are deriding them (Mainichi Shimbun, 15 June 1993, p. 30).

Newspaper editorials were also very critical of those who wrote the poems and of the journal editors. 'Many of the poems express case workers' dissatisfaction and dislike toward the handicapped' (Mainichi Shimbun, 15 June 1993, p.30). 'A majority of poems deride the lives of welfare benefit recipients or single mother families' (Yomiuri Shimbun, 15 June 1993, p.30). 'Most of the poems are hurtful for the welfare recipients' (Asahi Shimbun, 15 June 1993, p. 31).

Many people who read the media reports must have thought that 'writing and publishing such poems are appalling and inexcusable.' I understand their anger as I was also appalled when I read these poems.

However, once I calmed down and thought about it, I felt that the root cause of this incident existed somewhere a lot deeper than in the reported phenomenon.

What brought this intuition to me was a somewhat peculiar atmosphere created by these poems and a sense of urgency surrounding them.

The power of *senryū*

The poems reported in the newspapers included the following:

> On home visit day, I hope my client is well and out.
>
> Putting on a sincere face, I can't get through if I get serious.
>
> No thanks, a cup of tea and you will make me stay for an hour.
>
> At a single mother's home, a strange man is house-sitting.
>
> I'm nodding to the same story on every visit.

Can you picture the vivid scene in which a case worker is having a long talk with his or her client in the living room?

Perhaps an endless stream of complaints and stories are flowing out of the client's mouth as a result of his or her worries about job hunting or dissatisfaction with the present job. The case worker frequently looks at his or her watch and breathes a sigh. You can clearly see an expression of impatience or irritation on their face.

By the way, what is irritating the case worker so much?

Actually, a social worker's work is not limited to independent living support such as providing advice and encouragement so that welfare recipients can lead independent living.

On the other hand, case workers are required to apply the welfare entitlement criteria strictly. To check if welfare recipients (or applicants) are eligible for welfare benefits, they regularly carry out investigations into their assets including savings deposits, dependant carrying capacity of a supporting family member, and the earned income from their work.

And if they find that their clients had savings or income exceeding certain levels or someone who was capable of providing for them, they must begin proceedings to stop the payment of benefits.

It must be a tough job, physically and mentally.

It is an acrobatic feat to conduct a strict eligibility assessment (i.e. stop paying benefits to those who do not meet the criteria) while supporting and leading them to independence. In other words, the job of a case worker demands a contradictory attitude of giving and taking, and trusting and being suspicious all at the same time.

In this sense, even an encounter with a 'strange man' at one client's house, which is a scene of everyday living to be smiled at (or congratulated on), bears down on the case worker's shoulders as a new problem he or she must investigate…

Just several *senryū* poems.

But the pictures drawn by them in our mind, reveal to us, the difficult situations faced by today's welfare field workers.

And more than anything else, they grabbed in both hands and showed us some sort of sludge settling at the bottom of each case worker's heart which we usually cannot see…

Preparedness for discriminatory expressions

In my view, these *senryū* poems published in the welfare journal can be called black humor.

However, I know this comment will immediately prompt the next question: 'Even if it is so, isn't it wrong to deride or hurt welfare recipients by using expressions that promote discrimination or prejudice?'

My answer to this question is 'yes' and 'no.'

I think it is best not to use discriminatory expressions in principle but certainly there are certain situations which permit their use.

Please try and read the poems once more.

Some of them seem to deserve criticism for being disrespectful of people's death and ill health. However, all the poems, including these, have the power to shake the readers violently although their response may be different—some may smile wryly, others may burst into laughter or become speechless or take offense.

And did you notice that all of the poems were ultimately trying to tell us one thing in all sorts of ways? Please try to listen carefully to the silent voices of the case workers echoing in the poems.

Can you hear them? The voices of case workers that sound like cries of pain.

Can you hear the SOS signals they are sending?

The one thing repeatedly put forward by these poems is none other than the harsh, demanding working conditions surrounding case workers.

I believe that the real cause of this incident cannot be discussed without considering their working conditions. (Strangely enough, none of the newspapers mentioned this point at all).

I regard these poems as a form of black humor. The case workers are ringing an alarm bell to the current welfare system by expressing, in the form of *senryū*, the reality of the front line of social welfare, which compelled them to have some sort of discriminatory feelings.

I do believe that there are cases like this one in which the use of discriminatory expressions are unavoidable.

They include the following cases in which:

1. The deliberate use of discriminatory expressions helps people identify contradictions and problems with a society or system, which forces them to use such expressions; and
2. The use of discriminatory expressions is expected to help change fundamentally the social relationships between those who discriminate against and those who are discriminated against, which has created such expressions.

Of course, the following qualifications should be fully considered even in such cases.

Firstly, those who use discriminatory expressions (or expressions considered to be discriminatory) should listen with humility to criticisms and protests by those who are (or feel) discriminated against. Secondly, they should be fully prepared to continue to be aware of the fact that certain people or an unspecified number of people were hurt by their use of discriminatory expressions. In other words, it is a resolve to live with a heavy heart as a person accused of being a perpetrator of discrimination.[6]

Life-threatening

For those who still think that the discriminatory expressions used in those poems are too bad, beyond acceptable limits, I recommend a book to read. The title of this book is precisely '*Seikatsuhogo kēsu wākā funtōki* (Struggles of a welfare case worker)' and it is written by Yōko Mitsuya based on her own experience of working as a case worker for eight years and as an interview officer for five years with a social welfare office (Mitsuya 1996).

She repeatedly states in the book that the job of a case worker is a 'stressful' and 'life-threatening' job burdened by systematic contradictions in the social welfare law.

'Life-threatening' is a rather strong word.

However, I gradually realized that it was not an exaggeration as I read the real-life episodes of Ms Mitsuya and her colleagues in which they were threatened by a gang member whose application for welfare benefits was rejected and who yelled: 'I would only get eight years (in prison) even if I killed you all!' Or desperate words were exchanged between them and an alcohol dependent recipient who was in and out of hospital: 'Find a hospital by yourself if you want to go into a hospital!' 'Are you taking me lightly? I'll kill you!'

And there was a client who had been arrested and detained for suspicion of fraud, extortion, assault and criminal damage on more than a dozen occasions. She writes that it took the whole welfare section of the welfare office to deal with his violence as his case was beyond what one case worker could handle. I was reminded of the world portrayed by those *senryū* poems when I read that a case worker who cared about this man and tried to help him to the end, unexpectedly blurted that he felt 'relieved' when this man passed away.

The highlight of the book is the comment made by the ailing manager of the welfare section two months before his death. I will quote that part in full:

> And at around the same time, there was an incident in which my client heaped abuse on one aged welfare field officer from frustration of not being able to find a place in a nursing home for his parent. This client was always somewhat antisocial in his attitude but the young officer patiently endured a barrage of derogatory words thrown at him...Then, the section manager blurted out in a whispering but angry voice, 'Why someone like him is still alive? It's unforgivable. I hope he dies.' I could not believe my ears. These are the words that should not be uttered by

anyone involved in welfare administration. And I heard them from the mouth of my section manager who was gentle, patient and had a habit of saying that we were always learning from our clients...(Mitsuya 1996: 187–188).

To Editor M

I read in one of the papers that in a short space of time after the poems were published in the journal, more than 1,000 complaints were received by various welfare offices and the editor of the journal appeared completely exhausted by a barrage of daily phone calls of protest.

Editor M, you expressed your regret in the media that 'the *senryū* format failed to convey real intentions properly.' You also said that 'publishing (them) was an error of judgment.'

I do not think your judgment to publish the poems in the journal was wrong at all.

It is undeniable that the poems used some expressions that might hurt welfare recipients or promote discrimination. Nevertheless, I believe that there are some social situations about which discriminatory expressions in public are unavoidable; the current state of affairs surrounding social welfare portrayed by the poems is precisely the type of situation that justifies it.

A significant cut in the government's welfare budget and a reduction in the number of case workers working at welfare offices, brought on by the welfare benefit 'optimization' policy in 1982, have created many distortions on the front line of social welfare. Welfare recipients and also the case workers, who were caught between the government and the recipients, were directly affected by them.

One newspaper carried a letter from a case worker.

> It was wrong to publish them. But I have personally experienced most of the things described in the poems and I could not help but smile wryly or laugh when I read them. I showed them to my colleagues and their response was: "I know, I know..." There is too large a gap between the ideals of social welfare and the reality. I feel that the public and the government do not understand welfare enough (Mainichi Shimbun, 7 July 1993, p. 4).

Clearly there were quite a few case workers who identified with the feelings expressed in the poems.

Not only that, it is not so difficult to imagine that we, too, would have the (seemingly) discriminatory feelings expressed in the poems if we were assigned to work in such an office.

It means that your gloom over your role in triggering this incident would have been ours if we were in your position.

Of course, you and others who were involved in the publication are responsible for the pain suffered by the recipients and the handicapped who read the poems.

However, I do not think that your responsibility has been discharged by the suspension of the journal publication.

I believe that what you are required to do now is to publish in the journal all the criticisms received for the poems as well as reports on the background (or even self-justification) written by the authors of the poems so that a dialogue between case workers and welfare recipients can begin.

The use of discriminatory expressions can have a positive meaning only if it leads to a review of the existing welfare system or if it helps rebuild the relationship between case workers and recipients.

I think that we need to change our attitude toward discriminatory expressions in order to create the right environment for this.

It is easy to criticize discriminatory expressions as wrong or unforgivable.

I believe that one of the options we should take is to try to understand the heavy heart of the perpetrator of (inadvertent) discrimination by placing ourselves in his/her position and to search for a possibility of dialogues with those who were hurt by the discrimination from the standpoint of someone who shares the heavy heart.

Third letter: can you be my hand?

My backside and someone else's backside

I am sorry to open this with a smelly story.

'Why are you doing that?' My three-year-old daughter mumbled while standing and watching me sitting on the toilet.

'...?' I didn't know what she was asking me about at that moment. Then I casually shifted my eyes to my hands and found that I was crumpling folded toilet paper sheets in my hands to soften them.

I didn't notice it instantly perhaps because it had become my habit and I was not aware of doing so. Since when I had piles some time ago,

I have got into a habit of softening toilet paper before use.

When I began to understand my daughter's question, I suddenly realized something with a startle and felt ashamed in my heart.

Around that period, it was my daily routine to drop everything and run to the toilet to wipe my daughter's bottom as soon as she called loudly: 'I've finished!'

If I wiped her bottom even a little too vigorously, she would complain: 'Ouch!' So, I thought I was very careful and gentle when wiping her bottom but I obviously did not do it the way I wiped my own bottom.

This fact is clearly highlighted by my action to soften toilet paper only when I wipe my own bottom.

However, there was another reason for my surprise at the curious face of my daughter.

At that moment, a painful memory from nearly forty years ago instantly came back to me. I saw myself in my childhood, standing, bewildered by a baffling behavior of one girl who was of the same age as I was...

It happened when I was a pupil at a kindergarten in a Tokyo metropolitan area. Partly because my family and I moved to Tokyo from a rural village in Yamaguchi Prefecture and partly because I was absent from the kindergarten for nearly a half of the year from illnesses, it was difficult for me to make friends.

I was sitting alone in a corner of the classroom or the playground most of my time at the kindergarten and I have no memory of talking with others very much. However, just once, I gathered all of my courage to talk to a girl. It was probably a bout of puppy love.

The girl was initially listening and nodding to me. Then, she suddenly started laughing even though I did not say anything funny. And she had a kind of frosty, derisive expression on her face. I think I just panicked and clammed up then.

The painful memory from forty years ago is just that when I put it on paper.

But it left an unexplainable scar inside me until I grew up past my teens. The experience not only reinforced my preconception that I was shy but also created some sort of complex toward women which cast a dark shadow on my adolescence...

By the way, why was my childhood experience from decades ago awakened by my experience of wiping my daughter's bottom?

It turned out that a daring question raised by one woman was behind all of this.

My helper is my hand

Let us go back to the story about the bottom.

This time, it is not my bottom. This is a story about Ms Michiko Osanai, a self-proclaimed 'professional care recipient' whose bottom has been wiped by others thousands of times due to her physical disability.

Reviewing the act of care giving from the standpoint of care recipients has always been her aim in her involvement in the independent living movement by the handicapped. At the starting point of her endeavor was the following experience:

> When we are unhappy about the way our bottom is wiped, we cannot say, 'Please wipe it again.' We hold our tongue, fearing that the carer may be offended if we say it. When I moved into a facility and had my backside wiped by a nurse for the first time, it felt like my bottom was still dirty and unpleasant. But I could not ask her to wipe it again. I just kept repeating a question in my mind: 'Do you wipe your own bottom in this way?' (Osanai 1997: 24)

I try to imagine myself being in a position to receive care.

Anyone would like to make your carer's job as pleasant as possible. Therefore, I would try not to say anything that might sound like a criticism of my carer's work. (For example, 'Please wipe it again' would be almost the same as saying: 'You didn't wipe it properly!')

Ms Osanai has been trying to tell us, based on her own experience, how much discomfort care recipients have had to endure for such a long time because of the asymmetrical relationship that lies between care givers and care recipients (a paternalistic relationship between the helper and the helped).

Certainly, the 'unpleasant bottom' would be one of the worst discomforts of all.

So what has been tried in order to change this asymmetrical relationship? Firstly, emotional elements (such as 'I would like to make my carer's job as pleasant as possible') should be separated from the carer-recipient relationship and replaced by a purely monetary relationship.

Ms Osanai clearly states this:

> A care recipient must be the boss (to a carer). Care giving is all about giving what a recipient wants. A carer should not force his/her ideas

upon a recipient. A recipient must learn to be brave enough to say no if he/she does not like the way care is given (Osanai 1997: 24–25).

I wonder how many hardships and failures this girl, who could not ask her nurse to wipe her bottom again on her first day in the facility, had to go through to get to this stage. To be honest, it is far beyond my imagination how many difficulties she had to overcome.

So what is this new carer-recipient relationship like? I think its characteristics are clearly portrayed in the following episode told by Ms Osanai:

> An old man gets angry if the washing machine is not set to the longest wash time. His helper tells him that it may damage the fabrics but he wouldn't change his way. But you should not think he is a stubborn old man. A helper is his hand, not his wife. *A helper should simply accept and follow his instruction even if it is wrong.* Many helpers are still unsure about this. I burst into laughter when I heard about this story about washing but I believe the principle of care giving can be found there (Osanai 1997: 55–56) (Emphasis added by the author).

Do you understand how different the concept is of 'my helper is my hand,' from the conventional paternalism? Paternalistic care giving has been done from the point of view of a protector as in the case of parents caring for their child (or the wife looking after the husband). (Care giving at hospitals and nursing homes would have been the same).

However, those who aim for independent living including Ms Osanai are saying that a carer should concentrate on being a servant (i.e. hands and feet of the handicapped), not a protector. This change in thinking alone is quite dizzying. (If we became helpers, could we silently follow through on the recipient's instruction even if we thought it was wrong?)

The feel of the hand

All the remarks of Ms Osanai have been quoted from her book, *Anata wa watashi no teni naremasuka—Kokochiyoi kea wo ukerutameni* (Can you become my hand—To receive comfortable care) (Osanai 1997).

At a first reading, she appears to demand that helpers should become their recipients' hands and feet. Some of the readers may be offended, thinking that her attitude is arrogant.

As we see next; however, her argument was intended as a fundamental criticism of the so-called professionals in the field. (It should be noted that there is a sense of self-reproach in it at the same time).

> Becoming confident about their work and more professional is fine, but when you become over-confident and stop wondering if you are doing [it] the right way, I think you will fall into a large pit. When I have my bottom wiped by nursing staff, nurses or helpers who have many years of experience, their lack of doubts or hesitation makes me wonder if they are over-confident. Every time *I feel the hand*, I tell myself not to become over-confident about my own way of living either (Osanai 1997: 30) (Emphasis added by the author).

The irony of the situation is that in which professional care-givers with many years of experience are less competent than others when it comes to wiping other people's bottoms.

Actually, it may not be ironic at all. In fact, Ms Osanai makes this mysterious remark elsewhere:

> I think that a real volunteer is someone who doesn't think he or she can be your hand, just like the title of this book (Osanai 1997: 33).

Her request for helpers to be her hand was coming from the very edge of her desperation with an understanding of its impossibility. In other words, what is meant by the question: 'Can you be my hand?' was the message that the practice of care giving could only start from the acceptance of your inability to be her hand.

In this sense, the whole book seems to be wrapped in Ms Osanai's deep sense of resignation or despair (although I may cause misunderstanding by saying this).

It goes without saying that her resignation or despair is brought by the 'feeling of the hand' when a nurse or helper is wiping her bottom toward which she 'sometimes even feels hatred.'

However, it was not just the fault of professional care givers such as nurses and helpers alone.

Because, from my own experience of wiping my daughter's bottom almost everyday, it is a definite fact that the person who wipes another person's bottom can never feel the 'feeling of the hand' on the latter person's bottom.

I can surely feel the feeling of my hand that is wiping someone's bottom. But I wouldn't know what the 'feeling of the hand' on that person's bottom is like unless that person expresses it in words or gesture.

Even if I get such a response, I can only guess what the 'feeling of the hand' is like, based on the person's mannerism or tone of voice.

And in our hectic daily life, we rarely have time to conduct communication with regard to the way the bottom is wiped.

In that case, the sense of resignation or despair felt by Ms Osanai is not limited to individuals but it is a universal, and at the same time very fundamental, feeling for human beings.

Beyond empathy

With regard to the link between my unhappy experience at the kindergarten and my ordinary everyday experience of wiping the bottom, the fundamental question: 'Can you be my hand?' asked by Ms Osanai had in fact a lot to do with it.

And thanks to the same question, I was able to reaffirm that my stance on the issue of discrimination reflects my childhood experience I am going to talk about below.

There is a sequel to that experience.

I went to university. When I was reading a psychology book one day, I came across one passage which totally riveted me. And I was feeling that the inexplicable mystery which had troubled my mind since my childhood was dissolving away at once...

I think it was a book about developmental psychology. It explained how important the period of age three to four was for children in acquiring their mother tongue.

I came to Tokyo when I was in the later half of that period. What kind of mother tongue was I speaking at the time?

As I thought about it, I clearly realized why the girl laughed.

Even though I had spent one year in Tokyo by then, I was still speaking the language strongly influenced by the back-country Yamaguchi dialect. And because I grew up among my mother and sisters, I would have been speaking in the women's dialect.

I have no signs of the dialect in my speech now except some fragmented memories of it (for example, I used to call myself *uchi* (a female word for 'I') instead of *boku* (a male word for 'I')).

It is not so difficult to imagine how strange and funny it sounded to the little girl's ears when she heard the unfamiliar Yamaguchi dialect with unique vocabulary and intonation.

When I realized that the derisive look I saw on her face was my misperception, I felt an indescribable sense of relief. Also a sense of amusement about myself who had been troubled by a complex I took upon myself.

It may sound like a funny anecdote from my adolescence. But it only lasted for a short while and I was in an abyss of confusion again. I will explain why.

I understood that the girl had no malice. But it is also true that her gaze had managed to trouble me for over a decade.

It means that harmless, or even innocent, extremely ordinary gestures or facial expressions can hurt others more often than not. And the person who did this has no way of knowing that he or she has hurt someone.

I was dumbfounded by this fact for a while.

'You should become the kind of person who can understand another's pain.' This teaching had never sounded so hollow until then.

Getting back to the experience of wiping another's bottom, we have seen that the way one wipes another's bottom in the belief that it is quite 'harmless and ordinary' can end up hurting the person irreparably deeply in some cases.

'Can you be my hand?' What this seemingly provocative question was trying to tell us was the fact that there were some areas around us where we could not fully empathize with the pain of others no matter how hard we tried.

Ms Osanai admits this point straightforwardly:

> Even for the handicapped, those who can walk do not understand how those who cannot walk feel. Those who are able to use hands would not understand how terrifying a runny nose could be. They just cannot know it by direct experience. There are so many things that are unknowable (Osanai 1997: 94).

What we need to do first is to recognize the fact that there is a vast expanse in front of us that we cannot empathize with, rather than trying to find an easy way to empathize.

Once we have recognized the fact, then we need to have enough composure to listen calmly to unexpected complaints or requests coming from our counterpart (e.g. 'do it more gently, once again!'). I think this is what is required of each of us.

Postscript (in lieu of conclusion)

This thesis can be called an attempt to face squarely a certain type of ill-being that is almost inevitably contained in the 'helper/helped' or 'care giver/care recipient' relationship in modern society. 'Structural discrimination' is just another name for this type of ill-being.

And what has come to light as a result? Various forms of ill-being such as the 'heavy heart' of care workers and a 'sense of resignation' of handicapped people should not necessarily be rejected totally in themselves. In other words, what these examples showed us was an undeniable truth that the pursuit of real well-being could only be accomplished by fully embracing such ill-being or enjoying such ill-being to the limit, rather than by political measures such as the removal or exclusion of ill-being phenomena.

I should note; however, in order to avoid misunderstanding that 'enjoying ill-being' does not mean I am recommending the use of 'despair' simply as a psychological mechanism to attain well-being, as suggested by Comte-Sponville (2000). It means to 'enjoy ill-being' to achieve our objectives, including a thorough analysis of various social systems which have generated ill-being, and the rearrangement of such relationships.

In this sense, the following comment made by a woman living in a *hisabetsu buraku* appears to explain the dialectic of well-being and ill-being aptly:

> As far as I'm concerned, I enjoy listening to discriminatory views of people very much because I realize there are people who have interesting views (laughs). When I hear them, I don't get depressed now, I really think, ah, that's how they see things, and I think I really enjoy it very much (Interview by the author).

13
In Search of Evidence of a Child's Best Interests: Bridging Research and Practice in Social Work

Matsujiro Shibano

Foreword

'Social protective care' was defined in the Social Security Deliberative Council's Child Welfare Panel report issued in November 2003, by the words 'a child's best interests' (2003: 2). Despite the fact that the Child Welfare Law has been repeatedly revised, the fundamental principle of 'a child's best interests' has never been defined.

Article 3 of the *Convention on the Rights of the Child*, adopted by the United Nations in 1989, is generally regarded as the provision which deals with children's 'best interests.' In Paragraph 1 of this Article, it is stated that: 'In all actions concerning children, whether undertaken by public or private social welfare institutions, courts of law, administrative authorities or legislative bodies, the best interests of the child shall be a primary consideration' (United Nations 1989: 5). This means that all treatment of children must be carried out in each child's best interests. Unfortunately there is no definition of what exactly constitutes best interests.

The preamble to the *Convention on the Rights of the Child* does; however, include the following description:

> Convinced that the family, as the fundamental group of society and the natural environment for the growth and well-being of all its members and particularly children, should be afforded the necessary protection

and assistance so that it can fully assume its responsibilities within the community...Recognizing that the child, for the full and harmonious development of his or her personality, should grow up in a family environment, in an atmosphere of happiness, love and understanding... (United Nations 1989: 3).

This is a clear indication that, in order for the child to grow within the community and to be able to take its place in the world as a human being, 'the place of growth,' that is the family environment, is essential. We can assume that it is the guarantee of this family environment, representing the child's best interests that must be considered in the treatment of the child. Therefore, it is only natural that, as is evident in the Social Security Deliberative Council's Child Welfare Panel report of 2003, a move for a renewed recognition of the importance of 'family-like care' in social protective care—something that has been difficult to establish in Japan—is taking place. This recognition is occurring by the incorporation of the fundamental principle of 'the child's best interests' into 'social protective care' (the care, by society, of a child who, for whatever reason, is not able to remain with his or her own family).

The major issue remains of how exactly to define and convey 'best interests' in social work. That is, how to demonstrate evidence of 'a child's best interests' in a way that anyone can understand. In particular, this paper will consider the interface between research and practice by examining the way in which to convey a child's best interests. And more specifically, it will explore the question of what perspective should be taken in examining evidence of 'best interests' by the social work profession. The aim is to consider ways of bridging the two—something which has been a long-standing issue in social work—by referring to the developmental study that my colleagues and I have been involved in.

The ongoing search for evidence of best interests in the USA

The 1974 Act to address child abuse

It is approximately forty years since the 'battered child syndrome' shocked the people of the United States of America. As the Program Director of the 1961 Meeting of the American Academy of Pediatrics, Henry Kempe planned an interdisciplinary meeting and reported on examples of child abuse. In the following year, a thesis that appeared in an academic journal graphically described children who had been cruelly abused by their actual parents (Kempe et al. 1962) and child abuse was immediately recognized as a major social issue. In 1968, Helfer and Kempe published a book titled *The Battered Child*, which has since been revised and republished numerous times and is regarded as the most detailed and reliable specialist textbook on child abuse to date (Helfer and Kempe 1968; Helfer et al. 1997).

As a result of strong public demand, the Child Abuse Prevention and Treatment Act was enacted in the United States of America in 1974. 'Saving children's lives' was the essence of this legislation. Children who were being abused were successfully separated from the perpetrating parent/s under the banner of 'rescue' and 'protection.' The children separated from their families in this way were then placed under protection in institutions and foster families to guarantee their safety. The new law was effective. At the same time, however, the children also lost an environment that was vital to their growth. There was no way in which parents, whose children had been taken away from them, would have been able to have their child returned unless conditions changed. This required both specialist and non-specialist support. In a situation that does not offer this support; however, the child loses the growth environment that they can return to. The child who was abused and placed in protection (separated from his/her family) was not able to return home and therefore found him/herself frequently moving between foster families and institutions. This is the 'drift' or 'limbo' phenomenon. The 1974 Act would prove to have unexpected consequences.

The North American interpretation of 'a child's best interests'

All children need a stable growth environment and it took some time before North American society understood this basic fact. Assisting this understanding was the research by Goldstein et al. (1979). In their book, *Before the Best Interests of the Child*, which represented the results of extensive research carried out by the authors, Goldstein, Freud and Solnit claimed that children require a stable family environment in which a psychological parent is present. According to the authors, this parent does not necessarily have to be a biological parent—as long as he or she is an adult who has the ability to develop a strong psychological bond with the child. The physical and functional place where this adult is present is the family environment.

This is arguably the North American interpretation of 'a child's best interests.' However, I believe that this has a universal significance that transcends North American or Western society and can also be seen in the preamble and Article 3 of the even more universal *Convention on the Rights of the Child* (United Nations 1989), referred to at the beginning of this paper.

Goldstein et al.'s research altered national policy and new legislation was enacted along with the establishment of a new system. As a result, the Adoption Assistance and Child Welfare Act, which proved to be highly significant in North American history, was enacted in 1980. Government policies are seen as being generated as the result of two situations: when public opinion moves politicians and a policy is devised over a relatively short term as a political response to public opinion; and when a policy is devised over the long-term based on systematic research undertaken to understand the issue (Pecora et al. eds 1992). The former can be effective over time but can just as equally be a haphazard and symptomatic therapeutic policy that is short lived. The latter may, in some cases, not be as effective over the long-term as initially anticipated, but as a solid policy addressing the issue may alter history and have a long shelf life. This child welfare policy and the 1980 Act, that are based on the results of Goldstein et al's research, are the product of both: a maturation of public opinion in response to the drift phenomenon; and a long-term, systematic research and investigation that sought to understand this phenomenon and altered North American history, continuing to wield its influence today.

Due process in realizing permanency

Three characteristics are attributed to the 1980 Act, which is known as the Permanency Law (Schuerman et al. 1995; Shibano 2001). These are firstly, least restrictive alternatives: secondly, reasonable efforts and; thirdly, permanency planning. Figure 13.1 represents an assistance procedure flow diagram. The due process based on the 1980 Act (legal procedure based on the law, in which specialist professions have a duty of execution and are responsible for this, while the person receiving the support has the right to demand that this be executed appropriately) will be reviewed by following this flow diagram.

Firstly, a child who is determined as being abused is not immediately separated from the perpetrating parent and instead *reasonable efforts*

Figure 13.1: Process of permanency planning based on 1980 Act

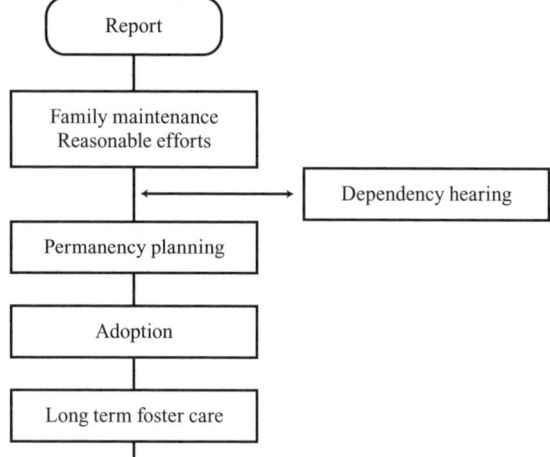

are made to maintain the family (family maintenance) as the child's growth environment. If it is determined that, regardless of these efforts, the family is not able to be maintained, a hearing into whether the child should be separated from the parent (guardian) and placed outside the family (dependency hearing) is held. If it is determined that the child must be removed from the family, parental rights are transferred to the juvenile court, and *reasonable efforts* are made to provide a growth environment for that child. This is permanency planning. In the 1980 Act, a hierarchy was established in this planning in order of the least restraint of the child. Adoption is at the top of this hierarchy, and represents *the measure in which the rights of the child is least restrained.* This is because it provides the child with a stable family that most resembles the child's birth family. If child adoption is difficult, long-term foster care in the form of a foster family or institution, (although few institutions remain today), becomes an option. In Japan a differentiation is made between placing the child in family-like care, in the form of foster parents, and placing the child in institutional care, with the former being seen as the provision of a family environment. In the USA, however, due to legal and psychological restraints, these two forms of care are seen as being equal. If these measures cannot be realized, there is the option of assistance and support towards autonomy and emancipation.

Safety, permanency and well being: The 1997 Act

The American Permanency Act has been repeatedly revised, and was last revised in 1997 to become the Adoption and Safe Families Act. In this Act the hierarchy of permanency planning has been altered to enable flexibility in response to each child's situation as well as that of his or her family. Moreover, when abused children are placed into protective custody or temporary custody, the family environment is improved and safety achieved through direct assistance of and support for the family, including the perpetrating parent (guardian), in order to guarantee that a stable and continuous family environment (permanency; more stable and permanent growth environment) is provided more promptly. As a result, this law indicated even more clearly that family reunification or adoption, if the former was not possible, must be carried out.

The goal of the Safe Families Act is the realization of safety, permanency and well-being. Although the process for achieving this goal is obviously important, this law arguably places greater importance on results rather than process. The 1997 Act made it clear that it was society's accountability that must clearly indicate whether as a result of efforts that, assistance, safety, permanency and well-being were achieved.

Surprising though it may be, the Convention on the Rights of the Child has not yet been ratified in the USA. As we have seen; however, based on the Permanency Act (1980) and the Safe Families Act (1997), that incorporate 'best interests,' due process for achieving best interests and the goal as the result is clear. The reasons given for why the USA has not ratified the *Convention on the Rights of the Child* include the traditional isolationism of the USA and its resistance to the child's right to autonomy and social rights. However, I believe that this represents pride in the fact that legal procedures to guarantee best interests already exist. This can be interpreted as representing ongoing continued efforts to clarify evidence of best interests and a strong will to continue with these efforts.

A child's best interests: a legal system that demands evidence

The positioning of a child's best interests in Japan

Stories of child abuse and neglect have frequently appeared in newspapers in Japan over the last decade. A private organization (Child Abuse Prevention Association—a voluntary and currently non-profit organization) was established in 1990 in Osaka to deal specifically with child abuse and neglect. This was followed by an exponential increase in the number of reports of abuse and neglect reported to child and family centers, and this in turn influenced public opinion and politics. A bipartisan members' bill in 2000 resulted in the enactment of 'legislation related to the prevention of child abuse and neglect' (Child Abuse Prevention Law). However, there is no mention of a child's best interests in this legislation. In Japan, as indicated by the energetic activities as a result of the establishment of private organizations throughout the country such as JaSPCAN (Japan Society for Prevention of Child Abuse and Neglect), it was the private sector that were the leaders in publicly addressing this issue.

Japan ratified the *Convention on the Rights of the Child* five years after the Convention was adopted by the United Nations. Legislation was not newly enacted with the ratification and the issue was addressed through the application of the Child Welfare Law. Therefore, in Japan, the child's best interests are yet to be clearly defined within a legal context. It is well known that the United Nations has issued a strong request for this to be carried out. The revision of the Child Welfare Law, the enactment of the Child Abuse Prevention Law and the revisions that have followed, have each been carried out in response to the reporting of high-profile incidents, popular opinion and various political considerations. They are arguably typical examples of policy and legislation that is transitory, haphazard and symptomatic.

As is evident from this type of situation, permanency planning that substantiates a child's best interests clearly does not exist in Japan. The effect of this is evident in the frequently unprofessional response by the staff in child and family centers. This may seem an extreme argument, but I believe it is indicative of the lack of measures in Japan's child and family social work to identify accountability. Public opinion quickly becomes heated, and politicians respond unconditionally and reflexively, resulting in a series of inconsistent new legislation and minor legislative amendments. After this, people's emotions rapidly cool and nothing is done until the next high-profile incident. This pattern is simply repeated without any fundamental reform taking place, and as a result, the principle of permanency cannot be established and matured in Japan.

A legal system without a backbone

In such an environment, there are few attempts in demanding evidence of a child's best interests. In Japan, both general citizens and professionals are obliged to report child abuse and neglect under Article 25 of the Child Abuse Prevention Law. But depending on the local government, there are differences in the ways the child and family centers, to whom the reports are directed, handle these notifications. With the enactment of the revised Child Welfare Law in 2004, some of the functions of child and family centers were transferred to local authorities, which resulted in even greater disparities in the way reports were dealt with. Furthermore, in a situation in which parental authority—prescribed in the civil code of the Meiji Period—remains effective, and in an absence of the principle of permanency which underpins the child's best interests, *reasonable efforts* for *family maintenance* are not carried out. As a result, the child's protection through his or her removal from the family, the child's return to the family, or family reunification is carried out while parental rights remain in place. Consequently, there is little judicial involvement in assisting the child who has been abused or neglected. Any assistance is carried out without the provision of safety based on due process backed by legislation, the execution of which is mandatory, and without goals such as the permanent provision of a family environment in place. As the only goal is the securement of the child's safety and protecting the child's life in the immediate future, the assistance provided is both unplanned and momentary. It comes nowhere near a form of assistance in which goals such as long-term safety, the securement of a growth environment (permanency) and well-being are established. Social workers (such as the child welfare officers and workers at the child and family centers operated by local authorities) can only rely on the dim light of 'immediate safety' as they proceed through a jungle without any maps or equipment. A legal system, that can be a backbone to enable evidence of a child's best interests to be provided, is necessary.

Flow or phase?: a discussion

The USA and Japan are two countries, which have responded differently to these situations. They have been compared, and there has been a consideration of the position of the legal system in terms of a child's best interests, the due process based on this, and whether goals actually exist. The establishment of a system guaranteeing 'a family that includes a psychological parent' as a social responsibility, in other words, that provides 'a safe and stable growth environment,' is what realizes a child's best interests. Evidence of safety, permanency and well-being in the form of the permanency planning (process), and its results, must be explicitly provided as definite goals.

Practitioner and researcher

I have been involved in developing a best practice model that is able to convey the accountability of social work as professional assistance in child abuse and neglect cases. My interest lies in improving the quality of professional practice by: viewing the response to child abuse and neglect in child and family centers in the form of case management; to store this process in the form of digital information; and to provide feedback to appropriate assistance and support practices.

In the past, evaluation of social work practice was primarily nomothetic (an approach in which groups are used to obtain a universal conclusion), or summative (an approach in which there is an attempt to achieve a cumulative and recapulative conclusion). In order to maintain objectivity, the assessor or researcher cannot, as a rule, also be the practitioner. In many cases, however, the results of these forms of research were not utilized in practice, and there were concerns about the separation of research and practice (Shibano 2004b). Studies carried out by research specialists who seek universality or principle, mainly provide average, explanatory and static knowledge. However, what is sought in practice is individual and dynamic knowledge and skills that will be useful in providing assistance (Schuerman 1983). Jayaratne and Levy (1979) argued that research education in social work was insufficient in educating the consumer—who uses the research results obtained by research specialists—and that there was a need for education and training to teach professionals how to plan and implement one's research and reflect this in one's own practice. This is the definition of the concept of 'practitioner-researcher.'

The necessity of filling the void between research and practice has since continued to be argued but the anticipated results have not emerged. In recent years, however; Gibbs and Gambrill (1999) have presented a detailed method of critically interpreting research results and reflecting this in practice, arguing for the importance of evidence-based practice (or EBP). Although the importance of EBP in social work is being rapidly recognized, the image of the social worker as a consumer with a slightly higher knowledge of research results still prevails. I have continued to argue for the importance of EBP as practitioner-researcher (Shibano 2004a; 2004b). By this, I mean the importance of a pragmatic cycle in which research is implemented in practice and the results reflected in practice. The implementation of social work in the child's best interests—in other words case management—is represented by EBP in which the social worker as practitioner-researcher carries out his or her own research, and utilizes the results to provide assistance.

EBP as a bridge to connect research and practice

In comparison to other similar professions, it has been pointed out for many years that there are few detailed procedures in social work practice (Thomas 1978; Reid 1979; Mullen 1978). Despite this, however, no major improvements have taken place. This is particularly pronounced in Japan. Although various practice methods as new responses to issues and problems are being developed in many different places, little modeling is carried out for the dissemination of these practice methods, and research and development with the clear goal of dissemination is required. The modeling of practice procedures that has been developed with the aim of dissemination is called a practice model (Reid and Smith 1981; Shibano 2002a).

Rothman and Thomas (1994) gave the name 'Design and Development' (D & D) to the procedure of research and development with the aim of dissemination. I have amended and simplified this D & D so that not only researchers but also social work practitioners can also develop practice models at the workplace. This version was released as Modified Design & Development (M-D&D) (Shibano 2002a). Although I am unable to elaborate on M-D&D in this paper, it can be simply described as a procedure for the development and dissemination of a practice model that is comprised of the following four phases (refer Figure 13.2). First, the assessment and analysis phase; second, the tentative practice model design phase; third, the pilot testing and improvement phase and; fourth and finally the dissemination and tailoring phase. The tentative practice model is pilot tested in the third phase and the model refined through repeated testing. This process is called iteration and is an important feature of M-D&D. The improved final model is advertised and disseminated in Phase four and is customized to suit the practice site where the model

Figure 13.2: The modified design & development (M-D&D) process

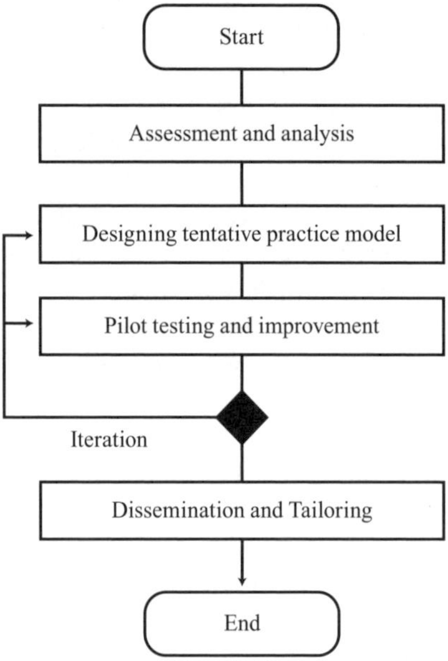

```
Start
  ↓
Assessment and analysis
  ↓
Designing tentative practice model  ←┐
  ↓                                   │
Pilot testing and improvement  ←──┐   │
  ↓                               │   │
  ◆  Iteration ────────────────────┴───┘
  ↓
Dissemination and Tailoring
  ↓
End
```

is to be utilized. This dissemination and tailoring phase is also an important feature of M-D&D.

The development and dissemination of the practice model first comes into its own when research and practice is linked. In this sense, the authors believe that it can fill the gap between research and practice, which is the eternal issue of social work. The practice model which was created in this way also contributes to the realization of EBP.

A practice model that realizes a child's best interest

The development of a practice model is not simply for the realization of EBP. There is another practical significance—to provide a solution for the common dilemma found amongst professionals who are directly in contact with the recipient of assistance or a user. Lipsky (1983) called the professionals working on the fringes of bureaucratic organizations 'street-level bureaucrats' (SLB). He described them as those who have the most discretion, despite being the most restricted, as a result of being at the fringe of the organization. In the social work sector, the demand is always greater than the level of services that can be provided and Lipsky argues that, within such an environment, it is the

SLB's discretion that determines the equity of services. The SLB has considerable discretion in relation to providing assistance to the user, such as through the provision of information on services available and deciding to what extent and how management is to be carried out. As a result, inequality in the provision of services, such as the favoring or disfavoring of certain users can happen quite easily. However it is also true that, because of the discretion that the SLB has, the SLB is able to provide—from the limited service resources available—more resources to more people that require them, rather than parity-based resource provision. Mary E. Richmond (1922) quoted Plato who said: 'treat unequal things unequally,' to describe the essence of casework. She claimed that it was individual assistance-based casework that represented the very essence of casework. Arguably, the aim of the SLB's discretion is the realization of this. However, although the SLB wants to effectively use its discretion to ensure that more services are provided to more people that need them, any unfairness must be avoided, and this is where the SLB faces a dilemma. The same applies to the organization. Although the intention is to utilize the SLB's discretion and realize a fair though not equal service, because of the risk of unfairness being generated, the organization finds itself having to solve the extremely difficult problem of minimizing such unfairness. The development of a practice model and its utilization as a guide in the provision of assistance or as a navigatory tool represents one solution for the dilemma surrounding the discretion of the SLB. I believe that there is a need to develop a practice model that utilizes the advantages of the SLB's discretion and at the same time minimizes its weaknesses.

Thinking along these lines, the clear presentation of evidence of a child's best interests requires three key elements. Firstly, the establishment of a legal system that reinforces the idea of permanency; and secondly, the design and development of a practice model based on this legal system. Thirdly, the manualization of a practice model (the presentation of a more detailed set of procedures and guidelines arguably implies detailed due process), with the discretion of the social worker who is the SLB being monitored and flexibly controlled to effectively utilize the SLB's discretion towards the realization of practice that is fair and of a high standard (Shibano 2002a; 2002b).

Flow or phase?

Through a research grant from the Ministry of Health, Labor and Welfare, my colleagues and I developed a practice model for child welfare officers involved in child abuse and neglect cases at child and family centers, and believe that this model has the potential to provide a solution to social work as evidence of a child's best interests. However, a major problem was encountered during the development of this model. As described in the previous section, in Japan, the concept of permanency—essential to the child's best interests—does not exist in either the Child Welfare Law or the Child Abuse and Neglect Prevention Law. As a result, no due process for assessing the assistance process to realize the child's best interests, nor the goals to assess the results of this assistance, exist. Haphazard legislation and repeated legal amendments which are simply minor amendments to the legislation have resulted in a patchwork of laws, and the reality is that we have almost lost sight of the inherent purpose of the Child Welfare Law and the Child Abuse and Neglect Prevention Law. The response of the child welfare officer is equally haphazard and their response represents nothing more than an attempt to solve the immediate problem. Indeed, in most cases nothing is actually done for permanency. Furthermore, there has been only a slight increase in the number of professionals dealing with the exponentially increasing cases of abuse, creating a situation that allows the child welfare officer or the SLB's discretion to be directed in the wrong direction. This situation was revealed as a result of the interview survey that we carried out several years ago on child welfare officers at a child and family center in City A (Kimura et al. 2002). As a result of analyzing deviant behavior recorded in child welfare officer's handbooks based on the *Guidebook to Dealing with Child Abuse and Neglect* edited by the Children and Families Bureau, the Ministry of Health, Labor and Welfare (1999), it was apparent that decision-making based on insufficient information was chronic, while there was marked deviation from the assistance process outlined in the handbook, that is, the assistance flow that the officers were required to follow. Although legislation exists and something akin to due process is presented as a set of guidelines, because of the absence of the concept of permanency as a backbone to support this process, there are no goals. As a result, an assistance plan (treatment guidelines) to realize case assistance is not being established and reasonable efforts to assist appropriate to that plan, are not being carried out. Because of this, and as a result of their discretion, the SLB typically ended up 'deciding not to make a decision' and a significant deviation from the flow was evident. In Japan, there was a need to first raise the issue of thoroughly carrying out the basic decision-making process before depicting a flow. We realized that, rather than conducting the child welfare officer through a fixed process backed by the law, a practice model to guide the professional to ensure the best decision-making was needed in the decision-making phases that the professional passes through during this process.

Meanwhile, a flow can be depicted in countries such as the USA where permanency, as a principle to ensure the child's best interests, is clearly defined. Family maintenance and permanency planning as due process based on this principle exists, and there are goals that provide a standard upon which to assess the results of the implementation of the assistance plan. The careful recording of the social worker's actions in the form of assistance activities referring to this flow and the child and family's situation (safety, permanency and well-being as goals) becomes the evidence of a child's best interests. Therefore, it is the existence of a legal system (or lack thereof) that acts as a backbone for this process that determines whether the model is a phase-mode or flow-mode model.

A framework for a practice model for a child's best interests

In this section, the structure and features of the practice model developed by my colleagues and myself will be introduced and the link between research and practice considered. The phase-mode practice model under the Japanese legal system and the flow-mode practice model under the American legal system will be introduced and details of social work-based and professional solutions as evidence of a child's best interests are considered while comparing the two modes. In addition, the mechanism in which the social worker as SLB monitors the process involved in utilizing this practice model to carry out assistance, and then transfers this to the database will be considered, while emphasizing the importance of storing and utilizing process evidence and outcome evidence.

Two practice models: the phase and the flow modes

As we have seen so far, whether due process is depicted as a flow, or as a flexible combination of the decision making phases in the assistance process, is determined by whether a child's best interests is clearly defined by child welfare and child abuse and neglect related legislation. Therefore, when dealing with actual abuse cases, there are two practice models guiding the social worker or SLB—the phase-mode model and the flow-mode model.

The phase-mode practice model applies to assist a child who has been abused when a child's best interests is not clearly defined in child welfare or child abuse prevention legislation as 'the guarantee, as a social responsibility, of a safe and stable family environment as a place for the child to grow up in.' The situation in Japan is one in which the child and family center (as the public agency prescribed by the Child Welfare Law which has to provide various advice related to children), must provide both initial assistance requiring mandatory protective intervention, as well as intermediate and later assistance. This comprises of non-mandatory protective assistance, which is provided for family reunification or the autonomy of the child and family (a form of assistance which emphasizes a favorable relationship between the child and its family). In other words, the social worker must be both 'good cop' and 'bad cop.' In some situations, the due process backed by legislation is not clear and the only assistance process given is that outlined in operational guidelines or a handbook. In other situations, because the assistance target of providing a safe and permanent environment for growth and achieving a child's healthy growth or well-being in this environment is not made clear, the onus of planning short-term, mid-term and long-term assistance targets is left to the discretion of the social worker. In addition, situations exist in which assistance must be provided while accepting the existence of parental authority based on the family system of the civil code of the Meiji period. These various situations create vast inconsistencies in the way that some of the 180 child and family centers in Japan deal with cases, allowing for haphazard responses on the part of social workers and preventing the depiction of a flow that could be put into practice. As a result, there is no choice but to create a practice model that represents a flexible combination of decision-making phases such as 'temporary protection,' 'on-the-spot inspections' and 'Article 28 motion' (Shibano 2002b; 2003; 2004b; 2004c).

The *Guidebook to Dealing with Child Abuse and Neglect*, issued by the Children and Families Bureau, the Ministry of Health, Labor and Welfare (1999; 2000) and the results of the survey, confirmed the existence of situations demanding important decisions to be made in terms of providing assistance in child abuse cases, as indicated in the rhomboid diagram in Figure 13.3, in Kimura et al. (2002). These decision-making phases are positioned in the strategic stages of the assistance process in response to a report to the child and family center following the discovery of child abuse in the region. The initial stage requires urgent and mandatory protection of the child by the child and family center (or welfare office) in which temporary protection is considered. The intermediate stage is that in which the protective care policy such as care in the home or in an institution is determined after the obtainment and analysis of sufficient information; through to the final stage in which the decision to return the child to his/her family or family reunion is made and executed. When these phases are scrutinized, eight phases similar to those in Figure 13.4 were confirmed (Shibano 2002b; 2003, 2004c). As indicated in Figure 13.4, the important phases in the phase-mode practice model to be applied under the Japanese legal system, is not part of a linear flow. Instead, it is non-linear and reversible and phases can be skipped. Therefore, the features of the phase-mode model can be represented by placing the phases in a circle as shown in Figure 13.4. Furthermore, risk assessment, vital in dealing with child abuse and neglect cases, must be repeatedly carried out and updated. A more detailed decision-making process for each phase based on the updated assessment results must also be implemented. This is represented in the diagram by positioning risk assessment in the middle of the decision-making phases positioned in the circle.

The independence of each decision-making phase is strong in this phase-mode practice model and each phase can be modeled as an independent decision-making unit or module. The independent module of each decision-making phase can be seen as a conglomerate of procedures in which the decision-making process based on the IF=THEN rule (the rule in which IF certain information is available THEN specific assistance is carried out) represents the core. The feature of this type of module is that the SLB's negative discretion is suitably controlled so that its function encourages appropriate action. In other words, it carries out a navigational function and an educational function in the form of on-the-job-training so that the child welfare officer or the SLB can carry out the appropriate decision-making that forms the core of each phase (for example, whether to carry out temporary protection or whether to carry out an on-the-spot inspection) (Shibano 2004c).

Meanwhile the flow-mode practice model is a model that is applied when a legal system exists within which the concept of a child's best interests is clearly defined. This model is viable when due process as part of family maintenance and permanency planning is made clear, as can be seen in the 1980 Act (the Permanency Act) or the 1997 Act (Safe Families Act) of the USA. Figures 13.5 to 13.8 represent due processes in dealing with child abuse prepared by the Department

Figure 13.3: The Japanese-style management process in dealing with child abuse cases

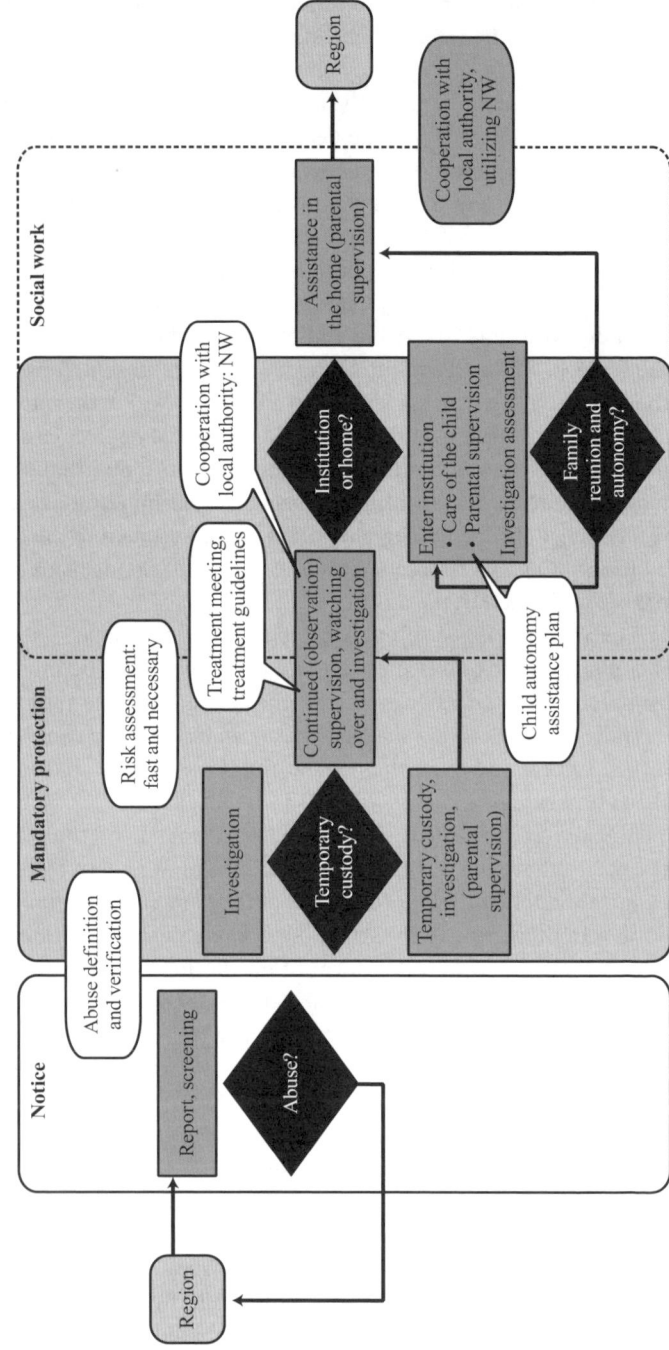

In Search of Evidence of a Child's Best Interests 289

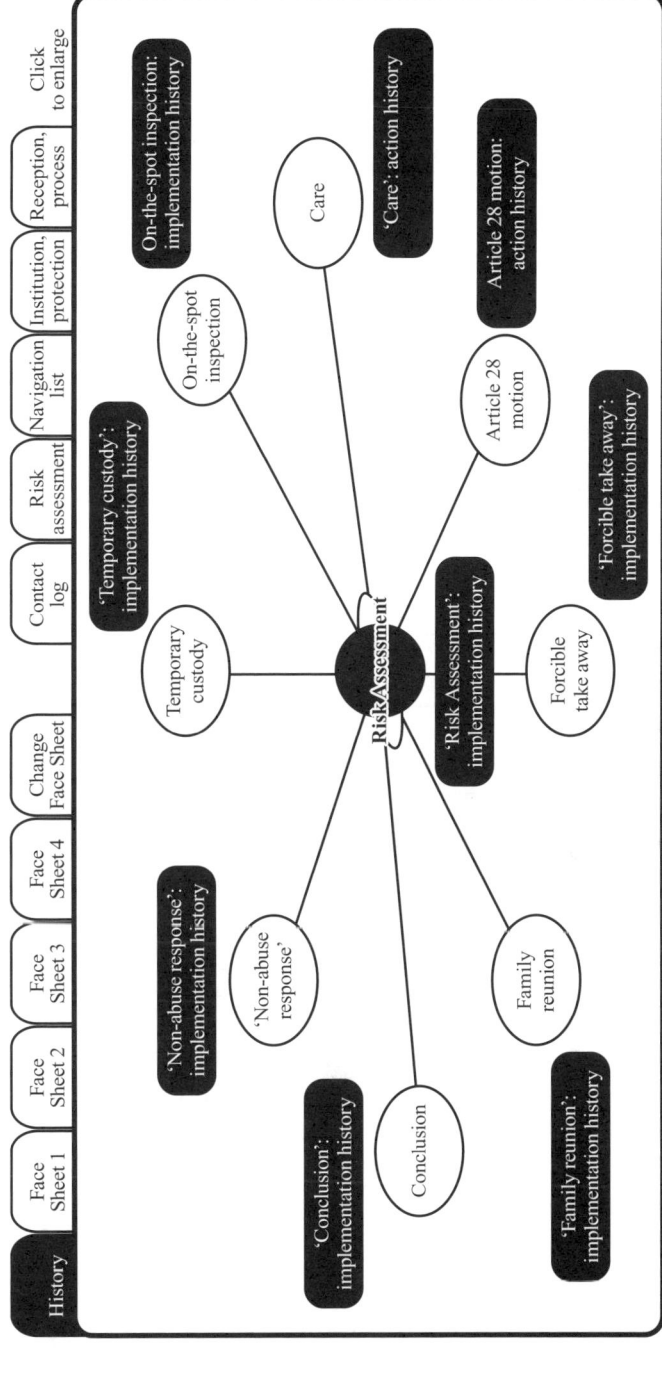

Figure 13.4: The practical navigational database system's decision-making phase and risk assessment phase based on the phase-mode practice model

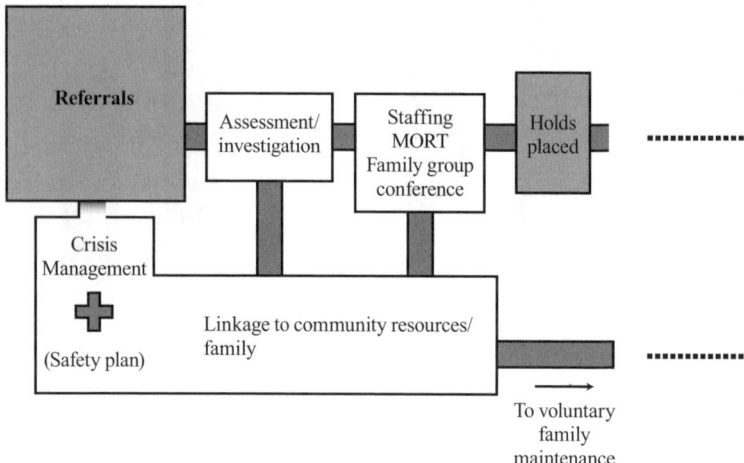

Figure 13.5: Fresno County due process 1: Referrals and investigation

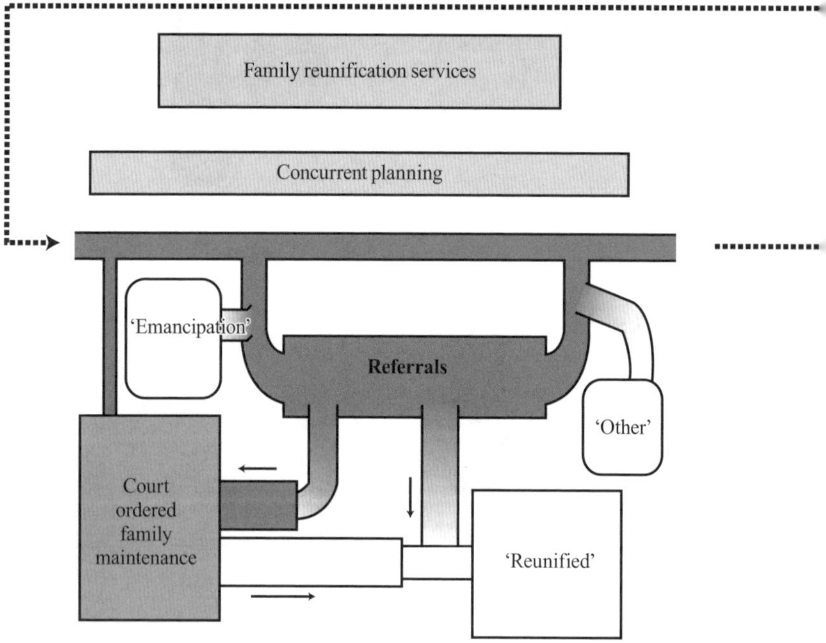

Figure 13.7: Fresno County due process 3: Family maintenance, protection hearing and family reunification

In Search of Evidence of a Child's Best Interests 291

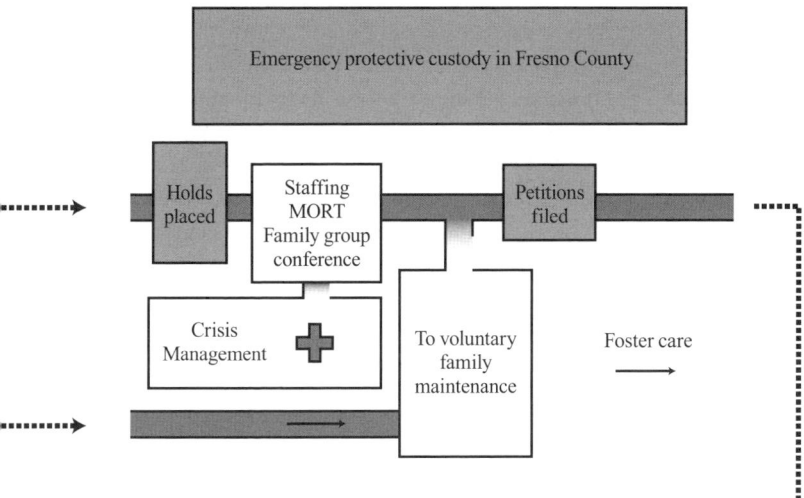

Figure 13.6: Fresno County due process 2: Family maintenance

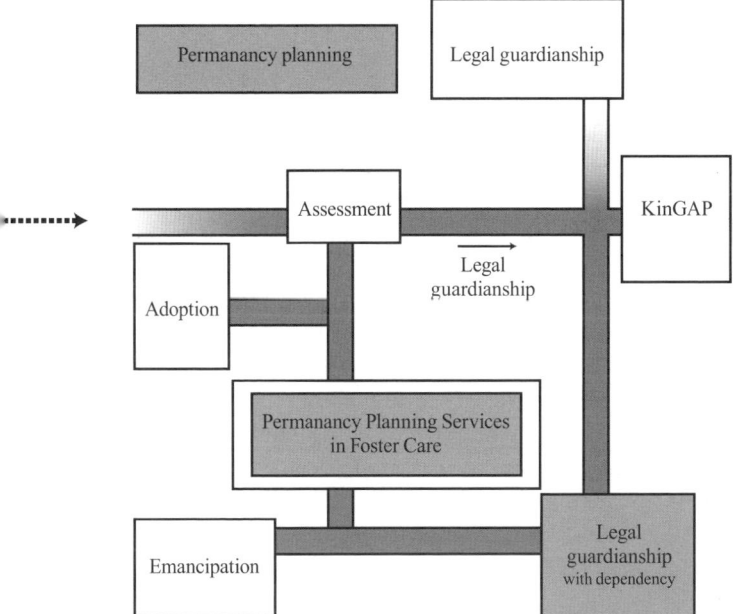

Figure 13.8: Fresno County due process 4: Permanency planning

of Child and Family Services in Fresno County, California. They are divided into four processes but when linked form a single management flow. Figure 13.5 represents the investigation stage (the meaning of the word 'investigation' here represents the process of confirming a child's safety) carried out together with the region based on a referral (or placement into custody). Fresno County's plan is ground-breaking as it has introduced the family group conference, first developed in New Zealand, and has been attracting attention in the USA over the last decade. This plan provides assistance so that problems can be solved first by the family, including the extended family.

Figure 13.6 represents the emergency protective custody stage and provides active assistance for voluntary efforts to maintain the family. Family maintenance is attempted through such *reasonable efforts for assistance* in these two initial stages.

Figure 13.7 represents the stage in which official family maintenance is attempted when the child has been placed into protection (placed outside the family; the majority of cases in the USA involve foster care). Returning the child to the family and family reunification are defined as clear goals. If efforts in accordance with these due processes are not successful, permanency planning depicted in Figure 13.8 is carried out. Although adoption has been prioritized since the review of the hierarchy clarified in the 1980 Act, the options of legal guardianship and emancipation are also clearly defined and there is a clear framework for guaranteeing a child's best interests. This flow-mode practice model allows the incorporation of a mechanism that determines the extent to which the social worker as SLB adheres to the legally prescribed procedures, in other words to monitor the SLB's level of compliance. In addition, preliminary and thorough training and education enables the clarification of ways to improve professionalism and the quality of assistance. As a result, the efforts being made to improve the social worker's response and quality of response are more transparent, also favorable from the perspective of accountability.

In this COE-designated research project, which is the development of an international version of this model, only the essentials of management procedures in addressing child abuse cases have been modeled. These have been based on the flow-mode practice model, and as indicated in Figure 13.9, enable the flexible adoption of the model to suit the situation in each country or region (local government). Although this model includes the procedures for dealing with referrals when a referral is received, and screening is carried out to determine whether the case is a child abuse case, it has not been

Figure 13.9: Essential flow of the navigational database system based on the flow-mode practice model

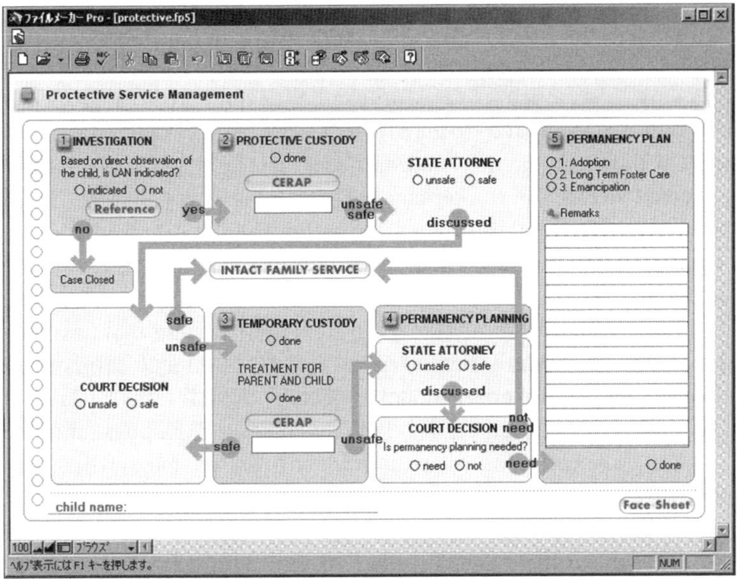

included in this diagram as it is an independent module. As a result, the starting point differs from that in the Fresno County flow chart in which it begins with the report to the Reports Registration Center. However, the characteristics of the flow-mode process that follows the initial, report response stage are the same.

The shift from the Japanese style phase-mode model to the North American style flow-mode model needs to be considered within the context of the differences in the legal systems of each country, in the maturity of the profession, and the specific situations in each region. In developing this practice model, I believe that placing the models of these two countries at opposite poles will enable the design and development of European, Asian, African and South American models as phase-mode or flow-mode models catering to differences in each region.

Compiling a process and outcome evidence database

There are two ways of compiling a database of evidence of a child's best interests, regardless of whether a practice model is a flow-mode or phase-mode model. The first is to compile a process evidence database, while the other is to compile an outcome evidence database. The issue in compiling a database is that the database system that is compiled—one that incorporates a people-friendly dialogue-based interface and which prompts the entry of evidence—must function in a way that navigates the worker or SLB so that the appropriate assistance is provided. Whether phase-mode or flow-mode, it is a system in which the information necessary for decision-making is collected so that the worker can be directed in a way that facilitates prompt decision-making. The information and the decisions that are made are added, in real time, to the database. I have designed and developed the Japanese version of the phase-mode practice model into the 'Navigational Database' system. The system that has been developed is currently being trialed and assessed as a Ministry of Health, Labor and Welfare model project, by three local governments. Figure 13.4, described earlier, is an overview of the phase module and the assistance progress situation confirmation page, which was adopted by Local Government B and in which trialing and assessment has commenced. Although the appearance and the framework is similar to the systems used by other local governments, as mentioned earlier, it was not possible to create a model common to all child and family centers. The assistance process currently adopted by each local government is different, with different categories and names of the type of information to be collected and different forms to be used in the measures carried out, requiring extensive customization. This is a good indicator of the current situation in Japan.

The North American version of the flow-mode practice model is being developed as one of the twenty-first century COE program research subjects with the collaboration of the School of Social Science Administration at the University of Chicago and UCLA Berkeley. Figure 13.9 represents one screen of the prototype developed as the essence of the flow-mode practice model, as described earlier, in the form of a navigational database system. Both programs were developed with FileMaker Pro 6 (FileMaker Inc.), the general-purpose database software. The advantages of using general purpose software at this stage is that it makes it easier to address the frequent amendments and revisions characteristic to iteration, (the repetition of trials and improvements in order to develop a better system), during the process of prototype development. Another advantage is the simplicity of building an interface that is both easy to look at and use. That FileMaker Pro is one of the few examples of software, compatible with both Windows OS and Macintosh, is another advantage. Its disadvantage is the fact that, although at this stage the protection of individual information is the priority, and it is a stand-alone system for each of the sites (child and family centers) that it is used in, in future, processing speed during searches could be an issue as it becomes used as part of a wide area network on either a prefectural or national level. It is clear; however, that the prototype development of this system will facilitate the development of a system that can be used in a wide area network.

Process Evidence

Process evidence will now be examined. In the flow-mode practice model, it is the record of whether the social worker who is the SLB acted in accordance with the procedures (due process) prescribed by the law—in which the child's best interests is made clear—that represents the process evidence. In the phase-mode practice model, it is whether the worker adequately carried out decision-making in each phase that represents the evidence. In other words, process evidence must be indicated in the form of professional achievements as an SLB rather than an outcome that determines whether the family environment, as a safe and stable environment for growth that a child needs has been prepared. Process evidence is the explanation that reasonable efforts have been made by the social work profession, in other words, accountability.

Process evidence in the case of the flow-mode practice model will now be examined by following Figure 13.9. This diagram begins with the social worker as investigator carrying out an investigation into the degree of child abuse. In fact, prior to this stage, there is the screening stage (Figure 13.10) in which a check is carried out to determine whether, based on the information obtained in the report, the definition of abuse applies. In the USA, all reports are linked to the central registry in each State capital. At this registry, workers with specialized training determine whether the details of the report conform to the definition of abuse prescribed in that State. Cases that are determined as conforming to the definition are then sent to the Department of Child and Family Services (DCFS) in the applicable county and assistance provided as an abuse case. Figure 13.10 represents the model, in the format of a module, of the screening procedure based on the definition of Cook County in the State of Illinois. In the initial stages represented by [1] and [2] in Figure 13.9,

Figure 13.10: Flow-mode navigation database system screening model

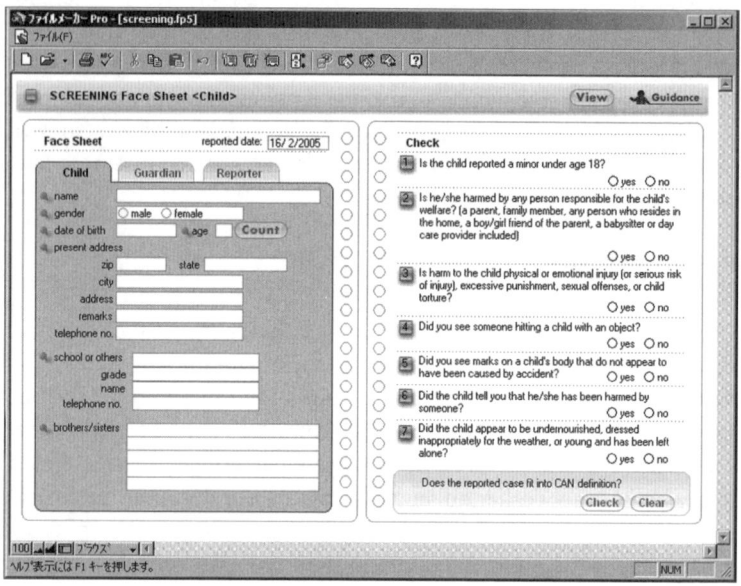

the worker (investigator) to whom the information has been sent investigates whether abuse is (has) in fact taking (taken) place and to what degree the abuse constitutes, and determines whether the child should be placed into protective custody. In the case of the State of Illinois, this decision must be made within twenty-four hours of receiving the information from the central registry by, for example, visiting the home. Although the basis of making the decision differs depending on the State, a meticulous on-the-spot investigation must be carried out. The worker must determine, in [1] of the Figure, whether, as a result of the investigation, abuse is indicated. When the corresponding radar button is clicked, the decision is registered and stored in the database. This is not the decision of whether the case corresponds to the definition of abuse, as carried out in the screening stage, but is the decision of whether abuse is in fact taking place. As referred to previously, this development version only represents a model of the essence and does not represent the detailed checklist used during an investigation or the navigation module that is obtained by utilizing this list. (Although the checklist-based investigation module used by the State of Illinois has already been developed, this can differ slightly between States. However, customization would not be difficult as discrepancies are not as significant as those found in Japan).

Once it has been determined that abuse is being carried out, the worker follows the arrow and must next decide whether temporary custody is necessary ([2] in Figure 13.9). In many States, the investigator and the caseworker in place, after the decision to place the child in temporary custody has been made, are different individuals. This is because there is a significant difference in the work involved in verifying a rescue or a criminal act such as abuse and that involved in providing assistance or support while emphasizing relationships, family maintenance or family reunification, for example. As a result, for a single worker to simultaneously wear both hats is seen as being extremely difficult. As has already been mentioned, this division of roles is unusual in Japan and consequently has a negative influence on the establishment of a system.

If a child has been temporarily placed into protection as in [2] of Figure 13.9, a decision is made, within twenty-four hours, as to whether that child is to be placed into temporary custody outside the family by using an assessment tool called CERAP (Child Endangerment Risk Assessment Protocol) based on fourteen items (Figure 13.11). Based on the information that has been collected, the caseworker responds to the main questions (the questions marked by large numbers) to determine whether the child is safe or not. However, each main question is accompanied by a supplementary question (questions marked by smaller numbers). These are questions related to the mitigating factors in relation to the danger (non-safety) in the main questions. Based on the information that has been collected, the worker, by answering these supplementary questions, determines whether the main questions are mitigated and therefore, whether danger is alleviated. In the CERAP module, the worker only has to collect the information and answer the main and supplementary questions based on this information. The program is designed to provide answers in accordance with the decision-making rules that have been programmed a priori. Although safety and non-safety in each main question is determined in accordance with the decision-making rules that have already been built in, the decision of whether the overall evaluation comprising the fourteen items, from the overall CERAP perspective, signifies safety or lack of safety is determined in accordance with the decision-making rules programmed a priori. The rules, which have been programmed in advance, represent the decision-making rules based on questionnaire-based quantitative surveys, qualitative surveys by interviewing experts (expert modeling),

Figure 13.11: The CERAP module

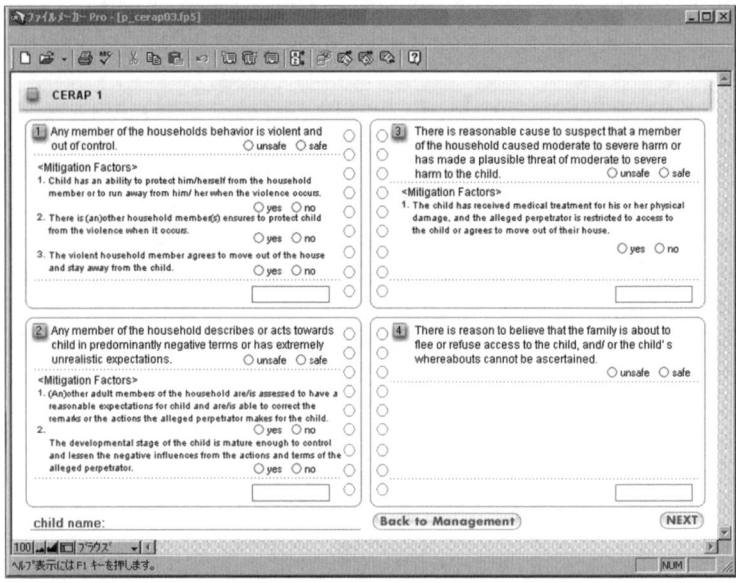

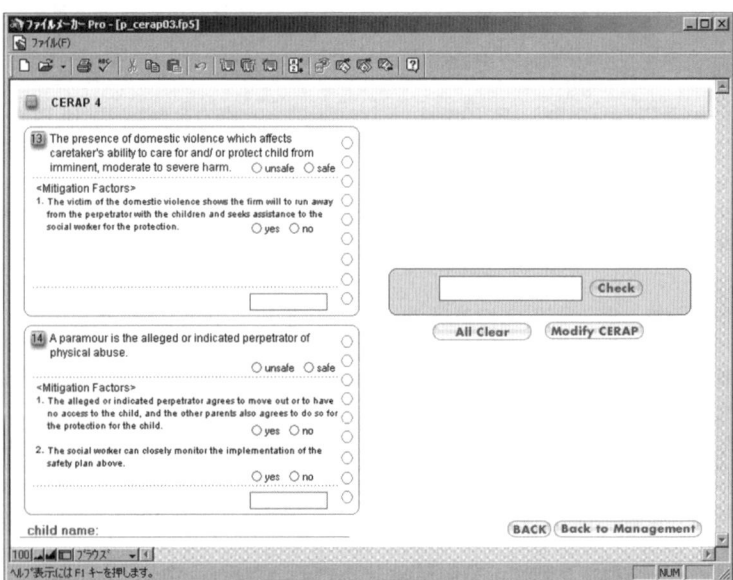

and document research. It is the provision of assistance by respecting the decisions indicated by the rules that suppresses any negative influence that the SLB's discretion may have on that worker's decision. However, the decision-making rules are not absolute or final, and areas for improvement remain. The decisions made by the worker in individual cases and the achievement of assistance targets are recorded by using this navigational database system, and it is by analyzing this database that the decision-making rules can be scrutinized, amended, improved and developed.

Through longitudinal analysis by individual cases or cross-sectional analysis through groups of cases of the practical information that has been added to the database as the worker follows the flow chart and makes entries, the decision making rules and the system itself are improved, enabling improvement of the quality of practice and development of the practice model. This represents the linking of research and practice and contributes to the development of the practitioner-researcher. In other words, I believe that this contributes to solving this long-standing issue in social work.

The process evidence can be seen as the database itself in which the social worker who is the SLB, by using the database navigational system that represents the programming of the flow-mode practice model, enters the necessary information in order to make a decision (IF information) and the results of the decision (THEN information) by following due process. There has been a deep-rooted resistance to transferring and storing, in digital format, the narrative-based analogue information that remains in the form of paper-based case records. Although the navigational database system that my colleagues and I have been developing towards the digitization and storage of practice information, is one that attempts to obtain, as much as possible, feedback from the practice information and practice determined as to be important through careful and thorough research. Obviously it is not able to cover all information that is important in practice. In reality; however, the social worker only utilizes a small portion of the enormous quantity of narrative-based information that has been stored. We believe that digitizing, organizing and storing (in database format) practice information will improve the degree of utilization of this information.

In the case of process evidence in the phase-mode practice model, it is not possible to obtain evidence by entering the necessary data by following the flow—as is possible in the flow model—due to the absence of due process backed by permanency in a child's best interests. It is the selection of the appropriate phase from the eight phases together with the development of the assistance and determining whether the best decision was made that represents the evidence. For example, if this is the 'on-the-spot-investigation' module, this module in Figure 13.13 is undertaken after first carrying out the risk assessment (refer to

Figure 13.12: Risk assessment module

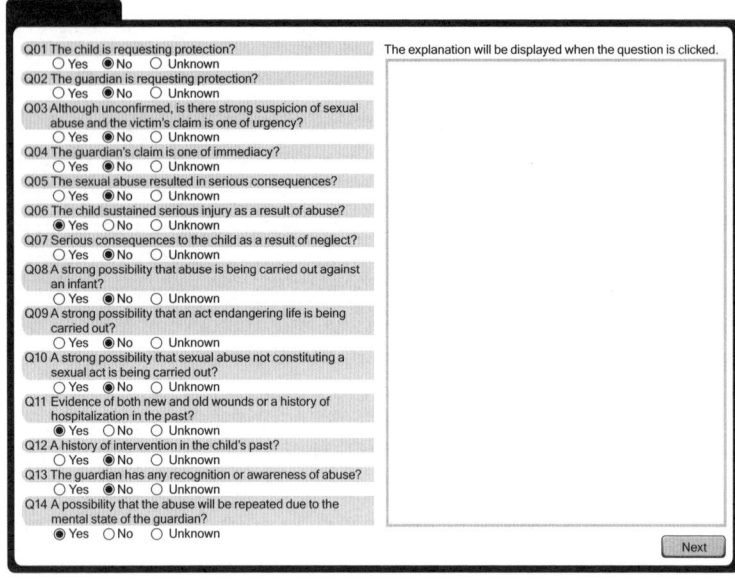

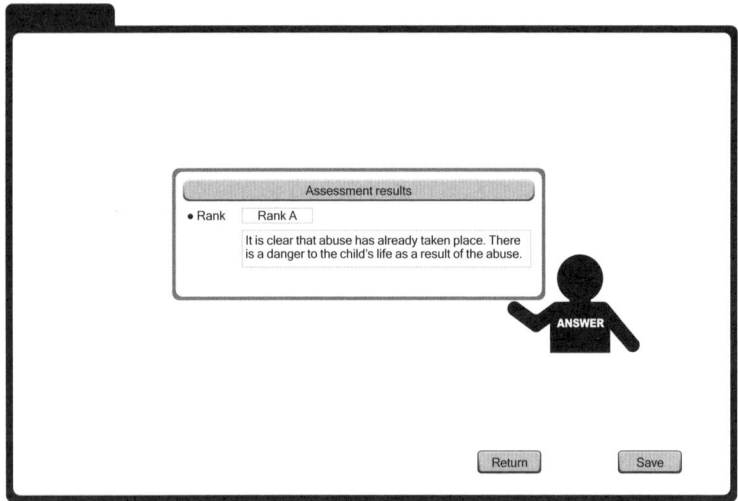

the checklist displayed in Figure 13.12). Looking closely at Figure 13.13, we can see that the risk assessment result is automatically reflected in the first question (Q1) of the information (question) for making the decision. By answering the second question onwards (Q2) using the

Figure 13.13: On-the-spot-investigation module

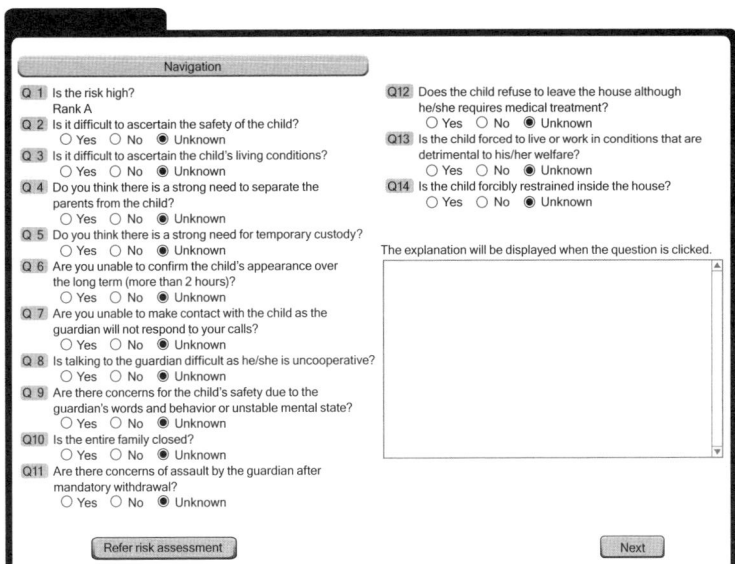

information that has been collected, the necessity of an on-the-spot-investigation is indicated. As in the flow-mode, the rules obtained as a result of thorough research have been built in a priori and it is the decision based on these that are displayed.

Decision-making involves information as IF information (making entries into the list of questions) and then selecting (THEN) the optimal alternative from the assistance options, in accordance with the IF = THEN rule. In the phase-mode navigational database system, into which the information is entered into the questions list, the options selected by the system and whether or not the worker has implemented those options (and the reasons if not) are entered into the database in real time. These are entered along with the implementation of the module, and the information database then becomes the process evidence.

The system based on the phase-mode practice model is extremely complex and considerable time is required to customize the model to suit the requirements of different local governments. In addition, entry is also time-consuming and as a result continued use could pose difficulties. Not only are considerable adjustments necessary to improve the usability of the interface, but incentives on the part of the worker to enter information into the interface is also necessary. If, however, the entries are carried out correctly, this will not only assist the worker as SLB to act appropriately but there is also the added advantage that an educational effect equivalent to on-the-job training can be anticipated. Many simple errors are generated in the assistance carried out by Child Welfare officers at child and family centers in Japan, and when we consider that this is often linked to tragic and major incidents, the introduction of the phase-mode program which functions as on-the-job training would be the appropriate measure. However, as society matures and the legal system is improved, the role of the phase-mode practice model and the phase-mode practical navigation database system based on this model will no doubt come to an end.

Outcome Evidence

Outcome evidence can be seen as evidence that can be determined by referring to the results of permanency and well-being. As referred to earlier, the 1997 Act of the USA states that one of the principles of the Act is the focusing of results and accountability. Therefore in the flow-mode practice model, social work accountability lies in whether the facts that indicate safety, permanency and well-being have been obtained as a result of the provision of professional assistance. During the process from investigation to temporary protection, it is the collected information indicating the validity of intact family service that indicates safety. In the case of temporary protection, evidence of safety is represented by an indication that family reunion is valid as a result of providing assistance. In this case, it is not only information related to the perpetrating parent, but information about the district (such as information about neighbors), the school and kinship (such as relatives), as well as information on the child's mental and physical state and the child's own wishes, that indicate the safety and permanency of the actual family. This information on the state of the child or the state of the family environment is also entered into the database as evidence in the form of the results of assistance.

During the process in which it is determined by CERAP that the child is not safe and that formal temporary custody is to be carried out, the information indicating that the child needs to be placed outside the family, despite the provision of assistance, becomes the evidence. It is information regarding whether the foster parents, relatives and foster parents or the caregiver at the children's home (very rare in the USA) understands the child; is able to establish a good relationship of trust, and can assist in the growth of the child; and how the child views the foster parents or the institution; represents the outcome evidence supporting the need to remove the child from the family, in the child's best interests. It is this evidence that is added to the database. The CERAP results also represent evidence and these are also entered into the database. In cases in which a child is removed from the home for an extended period (as a rule, placing the child outside the home is prescribed by State law as a short-term measure to the extent that the term 'temporary' is used and in this sense differs from the Japanese phase-mode model), or if it is determined by CERAP and others that returning the child to the family poses difficulties, permanency planning becomes the evidence. The decision and planning of whether permanency planning is to take the form of adoption, long-term foster care, in the care of an institution, or assistance towards the autonomy of the child represents the outcome evidence and is entered into the database. The 1980 Act provided a clear hierarchy of such options but this hierarchy was deleted from the 1997 Act. However, the principle of least restrictive alternatives remains and it is the social worker's responsibility to make the utmost efforts to realize adoption.

In this way, the flow-mode practice model's outcome evidence determines, during the assistance process, whether reasonable efforts have been made to guarantee a safe and stable (permanent) environment for the growth of the child, and whether this environment has been realized. In other words, it represents evidence of safety and permanency. However, there is still no clear definition of the third item—'well being'—and in what way, at what stage and through what kind of information (evidence) this is to be indicated, remains a major issue. In fact, this represents the very core of a child's best interests, but even in the USA, debate and research on direct evidence to indicate well being has only just commenced.

It is more difficult to indicate evidence as outcome with the phase-mode practice model than with the flow-mode practice model. As we have seen so far, in the phase-mode practice model, because the idea of permanency has not been clearly defined in the legal system, the consequence of this is solutions in which due process remains ambiguous. Unlike the flow-mode, both aspects—safety and well-being—are emphasized in the evidence. However, as the idea of permanency is not clear, safety and well being are transitory and because these must be confirmed by each phase, it is extremely difficult to establish targets for achieving a long-term, safe, and stable growth environment and the resulting well-being of the child. For example, with emergency temporary protection, as we can see by looking at the Fresno County example (refer Figures 13.5 to 13.8), the flow-mode model requires the worker to consider not only protecting the child from an emergency and critical situation, but also the child's best interests such as family maintenance or permanency planning. In contrast, in the case of Japan's phase-mode model, temporary protection is completed at the actual protection of the child. In the flow-mode model, it is made clear as due process that as much support as possible is provided to the perpetrating parent during the emergency temporary protection and that preparations are made to provide a safe and stable environment for growth to enable family reunion. In the case of the phase-mode; however, the aim of temporary protection is seen as simply to avoid danger at the present time or to carry out a rescue. Therefore the reality is that little assistance is provided to prepare the family environment during the maximum temporary protection period of two months. In such a situation, the record of whether the worker collected the necessary and sufficient information to determine the necessity of temporary protection; whether, based on this information, temporary protection was carried out; whether danger was avoided as a result; and whether the rescue was successful—these are the outcome evidence that is entered into the database. The phase-mode Navigational Database System, which my colleagues and I have developed has also been designed so that data related to the collecting of appropriate information (IF) and the execution of appropriate professional support (THEN) is entered into the database. Also incorporated into this system is a check to be carried out by the supervisor to confirm whether the decision-making was appropriate, with the check results being able to be retained as evidence.

A major problem with the phase-mode practice model is the inability to evaluate the results or outcome of assisting with permanency—believed to be directly related to a child's best interests. Although it is possible to evaluate the outcome of each phase, it is extremely difficult to evaluate the outcome of the case assistance as a whole. As a solution to this problem, the program that we have developed incorporates a 'family reunion' phase and a 'conclusion' phase as modules. In the current situation; however, as family reunion is often not established as a medium term or long-term target during the creation of an assistance plan by the child welfare officer at a child and family center, the forced removal of the child from parents retaining parental authority is often not possible. This situation has also been considered, and mandatory removal from the family has also been modeled as a phase.

In reality; however, this is rarely defined clearly as a procedure by child and family centers. Similarly, with the 'termination' module, a 'termination' category does not exist in some centers nor is the matter being actively addressed. However, outcome evaluation cannot be carried out at all in the phase-mode unless the system enables this phase to be properly executed, thereby resulting in the inability to convey accountability in social work.

Conclusion: Modified design and practice model

Summary

While considering 'a child's best interests,' something that is finally being mentioned in Japan, I have also considered whether the development of a flow-mode practice model or a phase-mode practice model is appropriate depending on whether permanency has been clearly defined in the legal system and whether the assistance procedures as due process are made clear. I have also stated that, with the flow-mode practice model, it is the faithful and clear entry of the compliance with the worker's due process into the database, the analysis of the information and the conveying of results in an easy to understand way that represents process evidence of a child's best interests. It was stated that, as far as evidence of outcome is concerned, the discovery of detailed indicators related to safety, permanency and well being, the addition of this information to the database and the analysis of this information is necessary in view of the emphasis on results, which represents one of the principles of the 1997 Act and of accountability. The Navigational Database System that has been developed as a flow-mode practice model has the potential to function both as a system to generate process evidence, as well as a system to generate outcome evidence. Obviously there is a need for continued on-site testing and improvement. The features of this system; however, lie in the fact that these improvements are already built into the system itself through ongoing analysis of the database and feedback of the results.

Although the phase-mode practice model is the most appropriate for the current Japanese legal system, carrying out planned assistance with a medium and long-term perspective in order to indicate process evidence and outcome evidence poses difficulties. As signified by the words 'permanency planning,' social work requires planning. And yet, this element of planning remains tenuous in the phase-mode model. The only method available, therefore, is to determine process evidence by entering, into the database, information that enables the determination of the soundness and validity of the decision-making process in each phase. As far as outcome evidence is concerned, this means that there is no way of knowing what it is that should be conveyed and when. Despite these issues, however, we believe that the phase-mode practice model that we have developed is the best under the current Japanese legal system. The conversion of the phase-mode model to the flow-mode model should not pose that much of a difficulty when permanency or an idea similar to this is eventually defined by law and due processes made clear. By then, the flow-mode practice model that will become the international standard will one day be developed and popularized in Japan as well.

The integration of research and practice

The example of a phase-mode and flow-mode practice model navigational database system that has been described as an example in this paper is still being developed and is currently positioned between the third modified design and development stage (the testing and improvement phase) and the final phase (the dissemination phase). The former has been introduced by several local governments as a Ministry of Health, Labor and Welfare model program, and evaluation has commenced. While writing this paper, I received the news that the phase-mode practice model navigational database system will be introduced into all child and family centers in Osaka Prefecture from 2006 (Nihon Keizai Shimbun, 26 February, 2005). So it is Osaka that has made the first move in its implementation.

As we have seen, the Navigational Database System has been designed and developed as software to realize evidence-based practice (EBP). We believe that this system represents the realization of the 'practitioner-researcher'—something that has remained a long-standing issue in social work—and realizes the collaboration between research and practice. The authors propose a pragmatic approach to 'the theorization of social work' that is once again being debated in recent years (Shibano 2005). The clinical (practice) cycle represents the EBP cycle, in which practice is carried out by searching for, selecting and utilizing the appropriate model from amongst various practice models that have been stored in the data-base, the results of which are then fed back into practice and into the database. In the innovation cycle, the development of a practice model (M-D&D)

enriches the practice model database and renews the database as necessary.

The theorization of a pragmatic form of social work based on this practice must also be reflected in the development of assistance practice models for abuse cases in order to ensure a child's best interests. Furthermore, we believe that developing and improving such practice models and enriching the database will contribute to improving the quality of the social worker. It is in anticipation of this and with a sense of responsibility to realize this that I conclude this chapter.

Notes

Preface

1 It is possible to see this kind of conceptualizing in Kizaemon Aruga's lifestyle theory which dates back over fifty years. According to Aruga, the context of lifestyle is a context that continually demands the creation of a pluralistic cooperativity. However, this cooperativity was not something to be fixed as a historical necessity. Rather, the stipulation of certain lifestyle conditions would lead to the appearance of individualism in some instances, while the stipulations of different lifestyle conditions might lead to closed, exclusive communities. Further, in the early 1980s Hiroyuki Torigoe advocated a lifestyle environmentalist methodology after conducting joint research at Lake Biwa. The research was based on Kizaemon Aruga's lifestyle theory and led to the adoption of a methodology, to consider the issue of the self and the other in fieldwork, from Aruga's theoretical perspective. Kada, Matsuda and Furukawa—who have collaborated in the present volume—were also joint researchers with Torigoe in the Lake Biwa project. Please refer to Torigoe (1997) for details of lifestyle environmentalism.

Chapter 1

1 A draft version of this paper has been published in *Sociology Critique*, 53–4.
2 In the opening of his book, *Argonauts of the Western Pacific*, Malinowski refers to the methods of depicting the real mind of native people and the reality of the tribal life world as the 'ethnographer's magic.' This phrase is used in the negative context of a critique of ethnographies as making use of the monstrous mechanisms of power (Malinowski [1922] 1967: 72–73).
3 Kovats-Bernat, who carried out fieldwork in a section of Port-au-Prince in Haiti, examines research methods for the riskier field seen in present day Africa and Central and South America, based on his own life-threatening experiences in situations of political and social turmoil. It was a revision of research methodology from the viewpoint of a fieldworker, hurt and fleeing from the turmoil and disorder in which he was caught up, a field over which he had absolutely no control (Kovats-Bernat 2002: 208–22).

4 The arguments put forward by Firth are one example. Firth created the concept of a social system as a realm for the specific existence of one-off occurrences that are the cornerstone of individual choice, separate to established social structures, which fix in place the permanency and continuity of behavior.
5 Referring to their exchanges as a 'debate' requires qualification. Nakano placed his main emphasis on scrutinizing his own view of research in the form of a critique of the theory of a joint project. On the other hand, at the time in the 1970s, Nitagai never directly argued against Nakano. Consequently, both parties might object to my declaring it a 'debate.' However, in the context of a critical restructuring of research methods in this article, progressing the argument with both parties at one of two extremes is valuable, hence the term 'debate.'
6 As an ethnographic critique, *Writing Culture: The Poetics and Politics of Ethnography*, wholeheartedly dismantled the creative behavior of ethnographies as a (re)production of text. While, at first glance, Clifford's *The Predicament of Culture* may seem to be putting forward the same argument, the latter has present day relevance in that it foresaw the reformulation of anthropology in his astute critique of ethnographic authority, so much so that it is hard to believe it was published some fifteen years ago. It does not restrict itself to dissecting the Orientalist hegemony that is part of the process of perceiving foreign cultures as subjects of research, but covers the creative function of cross-cultural understanding that is expressed after being differentiated and made relative. Yoshinobu Ota's superior translation, complete with an excellent commentary, is available. See Clifford ([1998] 2003) translated by Yoshinobu Ota et al.
7 In 'Post Modern Ethnography: From Document to the Occult to Occult Document,' Tyler develops the most radical critique of ethnographies. She denies the relatedness of the observer and the observed and claims that the only thing that exists between the two is the one-way production of discourse (Tyler 1986: 122–40). It was Fox who metaphorically referred to this radicalism as '*sans-culottism*' (Fox 1991: 7).
8 Sugishima (1995) gives us one example in Japanese fieldwork theory. Sugishima, an ethnographer known for his precise, empirically based fieldwork was one anthropologist who was the most pure minded in his reaction to critiques of ethnography at the time.
9 This is common to Butler's argument that critiques the established cooperativity in understanding it as a forced categorization based on symbols of oneness. Butler finds new potential for cooperativity in solidarity based on a naturally emerging group formed pluralistically by experiencing divisions and separation and accepting them (Butler 1997).
10 However, Maruyama's coherent logocentrism is prescribed by the circumstances surrounding the history of thought in the 1950s. In his later years, Maruyama's thinking suggested a move towards overcoming logocentrism in his emphasis of the importance of 'the sensation of otherness' (Maruyama 1986: 321–335). This was carefully pointed out to me by an anonymous reviewer on the editorial committee of the journal *Sociology Critique*. I am grateful for the precise and astute comments.
11 We can see that Yanagita uses expressions in his explanations and descriptive accounts that are not 'empirical' as required by 'science.' Apparently

Torigoe felt that the unscientific quality in this sense could be traced back to Yanagita's literary proclivities and to his disposition. He felt that this artistry was 'too crude a method for resolution.' Here, Torigoe found the kernels of a separate epistemology and ontology (Torigoe 1988: 38).

12 Yanagita's mental theory is given to being misunderstood as an exclusivist perception that can never presume cooperativity in claims that the mind of a person can only ever be understood by people who live in the same area. However, as pointed out by Kenji Satō, this emphasis on the sameness of living circumstances merely equates to an emphasis of a method of self-reflection. Directing it towards epistemology and it becomes an expression of the 'will to create a macrocosm out of sensory order' (Satō 1987: 262–7).

Chapter 3

1 For example Takatoshi Imada (2000: 15) says: 'The aim of analyzing individual case studies is not a generalized recognition of the whole, or a universal recognition which stands irrelevant of time or space. The aim is the recognition of the essential nature concealed deep inside the case study.' Harutoshi Funabashi (1999: 30) says: 'When a limited subject is deeply and thoroughly pursued, at one point one reaches a universal theoretical viewpoint or insight which all of a sudden enables the 'discovery of meaning' and 'discovery of regularity' of various events.
2 The case study is based on the research undertaken on Malaita Island, Solomon Islands, which has occurred almost every year between 1992 and 2004. P's life history is further detailed in Miyauchi (2002). The meaning of P and others' migration plan to the inland is discussed in detail in Miyauchi (2003a).
3 The interview took place on 14 August 2002.
4 The case study of the Saitama NPO Center is based on the interview on 19 November 2004 with Tadashi Nishikawa and Akiko Wakao (both were staff of the Saitama NPO Center at the time of the research project, and were in charge of the project) and Saitama NPO Center (2001, 2002) and Saitama Prefecture (2002).
5 Personal interview with Akiko Wakao (19 November 2004).
6 Personal interview with Tadashi Nishikawa (19 November 2004).
7 Personal interview with Akiko Wakao (19 November 2004).
8 Personal interview with Akiko Wakao (19 November 2004).
9 Personal interview with Akiko Wakao (19 November 2004).
10 Personal interview with Akiko Wakao (19 November 2004).
11 Personal interview with Tadashi Nishikawa (19 November 2004).
12 See Miyauchi (2003b) for a detailed discussion on the meaning of research by citizens.

Chapter 4

1 The method to describe something exactly as it is seen is discussed a little in this article, but closer inspection would be required to determine what sort of deformation of reality is involved. As this article is an 'introduction,' detailed discussion will be left to another opportunity.

2 The aim of this article is not to cut up this mixed-up concept but to suggest that there should be at least as much discussion on the topic of '(participant) observation' to balance the discussion on the topic of 'participant (observation)', and to suggest that at the point where both exist in balance, the possibility may be found for participant observation to fully demonstrate its jumbled nature.
3 Satō developed his discussion here, based on sociology in the USA. For information about his source, refer to the original reference.
4 Obviously, some items could not be carried outside and these are mentioned as 'Items not seen in the big pictures' (Material World Project 1994: 18, passim).
5 Thinking in relation to this COE program, it is interesting that the family lives grasped and described in this way can lead to a sort of eudemonics. The same book suggests that the key to family life does not depend on movable and immovable assets but on the composition and size of the family.
6 Refer to Kawazoe (2004) for a chronological record.
7 Refer to Kawazoe (2004: 381–90) for his comments on Wajirō Kon.
8 The name of the questioner reveals that this is a fabricated question. The name, Ineko Ise, is the same as that of Yanagita's first love, according to explanatory notes in the book (p. 746).
9 Refer to Satō (1987) as to how these were not a simple rewording, but a classification plan, to make humans relative and make the structural analysis of society three dimensional.
10 I began to think that it was not only my strained interpretation to recognize the three-part categorization in '*Meiji Taishō-shi sesō-hen*' ([1931] 1998a) after seeing the following passage by Kenji Satō: 'It was a complex setup, a language strategy, in which the transformation of street customs and social trends as a subject of discussion, and the changes in the essence that wove Meiji Taishō history, an integration of these customs and trends, were superimposed and revealed. There seems to be a similar logic in the frame of this correlated setup between the subject and the essence, to that in the above diagram [A diagram of the three-part categorization concept-author] from my previously discussed methodology for rural area study' (Satō 2001: 119).
11 Jun'ichi Koike provided the information about this reference. I express my gratitude.

Chapter 5

1 This article only discusses the research method of drawing. For details about the research findings, please refer to related reference materials (Kamei 1997, 2001a, 2001b, 2001c, 2002a, 2002b, 2002c, 2005).
2 One sketch is usually a combination of more than one picture. For example, when observing a fruit, the appearance, cross-section and seeds are drawn. In the case of a dish, the cooking process was recorded in a series of pictures. Therefore the number of actual drawings may reach two to three times the number given here.
3 Some tricks to communicating in the field independent of language include expression with the body such as body language, miming and dancing.

These methods are effective when communicating, for example, with deaf children who have not fully acquired sign language.
4 The potential of comics as a descriptive format for science will be discussed at another opportunity. However, with the so-called 'study comics,' which are translations of existing scientific knowledge into narrative comics, it cannot be said that the potential is sufficiently realized. For comics to become a descriptive format responsible for the production of knowledge, would depend on whether innovation in social science philosophy is achieved, as well as innovation in comics. Will the day come when an article consisting of comics is accepted in a reputable academic journal?

Chapter 6

1 Kenji Kiyono confessed that anthropology was not his main occupation but *'Anthropology is a pastime* for me as a pathologist...I first became interested in the constitution of old races, especially their bone structures...then started taking part in archaeological excavations' (Kiyono 1930: 82) (emphasis added).
2 This kind of tobacco was called 'compressed tobacco' and sold at a tobacconist.
3 Seiichi Izumi moved from a preparatory course to a regular course at his university in April 1934. He climbed Mt Halla in Chejudo Island in July of the year (Iiyama 1972: 6–8). While climbing the mountain in January 1936, Izumi's party met with an accident in which he lost his friend. After that, he transferred his specialty from Japanese literature to sociology (Kimiko Izumi 1972: 32). The time of that transfer was likely to be in April 1936. Assuming that he first met Professor Takashi Akiba for his enrolment in sociology immediately after the accident, the period of his anthropological training prior to the commencement of his research could be six months at longest. On the other hand, if he first met the professor in April, the period of his anthropological training could be as short as three months.
4 There are three passages discussing matters related to opium in a judgment of the Tokyo Trial 'Part B Chapter 5: Japanese invasion of China.' One passage discusses Japan's political intention as follows:
   The trade was related to military operations and political development. This generated the majority of funds for a variety of local administrations established by Japan...Opium was among the various items that were under the control of Japan's state institution called *Kōa-in*. It investigated the demand situation for opium in rural areas of China and took charge of its provision to Mongolia as well as North, Middle and South China (Eguchi 1988: 7).
5 Of the Sections 135 to 141 of the Japanese Criminal Code, which are devoted to 'opium-related crimes,' Section 140 takes up the issue of 'opium possession.' Since its enactment in 1907, this criminal code has undergone minor revisions but maintained its basic form until 1995. This may raise a question about how we should evaluate Izumi's action of carrying opium in Manchukuo as a subject of the Great Empire of Japan in 1936.
6 Opium-related problems of the Orochon were reported by Imanishi and Ban. They note:

> The situation of the Horse Orochon is miserable. For example, in case of the Horse Orochon residing in the middle part of Daxinganling, opium addicts account for 83 (60 percent) out of 138 adults over 25 years old. They spend the majority of trade earnings on opium. Opium was first introduced approximately 40 years ago by Chinese coolies who engaged in deforestation in the closing days of the Qing Dynasty and became an essential part of the life of the Horse Orochon. With no medical facilities or medications available to treat the sick and wounded, along with bitter hardships of the hunting life, it was a sole remedy for physical and psychological pains in their lives. Unlike Chinese who smoke opium, the Horse Orochon eat opium raw as they believe its negative effects on the human body are somewhat reduced in this way...Opium created physiological and economic problems for them. Opium is too expensive to obtain through legitimate channels. The Horse Orochon have been mercilessly exploited by Chinese traders who take mean advantage of their situation...A strict enforcement of the Opium Control Law since the establishment of Manchukuo forced dishonest traders to engage in secret maneuvers. This created a situation in which the Horse Orochon have no choice but to spend the majority of their earnings on opium. Some lose horses that are their sole possession. Extreme poverty resulting from opium addiction and a strong craving for opium even impel them to steal others' cattle (Imanishi and Ban 1948: 57).

And further they state that: 'Compared to the situation in 1936 when Seiichi Izumi conducted his research into the Orochon residing in the southeast of Daxinganling, the situation seems to have been slightly improved under the guidance of concerned authorities (Imanishi and Ban 1948: 61).

7 'I prepared my research paper under the lead of Professor Akiba who made a thorough revision of my rough manuscript' (Izumi 1937: 42).

8 In 'Honkan ni notta ronbun to essei (Papers and essays appearing in this book)' of 'Hensha atogaki (A postscript by the editor)' (Satō 1972: 426), the editor of the Izumi's collection published in 1972 mentioned the original record published in January 1937 but not his subsequent revised version published in May 1969. This may raise the question of whether or not the appearance of the revised version in the collection was in fact a deliberate intention of the editor. On comparison of the publications, the contents of the collection are identical with those of the 1969 version. If the editor had clearly referred to the source of the article as the 1969 version, there would not have been any unnecessary misunderstanding and we could have been convinced that the editor was unaware of the revision of the original record during the production process and that the revision was made by Izumi himself in 1969.

9 Nobuhiko Ogawa mentioned the process of deleting the parts of Izumi's original record, though his comment is recorded in a generally inaccessible report published in 1996.

10 According to a talk by given Professor Robert Spencer, who was a student advisee of Professor Alfred Kroeber, during his anthropology seminar at the University of Minnesota in the autumn session of 1979.
11 Sugiura introduced the conference based on his knowledge from a paper by Wilhelm Koppers, 'Das Schicksal der Ethnologie unter dem Sowjet-Regime (Fate of ethnography under the reign of the Soviet government)', compiled in *Anthropos*, 27, pp.501–23. He seemed to have memorized the month of the conference incorrectly, saying it was August though it actually was April (Koppers 1929: 501).

Chapter 7

1 See the fourth edition of Whyte's *Street Corner Society* translated into Japanese by Okuda and Arisato ([1993] 2000). Japanese readers should pay attention to the translators note. See also Okuda and Arisato (2002).
2 See especially Michihiro Okuda (2000), 'Asian newcomers in the Shinjuku and Ikebukuro areas,' 1988–1998: Reflections on a decade of research, *Asian and Pacific Migration Journal*, 9 (3), pp. 343–348.
3 See Lie and Ishida (1995) for the ethos of the American Koreans. For the background of the resurrection of spiritual life in the community, see, for example, Baltzell (1979).
4 For one example, see Okuda (ed.) (1989, 2003).
5 See Lie and Ishida (1995: 45–113) for a detailed analysis of the process of how Americans of Korean descent were accepted in the wider society by the mid 1980s as a spectacularly successful minority.
6 See also Levitt and Waters (eds) (2002).
7 See the large sociological monograph by Li (2000) who was working on the Okuda seminar at the time we were carrying out our fieldwork in Ikebukuro and Shinjuku. Li researched the Xinjiang Uyghurs' domestic and international migration patterns and processes, using observation and participatory research in China's western most Xinjian Uygur Autonomous Region as well as in Beijing, Shanghai and Guangzhou.
8 For reviews on the 'manners of co-existence,' see Machimura and Nishizawa (2000: 347–349).
9 With regard to the fiftieth commemorative extended revised edition of Whyte ([1943] 1993), see also the translated edition by Okuda and Arisato (Whyte [1993] 2000).
10 Okuda and Arisato wrote the foreword to the Japanese edition of the fourth edition of *Street Corner Society* by Whyte ([1993] 2000: ii).
11 An example of individual participatory action research following our research in Ikebukuro and Shinjuku (1998–2003), see Watado, Hirota and Tajima (eds) (2003).
12 See also Abbott (1999).

Chapter 8

1 Compared to the number of cases in *Good Deeds of the Taishō Earthquake* by the Tokyo government (Tokyo-fu hen 1924), the total number of cases cited in the list provided in Chapter 4: 'Person of Merit,' in the publication

Record of Tokyo Earthquake; Separate edition (Tokyo-fu hen 1926b) was far greater. Both of the documents were based on the information collected by organizations such as the government, the army, police, and schools during the rescue operation of the earthquake. In that sense, both of them had the same system for collecting the information. They share the same cases and the cases of awards, because of the background I mentioned previously. Whether or not the results of investigations were linked directly to the system of awards, is a subject for further investigation.

2 As of the third of October, 5,440 people were supposed to be placed in the barracks built in the burnt remains of eight primary school sites in Fukagawa-ku (Kotō-ku 1997: 588–589). As with the case of Rekisen Primary School in Koishikawa-ku, some of the teachers were asked to perform rescue administration and managed the rescue operation office with the support of the youth organization run by the graduates of each school (Suzuki 2004: 178–180).

3 *Hifuko-sho-ato* originally referred to a large warehouse where military uniforms had once been manufactured and stored. During the earthquake, approximately 40 000 people ran into this warehouse to seek protection, but a fire storm came through the area and all of the people were burnt to death. Subsequently, the area of *Hifuku-sho-ato* came to be memorialized as a tragic symbol of the Great Kanto earthquake.

4 Refer to Kawai (1991) for the first national survey. The fact that those conducting the survey tried to achieve direct and precise results, overcoming the difficulties with the authority of the nation on their shoulders, is the main theme of the *bidan* stories of the national survey, that were issued after the survey was completed (Satō 2001).

5 Refer to Ōyane (1991) for a discussion about the toll of the sufferers and its relation to the reconstruction operation after the earthquake.

6 Suzuki (2004) reconstructed and examined the entire system of the rescue operation and pointed out that participation by individuals voluntarily in the activities of the youth and veteran's associations, resulted in a lack of control. Reflection on this problem led to the improvement of the operation, through 'strengthening the leadership of each organization' and the 'organization of town committees,' which had the characteristic of government subcontractors.

7 Refer to Shigenobu (2000) about *bidan* stories of the home front.

Chapter 9

1 *Mura no nikki—Gōshū Chinaimura 'Kiroku' (1)–(12), (Ho)* (Diary of a village—'Records' of Chinai Village, Gōshū, (1) through (12) and (Sup.)) is published jointly by Yasuhiro Itō and the author in Chūkyō Daigaku Shakaigakubu Kiyō (Chukyo University School of Sociology Bulletin), Nos. 2-1 through 8-1. *Mura no nikki—Gōshū Chinaimura 'Kiroku' (13)–(14)* (Diary of a village—'Records' of Chinai Village, Gōshū, (13) and (14)) was published by Yasuhiro Itō and Kaoru Kamatani in Kwansei Gakuin Daigaku Shakaigakubu Kiyō (Kuwansei Gakuin University School of Sociology Bulletin), Nos. 97 and 98. Unless otherwise noted, excerpts are from the *Kiroku*.

2 Brackets ([ ]) appearing in the excerpts from *Kiroku* indicate the author's note.
3 All descriptions in the *Kiroku* directly referring to flood damage are discussed in the present paper.
4 The mechanism created by the village in order to maintain its quiet life is discussed in Furukawa (2004), Chapter 2, Section 4, 'Disaster and quiet life of the village—the mechanism called the 'fishing system specifically for the poor.'
5 For further information on Chinai District and the *Kiroku* of Chinai Village, refer to Furukawa (2004). Movements of the new community are also discussed in Furukawa and Matsuda (eds) (2003).
6 The circumstances surrounding the dredging of the Seta River at that time are detailed in Kada and Furukawa (1984).
7 At that time, the post of guardian of the village shrine was not hereditary but rotated among villagers, and the shrine guardian was elected from among villagers by lot. Those who were eligible for the post of shrine guardian were called *Morotō*, and all *Morotō* villagers constitute *Miyaza*. This rotation system was abolished in 1872 and the post became fixed and occupied by a professional priest.
8 For further information refer to Furukawa (2004: 102–103).
9 For information about structural change in the village refer to Furukawa (2004: 75–101).
10 Examples include, the Land Tax Reform (1875), billeting of soldiers in the village for military exercises (first mentioned in the article written on 3 October 1898), the consolidation of Chinai Primary School into Momose Primary School (the article written on 31 March 1906), the designation of shrines which shall present offerings for Shintō gods (the article written on 29 April 1908), and the holding of the farmer's cooperative rice, cereal and vegetable show (the article written on 5 December 1910).
11 For example, Nagao Nishikawa (1995).
12 This way of processing information, however, could be a force to maintain the village as a whole but, for example, cannot protect each individual villager who goes to the front. In his book *Nippon no mura no hyakunen* (One hundred years of Japanese villages) mentioned in the beginning, Toshinao Yoneyama (1967) commenced his descriptions of Chinai Village with a description of the graves of former villagers who were killed in war as soldiers. He saw this as evidence to illustrate the idea that the village has always been open to the outside world, rather than being a quiet, closed system. A village which is open to the outside world and moves toward a system supportive of the militant government was able to exist, at the same time as a village with the ability to collect, process and use information to negotiate with the state. This point will be discussed elsewhere.

Chapter 12

1 Discussions in Katsurayama (2000) were helpful with regard to the characteristics of an epistolary style.
2 'Discrimination occurred by circumstances' and 'discrimination occurred psychologically,' here refer to the methods of thinking, which attempt to

explain the causes of discriminatory phenomena by way of circumstantial factors of society such as poverty, occupation and educational levels, and psychological factors such as prejudicial or discriminatory perceptions, respectively.
3 In disability studies there is a body of work which has expanded this line of research (Ishikawa and Nagase eds 1999; Ishikawa and Kuramoto eds 2002).
4 It seems strange to me that, while terms such as 'sociometry' and 'sociogram' are positioned within the field of sociology, despite their leaning toward psychology, the term or genre of 'sociography' does not exist in sociology.
5 While ethnography is characterized by 'thick description' about culture as discussed by Geertz (1973), it can be said that sociography is characterized by 'in-depth description.' Of course, just like Van Maanen (1988) arrived at ethnography as a consequence of building up many layers of description about social relationships, it is very likely that there are some areas of overlap between ethnography and sociography. However, the world portrayed by many layers of 'in-depth description' about social relationships will have a far broader scope than the world portrayed by the conventional ethnography.
6 Tanaka (2001) was a helpful reference with regard to discriminatory terms and expressions.

Bibliography

Abbott, Andrew (1999), *Department and Discipline: Chicago Sociology at One Hundred*, Chicago: University of Chicago Press.
Akamatsu, Chijō and Takashi Akiba (1941), *Manmō no minzoku to shūkyō* (The races and religions of Manchuria and Mongolia), Tokyo: Ōsakaya Shoten.
Alba, Richard and Victor Nee (2003), *Remaking the American Mainstream: Assimilation and Contemporary Immigration*, Cambridge: Harvard University Press.
Anderson, Elijah (1978), *A Place on the Corner (Studies of Urban Society)*, Chicago: University of Chicago Press.
Anderson, Elijah (1990), *Streetwise: Race, Class and Change in an Urban Community*, Chicago: University of Chicago Press. [Translated into Japanese by Michihiro Okuda and Keiko Okuda (1990) Tokyo: Harvest-sha].
Anderson, Elijah (1999), *Code of the Street: Decency, Violence and the Moral Life of the Inner City*, New York: W. W. Norton and Co.
Anon, nd, *Chinai Gyogyō Kumiai enkaku-shi* (The history of Chinai Fishermen's Association), Unpublished document.
Aruga, Kizaemon ([1948] 1969), 'Toshi shakaigaku no kadai—Sonraku shakaigaku to kanren shite (Topics in urban sociology—In relation to rural sociology),' in *Aruga Kizaemon chosaku-shū VIII* (Collection of works of Kizaemon Aruga, Vol.8), Tokyo: Miraisha, pp. 147–204.
Asaka, Junko, Fumiya Onaka, Masayuki Okahara and Shinya Tateiwa (1995), *Sei no gihō—Ie to shisetsu o detekurasu shōgaisha no shakaigaku* (The technique of life—Sociology of the handicapped who moved out of their family and nursing homes to live independently) (new edition), Tokyo: Fujiwara Shoten.
Baltzell, E. Digby (1979), *Puritan Boston and Quaker Philadelphia: Two Protestant Ethics and the Spirit of Class Authority and Leadership*, Boston: Beacon Press.
Barth, Frederik (1974), 'On Responsibility and Humanity: Calling a Colleague to Account', *Current Anthropology*, 15 (1), pp. 99–102.
Bean, Frank D. and Gillian Stevens (eds) (2003), *America's Newcomers and the Dynamics of Diversity*, New York: Russell Sage Foundation.
Binford, Henry C. (1985), *The First Suburbs: Residential Communities on the Boston Periphery, 1815—1860*, Chicago: University of Chicago Press.
Boas, Franz (1919), 'Scientists as Spies', *The Nation*, 109 (#2842), p. 797.

Bohannan, Laura (1966), 'Shakespeare in the Bush', *Natural History*, 75 (7), pp. 28–33.
Boon, James (1982), *Other Tribes Other Scribes*, Cambridge: Cambridge University Press.
Borofsky, Robert (2002), 'The Four Subfields: Anthropologists as Mythmakers', *American Anthropologist*, 104 (2), pp. 463–80.
Bourdieu, Pierre ([1980] 1990), *The Logic of Practice*, translated into English by Richard Nice, Cambridge: Polity Press.
Brymann, Alan (2001), 'Introduction: A Review of Ethnography', *Ethnography (1)*, London: Sage, pp. ix-xxxix.
Burgess, Ernest W. and Donald J. Bogue (eds) (1964), 'Research in Urban Society: A Long View', *Contributions to Urban Sociology*, Chicago: University of Chicago Press, pp. 1–14.
Butler, Judith (1997), *Excitable Speech: A Politics of the Performativity*, New York: Routledge.
Chen, Hsiang-Shui (1992), *Chinatown No More: Taiwan Immigrants in Contemporary New York*, Ithaca: Cornell University Press.
Chun, Kyung-soo (2001), 'Malinovusukī ui munhwa iron—Maekrak-ron urobuto kinung-ron uro (Malinowski's cultural theory—From contextualism to functionalism)', *Hankuk munhwa inryuhak* (Korean cultural anthropology), 34 (1), pp. 3–27.
Clifford, James (1988), *The Predicament of Culture,* Cambridge, Mass.: Harvard University Press.
Clifford, James (1988), *The Predicament of Culture,* Cambridge, Mass.: Harvard University Press. [Translated into Japanese by Yoshinobu Oota et al. (2003), *Bunka no kyuujoo* (The Predicament of Culture), Jimbun Shoin].
Clifford, James and George E. Marcus (eds) (1986), *Writing Culture: The Poetics and Politics of Ethnography*, Berkeley: University of California Press.
Comrie, Bernard, Stephen Matthews and Maria Polinsky (eds) (1996), *The Atlas of Languages*, New York: Chackmark Books.
Comte-Sponville, André (2000) *Le bonheur deséspérement*, Nantes: Édition Pleins Feux. [Translated into Japanese by Hajime Kida, Ken Osuda, et al. (2004) *Kōfuku wa zetsubō noueni* (Happiness is above despair), Tokyo: Kinokuniya Shoten].
Douglas, Mary and Aaron Wildavsky (1982), *Risk and Culture: An Essay on the Selection of the Technical and Environmental Danger*, Berkley: University of California Press.
Durkheim, Émile ([1897] 1952), *Suicide: A Study in Sociology*, translated into English by John A. Spaulding and George Simpson, edited with an Introduction by George Simpson, London: Routledge and Kegan Paul Ltd.
Eguchi, Keiichi (1988), *Nicchū ahen sensō* (Japan-China opium war), Tokyo: Iwanami Shoten.
Endō, Sōsen (1924), *Zenkō Sōsasha no Shuki* (Memoir of a Good Deed Investigator), Tokyo: Bunka Shobō Hakubunsha.
Flick, Uwe (1995), *Qualitative Forchung*, Hamburg: Rowohlt.
Fong, Timothy P. (1994), *The First Suburban Chinatown: the Remaking of Monterey Park, California*, Philadelphia: Temple University Press.
Fox, Richard G. (ed.) (1991), *Recapturing Anthropology: Working in the Present*, Santa Fe, New Mexico: School of American Research Press.

Fujibayashi, Yasushi and Taisuke Miyauchi (eds) (2004), *Katsuo to katsuobushi no dōjidai-shi* (Contemporary history of bonito and dried bonito), Tokyo: Commons.
Fujise, Kazuya (1992), *Shōwa rikugun 'ahen bōryaku' no daizai—Tenpōsengumi ha ikani kikaku jikkō shitaka* (Serious crimes of the Shōwa Japanese Imperial Army through the opium stratagem—How it was conceived and employed by the graduates of the prestigious Military Staff College), Tokyo: Yamate Shobō Shinsha.
Fukutake, Tadashi ([1958] 1984), *Shakai chōsa hoteiban* (Social research: revised and enlarged), Iwanami Shoten.
Fumio Shiozaki (ed.), *Tokyo Kantō Daishinsai zengo* (Before and After the Great Kanto Earthquake), Tokyo: Nihon Keizai Hyōronsha, pp. 353–390.
Funabashi, Harutoshi (1999), 'Kankyō-shakaigaku kenkyū ni okeru chōsa to riron (Research and theory in environmental sociology)', in Harutoshi Funabashi and Akira Furukawa (eds), *Kankyō-shakaigaku nyūmon: kankyō mondai kenkyū no riron to gihō* (An introduction to environmental sociology: theory and methodology of environmental issues study), Tokyo: Bunka Shobō Hakubunsha, pp. 17–54.
Furukawa, Akira (2004), *Mura no seikatsu kankyō-shi* (Histories of the living environment of villages), Kyoto: Sekai Shisōsha.
Furukawa, Akira and Yasuhiro Itō (1988a), 'Mura no nikki—Gōshū Chinaimura 'Kiroku' (1) (Diary of a village—'Records' of Chinai Village, Gōshū (1) 1867–1888)', in *Chūkyō Daigaku Shakaigakubu Kiyō* (Chukyo University School of Sociology Bulletin), Nos. 2–1.
Furukawa, Akira and Yasuhiro Itō (1988b), 'Mura no nikki—Gōshū Chinaimura 'Kiroku' (2) (Diary of a village—'Records' of Chinai Village, Gōshū (2) 1889–1903)', in *Chūkyō Daigaku Shakaigakubu Kiyō* (Chukyo University School of Sociology Bulletin), Nos. 2–2.
Furukawa, Akira and Yasuhiro Itō (1989a), 'Mura no nikki—Gōshū Chinaimura 'Kiroku' (4) (Diary of a village—'Records' of Chinai Village, Gōshū (4) 1904–1912)', in *Chūkyō Daigaku Shakaigakubu Kiyō* (Chukyo University School of Sociology Bulletin), Nos. 3–2.
Furukawa, Akira and Yasuhiro Itō (1989b), 'Mura no nikki—Gōshū Chinaimura 'Kiroku' (5) (Diary of a village—'Records' of Chinai Village, Gōshū (5) 1919–1926)', in *Chūkyō Daigaku Shakaigakubu Kiyō* (Chukyo University School of Sociology Bulletin), Nos. 4–1.
Furukawa, Akira and Yasuhiro Itō (1991), 'Mura no nikki—Gōshū Chinaimura 'Kiroku' (7) (Diary of a village—'Records' of Chinai Village, Gōshū (7) 1938–1940)', in *Chūkyō Daigaku Shakaigakubu Kiyō* (Chukyo University School of Sociology Bulletin), Nos. 5–2.
Furukawa, Akira and Yasuhiro Itō (1992b), 'Mura no nikki—Gōshū Chinaimura 'Kiroku' (9) (Diary of a village—'Records' of Chinai Village, Gōshū (9) 1745–1818)', in *Chūkyō Daigaku Shakaigakubu Kiyō* (Chukyo University School of Sociology Bulletin), Nos. 6–2.
Furukawa, Akira and Yasuhiro Itō (1994a), 'Mura no nikki—Gōshū Chinaimura 'Kiroku' (12) (Diary of a village—'Records' of Chinai Village, Gōshū (12) 1831–1832)', in *Chūkyō Daigaku Shakaigakubu Kiyō* (Chukyo University School of Sociology Bulletin), Nos. 8–1.

Furukawa, Akira and Yasuhiro Itō (1994b), 'Mura no nikki—Gōshū Chinaimura 'Kiroku' (Ho) Mura Kiyaku (Diary of a village—'Records' of Chinai Village, Gōshū (Sup) bylaws of village)', in *Chūkyō Daigaku Shakaigakubu Kiyō* (Chukyo University School of Sociology Bulletin), Nos. 8–2.

Furukawa, Akira, Yasuhiro Itō and Kaoru Kamatani (2004–2005), 'Mura no nikki—Gōshū Chinaimura 'Kiroku' (13)–(14) (Diary of a village—'Records' of Chinai Village, Gōshū, (13) and (14))', in *Kwansei Gakuin Daigaku Shakaigakubu Kiyō* (Kwansei Gakuin University School of Sociology Journal), Nos. 97 and 98.

Furukawa, Akira and Motoji Matsuda (eds) (2003), *Kankō to kankyō no shakaigaku* (Sociology of tourism and environment), Tokyo: Shin-yo-sha.

Furuno, Kiyoto (1967), 'Oikawa kun no tsuioku (In memory of Oikawa)' in Hiroshi Oikawa (ed.), *Dōzoku soshiki to sonraku seikatsu* (Homogeneous organizations and village life), Tokyo: Miraisha, pp. 251–262.

Gans, Herbert J. (1962), *The Urban Villagers: Group and Class in the Life of Italian-Americans*, New York: Free Press of Glencoe.

Geertz, Clifford (1973), *The Interpretation of Cultures*, New York: Basic Books.

Geertz, Clifford (1988), *Works and Lives: The Anthropologist as Author*, Stanford: Stanford University Press.

Gibbs, Leonard E. and Eileen D. Gambrill (1999), *Critical Thinking for Social Workers* (revised edition), Thousand Oaks: Pine Forge Press.

Giddens, Anthony (1995), 'Epilogue: Notes on the Future of Anthropology', in A. S. Ahmed and C. N. Shone (eds), *The Rise and Fall of Scientific Ethnography*, London: Athlone, pp. 272–277.

Glazer, Nathan and Daniel Patrick Moynihan (1963), *Beyond the Melting Pot*, Cambridge: MIT Press and Harvard University Press.

Goldstein, Joseph, Anna Freud and Albert J. Solnit (1979), *Before the Best Interests of the Child*, New York: Free Press.

Griaule, Marcel (1957), *Methode de l'ethnographie*, Paris: Presses Universitaires de France.

Hara, Kimika (2005), *Shōgatsu ryōri no shūshū to bunseki* (Collection and analysis of New Year dishes), An assignment for '2004 Cultural Anthropology B,' Otsu: Seian University of Art and Design.

Harada, Katsumasa (1997), 'Sōryokusentaisei to bōkūenshū: Kokumin dōin' to minshū no saihensei (Total War and Air Defence Drills: National Mobilization and Organization),' in Fumio Shiozaki (ed), *Tokyo Kanto Daishinsai Zengo* (Before and After the Great Kanto Earthquake), Tokyo: Nihon Keizai Hyōronsha, pp. 353–390.

Harvard G.S.D Tokyo seminar (1989), *Beikoku/Nihon no toshi kaihatsu to kenchiku, aaban dezain o megutte* (On urban design and city planning in the USA and Japan), March 28, 1989, Report summary in the August issue of SD, Tokyo: Kajima Shuppankai, pp. 61–76.

Hase, Masato and Hideyuki Nakamura (eds) (2003), *Eiga no seijigaku* (Political science of films), Tokyo: Seikyūsha.

Hattori, Tamio (1974), 'Kankō no motsu mondaiten ni tuite (Problems inherent in publication)', in *Suzuki Eitarō chosaku-shū V—Chōsen nōson shakai no kenkyū* (Collection of Eitarō Suzuki—Research into rural societies in Korea), Tokyo: Miraisha, pp. 48–56.

Helfer, Mary E., Ruth S. Kempe and Richard D. Krugman (1997), *The Battered Child* (Fifth Edition), Chicago: University of Chicago Press.
Helfer, Rany E. and C. Henry Kempe (1968), *The Battered Child*, Chicago: University of Chicago Press.
Hijikata, Hisakatsu (1943), *Ryūboku* (Driftwood), Tokyo: Oyama Shoten.
Hirano, Kenichiro et al. (eds) (2000), Special Issue: Asian Migration and Settlement—Focus on Japan, *Asian and Pacific migration journal* (APMJ) 9–3.
Hirota, Yasuo (2003), *Shinpan esunishitii to toshi* (Ethnicity and the city, new edition), Tokyo: Yushindo Kobunsha.
Iiyama, Tatsuo (1972), 'Shōnen jidai no Seiichi-kun (What was Seiichi like in his boyhood)', in Seiichi Izumi (ed.) *Izumi Seiichi chosaku-shū* (Collection of Seiichi Izumi), 3 (6), Tokyo: Yomiuri Shimbunsha, pp. 6–8.
Iizuka, Tetsuei (ed.) (1923), *Daishinsai no Aiwa to Bidan* (Stories of Sorrow and Good Deeds of the Great Earthquake), Second Edition, Tokyo: Kinnotori-Sha.
Imada, Takatoshi (2000), 'Riaritī to kakutō suru: shakaigaku kenkyūhō no sho-ruikei (Wrestling with reality: various patterns of sociological study methods)', in Takatoshi Imada (ed.), *Riaritī no toraekata: shakaigaku kenkyūhō* (How to grasp reality: sociological study methods), Tokyo: Yūhikaku pp. 1–38.
Imanishi, Kinji and Yutaka Ban (1948), 'Daikōanrei ni okeru Orochon no seitai: 2 (The way of life of the Orochon in Daxinganling: 2)', *Minzokugaku kenkyū* (Ethnographic research), 13 (2), pp. 42–61.
Inoguchi, Takashi (2003), 'The usefulness of international comparative research', Paper presented to the Second International Symposium *On the study of social research improving human happiness*, Kwansei Gakuin University 21st Century COE Program, Japan, 12 December 2003.
Isaka, Tadashi and Gamō Yakōgen Kurabu (eds) (2001), *Tanken, hakken, hottoken—Kodomo to aruita biwako, mizunosato no kurashi to bunka* (Explore, discover, action—Lake Biwa explored with children, life and culture of the water country), Kyoto: Shōwadō.
Ishikawa, Jun and Osamu Nagase (eds) (1999), *Shōgaigaku eno shōtai—Shakai, bunka, disability* (Invitation to disability studies—Society, culture and disability), Tokyo: Akashi Shoten.
Ishikawa, Jun and Tomoaki Kuramoto (eds) (2002), *Shōgaigaku no shuchō* (Propositions of disability study), Tokyo: Akashi Shoten.
Ishimure, Michiko (1969), *Kukaijodo—Waga Minamatabyō* (Paradise in the sea of sorrow: Our Minamata Disease), Tokyo: Kōdansha.
Izumi, Kimiko (1972), *Izumi Seiichi to tomo ni* (With Seiichi Izumi for life), Tokyo: Fuyō Shobō.
Izumi, Seiichi (1937), 'Daikōanrei tōnan-bu Orochon-zoku tōsa hōkoku (The fieldwork report on the Orochon residing in the southeast of Daxinganling)', *Minzokugaku kenkyū* (Ethnographic research), 3 (1), pp. 39–106.
Izumi, Seiichi (1969), *Fīrudowāku no kiroku—Bunkajinruigaku no jissen* (The record of fieldwork—Practice of cultural anthropology), Tokyo: Kōdansha.
Izumi, Seiichi (1972), *Izumi Seiichi chosaku-shū* (Collection of Seiichi Izumi), Tokyo: Yomiuri Shimbunsha.

James, Wendy (1988), *The Listening Ebony: Moral Knowledge, Religion, and Power among the Uduk of Sudan*, Oxford: Clarendon Press.
Jayaratne, Srinika and Rona Levy (1979), *Empirical Clinical Practice*, New York: Columbia University Press.
Kada, Yukiko (1989), 'Nichijō seikatsu to kankyō ninshiki (Everyday life and environmental awareness)', in Hiroyuki Torigoe (ed.), *Kankyō mondai no shakai riron* (Social logic of environmental problems), Tokyo: Ochanomizu Shobō, pp. 146–165.
Kada, Yukiko (1992), 'Hotaru no fūkeiron—Hotaru o tōshitemita mizu kankyō ninshiki (A discourse on the firefly in the landscape—Water environmental awareness seen through the firefly)', in Akira Furukawa and Yukio Ōnishi (eds), *Kankyō imējiron—Ningen kankyō no jūsōteki fūkei* (Environmental image theory—Multi-layered view of human environment), Tokyo: Kōbundō, pp. 35–79.
Kada, Yukiko (1997), 'Seikatsu jissen kara tsumugidasareru jūsōteki shizenkan (Multi-layered view of nature woven from life practices),' *Kankyō shakaigaku kenkyū* (Environmental sociology research), 7, pp. 72–85.
Kada, Yukiko (2000), 'Mijikana kankyō no jibunshi—Kagakuchi to seikatsuchi no taiwa o mezashita hotarudasu (One's own history of the familiar environment—The firefly research for a dialogue between scientific knowledge and life knowledge)' in Mizu to Bunka Kenkyūkai (ed.), *Minnade hotarudasu—Biwako chiiki no hotaru to mijika na mizu kankyō chōsa* (Let's research the firefly together—Research into the firefly in the Lake Biwa region and nearby aqueous environs), Tokyo: Shin-yo-sha, pp. 192–220.
Kada, Yukiko (2001), *Mizubekurashi no kankyōgaku—Nihon to sekai no mizuumi kara* (Environmental study of the waterside life—From lakes of Japan and the world), Kyoto: Shōwadō.
Kada, Yukiko (2002), 'Shizen to seikatsu no kyori—Shōwa 30-nendai o miru me (A distance between nature and life—Looking at the 30s of the Shōwa era), *Kagaku* (Science), January 2002, pp. 34–44.
Kada, Yukiko (2003), *Mizu o meguru hito to shizen—Nihon to sekai no genba kara* (People and nature around water—From fields of Japan and the world), Tokyo: Yūhikaku.
Kada, Yukiko and Akira Furukawa (1984), 'Mizu to mura (Water and villages)', in *Mizu to hito no kankyō-shi* (The history of environment in terms of water and people), Tokyo: Ochanomizu Shobō, pp. 25–46.
Kada, Yukiko and Akira Furukawa (2000), *Seikatsu saigen no ōyōtenjigaku-teki kenkyū—Hakubutsukan no esunogurafī toshite* (Applied exhibitory study of recreated life scenes—As museum ethnography), Kusatsu: Lake Biwa Museum.
Kada, Yukiko and Yukio Ōnishi (1992), 'Yagai chōsa to denen nettowāku—Pasokon tsūshin niyoru chiiki jōhō no hasshin to soshaku (Field research and electronic network—Dissemination and assimilation of local information via personal computer communication)' in Masakazu Nomura (ed.), *Jōhō to nihonjin* (Information and the Japanese), Tokyo: Domesu Publishers, pp. 83–105.
Kada, Yukiko and Masahide Yūma (2000), *Mizube asobi no seitaigaku—Biwako chiiki no sansedai no katari kara* (Ecology of waterside plays—From stories

told by three generations of the Lake Biwa region), Tokyo: Nōbunkyō (Rural Culture Association).

Kada, Yukiko (ed.) (1992), *Shirōto saiensu no saiensu* (The science of amateur science), Ōtsu: Lake Biwa Environmental Research Institute.

Kamei, Nobutaka (1997), 'Research on the material culture of the children of the Baka: Tools and toys', in Nobutaka Kamei (ed.), *A Study of the Transitional use of Tropical Forest*, Intermediate report (10), Ministry of Scientific and Technical Research, Republic of Cameroon, pp. 5–12 and 19–24.

Kamei, Nobutaka (2001a), 'An educational project in the forest: Schooling for the Baka children in Cameroon', *African Study Monographs*, Supplementary Issue 26, pp. 185–195.

Kamei, Nobutaka (2001b), 'Shuryō-saishū-min Baka ni okeru kodomo no asobi (How the Baka children of Cameroon play?)', Paper presented to the 6th Annual Meeting of Japanese Society for Ecological Anthropology, Nanbuya, Aomori, Japan, March 2001.

Kamei, Nobutaka (2001c), 'Shuryō-saishū-min Baka ni okeru kodomo no asobi (How the Baka children of Cameroon play?)', in Mitsuo Ichikawa and Hiroaki Satō (eds), *Mori to hito no kyōzon sekai (Kōza: Seitai-jinruigaku 2)* (Hunter-gatherers in the Central African forests (Lecture series: Ecological anthropology, Vol. 2)), Kyoto: Kyoto University Press, pp. 93–139.

Kamei, Nobutaka (2002a), 'How the Baka children of Cameroon play,' Paper presented to the 9th International Conference on Hunting and Gathering Societies, Session 32: Recent Research on Forager Children, Edinburgh Conference Centre, Heriot-Watt University, Edinburgh, UK, September 2002.

Kamei, Nobutaka (2002b), 'How the Baka children of Cameroon play', Paper presented to the 101st Annual Meeting of the American Anthropological Association', Session 0–043, 'Culture and ecology of Forager Children', Hyatt Regency New Orleans, USA, November 2002.

Kamei, Nobutaka (2002c), *Shuryō-saishū-min Baka ni okeru kodomo no nichijō katsudō to shakai-ka katei ni kansuru jinruigaku-teki kenkyū* (An anthropological research on daily activities and socialization process of children of the Baka Hunter-Gatherers), Doctorate Thesis, Kyoto: Kyoto University, Japan.

Kamei, Nobutaka (2005), 'Play among Baka children in Cameroon', in Barry S. Hewlett and Michael E. Lamb (eds) *Hunter-gatherer childhoods: Evolutionary, developmental & cultural perspectives*, New Brunswick, NJ: Transaction Publishers, pp. 343–359.

Kami, Shōichiro (1988), 'Endo Sōsen', *Jidō bungaku jiten* (Dictionary of Children's literature), Tokyo: Tokyo Shoseki, p. 103.

Kamishima, Jirō (1961), *Kindai Nippon no seishin kōzō* (Mental structure of modern Japan), Tokyo: Iwanami Shoten.

Kano, Tadao (1946), *Tōnan-Ajia minzokugaku senshigaku kenkyū* (Anthropological and prehistorical research in Southeast Asia), Tokyo: Yajima Shobō.

Katō, Mikio (1996), *Eiga janru ron* (Discussion on film genres), Tokyo: Heibonsha.

Katō, Mikio (2004), *'Blade Runner' ron josetsu—Eigagaku tokubetsu kōgi* (An introduction to discussion on 'Blade Runner'—Film study special lecture), Tokyo: Chikuma Shobō.

Katsurayama, Yasuo (2000), *Yūai no rekishi shakaigaku—Kindai eno shikaku* (Historical sociology of friendship—A view to modern times), Tokyo: Iwanami Shoten.

Kawabata, Akira, (1998), 'Shakai chōsa no rekishi: keiryōteki shuhō o chūshin ni' (The history of social research: mostly on quantitative methods) in Kenji Kosaka and Yōsuke Kotō (eds), *Kōza shakaigaku 1: Riron to hōhō* (On sociology 1: theory and practice), Tokyo: University of Tokyo Press, pp. 239–270.

Kawai, Takao (1991), 'Kokusei Chōsa no kaishi: Minsei Chōsa kara Kokusei Chōsa he (Start of the National Population Census: From Minsei to Kokusei Census)', *Kindai nihon shakai chōsa shi II* (History of Research in Modern Japanese Society [II]), Tokyo: Keio Tsūshin, pp. 105–141.

Kawazoe, Noboru (2004), *Kon Wajirō—sono kōgengaku* (Wajirō Kon—his study of modern phenomena), Tokyo: Chikuma Shobō.

Kempe, C. Henry, F.N. Silverman, B.F. Steele, W. Droegmueller and H.K. Silver (1962), 'The Battered Child Syndrome,' *JAMA*, 181 (1): pp. 17–24.

Kimura, Daiji (2003), *Kyōzai kankaku: Afurika no futatsu no shakai ni okeru gengoteki sōgo kōi kara* (The sense of co-presence: the linguistic interactions of two African societies), Kyoto: Kyoto University Press.

Kimura, Motoi (2000), *Mura no seikatsu-shi—Shiryō ga kataru futsū no hitobito* (Life histories of villages—Ordinary people seen in historical documents), Tokyo: Yūzankaku.

Kimura, Yoko, Kaori Hara and Noriko Yamano (2002), 'Jidō gyakutai kēsu ni okeru enjo tetsuduki no kentō (A consideration of assistance procedures in child abuse cases),' *Kwansei Gakuin Daigaku Shakaigakubukiyō* (Kwansei Gakuin University School of Sociology Journal), 91, pp. 149–165.

Kitano, Seiichi (1967), 'Oikawa kun no tsuioku (In memory of Oikawa),' in Hiroshi Oikawa (ed.), *Dōzoku soshiki to sonraku seikatsu* (*Dozoku* organizations and village life), Tokyo: Miraisha, pp. 263–278.

Kiyono, Kenji (1930), 'Kōko zuiroku [1] (Archaeological essays [1]),' *Rekishi to chiri* (History and geography), 26 (4), pp. 82–7.

Kiyono, Kenji (1943), *Sumatora kenkyū* (Research in Sumatra), Tokyo: Kawade Shobō Shinsha.

Kobayashi, Hideo (1977), *Motoori Norinaga*, Shinchōsha.

Kon, Wajirō (1971), *Kon Wajirō shū 1: Kōgengaku* (Wajirō Kon collection 1: Study of modern phenomena), Tokyo: Domesu Publishers.

Kon, Wajirō (1987), 'Kōgengaku ga hamon no moto (Expelled because of *Kōgengaku*)', in Terunobu Fujimori (ed.), *Kōgengaku nyūmon* (An introduction to the study of modern phenomena), Tokyo: Chikuma Shobō, pp. 403–405.

Kondo, Dorinne K (1989), *Crafting Selves: Power, Gender, and Discourses of Identity in a Japanese Work Place*, Chicago: Chicago University Press.

Kōno, Seizō (1942), *Kōdō no kenkyū* (Research into the Japanese ideology centered on the Emperor), Tokyo: Bungakusha.

Koppers, Wilhelm (1929), 'Das Schicksal der Ethnologie unter dem Sowjet-Regime', *Anthropos*, 27, pp. 501–23.

Korzeniewicz, Roberto Patricio and William C. Smith (eds) (1996), *Latin America in the World Economy*, New York: Russell Sage Foundation.

Kosaka, Kenji (2004), 'Shikirini muko o sasshōshi—Kōfuku to fukō no shakaigaku josetsu (Killing many innocent people—An introduction to the sociology of well-being and ill-being)', *Sentan shakai Kenkyū* (Advanced Social Research), 1, pp. 1–52.

Kōtō-ku (1997), *Kōtō-ku shi, Chūkan,* (History of Kōtō-ku, middle edition), Tokyo: Kōtō-ku.

Kovats-Bernat, J. C. (2002), 'Negotiating Dangerous Fields: Pragmatic Strategies for Fieldwork amid Violence and Terror', *American Anthropologist,* 104 (1), pp. 208–22.

Kurasawa, Susumu and Tatsuto Asakawa (eds) (2004), *Shinpen Tokyo ken no shakai chizu 1975–90* (New edition, A social map of the Tokyo area, 1975–1990), Tokyo: University of Tokyo Press.

Kurihara, Akira (ed.) (2000), *Shōgen Minamata-byō* (Testimony Minamata disease), Tokyo: Iwanami Shoten.

Levitt, Peggy (2001), *The Transnational Villagers,* Berkeley and Los Angeles: University of California Press.

Levitt, Peggy and Mary Waters (eds) (2002), *The Changing Face of Home: The Transitional Lives of the Second Generation,* New York: Russell Sage Foundation.

Li, Tian-quo (2000), *Idō suru Shinkyo Uiguru jin to Chugoku shakai: toshi wo musubu dainamizumu* (Xinjiang Uyghurs on the move and the Chinese society: Dynamism connecting the cities), Tokyo: Harvest-sha.

Lie, John and Hiroshi Ishida (1995), 'Gendai Amerika no esunishitī to kaiso (Ethnicity and Class in contemporary America)' in Michihiro Okuda (ed.), *21 seiki no toshi shakaigaku 2: komyunitī to esunishitī* (The urban sociology of the 21st century: community and ethnicity), Tokyo: Keisō Shobō, pp. 45–113.

Lienhardt, Godfrey (1980), 'Self: Public and Private. Some African Representations', *Journal of Anthropological Society of Oxford,* 11, pp. 69–82.

Lipsky, Michael (1983), *Street Level Bureaucracy,* New York: Russell Sage Foundation.

Machimura, Takashi and Akihiko Nishizawa (2000), *Toshi no shakaigaku: Shakai ga katachi o arawasu tok*i (Sociology in the city: when the society shows its shape), Tokyo: Yūhikaku.

Makino-chō-shi Hensan Iinkai (The Editorial Committee for the History of Makino-chō) (ed.) (1987), *Makino-chō-shi* (The history of Makino-chō), Shiga: Makino-chō.

Makino Tatsumi sensei tsuitōroku kankō kai (ed.) (1977), *Makino Tatsumi sensei tsuitōroku* (A collection of memorial writings for Tatsumi Makino), Privately published.

Malinowski, Bronislaw (1922), *Argonauts of the Western Pacific,* London: Routledge & Kegan Paul. [Translated into Japanese by K. Terada and Y. Masuda (1967), 'Seitaiyo no enyokokaisha' (Ocean Voyagers on the Western Pacific), *Sekai no meicho 59 Marinofusukii & Rebai Sutoroosu* (World Classics, 59, Malinowski & Lévi Strauss), Chūō Kōronsha, 6-342].

Malinowski, Bronislaw (1965), *Coral Gardens and Their Magic,* 2 volumes, Bloomington: Indiana University Press.

Malinowski, Bronislaw (1967), *A Diary in the Strict Sense of the Term,* translated into English by Norbert Guterman, London: The Athlone Press.

Maruyama, Masao (1957), 'Nihon no shisō', (Japanese Thought), *Iwanami kōza Gendai Shisō Gendai Nihon no Shisō 11,* (The Iwanami series: Contemporary thought—Contemporary Japanese thought, 11), Iwanami Shoten, 8–204 (Rerecorded: 1996, 'Japanese Thought', *Maruyama Masao-shū Dai 7 kan,* (Collected works of Masao Maruyama, volume 7), Iwanami Shoten, pp. 191–244).

Maruyama, Masao (1986), *'Bunmeiron no gairyaku' wo yomu (jō, chū & ge)* (Reading an 'Outline of theories of civilisation' [Volumes 1, 2 and 3]) Iwanam ishinsho (Rerecorded: 1996, '"Bunmeiron no gairyaku" wo yomu (ichi)' (Reading an 'Outline of theories of civilisation' (1)), *Masao Maruyama-shū dai 13 kan* (Collected works of Masao Maruyama, volume 13), 5–446 and '"Bunmeiron no gairyaku" wo yomu (ni)' (Reading an 'outline of theories of civilisation' (2)), *Masao Maruyama-shū Dai 14 kan* (Collected Works of Masao Maruyama, volume 14) Iwanami Shoten, 5–355).

Marx, Karl, ([1867] 1976), *Capital,* Volume 1: *A Critique of Political Economy,* London: Penguin.

Material World Project (Head: Peter Menzel) (1994), *Chikyū kazoku—sekai 30-ka-koku no futsū no kurashi* (A global family—ordinary lives in 30 countries in the world), Tokyo: TOTO Ltd.

Matsuda, Motoji (1995), 'Jinruigaku ni okeru kojin, jiko & jinsei' (The individual, self and life in anthropology), in Toshinao Yoneyama (ed.) *Gendai bunka jinruigaku wo manabu hito no tameni* (For students of contemporary cultural anthropology), Sekai Shisōsha, pp. 186–205.

Matsuda, Motoji (1996), 'Jinruigaku no kiki to senjutsu teki riarizumu no kanōsei' (The anthropology crisis and the potential of strategic realism), *Shakaijinruigaku nenpō* (The social anthropology yearbook), 22, pp. 23–48.

Matsuda, Motoji (1997), 'Jissenteki bunka sōtaishugikō—shoki afurikanisuto no chōyaku' (Investigating practical cultural relativism—The leap made by the early Africanists), *Minzokugaku kenkyū* (Enthnographic research), 62 (2), pp. 205–26.

Matsuda, Motoji (2001), 'Bunka/Jinruigaku—Bunka kaitai wo koete' (Culture and Anthropology: Overcoming the dismantling of culture), in T. Sugishima (ed.), *Jinruigaku-teki jissen no saikōchiku—posuto koroniaru tenkai igo* (The reconstruction of anthropological practice—After the post-colonial turnaround), Sekai Shisōsha, pp. 123–51.

Matsuda, Motoji (2002), 'Kojinsei no shakairiron josetsu—Hiseiō shakai no serufuzō o tōshite' (Introduction to the social theory of individuality: Through the analysis of the self-images of non-Western societies), *Gendai shakaigaku fōramu* (Contemporary sociology forum), Sekai Shisōsha, pp. 33–42.

Matsuda, Motoji (2003), 'Fīrudo chōsahō no kyūjō o koete (Beyond the plight of field research methodology)', *Shakaigaku hyōron* (Sociology review), 53–4, pp. 499–514.

Mauduit, J. A. (1960), *Manuel d'ethnographie,* Paris: Payot.

Mauss, Marcel (1947), *Manuel d'ethnographie,* Paris: Payot.

Mauss, Marcel (1967), *The Gift: Forms and Function of Exchange in Archaic Societies,* New York: Norton.

Ministry of Health, Labor and Welfare, Children and Families Bureau (eds) (1999), *Kodomo gyakutai taiō no tebiki* (Guidebook to dealing with child abuse), Tokyo: Japan Children Welfare Association.

Ministry of Health, Labor and Welfare, Children and Families Bureau (eds) (2000), *Kodomo gyakutai taiō no tebiki (kaitei)* (Guidebook to dealing with child abuse [revised]), Tokyo: Yūhikaku.

Mitsuya, Yōko (1996), *Seikatsuhogo kēsu wākā funtōki* (Struggles of a welfare case worker), Kyoto: Minerva Shobō.

Miura, Kōkichirō (1997), *Hisabetsu buraku eno gotsū no tegami* (Five letters to outcast villages), Ōtsu: Hansabetsu Kokusai Rentai Kaihō Kenkyūjo Shiga.

Miura, Kōkichirō (2004), 'Kategorī-ka no wana (The trap in categorization)', in Hiroaki Yoshii and Kōkichirō Miura (eds), *Shakaigaku-teki fīrudowāku* (Sociological fieldwork), Kyoto: Sekai Shisōsha, pp. 201–45.

Miyahara, Kojiro (2000), *Rinshō no shakaigaku* (Clinical sociology), Tokyo: Shin-yo-sha.

Miyamoto, Tsuneichi (1984), *Wasurerareta nihonjin* (Forgotten Japanese), Tokyo: Iwanami Shoten.

Miyauchi, Taisuke (1989), *Ebi to shokutaku no gendaishi* (Contemporary history of prawns and food system), Tokyo: Dōbunkan Shuppan.

Miyauchi, Taisuke (1998), 'Jūsō-teki-na kankyō riyō to kyōdō-riyō-ken— Soromon Shotō Maraita-tō no jirei kara (Mixed use of the environment and collective usufruct: a case study in Malaita, Solomon Islands)', *Kankyō shakaigaku kenkyū* (Journal of Environmental Sociology), 4, pp. 125–41.

Miyauchi, Taisuke (2000), 'Soromon Shotō Maraita-tō ni okeru dekasegi to ijū no shakai-shi (Social history of migration in Malaita Island, Solomon Islands)—1930s–1990s', in Masanori Yoshioka and Isao Hayashi (eds), *Oseania kindaishi no jinruigaku-teki kenkyū* (Anthropological studies on the modern history of Oceania), Bulletin of the Japanese National Museum of Ethnology, Osaka, Special Issue, 21, pp. 237–60.

Miyauchi, Taisuke (2002), 'Mori ni modoru hitobito—Soromon Shotō: ikiru senryaku neru Maraita tōmin (People who return to the forest—Solomon Islands: Malaita Islanders' survival strategy)', *Oseania* (Oceania), Japan-Oceania Society for Cultural Exchanges, 67, pp. 4–7.

Miyauchi, Taisuke (2003a), '"Jibun tachi no tochi e"—gendai meraneshia shakai ni okeru ijū, minzoku funsō, tochi shoyū ("To our land"—migration, ethnic conflicts and land ownership in modern Melanesian society)', in Shōgo Takekawa and Nobuyuki Yamada (eds), *Gendai shakaigaku ni okeru rekishi to hihan—gurōbaru-ka no shakaigaku* (History and criticism in modern sociology—sociology of globalism), Tokyo: Tōshindō, pp. 133–58.

Miyauchi, Taisuke (2003b), 'Shimin chōsa to iu kanōsei—chōsa no shutai to hōhō wo kuminaosu (A possibility of citizens' research—redefining the bearers and methods of research)', *Shakaigaku hyōron* (Japanese Sociological Review), 53 (4), pp. 566–78.

Mizu to Bunka Kenkyūkai (Water and Culture Study Group) (2000), *Minnade hotarudasu—Biwako chiiki no hotaru to mijika na mizu kankyō chōsa* (Let's research the firefly together—Research into the firefly in the Lake Biwa region and nearby aqueous environs), Tokyo: Shin-yo-sha.

Morrison, Joan and Charlotte Fox Zabusky (1993), *American Mosaic: The Immigrant Experience in the Words of Those Who Lived It* (revised edition), Pittsburgh: University of Pittsburgh Press.

Mullen, Edward U. (1978), 'The Construction of Personal Models for Effective Practice: A Method of Utilizing Research Findings to Guide Social Intervention,' *Journal of Social Service Research*, 2, pp. 45–63.

Murakami, Yōichiro (1979), *Kagaku to nichijōsei no bunmyaku* (The context of science and ordinariness), Tokyo: Kaimeisha.

Nagahama, Isao (ed.) ([1937] 1988), *Kokumin seishin sōdōin jisshi gaiyō dai 1 shū* (Practice of national spirit, volume 1), Fukkoku: Kokumin seishin sōdōin undō, Minshū kyōka doin shiryō shūsei 1 (Facsimile edition: National spirit mobilization movement 1), Naikaku Jyōho-bu (Information Department, Cabinet), Tokyo: Akashi Shoten.

Naigai Kyōiku Shiryō Chōsa Kai (Domestic and International Educational Material Research Institute) (1924), *Kyōiku shiryō: Daishinsai no bidan to sanwa* (Education Material: Stories of tragedies and good deeds of the Great Earthquake), Tokyo: Nankōsha.

Nagai, Yoshikazu (2000), *Bikōsha tachi no machikado: Tantei no shakai shi* (Street for tailers: Social history of detectives), Yokohama: Seori Shobō.

Nagata, Haruka (1939), *Manshū ni okeru Orochon-zoku no kenkyū: Dai-ippen* (Research into the Orochon in Manchuria: Volume 1), Fengtian: Chian-bu Sanbōshi Chōsa-ka (Security Department General Staff Office Research Division).

Nakanishi, Shōji and Chizuko Ueno (2003), *Tōjisha shuken* (The sovereign rights of the person concerned), Tokyo: Iwanami Shoten.

Nakano, Takashi (1975a), 'Rekishishakaigaku to gendaishakai' (Historical sociology and contemporary sociology), *Mirai* (Future), 101, pp. 2–7.

Nakano, Takashi (1975b), 'Shakaigaku-teki chōsa ni okeru hichōsasha tono iwayuru "kyōdō kōi" ni tsuite' (The so-called 'joint project' with subjects of sociological research), *Mirai* (Future), 102, pp. 28–33.

Nakano, Takashi (1975c), 'Shakaigaku-teki chōsa no hōhō to chōsasha/ hichōsasha tono kankei' (Sociological research methodology and the relationship between researchers and the subjects of research), *Mirai* (Future), 103, pp. 28–33.

Nakano, Takashi (1975d), 'Kankyō to ningen ni tsuite no kinkyū-chōsa to chōki-chōsa' (Emergency research and long-term research on the environment and people), *Mirai* (Future), 104, pp. 45–8.

Nakano, Takashi (1975e), 'Shakaigaku-teki chōsa to "kyodo kōi"' (Sociological research and 'joint project'), *UP*, 33, pp. 1–6.

Nakano, Takashi et al. (1990), *Fīrudo risāchi no hōhō* (Field research methodology), The Telecommunications Association.

Nakao, Katsumi (ed.) (2000), *Shokuminchi jinruigaku no tenbō* (The view of colonialism in anthropology), Tokyo: Fūkyōsha.

Narita, Ryūichi ([1996] 2003), 'Kantō Daishinsai no meta hisutorii no tameni: Hōdō, Aiwa, Bidan' (Great Kantō Earthquake meta history: Report, stories of sorrow and good Deeds), in *Kindai toshi kūkan no bunkateki keiken* (Cultural experiences of modern urban space), Tokyo: Iwanami Shoten, pp. 192–236.

Nash, D. and B. Wintrob (1972), 'The Emergence of Self-consciousness in Ethnography,' *Current Anthropology*, 13 (5), pp. 527–42.

Nishikawa, Nagao (1995), 'Nippon-gata kokumin-kokka no keisei (Creation of a Japanese style nation state)', in Nagao Nishikawa and Hideharu Matsumiya (eds), *Bakumatsu/Meiji-ki no kokumin-kokka keisei to bunka hen'yō* (Creation of a nation state and cultural transformation at the end of Edo period and during the Meiji era), Tokyo: Shin-yo-sha, pp. 3–42.

Nitagai, Kamon (1974), 'Shakai chōsa no magarikado—Jūmin undō chōsago no oboegaki' (The turning point of social Research—A memorandum after research on a social movement), *UP*, 24, pp. 1–7.

Nitagai, Kamon (1977), 'Undōsha no sōkatsu to kenkyūsha no shutaisei (jo/ge)' (Activists en bloc and researcher autonomy (1 and 2)). *UP*, 55, pp. 22–26, 56, pp. 28–31.

Nitagai, Kamon (1986) 'Komyuniti waku no tame no shakai chōsa' (Social research for community Work), *Kōshū eisei* (Public health), 50 (7), pp. 441–5.

Nitagai, Kamon (1996), 'Futatabi "kyōdō kōi" e: Hanshin daishinsai no chōsa kara' (Revisiting a 'joint project': From research of the Great Hanshin Earthquake), *Kankyō shakaigaku kenkyū* (Environmental sociological research), 2, pp. 50–62.

Noe, Keiichi (2005), *Monogatari no tetsugaku* (The Philosophy of narrative), Tokyo: Iwanami Shoten.

Ogata, Masato (narration) and Shinichi Tsuji (composition) (1996), *Tokoyo no fune wo kogite—Minamatabyō shishi* (Rowing the eternal sea—The story of a Minamata fisherman), Yokohama: Seori Shobō.

Ogawa, Nobuhiko (1996), 'Chiiki kenkyū seiritsu-shi no ichi danmen—Izumi Seiichi to Saishūtō (A cross section of the developmental history of area studies: Seiichi Izumi and Chejudo Island)', in Kiyotada Tsutsui (ed.), *Sōgōteki chiiki kenkyū seika hōkokusho sirīzu No.14 [Chiiki kenkyū seiritsu]* (Comprehensive area studies: Outcome reports series No. 14 [Development of area studies]), Monbu-shō Kagakukenkyū-hi Hojokin Jūten Ryōiki Kenkyū 'Sōgōteki Chiiki Kenkyū' Sōkatsu-han ([Comprehensive Area Studies] Coordination Unit for Priority Research Receiving the Education Ministry's Grants-in-aid of Scientific Researches), pp. 55–64.

Ogino, Masahiro (2005), Animation-based sociology 'Bōryoku no fūkei' (Landscape of violence), videotape.

Okuda, Michihiro (1996), 'Ishitsu kyōzon shakai e no kairo: Toshiteki sekai, komyunitī, esunisitī (A path towards the society of co-existence of heterogeneity: urban world, community and ethnicity)', in Yasuo Hirota (ed.), *Kōza gaikokujin teijū mondai 3: Tabunkashugi to tabunka kyōiku* (On the issue of the settlement of foreigners 3: Multiculturalism and multicultural education), Tokyo: Akashi Shoten, pp. 233 278.

Okuda, Michihiro (2000), 'Asian newcomers in the Shinjuku and Ikebukuro areas, 1988—1998', *Reflections on a decade of research*, Asian and Pacific Migration Journal, 9 (3), pp. 343–348.

Okuda, Michihiro (2004a) 'Tatoeba toshi shakaigaku chōsa ni okeru moderu kara ishitsu ninshiki he (For example, from model to recognition of heterogeneity in urban sociology research)', Paper presented to the Symposium *On the Study of Social Research Improving Human Happiness*, Department of Sociological Studies, Postgraduate School of Kwansei Gakuin University 21st Century COE program Gakushi Kaikan, Tokyo, 26 March 2004.

Okuda, Michihiro (2004b), *Toshi komyunitī no jiba: ekkyō suru esunishitī to 21 seiki toshi shakaigaku* (The magnetic field of the urban community:

transnational ethnicity and the urban sociology in the 21st century), Tokyo: University of Tokyo Press.

Okuda, Michihiro (ed.) (1989), *Mō hitotsu no kokusaika to shiteno Ikebukuro: Ajia kei gaikokujin no seikatsu kyotenka* (Ikebukuro, another internationalization: The settlement of migrants of Asian origin), Research report, Rikkyo University Okuda seminar.

Okuda, Michihiro (ed.) (2001), *Ajia no Shinjuku/Ikebukuro: genchi mensetsu chōsa kiroku korekushon 2000* (Shinjuku and Ikebukuro in Asia: A collection of research based on face to face interviews on the ground, 2000), Research report, Okuda seminar, Sociology Department, Faculty of Arts, Chuo University.

Okuda, Michihiro (ed.) (2002), *Ajia no Shinjuku/Ikebukuro: genchi mensetsu chosa kiroku korekushon 2001* (Shinjuku and Ikebukuro in Asia: A collection of research based on face to face interviews on the ground, 2001), Research report, Okuda seminar, Sociology Department, Faculty of Arts, Chuo University.

Okuda, Michihiro (ed.) (2003), *Ajia no Shinjuku/Ikebukuro: Genchi mensetsu chōsa kiroku korekushon 2002* (Shinjuku and Ikebukuro in Asia: A collection of research based on face to face interviews on the ground, 2002), Research report, Okuda seminar, Sociology Department, Faculty of Arts, Chuo University.

Okuda, Michihiro (ed.) (2004), *Ajia no Shinjuku/Ikebukuro: genchi mensetsu chōsa kiroku korekushon 2003* (Shinjuku and Ikebukuro in Asia: A collection of research based on face to face interviews on the ground, 2003), Research report, Okuda seminar, Sociology Department, Faculty of Arts, Chuo University.

Okuda, Michihiro and Junko Tajima (eds) (1991), *Ikebukuro no Ajia kei gaigokujin: Shakaigaku-teki jittai hōkoku* (Asian migrants in Ikebukuro: a sociological report), Tokyo: Mekong.

Okuda, Michihiro and Junko Tajima (eds) (1993), *Shinjuku no Ajia kei gaigokujin: Shakaigaku-teki jittai hōkoku* (Asian migrants in Shinjuku: a sociological report), Tokyo: Mekong.

Okuda, Michihiro and Kumiko Suzuki (eds) (2001), *Esunoporisu Shinjuku/ Ikebukuro: rainichi 10 nenme no Ajia kei gaigokujin chōsa kiroku* (The ethnopolis Shinjuku and Ikebukuro: a research report on foreigners of Asian origin, after ten years in Japan), Tokyo: Harvest-sha.

Okuda, Michihiro and Norizo Arisato (eds) (2002), *Howaito (Sutorīto kōna sosaetī) o yomu: toshi esunogurafī no atarashii chihei* (Reading Whyte (Street Corner Society): a new horizon for urban ethnography), Tokyo: Harvest-sha.

Osada, Hiroshi (1984), *Ichininshō de kataru kenri* (The right to speak in the first person), Tokyo: Heibonsha.

Osanai, Michiko (1997), *Anata wa watashi no te ni naremasuka—Kokochiyoi kea wo ukeru tameni* (Can you be my hand?—To receive comfortable care), Tokyo: Chūō Hōki.

Ōyama, Hikoichi (1943), 'Orochon chōsa no tabi (The journey of the Orochon research)', *Kenkoku Daigaku Kenkyū-in geppō* (National Foundation University Research Institute monthly), 25, pp. 2–3.

Ōyane, Atsushi (1991), 'Shinsai 'Fukko' to 'Sarubekihito', 'Kurubekihito': 'Shinsai Chōsa Hōkoku' wo meggutte (Post-quake Reconstruction, 'People gone', 'People come': On Earthquake Research Report)', in Takao Kawai (ed.) *Kindai Nihon Shakai Chōsa shi (II)* (History of Modern Japan Social Research [II]), Tokyo: Keio Tsūshin, pp. 213–241.

Pecora, Peter J., James K. Whittaker and Anthony M. Maluccio (eds) (1992), *The Child Welfare Challenge: Policy, Practice and Research*, New York: Aldline de Gruyter.

Polanyi, Michael (1983), *The Tacit Dimension*, Gloucester: Mass Peter Smith.

Portes, Alejandro (1996), 'Transnational communities: their emergence and significance in the contemporary world system,' in Roberto Patricio Korzeniewicz and William C. Smith (eds), *Latin America in the World Economy*, Westport Conneticut: Greenwood Press.

Price, David (1998), 'Cold War Anthropology: Collaborators and Victims of the National Security State', *Identities*, 4 (3–4), pp. 389–430.

Price, David (2002), 'Past Wars, Present Dangers, Future Anthropologies', *Anthropology Today*, 18 (1), pp. 3–5.

Proctor, Robert (1988), 'From Anthropologie to Rassenkunde in the German Anthropological Tradition', in George W. Stocking Jr. (ed.), *Bones, Bodies, Behavior: Essays on Biological Anthropology*, Madison: University of Wisconsin Press, pp. 138–79.

Rabinow, Paul (1977), *Reflections on Fieldwork in Morocco*, University of California Press.

Rapport, Nigel (1997), *Transcendent Individual: Towards a Literary and Liberal Anthropology*, London: Routledge.

Reid, William J. (1979), 'The Model Development Dissertation,' *Journal of Social Service Research*, 3, pp. 215–225.

Reid, William J. and A.D. Smith (1981), *Research in Social Work*, New York: Columbia University Press.

Reynolds, T. (2002), 'Re-thinking a Black Feminist Standpoint', *Ethnic and Racial Studies*, 25 (4), pp. 591–606.

Richmond, Mary E. (1922), *What is Social Case Work?* New York: Russell Sage Foundation.

Roberts, John Morris (2000), *The Illustrated History of the World*, Oxford: Oxford University Press.

Rosaldo, Renato ([1989] 1993), *Culture and Truth: The Remaking of Social Analysis*, London: Routledge.

Rothman, Jack and Edwin J. Thomas (1994), *Intervention Research: Design and Development for Human Services*, New York: Haworth Press.

Rumbaut, Rubén and Alejandro Portes (2001a), *Ethnicities: Children of Immigrants in America*, Berkeley: University of California Press.

Rumbaut, Rubén and Alejandro Portes (2001b), *Legacies: The Story of the Immigrant Second Generation*, Berkeley: University of California Press.

Said, Edward (1978), *Orientalism*, First edition, New York: Pantheon Books.

Saitama NPO Center (2001), *Saitama kaigo hoken sapōtāzu kurabu hōkoku-shū* (Reports collection of the Saitama public nursing-care insurance supporters' club), Urawa: Saitama NPO Center.

Saitama NPO Center (2002), *Kaigo hoken: mietekita genjitsu to kadai—Saitama kaigo hoken shimin chōsa no kiroku* (Public nursing-care insurance: reality

and issues coming in sight—a record of Saitama public nursing-care insurance research by citizens), Saitama: Saitama NPO Center.
Saitama Prefecture (2002), *Kaigo hoken no riyō jittai tō ni kansuru chōsa hōkoku-sho: jōkan riyōsha miriyōsha chōsa-hen* (Research report on the actual state of the use of public nursing-care insurance: Volume one: research of users and non-users), Saitama: Saitama-ken Kenkō Fukushi-bu Kaigo Taisaku-ka.
Sakurai, Atsushi (2002), *Intabyū no shakaigaku* (Sociology of interviews), Tokyo: Serika Shobō.
Satō, Ikuya (1992), *Fīrudowāku—sho o motte machi e deyō* (Fieldwork—let's take a book and go out to town), Tokyo: Shin-yo-sha.
Satō, Ikuya (1997), 'San'yo kansatsu (Participant observation)', in Noboru Kawazoe and Kenji Satō (eds), *Kōza seikatsugaku 2: seikatsugaku no hōhō* (Study on lifestyles 2: methodology in study of lifestyles, Lecture series), Tokyo: Kōseikan.
Satō, Kenji (1987), *Dokusho kūkan no kindai—hōhō toshiteno Yanagita Kunio* (The Modern era of reading space: Kunio Yanagita as a method), Tokyo: Kōbundō.
Satō, Kenji (1994), *Fūkei no seisan, fūkei no kaihō* (Production of scenery, liberation of scenery), Tokyo: Kōdansha.
Satō, Kenji (2001a), *Rekishi shakaigaku no sahō* (Manners in historical sociology), Tokyo: Iwanami Shoten.
Satō, Kenji (2001b), 'Shiryō to shite no bidan: Kokusei chōsa no monogatari (Stories of good deeds as historical data: Story of national population census)', *Monogatari no fūzoku: Gendai Fūzoku Kenkyū Kai nenpō 23* (Modern Culture Study Committee annual report 23: Cultures in stories), Tokyo: Kawade Shobō Shinsha, pp. 92–113.
Satō, Nobuyuki (1972), 'Hensha atogaki (A postscript by the editor)', *Izumi Seiichi chosaku-shū 1: Fīrudowāku no kiroku [1]* (Collection of Seiichi Izumi 1: (The record of fieldwork [1]), Tokyo: Yomiuri Shimbunsha, pp. 419–26.
Schuerman, John R. (1983), *Research and Evaluation in the Human Services*, New York: Free Press.
Schuerman, John R., Tina L. Rzepnicki and Julia H. Littell (1995), *Putting Families First: An Experiment in Family Preservation*, New York: Aldine De Gruyter.
Schutz, Alfred ([1932] 1967), *The Phenomenology of the Social World*, translated into English by George Walsh and Frederick Lehnert, Evanston, Illinois: Northwestern University Press.
Seiyama, Kazuo (1999), 'Gendai no kaisō shisutemu to sono hen'yō (Modern stratification system and its transformation)', *Shakaigaku hyōron*, (Japanese Sociological Review), 50 (2), pp. 3–23.
Seiyama, Kazuo (2004), *Shakai chōsahō nyūmon* (Introduction to social research), Tokyo: Yūhikaku.
Seki, Kazutoshi (1993), 'Shiawase no minzokushi: josetsu (Ethnography on happiness: introduction)', *Kokuritsu Rekishi Minzoku Hakubutsukan kenkyū hōkoku* (National Museum of Ethnology research report), 51, pp. 313–47.
Shibano, Matsujiro (author and editor) (2001), *Kodomo gyakutai kēsu manejimento manyuaru* (Child abuse case management manual), Tokyo: Yūhikaku (Teramoto, N., CD-ROM manual).

Shibano, Matsujiro (2002a), *Shakai fukushi jissen moderu kaihatsu no riron to jissai: Purosetikku apuroochi ni motozuku jissen modru no dezain ando deberoppumento* (The theory and practice of developing a social welfare practical model—the design and development of a practical model based on a prosthetic approach), Tokyo: Yūhikaku.

Shibano, Matsujiro (2002b), 'Jidō fukushi senmonshoku no jidō gyakutai taiō ni taisuru senmonsei kōjō no tameno maruchi media kyōiku kunren kyōzai oyobi denshi shoshiki no kaihatsuteki kenkyū (Multi-media education and training tools and electronic format developmental research for child welfare professionals to address child abuse),' *Ministry of Health, Labor and Welfare's Scientific Research Report 2001*, Tokyo: Ministry of Health, Labor and Welfare, pp. 419–500.

Shibano, Matsujiro (2003), 'Jidō fukushi senmonshoku no jidō gyakutai taiō ni taisuru senmonsei kōjō no tameno maruchi media kyōiku kunren kyōzai oyobi denshi shoshiki no kaihatsuteki kenkyū (Multi-media education and training tools and electronic format developmental research for child welfare professionals to address child abuse),' *Ministry of Health, Labor and Welfare's Scientific Research Report 2002*, Tokyo: Ministry of Health, Labor and Welfare, pp. 353–464.

Shibano, Matsujiro (2004a), 'Sōsharu wāku kenkyū ni okeru hyōka kenkyūhō—microreberu jissen ni okeru hyōka chōsa o chūshin to shite (Evaluation research methods in social work research—with a focus on evaluation studies in micro level practice),' *Sōsharu wāku kenkyū* (Social work research), 29, (4), pp. 293–301.

Shibano, Matsujiro (2004b), 'Fukushi (Welfare)', in K. Uchiyama and Y. Sakano (eds), *Ebidensu to kaunseringu* (Evidence and counseling), Tokyo: Shibundō, pp. 89–102.

Shibano, Matsujiro (2004c), 'Jidō fukushi senmonshoku no jidō gyakutai taiō ni taisuru senmonsei kōjō no tameno maruchi media kyōiku kunren kyōzai oyobi denshi shoshiki no kaihatsuteki kenkyū (Multi-media education and training tools and electronic format developmental research for child welfare professionals to address child abuse),' *Ministry of Health, Labor and Welfare's Scientific Research Report 2003*, Tokyo: Ministry of Health, Labor and Welfare, pp, 3–78.

Shibano, Matsujiro (2005), 'Ebidensu ni motozuku sōsharu wāku no jissenteki rironka—akauntaburu na jissen eno puragumatikku apurōchi (Practical theorization of evidence-based social work—a pragmatic approach to accountable practice),' *Sōsharu wāku kenkyū* (Social work research), 31, (1).

Shigenobu, Yukihiko (2000), 'Jūgo no bidan kara: Soryokusenka no 'seken' banashi, josetsu (Introduction, good deeds stories of home front: 'Rumors' during the total war)', *Kōshō bungei kenkyū* (Studies in folk-narrative), 23: pp. 69–84.

Skal, David J. and Elias Savada (1995), *Dark Carnival: The Secret World of Tod Browning–Hollywood's Master of the Macabre*, New York: Anchor Books.

Smith, Michael Peter (2001), *Transnational Urbanism: Locating Globalization*, Oxford: Blackwell.

Smith, Michael Peter and Luis Eduardo Guranizo (eds) (1998), *Transnationalism From Below*, New Brunswick: Transaction Publishers.

Social Welfare Deliberative Council's Child Welfare Panel (2003), *Jidō gyakutai e no taiō nado hogojidō oyobi yōshien katei ni taisuru shien no arikata ni taisuru tōmen no minaoshi no hōkōsei ni tsuite* (A report) (Directions in the reexamination of support of children in protection from child abuse and families requiring support), Tokyo: Equal Employment, Children and Families Bureau, the Ministry of Health, Labor and Welfare.

Soja, Edward W. (1996), *Thirdspace*, Oxford: Blackwell.

Sugishima, T. (1995), *Jinruigaku ni okeru riarizumu no shuen* (The demise of realism in anthropology), Tokyo: Kōbundō.

Sugiura, Ken'ichi (1933), 'Roshia ni okeru saikin no minzokugaku no keikō [2] (Recent trends of ethnography in Russia [2])', *Minzokugaku* (Ethnic studies), 5 (2), pp. 7–10.

Sugiura, Ken'ichi (1939), 'Yappu-tō minzoku chōsa nisshi-shō (Excerpts from a logbook of ethnographic research into the Yap Islanders)', *Minzokugaku kenkyū* (Ethnographic research), 5 (1), pp. 124–30.

Suzuki, Atsushi (2004), *Kanto Daishinsai: Shōbō, iryō, borantia kara kenshō suru* (Great Kanto Earthquake: Examination of fire-fighting, medical services and volunteers), Tokyo: Chikuma Shobō.

Swanson, Bert E. and Edith Swanson (1977), *Discovering the Community: Comparative Analysis of Social, Political, and Economic Change*, New York: Irving Publishers.

Tanaka, Katsuhiko (2001), *Sabetsugo kara hairu gengogaku nyūmon* (Introduction to linguistics through discriminatory language), Tokyo: Akashi Shoten.

Taub, Richard P., Taylor, D. Garth, and Jan D. Dunham (1984), *Paths of Neighborhood Change: Race and Crime in Urban America*, Chicago: University of Chicago Press.

Thomas, Edwin J. (1978), 'Mousetraps, Developmental Research and Social Work Education,' *Social Service Review*, 52, pp. 468–482.

Toda, Teizō (1933), *Shakai chōsa* (Social research), Tokyo: Jichōsha.

Tokyo-fu hen (1924), *Taishō Shinsai biseki* (Good deeds at the Taishō Earthquake), Tokyo: Tokyo Prefectural Government.

Tokyo-fu hen (1925), *Tokyo-fu Taishō Shinsai shi* (History of Tokyo-fu Taishō Earthquake), Tokyo: Tokyo Prefectural Government.

Tokyo-shi hen (1926a), *Tokyo Shinsai-roku chūshū* (Record of the Earthquake in Tokyo, Middle Edition), Tokyo: Tokyo City Government.

Tokyo-shi hen (1926b), *Tokyo Shinsairoku bettushū* (Record of the Earthquake in Tokyo, separate edition), Tokyo: Tokyo City Government.

Torigoe, Hiroyuki (1988), 'Yanagita minzokugaku ni okeru "shin'i" no imi' (The meaning of 'mind' in Yanagita Folklore), *Nihon minzokugaku* (Japanese folklore), 177, pp. 38–63.

Torigoe, Hiroyuki (1997), 'Environmental Awareness in Developing Countries: The Cases of China and Thailand', Papers and Proceedings of the Conference on 'Environmental Awareness in Developing Countries: The Cases of China and Thailand,' Tokyo, November 6–7, 1996. Conference Proceedings edited by Sigeki Nisihira, Reeitsu Kojima, Hideo Okamoto and Shigeaki Fujisaki, Institute of Developing Economies, Development and the Environment Series No. 3, Tokyo.

Torigoe, Hiroyuki (2002), *Yanagita minzokugaku no firosofī* (Philosophy of Yanagita's folklore), Tokyo: University of Tokyo Press.

Torigoe, Hiroyuki and Yukiko Kada (1984), *Mizu to hito no kankyōshi—Biwako hōkokusho* (The history of the environment for water and people—Lake Biwa report), Tokyo: Ochanomizu Shobō.

Tsuboyama, Hiroko (2005), *Shōgatsu ryōri no shūshū to bunseki* (Collection and analysis of New Year dishes), an assignment for '2004 Cultural Anthropology B,' Otsu: Seian University of Art and Design.

Tsurumi, Yoshiyuki and Taisuke Miyauchi (eds) (1996), *Yashi no mi no Ajia-gaku* (Asian studies through palms), Tokyo: Commons.

Tyler, Stephen A. (1986), 'Post-modern Ethnography: From Document of the Occult to Occult Document', in James Clifford and George E. Marcus (eds), *Writing Culture*, Berkeley: University of California Press, pp. 122–140

Uchiyama, Takashi (1998), 'Kindaiteki ningen-kan kara no jiyū (Freedom from modern views of human beings)', in Takashi Uchiyama et al., *Rōkaru na shisō wo tsukuru* (Creating local thoughts), Tokyo: Nōbunkyō (Rural Culture Association), pp. 46–68.

Ueno, Seigo (2003), *Tatta hitori no Kureoru: Shikaku shōgaiji kyōiku ni okeru gengo ron to shōgai ninshiki ron* (A lone Creole: on linguistic and impairment recognition in education of visually impaired children), Tokyo: Studio Potto.

Umesao, Tadao (1969), *Chiteki seisan no gijutsu* (The art of intellectual production), Tokyo: Iwanami Shoten.

Umesao, Tadao (1971), 'Kaisetsu (Comment)', *Kon Wajirō shū 1: Kōgengaku* (Wajirō Kon collection 1: Study of modern phenomena), Tokyo: Domesu Publishers.

United Nations (1989) *Convention on the Rights of the Child*, New York: United Nations.

Van Bremen, Jan and Akitoshi Shimizu (eds) (1999), *Anthropology and Colonialism in Asia and Oceania*, Surrey: Curzon.

Van Maanen, John (1988), *Tales from the Field: On Writing Ethnography*, Chicago: University of Chicago Press.

Wakita, Kenichi (1995), 'Kankyō mondai wo meguru jōkyō no teigi to sutoratejī—Kankyō seisaku heno jūmin sanka, shigaken sekken undō saikō (Definition of the situation and strategy surrounding environmental problems—Rethinking resident participation in the environmental policy and Shiga prefecture soap movement)', *Kankyō shakaigaku kenkyū* (Environmental sociology research), 1, pp. 130–144.

Watado, Ichiro, Yasuo Hirota and Junko Tajima (eds) (2003), *Toshiteki sekai/komyunitī/esunishitī: posuto metoroporisu ki no toshi esunogurafī shūsei* (An urban world/community/ethnicity: a collection of ethnographies in the post metropolis days), Tokyo: Akashi shoten.

Wazaki, Yōichi (1977), *Suwahiri no sekai nite* (In the World of the Swahili), Tokyo: NHK Books.

Weber, Max (1919), *The Vocation Lectures: Science as a Vocation, Politics as a Vocation*, D. Owen and T. B. Strong (eds) (2004), translated into English by R. Livingstone, Indianapolis: Hackett Publishers.

Weber, Max ([1920] 1996), *The Protestant Ethic and the Spirit of Capitalism*, translated into English by Talcott Parsons, Los Angeles: Roxbury Publishing Company.

Wengle, John L. (1988), *Ethnographers in the Field: The Psychology of Research*, Tuscaloosa: University of Alabama Press.

Whyte, William Foote ([1943] 1993), *Street Corner Society: The Social Structure of an Italian Slum*, 50th year commemorative edition, Chicago: University of Chicago Press

Whyte, William Foote (1993), *Street Corner Society: The Social Structure of an Italian Slum*, 50th year commemorative edition. [Translated into Japanese and with a foreword by Michihiro Okuda, and Norizō Arisato, 2000, Tokyo: Yūhikaku].

Whyte, William Foote and Kathleen King Whyte (1984), *Learning From the Field: A Guide from Experience*, London: Sage Publications.

Wuthnow, Robert (1998), *Loose Connections: Joining Together in America's Fragmented Communities*, Cambridge: Harvard University Press.

Yamaji, Katsuhiko and Masakazu Tanaka (eds) (2002), *Shokuminchi shugi to jinruigaku* (Colonialism and anthropology), Nishinomiya: Kwansei Gakuin Daigaku Shuppankai (Kwansei Gakuin University Press).

Yanagishita, Kiichirō (2003), *Kōgyōshitachi no eigashi—Exploitation film zenshi* (Showmen's history of films—Full history of exploitation films), Tokyo: Seidosha.

Yanagita, Kunio ([1931] 1998a), 'Meiji Taishō-shi sesō-hen (History of the Meiji and Taishō eras through social trends)', *Yanagita Kunio zenshū 5* (Kunio Yanagita collection 5), Tokyo: Chikuma Shobō.

Yanagita, Kunio ([1934] 1998b), 'Minkan denshō-ron (On folk traditions)', *Yanagita Kunio zenshū 8* (Kunio Yanagita collection 8), Tokyo: Chikuma Shobō.

Yanagita, Kunio (1934), 'Minkan densho ron' (Folklore theory), *Gendaishigaku taikei dai nana kan* (Compendium of studies in modern history, volume 7), Kyōritsusha. Rerecorded: 1990, *Yanagita Kunio zenshū 28* (Collected works of Kunio Yanagita—28), Chikuma Shobō.

Yanagita, Kunio ([1935] 1998c), 'Kyōdo seikatsu no kenkyūhō (Research method on country life)', *Yanagita Kunio zenshū 8* (Collected works of Kunio Yanagita—8), Tokyo: Chikuma Shobō.

Yanagita, Kunio (1935), *Kyōdo seikatsu no kenkyūhō* (Folk life research methods), Tokyo: Tōkō Shoin.

Yanagita, Kunio ([1938] 1970), 'Bunrui gyoson shūzoku (Classification of fishing village customs—introduction)', *Teihon Yanagita Kunio shū 30* (Collected works of Kunio Yanagita -30), Tokyo: Chikuma Shobō.

Yanagita, Kunio ([1941] 2003), 'Josei seikatsu-shi (History of women's life)', *Yanagita Kunio zenshū 30* (Collected works of Kunio Yanagita—30), Tokyo: Chikuma Shobō.

Yanagita, Kunio ([1956] 1999), 'Yōkai dangi (Discourse on ghosts)', *Yanagita Kunio zenshū 20* (Collected works of Kunio Yanagita—20), Tokyo: Chikuma Shobō.

Yanagita, Kunio ([1959] 1997), 'Kokyō 70 nen (Hometown, 70 years)', *Yanagita Kunio zenshū 21* (Collected works of Kunio Yanagita—21), Tokyo: Chikuma Shobō.

Yonebayashi, Tomio (1960), *Shakaigaku ni okeru jinkoshigaku-teki kenkyū hōhō ni tsuite* (On demographical study methods in sociology), Privately published.

Yoneyama, Toshinao (1967), *Nippon no mura no hyakunen* (One hundred years of Japanese villages), Tokyo: NHK Books.

Yoshii, Hiroaki (2004), 'Hiroshima no esunomesodorojī (Eiga ni miru Hiroshima hyōgen no kaidoku, sono hensen) (Ethnomethodology of Hiroshima (An analysis of expressions of Hiroshima in films and their changes)', in *Heisei 13–15 nendo kagakukenkyūhi hojokin (kisokenkyū (C)(2)) kenkyū seika hōkokusho* (Basic Research (C)(2)) Research Outcome Report, 2001-2003 Scientific Research Grant, University of Tsukuba.

Yoshii, Hiroaki and Kōkichirō Miura (eds) (2004), *Shakaigaku-teki fīrudowāku* (Sociological field work), Kyoto: Sekai Shisōsha.

Yoshimoto, Tetsuro (2001), 'Kaze ni kike, tsuchi ni tsuke—Kaze to tsuchi no jimotogaku (Listen to the wind, touch the land—The study of local neighborhood by the wind and the land)', *Zōkan gendai nōgyō* (Modern agriculture extra issue), 52, pp. 190–255.

Yūma, Masahide (1992), *Hotaru no mizu, hito no mizu* (Firefly's water, people's water), Tokyo: Shinhyōronsha.

Index

abnormality 239
academia 39
academic paper 28, 84, 87–8, 104, 113, 125, 253–4
academic world 39, 41, 113, 117, 125
accountability 277–8, 280, 292, 295, 302, 305
achieved status 145
actor's meaning-world 27
actor's subjective meaning-world 27
Adoption Assistance and Child Welfare Act 275
advanced case 40, 45
Akiba, Takashi 109–12, 312–13
allocation 192
American Mosaic 137
Americans 143, 151, 153, 205, 314
analogue data 202
Anderson, Elijah 128, 150–4, 156
animation based ethnology 97
animation based sociology 95–6
anomie 23, 25
anomie narrative 23
anthropology ix–xi, 2, 12, 53–5, 73, 78, 96, 101, 105, 108–9, 112–15, 117, 119, 120–5, 309, 312, 314
  Japanese 123

anti-air-raid 180
A Place on the Corner 153
'A record of street custom in Ginza, Tokyo' 59
Army personnel 162
ascribed status 145
Asian newcomers to Japan 126–7, 129–30, 314
Asia Pacific region 155
assimilation 139, 142–3
  theory 142
association-type motive 214

being urban 129
Beyond the Melting Pot 127
bidan stories 158–62, 164, 168, 171–2, 176, 178–81, 315
Binford, Henry 133
biology 74–9
bird's eye/bug's eye method 62
bird's eye perspective 62, 207
bird's eye view 62–3, 84
Biwako Museum 216–17
black community 13, 140, 153
black humor 260–1
Bohannan, Laura 115–18, 121–2, 124
Boon, James xii, 12–13
Borofsky, Robert 2–3
Bourdieu, P. 203, 218
Browning, Tod 237–8

bug's eye views 62
Burges, E. W. 157

Cameroon 78, 86–7, 98
care 50, 255, 266–8, 271–3, 276, 287, 292, 303
 -nursing 48–51
 medical 44
carer-recipient relationship 266–7
case management 280–1
case study 3, 39–41, 44–8, 51–2, 126, 134–6, 151, 155, 310
case study description 52
case worker 258–64, 297
categorization 57, 67–8, 71, 131, 251–2, 309, 311
Central Business District (CBD) 129
Chen Hsiang-Shui 132
child abuse and neglect 278–80, 283, 285, 287
Child Abuse and Neglect Prevention Law 284
Child Endangerment Risk Assessment Protocol (CERAP) 297, 302–3
children of immigrants 133, 139, 142–3
child's best interests 272–5, 278–81, 283–7, 292–3, 295, 299, 303–5, 307
Child Welfare Law 272, 278–9, 284, 286
child welfare officers 279, 283–4, 287, 302, 304
Chinai River 188–9, 192, 194–5, 197, 200–1
Chinai Village 183, 186–8, 190–9, 202, 315–16
Chinatown No More 132

classification-and-statistics method 59, 61
class narratives 34
Clifford, James 10, 309
code (coding) 47, 54, 138, 143, 147, 154, 241–3, 279, 286, 312
Code of the Street 153–4
collective other xi
colonialism 100–1, 112, 119, 122–5
 and war in Japanese anthropology 119, 122–3
common knowledge 33
common paradigm 253
commonsense 67, 233, 235, 238, 240, 251–2
common true value 20
community-type motive 214
complex city 128, 141, 146, 155
Comte, Auguste 33, 271
conceptualization 47, 160
constructionism xi, 210
construction of a society that promotes cultural diversity 146, 154
control 14–15, 100, 123, 147, 162, 187, 192, 199, 204–7, 210–12, 214–15, 229, 232, 241, 308, 312, 315
 -oriented discourse 207
 administrative 201, 230
 bureaucratic 206
 political 101
control theory 205–7, 211, 215, 229
conventional dichotomy 254–5
Convention on the Rights of the Child 272, 275, 277–8
coolheaded observer 254
cooperativity 12–14, 308–10

creation of a new vision 63
creativity 6, 13
cultural relativism x
custody 277, 292, 296–7, 302

database 87–8, 129, 207, 217, 285, 293, 296, 299, 302–7
data displaying research xiii
decency 154, 158
decontextualized discourses 204, 207
deep description 47–8
deep interviews 1
Department of the Interior 175
descriptive format 73, 75, 93–4, 97, 312
detective 171
detective investigations 171
dialectic of well-being and ill-being 271
digital data 201–2
disability studies 317
disabled 192, 238, 240, 243–5, 251, 258
disasters 181, 194, 201
discrimination 177, 239, 246, 249–50, 254, 258, 260, 263–4, 269, 316
  circumstantial 255
  perpetrator of 258, 261
  psychological 255, 316
  relational 255
  structural 255, *see* structural discrimination
  unintentional 255
  understood from a relational standard 255
discriminatory expressions 260–4
discriminatory perspective 238–40

discriminatory terms 317
documentary 95, 233, 235, 250
Douglas, Mary 205
drift 29, 274–5
due process 275, 277, 279–80, 280–7, 295, 299, 303, 305
Durkheim, Emile 23–6, 28, 36, 38
dynamic comparative method xiii, 128, 135, 146, 155

Eastern Xinganling Troop 109, 112
emic/etic dichotomy 34
empathic perspective 208
empathy xi–xii, 17, 210–12, 214–15, 228–9, 232, 238, 269
Emperor 100, 115–19, 122–3, 173, 179–81, 196–7
empirical generalization 19–20
enclave 134
Endō, Sōsen 160–1, 165–78, 182
enigmatic self xi
Enlightenment 8, 9, 13, 233
environmental sociology 204, 232
epistolary style 253–4, 316
essential narrativity theory 32
ethics 76, 100–1, 105, 112, 121–2, 164, 241–3
ethnic community 140
  local 133, 140
ethnographer 2, 10, 104, 109, 118, 308–9
ethnographic description methodology xiii
ethnography x–xiii, 1–3, 6, 10–12, 23, 41, 53, 67, 96, 102–6, 109, 117, 123,

149–51, 153, 257, 308–9, 314, 317
experimental ix–xi
ethnomethodology xi
Eutrophication Prevention Ordinance 204
everyday sense of reality 12
evidence 26, 72, 166, 170, 273, 277–80, 283–5, 293, 295, 299, 301–3, 305–6, 316
evidence-based practice (EBP) 280–2, 306
excessive empiricism 20
explanation 16, 23, 27–33, 38–9, 56–7, 67–8, 103, 117, 187, 204, 222, 243, 295
  vs. interpretation and understanding 27
exploitation film 237–8, 249–50
expression 39–40, 64, 73, 86, 88–90, 94–7, 103, 109, 134, 138, 147, 182, 211, 215, 243, 247–9, 254, 259, 265, 310–11

fact x–xi, 1, 5, 7–8, 13–14, 19–20, 22, 28–9, 31, 33–4, 37–8, 41, 43–4, 46–7, 64, 68, 70, 100–1, 103, 109–15, 118, 123, 125, 141, 167–9, 171–4, 178, 182, 186, 190, 192–3, 196, 198–9, 201, 208, 211, 213, 224, 229, 250, 254, 257, 261, 265, 268–70, 272, 274, 277, 295, 303, 305, 313, 315
family 24, 34, 41–4, 48–50, 61, 130, 156, 174–5, 185, 187, 193, 214, 219, 223–5, 236, 240, 251, 255, 260, 265, 272–4, 276–80, 284–7, 292, 294–5, 297, 302, 304, 306, 311
family environment 273–4, 277, 279, 286, 295, 302, 304
fantasies 233
fiction 11, 31, 236
field xi, xiii, 2–3, 5–8, 10–12, 14–15, 17–18, 43–4, 46, 48, 50, 53–4, 56–7, 63–6, 72, 76, 78–9, 82–3, 90, 96–8, 101–6, 109, 112–13, 115, 120, 124–6, 129, 135–7, 140–1, 144–7, 150, 154–8, 201, 210, 212, 215, 222, 251, 258, 260, 262, 268, 308, 311, 317
field research 3, 6, 54, 107, 120, 256
  of the life-world 256
fieldwork x–xiii, 2–3, 5–7, 9–12, 15–16, 18, 53–7, 63, 70–1, 73, 78, 85, 96, 98, 102, 104–6, 109, 114–15, 119, 124, 126–30, 132, 135–6, 139–41, 143, 148–51, 155–7, 182, 231, 308–9, 314
film 78, 84, 94, 105, 109, 233–43, 248–51
firefly 209–10, 212–16, 218
first-order interpretation 36
first-order versus second-order social theory 34
First World War 100, 116, 120, 180
fishing 65–6, 79, 82, 84, 194–5, 198, 219–20, 222, 316
flood 177, 185, 188–90, 192–4, 196–200, 202, 316
flood damage 188, 193, 196–7
flow-mode 285, 287, 292–5, 299, 301–3, 305–6

folklore 16, 54, 63–8, 70–1, 170, 172
folklore study methodology 66, 230
foreign residents 128, 140
Foucault, Michel 33, 96
Foucault's treatises on power 33
Freaks 233, 237–40, 246–7, 249–51
freaks 237–43, 248–50
from below 128–31, 134, 140, 142, 145–6, 148, 150, 156
Fukagawa-ku area 166
Fukutake, Tadashi 3–4
functionalism 55

Galton's principle of regression 19–20
Gans, H. 143
General Staff Office 112
'Genkaku no jikken' (Experiment of illusion) 70
ghetto 131, 150
Giddens, Anthony 12
Glazer, Nathan 127
GO 234
Goldstein, J. 274–5
good deed xiii, 159, 166, 173–6, 182
Good Deeds of the Taishō Earthquake 158–60, 162–7, 169, 174–7, 179–81, 314
government, local 40, 189, 232, 279, 292, 294, 301, 306
gray area 127, 129, 154
Great East Asian Co-Prosperity Sphere 101, 123
Great Empire of Japan 110, 118–19, 312
Great Kanto Earthquake 158–60, 162

habitus 203, 211, 218
handicapped 237, 239–40, 242–3, 245–6, 249–50, 255–6, 258–9, 264, 266–7, 270–1
Harada, Katsumasa 180
Hashiguchi, Ryōsuke 251
Helfer, R. E. 274
here and now 243, 246, 250–2
Hijikata, Hisakatsu 105–6
hisabetsu buraku (outcast villages in Japan) 45, 254, 271
historicize 159–60
Hughes, Everett C. 157
human being as a research tool 62
human rights 251, 253, 256
Hume, David 21
hunter-gatherer 78, 85, 89, 99
Hush! 251
hypothesis construction and verification 37

Ikebukuro 126–8, 130, 132, 134–41, 144, 146–7, 149–50, 154–5, 314
Imanishi, Kinji 14, 111–12, 312–13
Imperial
  education 160
  family 117
  Japan 100
  Japanese army 116
  script about building a national spirit 180
  script about capital reconstruction 180
  system, modern 159
independent living 255, 260, 266–7

independent living movement 255, 266
individualism 5, 13, 65, 308
individuality 5, 13, 68
inner-city 127, 129–32, 134, 136, 141, 145–6, 148–51, 153–6
　moral life of 154
Inoguchi, Takashi 131
insider's perspective 257
inter-subjectivity 31
international comparison 134
interpret 105, 220, 243
interpretation 23, 27, 36–7, 47, 274–5, 311
　first-order 37
　second-order 37
　third-order 37–8
interview 46, 49–50, 54, 57, 110, 114, 128, 133, 136, 139, 175, 207, 221, 254, 262, 310
interview survey 36, 284
Investigation Committee 165
investigations 162–3, 166, 170–1, 175–6, 184–6, 188–90, 192, 198, 201–2, 260, 315
investigator
　as a subjective performer 161
　subjectivity of 161, 165, 173, 182
　the scene of 165, 171
Itani, Junichirō 15
Izumi, Seiichi 107–15, 121–2, 312–13

Japanese
　anthropology and folklore x, 23
　army 116
　Society of Ethnology 113, 119
　sociology x

Jinruigaku zasshi
　(Anthropological magazine) 117
joint observation 21
joint project x, 6–12, 14, 309
justice 251

Keijō Imperial University 109, 112, 114
Keijō nippō 114
Kempe, Henry 273–4
Kimura, Daiji 148–9, 284, 286
Kiroku 183–92, 196–8, 200–1, 315–16
Kōgengaku 53–4, 58–9, 61–8, 70
Kon, Wajirō 58, 65–6, 311
Koreans 132, 166, 168, 177–8, 182, 314
　Japanese born 141
Kwansei Gakuin University xiv, 94, 98, 126, 134, 146, 154
Kwantung Army 109–13
Kyōdo seikatsu no kenkyūhō
　(Research method on country life) 66–7

Lake Biwa 183, 188–9, 192–3, 197, 200, 202, 204–5, 207–8, 210, 213, 218, 222–3, 225, 228–30, 232, 308
Land Tax Reform 191, 316
law of the average man 19
laws 4, 20, 22, 34, 284
Learning from the Field: A Guide from Experience 156
legacies 143
legend 170
letter-styled sociography xiii
Lévi-Strauss, Claude 3
Levitt, P. 128, 142–3, 314

Lewis, Oscar 6
life, to construct 43, 45–6, 52
life-world 203, 231–2, 236
limbo 274
living environment 222, 228
living together 147–8
local knowledge 104
local residents 57, 167, 205–6, 208–10, 213, 224
loose connections 146–7, 149

majority 254–6
Malaita Island 41, 43, 310
Malinowski, Bronislaw 3, 10, 23, 54–5, 102–9, 111, 115, 120–2, 308
Manchukuo 109–10, 312–13
Manchuria 107, 111
Manchuria National Foundation University 111
Manchurian Incident 123
Marcus, George E. 10
Martial Law Head Quarters 162
Maruyama, Masao 15–16, 309
Marx, Karl 74, 96
Marxism 33
massacre of Koreans 177–8, 182
material presentation-interview 218
mathematics 93–4
Matsuda, Motoji x–xii, 1, 231
Mauss, Marcel 36, 108, 120–1
Mead, George Herbert 23
meaning 12, 19, 21, 25–31, 34–6, 40, 44, 47, 55–6, 93, 116, 118, 138, 143, 145, 149, 159, 161, 185, 206, 209–13, 218, 222, 233–4, 250, 252, 264, 292, 310

meaning-world 27–31
measures 80, 147, 189–90, 194, 201, 204, 206, 229, 271, 277–8, 294
megalopolis 127–9, 130–6, 141, 145–6, 148–51, 154–6
Meiji era 185, 187, 190, 192–3, 230, 279, 286
Meiji government 191–2
Meiji Restoration 185
Memoir of a Good Deed Investigator 160, 166, 176, 182
Mendel's laws 20
meta-ethnography 102, 105–6, 117, 125
method of in-depth social description 256–7
methodology xii–xiii, 1–2, 4–5, 7, 10, 16–17, 46, 53–6, 58, 61, 65–8, 71–2, 75, 92, 95, 104, 106, 120, 122, 124, 153, 218, 230, 232, 308, 311
methodology of seeing 53–4, 67, 71
migration 43–4, 126, 133–4, 140, 142, 310, 314
military police 162
Minamata disease 206, 228–9, 231–2
Ministry of Education xiv, 98, 164
Minkan denshō-ron (On folk traditions) 66–7
minority 113, 254–5, 314
Minzokugaku kenkyū (Ethnographic research) 114, 117, 119
missed opportunity 228–9, 231
Mitsuya, Yōko 262–3
Miyamoto, Tsuneichi 207

mobile phone 97
mobilization
  national 181–2
  of public opinion 147
modernization 38, 187
Modified Design & Development (M-D&D) 281–2, 306
Motoori, Norinaga 16–17, 231
mutual references xiii
mutual relationships 186
mutual understanding xii, 7, 14–15

Nakano, Takashi x, 4, 6–9, 14, 17, 223–5, 231, 309
Narita, Ryūichi 159–60, 178
narratives 11, 22–3, 25–34, 37–8, 41, 251, 299, 312
  anomie 23
  class 34
  narrativity 23, 25–6, 28, 32–3, 34, 48
  triple-layered 26
  theory
    essential 32
    negative 32
nation, the 101, 179, 181, 185, 200–2, 315
national census 169–70, 184–5
nation state 130, 185, 198–9, 202
natural history 74–5, 78, 94, 97
natural sciences 1, 27, 54, 74, 94
navigational database system 294, 299, 301, 304–306
negative narrativity 32
neutral third party 254
New Cinema Paradiso 234
newcomers 127–30, 132, 134, 136, 139, 141, 145, 155
newest arrivals 140

newspapers 94, 159, 163–4, 166, 171–2, 180, 258–9, 261, 278
Nitagai, Kamon x, 6–9, 14, 231, 309
Noe, Keiichi 29
nomothesis 19–20
  fallacy of 19
normative narrativity 32

observation 4, 20, 22, 36, 46, 53–9, 61–3, 65–7, 71, 75–6, 78, 82–4, 90, 102–3, 112, 120, 123, 136, 139, 153, 214–5, 311, 314
observer's meaning-world 27
Okishima 218, 221–2
opium 106–8, 110–14, 122, 312–13
Opium Control Law 110, 313
Orientalism 10, 13
Orochon 106–7, 109–14, 122, 312–13
Osanai, Michiko 266–70
ostracism 242, 246, 249–50
outsider's perspective 257

Pacific basin 130, 134
Palau Islands 116
Parsonian theory 33
participant observation 53–9, 71, 102, 105, 120, 311
participation 7, 55–7, 136, 162, 214, 230, 257, 315
participatory action research (PAR) 129, 148, 150, 156, 314
paternalism 256, 267
Path of Neighborhood Change, The 140
permanency planning 275–8, 280, 285, 287, 292, 303–5

personal encounters 102–7, 110, 117, 121–2, 125
phase-mode 285–7, 293–5, 299, 301, 303–6
phenomenological sociology xi
photograph 61, 78–9, 84, 88, 104, 107, 133, 217–19, 221–5
photo message 97
pictures 72, 74–5, 97–8, 143, 260, 311
Polanyi, M. 203, 218
police station 166–7, 178
policy 39–40, 110, 117, 131, 134, 150, 169–70, 173, 204, 206, 209–10, 229–30, 232, 263, 275, 278, 287
politics and ethics ix, xi
Politics as a Vocation 26
pollution 8, 204–8, 210, 220, 229, 231
 environmental 205
 indicators 205–6
 risks 205
 water 204, 206, 209, 229
Portes, Alejandro 128, 142–3
positivism 1, 54, 204, 206, 210, 232
post-quake reconstruction 180
power 39, 233
power of enlightenment 237, 240, 249
practical knowledge 236, 239, 251
practice xii, 14, 16, 54, 92, 151, 171, 181–2, 202, 257, 268, 273, 280–7, 292–5, 299, 301–7
prejudice 137, 141, 255, 260
primary school 42, 44, 136, 145, 163, 167, 315
probability theory 19

professionals 94, 141, 230, 256, 266, 268, 279–80, 282, 284–5, 295, 302, 304, 316
Protestant Ethic and the Spirit of Capitalism 26
public nursing-care insurance 48–9, 50–1
public policy 205
public work 206

Qiqihar Secret Military Agency 112
qualitative research 1, 3–5, 17, 23, 27, 32
qualitative social research 1
qualitative surveys 21–2, 297
qualitative versus quantitative research xii
quantitative social research 19, 22, 34
Quételets law of the average man 19
quiet life 185–6, 194, 196, 198, 200, 316

Rabinow, Paul x–xi
Radcliffe-Brownian 5
rapport x, 56, 84–5, 87, 110, 120–1
reactive ethnic theory 142, 144
real and imagined place 129
record 3, 23, 49, 59, 61–3, 67, 76–7, 80, 90, 94, 96, 104–5, 114, 159, 163–4, 169, 183–4, 188, 190, 191, 196, 202, 211, 295, 304, 311, 313
recording 17, 61, 63, 73–4, 78, 83–4, 90, 94, 96, 202, 207, 285
Redfield, Robert 6
relational gaps 256–7

relational standard 255–6
representation 29, 65, 86, 204
representative individual 19
research ix–xiv, 1–19, 22, 23, 25–6, 29, 32, 34, 37–41, 43–59, 61–3, 71–5, 77, 80, 87–8, 90, 92, 97–8, 101, 105–6, 108–12, 114–15, 117, 119–22, 124–6, 131–2, 134, 136–7, 140–7, 150, 153–8, 160–2, 169, 182–3, 207–8, 210, 212–14, 218, 228, 230–2, 254, 257, 273–5, 280–3, 285, 292, 294, 298–9, 301, 303, 305–6, 308–14, 317
researcher ix–iii, 2, 5–7, 9–12, 14–16, 22, 38, 40–1, 45, 48, 59, 62, 76, 85, 90, 96–8, 102, 106, 124, 228, 231, 280–1, 299, 306
research ethics xiii, 2
research method ix
research methodologies ix, 17
research subject ix, xi–xii, 9, 11, 14–17, 231
resident research 231
resource 45–6, 57, 168, 283
revelation 48
revitalization 132, 134, 141, 147, 151
Reynolds, Tracey 13
Romanticism 12, 15
Rumbaut, Rubén 142–3
rumors 168–72, 178, 180–1

Said, Edward 10
Saitama NPO Center 48, 50–2, 310
sans-culottes 11–12
Schutz, Alfred 27

science 1, 3, 23, 33, 61, 73–5, 77, 92, 94, 97, 100–1, 103, 112, 115, 122, 124–5, 204–6, 215, 309, 312
  modern 1–2, 17, 54, 241
  natural 29
  social 1, 7, 45, 90, 92, 96, 98, 100–1, 312
Science as a Vocation 26
sciences
  natural 54
  social 1, 18, 53, 72–5, 90, 92–4, 97
scientific explanation 30–3
scribal selves 12
Second World War 101, 123, 180–1
Secret Military Agency 112
Seiyama, Kazuo xii, 19, 34
self/selves ix–xiv, 5–10, 12–17, 23, 28, 38, 41, 48, 58, 87, 102–3, 115–16, 118, 129, 152, 156, 159, 161, 172–3, 198–9, 217, 230–1, 264, 266, 268, 308, 310
  -consciousness ix, 5–6, 13–14, 231
  -interpretation-presenting 23, 38
  -promotion 173
  enigmatic xi
  heterogeneity of xi
senryū (5-7-5 syllabic poem) 257–63
Seoul National University 110
sewerage system 209, 222, 229–30
Shakespeare's Hamlet 122
Shiga Prefecture 183, 187, 192, 207, 213, 216, 230

Shinjuku 63, 126–8, 130–2, 134–8, 140–1, 144–7, 149–50, 154–5, 314
Showa era 171
sketch 59, 68, 72–80, 82–7, 89–90, 92–7, 218, 311
 definition of 95
 disadvantages of 90
Sketch Literacy 72
slum 127, 129, 131, 150, 154
social
 changes 224
 constructivism ix
 realism ix
 reality ix
 relationship between the helper and the helped 256
 research ix–xi, xiv, 1, 3–5, 7, 18–23, 27, 53, 72–4, 77–9, 82, 90, 92, 96–8, 126, 154, 157, 171, 207, 228
  unintentionally conducted 257
 research improving human happiness 146, 154
Social Security Deliberative Councils Child Welfare Panel 272–3
social welfare research xiii
social work 273, 278, 280–2, 284–5, 295, 299, 302, 305–7
sociogram 317
sociographical 257
sociography 257, 317
 of relationship 256
sociological
 methodology 27
 tales 32
sociology to analyze films, potential of 251
sociometry 317
Solomon Islands 41–4, 310
South Seas Agency 116
specialist knowledge 6, 17, 253
Spencer, Herbert 33, 314
static comparative paradigm 135–6, 146, 155
static knowledge 280
statistical
 indicators 20, 35–7
 software 22, 35
stories of good deeds 158–9, 162
Stories of Sorrow and Good Deeds of the Great Earthquake 171
storytelling 27
strategy 42, 180, 311
Street Corner Society 131, 150–1, 314
Streetwise 129, 150–1, 153–4
streetwise behavior, sense of 153
structural
 characteristics 20–1
 discrimination 253–6, 271
 functionalism 5
study of local neighborhoods 231
subjectivity 11, 21, 30–1, 182
suburban way of life 133
Sugiura, Ken'ichi 116–19, 121–3, 314
suicide 23–6, 36
suicide statistics 26
Sumerian letters 72
Supervisor of Social Education 163
support 44, 109, 169, 190, 194, 196, 215, 238, 255, 258, 260, 274–5, 277, 280, 284, 297, 304, 315

surveys 21, 61, 63–4, 171, 175, 188, 297
symbolic interaction theory xi

Taishō Earthquake 166, 176, 178, 181
Taishō era 171
tales (setsuwa) 31, 68, 70, 159, 165, 170, 172, 181, 240
Taub, Richard 140
temporary member 10
Temporary Rescue Operation Administration Office 175
text xiii, 10–11, 35, 54–5, 73–4, 76–7, 84, 87, 90–8, 309
The First Suburban Chinatown 132
The First Suburbs 133
The Transnational Villagers 143
The Urban Villagers 143
thick description 1, 317
thirdspace 127, 129, 131, 134, 141, 151, 155
Tiv 115–17, 122
tobacco 59, 106–8, 111, 121, 312
Toda, Teijirō 156–7
Tokyo government 158, 160–1, 165, 167, 172–3, 179, 181, 314
Tomikawa, Morimichi 14–15, 167
Torigoe, Hiroyuki 16, 206, 231, 308, 310
Tornatore, Giuseppe 234
transmigrants 128, 142–5
transnational 126–31, 133–9, 141–6, 150, 155–6
tribal selves 13
Trobriand Island 55
Trobriand Islanders 106–8, 111, 120–1
tropical rainforest 78

twenty-first century COE program 146, 294

Uchiyama, Takashi 4, 6, 109–10, 112, 131, 156, 186, 222, 231, 312
Umesao, Tadao 15, 64, 207
understanding x–xii, 2, 4–5, 11, 14–17, 22–3, 27–31, 34, 76, 82, 89, 92, 94, 100, 116–18, 122, 131, 142, 145, 153, 176, 207, 236, 243, 255–6, 268, 273–4, 309
uni-trend analysis 135
United Nations 272–3, 275, 278
University of Tokyo 114
urban
  characteristics of the changing urban community 134–5
  co-existence 128, 147–9
  ethnography 149–50
  of the twenty-first century 151
  sociological research 126, 129, 134
  villages 131

Van Maanen, John 317
video 61, 73, 92, 234, 237
village diary 183, 201
visual anthropology 61, 96

washing 209, 219–21, 223–5, 267
waterways 210–13
Wazaki, Yōichi 14–17
Weber, Max 26–7
welfare xiv, 50–1, 237, 251, 258–60, 262–4, 275, 285, 287
  child 278, 284, 286
  recipients 258–60
  social xiii, 261–3, 272
  system 261, 264

well-being 40–1, 50, 98, 154, 228, 232, 271–2, 277, 279–80, 285–6, 302–3
White Anglo Saxon Protestant (WASP) 133, 151
whole life 46
Whyte, William Foote 131, 150–1, 156, 314
Writing Culture x–xi, 2, 10, 309

Yanagishita, Kiichirō 238–9, 243, 249
Yanagita, Kunio x, 16–17, 63–8, 70–1, 207, 230, 309–11
Yap Island 117
Yonebayashi, Tomio 156–7
Yoneyama, Toshinao 183, 316
youth association 201
Yukisada, Isao 234